Essentials
of Active Learning in Preschool

Getting to Know the HighScope Curriculum

Essentials

of Active Learning in Preschool

Getting to Know the HighScope Curriculum

Ann S. Epstein

HIGHSCOPE
PRESS ®

Ypsilanti, Michigan

Published by

HIGHSCOPE® PRESS
A division of the
HighScope Educational Research Foundation
600 North River Street
Ypsilanti, Michigan 48198-2898
734.485.2000, FAX 734.485.0704
press@highscope.org

Editor: Jennifer Burd, HighScope Press
Cover design, text design, production: Judy Seling
Photography:
Chris Boisvert —199
Jennifer Burd — 47, 135, 141, 154
Patricia Evans — 55 (lower), 217
Gregory Fox — All other photographs

Library of Congress Cataloging-in-Publication Data
Epstein, Ann S.
  Essentials of active learning in preschool : getting to know the highscope curriculum / by Ann S. Epstein.
     p. cm.
   ISBN: 978-1-57379-300-1 (softcover : alk. paper)
   1. Education, Preschool--Curricula. 2. Active learning.
I. HighScope Educational Research Foundation. II. Title.
   LB1140.4.E77 2007
   820.9'35--dc22
                                        2006027713

Printed in the United States of America
10 9 8 7 6 5 4 3 2 1

Dedication

*To Dave Weikart, whose vision endures
in the continuing work of the HighScope Foundation.*

Contents

Preface

This book is written for several audiences — students in early childhood courses, program administrators, and teachers and caregivers — who want to learn about the HighScope Preschool Curriculum. For students who may be new to the field, this book is an introduction to a well-researched and comprehensive early childhood curriculum model that is widely used in the United States and abroad. Administrators may be deciding on a curriculum for their program, or they may have already chosen HighScope but want know more about it so they can support their staff in its implementation. For these decision makers, the book explains what children in this research-based curriculum learn and how the HighScope assessment system can meet demands for accountability. For teachers and caregivers, whose agencies use or are about to begin using HighScope, this book describes all the basic parts of the curriculum — how to create an effective learning environment and daily routine, interact with children using effective instructional strategies, and provide the content at the heart of preschool teaching and learning. We hope the information presented here will help all our readers understand and begin to use the principles of HighScope in their work.

What Is HighScope?

For readers new to HighScope, some background information on who we are and what we do may

be helpful. The HighScope Educational Research Foundation is an independent nonprofit organization headquartered in Ypsilanti, Michigan. The Foundation promotes the development of children and youth worldwide and supports educators and parents as they help children learn. The HighScope Curriculum is a set of *teaching practices* for adults and *content* for children's learning in all areas of development. There is also an *assessment system* to measure program quality and evaluate what children learn, and a *training model* to prepare teachers and caregivers to implement the HighScope Curriculum.

Mission and vision. To lift lives through education, the HighScope Educational Research Foundation engages in curriculum development, research, training, publishing, and communication. We envision a world in which all educational settings use active, participatory learning so everyone has a chance to succeed in life and contribute to society.

History. HighScope was established in 1970 to carry on the work that Dr. David P. Weikart began with disadvantaged children in the Ypsilanti Public Schools in 1962. The Foundation is best known for its preschool curriculum and studies of the lasting positive effects that high-quality early education can have on individuals and society as a whole. HighScope also has initiatives for infant and toddler programs, elementary schools, programs for youth, and intergenerational programs. The Foundation's curriculum, staff development model, research, and publications have influenced educational programming and public policy for over four decades.

Outreach. Today HighScope's curricula, staff development methods, assessments, and research findings are used in most every state in the United States and in 20 countries abroad. HighScope programs thrive in diverse settings that include Head Start, public school prekindergarten, center-based and family day care, corporate child care, university lab schools, and all other nonprofit and for-profit preschools and child care settings.

Because the curriculum builds on children's interests and community characteristics, it is appropriate for use with populations varying in culture and nationality, race and ethnicity, language, special needs, and geography. Through the Foundation's professional development program and dissemination efforts, an estimated 40,000 teachers and caregivers worldwide have been trained in the HighScope Preschool Curriculum. These practitioners are supported by a corps of 1,600 HighScope certified trainers and serve approximately 400,000 children and their families each year.

What Is in This Book?

This book is your introduction to the HighScope Preschool Curriculum. Each of the curriculum's four components — teaching practices, content for children's learning, an assessment system, and a training model — is discussed in its own section of the book.

Organization of this book. This book has five parts. **Part 1, Introduction and Overview,** has four chapters. Chapter 1 explains why educators should use a curriculum model; Chapter 2 is an overview of the HighScope Curriculum itself; Chapter 3 describes the theory underlying the curriculum; and Chapter 4 presents the research evidence supporting the curriculum. The remaining four parts each deal with one curriculum component.

Part 2, HighScope Teaching Practices, describes the methods HighScope practitioners use to create an active participatory learning experience for young children. Chapters 5 through 9 cover, respectively, strategies for interacting with children, arranging and equipping indoor and out-door learning environments, establishing a consistent daily routine that includes the plan-do-review sequence, working with parents, and maintaining effective staff communication to plan for children and continuously improve program quality.

Part 3, HighScope Curriculum Content, describes HighScope's key developmental indicators for preschool in five content areas that parallel the school readiness dimensions of the National Education Goals Panel (Kagan, Moore, & Bredekamp, 1995). These dimensions are widely accepted in the early childhood community and often form the basis for state and district standards. Chapter 10 addresses approaches to learning; Chapter 11 covers language, literacy, and communication; Chapter 12 addresses social and emotional development, and Chapter 13 deals with physical development, health, and well-being. Because the fifth content area, arts and sciences, embraces multiple subjects, it is divided into four chapters (14–17) covering, respectively, mathematics, science and technology, social studies, and the arts.

Part 4, HighScope Assessment, describes HighScope's validated assessment tools. Chapter 18 deals with child assessment, and Chapter 19, with program assessment. **Part 5, HighScope Training Model,** describes the HighScope approach to training early childhood practitioners. Chapter 20 explains how we apply the principles of active participatory learning to working with adults, and Chapter 21 briefly describes HighScope's training options and certification procedures to maintain quality.

Each chapter begins with a story or thought (titled "Think About It") to help you connect the topic to your own life and experience. Each chapter also includes a list of learning objectives and important terms used within the chapter to further assist the reader's learning and understanding. Terms appear in boldface upon first use within the chapter text. The suggested exercises or activities at the end of each chapter (titled "Try These Ideas Yourself") will help you apply the lessons learned to your own situation as a student, teacher, or supervisor. Documenting your responses to these questions and activities will help you reflect on the chapter and give you a record to look back on as you continue to develop your ideas.

Throughout the book you will also find many practical suggestions, illustrative examples, summary checklists, and observations and reflections from the diverse teachers, caregivers, and administrators who use the HighScope Preschool Curriculum.

Additional resources. Because this book can only serve as an introduction, we urge you to become more knowledgeable about the HighScope Preschool Curriculum as you begin to use its principles and methods. At the HighScope Web site, *www.highscope.org,* you can find additional resources to guide you toward further study and growth as an educator. HighScope training courses also provide additional information about the curriculum and how to implement it effectively in early childhood settings. It is our hope that learning about HighScope will help you grow as a practitioner and become an informed advocate for young children and their families.

Acknowledgments

Essentials of Active Learning in Preschool builds on over four decades of educational leadership by the HighScope Educational Research Foundation. Because contributors to the Foundation's international role are too numerous to list individually, these acknowledgments begin with major publications and services that collectively provided source material for this book. Foremost is the HighScope Curriculum manual *Educating Young Children,* which details the active learning model, teaching strategies, and program content that engage young children. Additional print and electronic resources used to write *Essentials* include step-by-step teacher idea books, assessment manuals, research-based policy papers, literally hundreds of articles in *HighScope ReSource* and *Extensions* (compiled in the *Supporting Young Learners* volumes) and in-depth publications on literacy, mathematics and science, conflict resolution, visual art, and movement and music.

HighScope practitioners have gathered an impressive archive of objective anecdotes about children and families. Their qualitative observations, when used to supplement the findings of quantitative research, helped bring many ideas to life in this volume. The HighScope training model, developed by the Foundation's staff and implemented by an international team of field consultants, was the standard I aspired to in introducing HighScope to this book's readers.

Complementing these group efforts are the individuals whose knowledge, skills, and support contributed significantly to this book. Founder Dave Weikart, to whom *Essentials* is dedicated, died two years before it was written. Yet my "conversations" with him while writing these pages aimed to capture his dual concerns for the individual child and for broad educational policy. The enthusiasm of HighScope President Larry Schweinhart was a motivating force in conceiving the book, and his comments helped bring it to completion. The HighScope Board of Directors also provided support and valuable feedback with regard to the book's overall content and potential audiences, with particular thanks to Harriet Egertson for reading and critiquing the entire manuscript.

A heartfelt "thank you" goes to the HighScope staff members who carefully reviewed and re-reviewed every chapter to verify both the accuracy and the spirit of the information. The first person to recognize is HighScope Senior Early Childhood Specialist Mary Hohmann, coauthor with Dave Weikart of *Educating Young Children* and its predecessor *Young Children in Action.* Not only was Mary's historical and current knowledge of the curriculum critical, but like all innovators, she delighted in updating it based on recent advances in theory, research, and practice. In addition, HighScope Early Childhood Director Beth Marshall's extensive knowledge of HighScope's curriculum and assessment procedures, as well as her leadership in developing adult training courses, made her input on these topics invaluable. Her background as a teacher, administrator, and trainer let her view the book from the perspective of multiple audiences.

HighScope Early Childhood Specialist Shannon Lockhart's dual background in research and program development permitted her to assess whether the manuscript clearly translated research results into practice. Her primary role in developing the infant-toddler curriculum also provided the context for understanding how the preschool years covered in this book fit along a developmental continuum. HighScope Early Childhood Specialist Polly Neill, who also brings both research and training expertise to this endeavor, carefully reviewed the assessment chapters. Her concern with capturing the authenticity and validity of HighScope instruments will enable readers to appreciate their value in supporting child development and program quality.

HighScope Early Childhood Specialist Karen (Kay) Rush, also an experienced trainer, made sure readers with different backgrounds could understand the information as it was presented. Her chapter-by-chapter approval guaranteed that practitioners would grasp what HighScope was about. Lead teacher Sue Gainsley, who teaches at the HighScope Demonstration Preschool and mentors practitioners at other sites, authenticated every example of child development and teaching practices. Coteacher Chris Boisvert verified the illustrations too, and contributed her special expertise in movement and music education.

Other content specialists contributed significantly to chapters in their subject areas. Andee DeBruin-Parecki, Director of the HighScope Early Childhood Reading Institute, reviewed the literacy information for accuracy and consistency with current research and standards. Karen Sawyers and Phyllis Weikart, present and former Director of Education Through Movement, respectively, reviewed the chapters on physical development and the arts with particular regard to teaching strategies that support active learning. Mary Hohmann and Beth Marshall supplemented their overall contributions with specialized knowledge in literacy and visual art, respectively.

Several HighScope Field Consultants who also work as college instructors, program directors, and teacher-trainers evaluated the book's ability to communicate with diverse audiences. Cathy Calamari, Moya Fewson, Debbie Handler, and Carol Montealegre guided the book's initial conceptualization, while Linda Weikel Ranweiler and Betsy Evans provided specific feedback on literacy and social development, respectively, topics on which they have written their own books.

Essentials would not be in the readers' hands without the knowledgeable efforts of HighScope's production and dissemination staff. Nancy Brickman, Director of Publications, was instrumental in shaping the book's tone and content from the beginning. HighScope Editor Jennifer Burd edited the manuscript with an eye toward its overall message, as well as an attention to detail. Every edit was carried out with thoughtfulness and respect and I always felt we were traveling on the same path. The photographs that helped the written message come alive were contributed primarily by Gregory Fox, with additional ones supplied by Chris Boisvert, Jennifer Burd, and Patricia Evans. Judy Seling designed the book to make sure it was both attractive and accessible. Kathy Woodard, HighScope Director of Marketing and Communications, asked meaningful questions about how *Essentials* could meet the needs of educators and then worked hard to make sure it reached them.

A resounding thank you goes to the teachers, children, and parents whose firsthand experience of the HighScope Curriculum continually informs our work and makes us better at fulfilling our mission — lifting lives through education. Finally, appreciation and encouragement are extended to you, the readers. My greatest hope and satisfaction rests with the potential for the words and images of *Essentials* to inspire active learning and active teaching on behalf of young children.

Essentials

of Active Learning in Preschool

Getting to Know the HighScope Curriculum

Part 1

Introduction and OverView

This part of the book provides an overview of the essential ingredients of the HighScope Curriculum and philosophy and discusses why the curriculum is effective.

Chapter 1 explains why educators should use a curriculum.

Chapter 2 provides an overview of the HighScope Curriculum.

Chapter 3 presents the child development theory behind the curriculum.

Chapter 4 describes the research on the effectiveness of the HighScope Curriculum.

Why Should Early Childhood Programs Use a Curriculum?

? ° ° Think About It

Many years ago, before there were good local bakeries in her town, Ann decided to bake her own bread. The ingredients looked simple enough (flour, yeast, water, sugar), and she'd been whipping up apple muffins and banana loaves for years. How hard could it be to bake bread?

She tried various recipes in cookbooks and magazines. Sometimes the dough didn't rise, either because the water was so hot it killed the yeast or so cold that the yeast never became "active." It was two months before Ann realized bread flour and cake flour were different. Arms aching after kneading, she was discouraged when the dough was as sticky as when she'd started. Every loaf smelled great coming out of the oven, but the results varied from inedible to incredible.

About a year later, books on bread-baking became popular — there were a lot to choose from. Some were so simple that Ann felt like an expert. Others were so complicated that she felt like a dunce. Finally she found one that worked for her. It began with simple recipes and advanced to more complex ones. Each step explained "why" as well as "how." Two weeks after buying the book, Ann had learned more than she had in a year of experimenting on her own. Now she could include "homemade bread" in her menu planning, confident of baking a reliably tasty loaf.

Adults can, and often do, learn by trial and error, in bits and pieces. But it's easier when learn-ing follows a logical order. The same holds true for children. It helps when their self-discovery is guided by a knowledgeable teacher who knows where the children have been and where they're going. Teachers in turn rely on the guidance of experts who have spent years studying how children learn. They don't have to reinvent the wheel each time they plan an educational experience. A **curriculum** lets teachers build on the knowledge that already exists in the field, add in their own experience and observations, and then adjust what they do for the individuals and groups in their class. This chapter explores the benefits of just such a process.

The Benefits of Using a Proven Curriculum

While no single curriculum ... can be identified as best, children who attend well-planned, high-quality early childhood programs in which curriculum aims are specified and integrated across domains tend to learn more and are better prepared to master the complex demands of formal schooling.

— *Eager to Learn,* National Research Council, 2000, p. 6

Before you begin reading about a particular curriculum — HighScope — you may be asking yourself, "Why should I, or my program, use any

4

Chapter Learning Objectives

By the end of this chapter, you will be able to

❖ Understand why using a curriculum helps teachers provide young children with a consistent learning experience

❖ Know why evidence of effectiveness is important in choosing a curriculum

❖ Relate your own experiences as a learner and decision-maker to choosing a proven curriculum model for young children

For children to get the full benefits of preschool, use a validated curriculum model with proof of effectiveness.

published curriculum? Why can't teachers invent their own curriculum, using what they know about child development and appropriate teaching practices?"

It is true that to be a good teacher, you have to know how children grow and learn. You must also know how to make children feel secure and excited about being in school. But this basic knowledge and set of skills is not enough to create an entire curriculum. So much learning happens in the early years — from understanding how books work, to figuring out how two children can use one computer, to mastering the zipper on a jacket — that it would be very difficult for an individual or even the entire staff of one agency to invent a complete curriculum from scratch. Developing a curriculum takes years of work by a group of thoughtful practitioners and researchers who pool their knowledge and talents.

Most important, it is not enough to offer a curriculum in the *belief* that it is good. There must be *proof* that it works. In order to get funding these days, administrators must show their program is using a curriculum that has **research-based evidence** of effectiveness. The word **validated** also describes such a proven curriculum. These terms mean scientific studies have shown that children in programs using the curriculum achieve certain educational goals. Further, the terms indicate that children achieve these goals more than children who are not attending any program or who are

enrolled in a program that does not use an identified curriculum — or possibly even one that uses a different preschool curriculum.

Proof of effectiveness is important to policymakers who want to make sure taxpayer dollars are invested wisely. It is also important to educators who want to be sure that what they do in the classroom truly benefits the young children in their care. Everyone concerned with early education therefore wants to make sure programs are of high enough quality to meet these objectives. (See the sidebar on p. 5 for a summary of the components of high-quality programs. The research base for these components is elaborated in Chapter 4.)

Using a validated or proven curriculum model means you get all of the following ingredients and instructions: a set of appropriate teaching practices for adults, a list of learning objectives for children, research tools to measure whether the program is meeting its goals, and a staff training model to make sure teachers understand and use the curriculum correctly.

For these reasons, HighScope urges early childhood educators to use a single and established curriculum rather than something homegrown and untested. A program that borrows bits and pieces from various models (sometimes called

---

Terms Used in This Chapter
• curriculum • research-based evidence • validated

an "eclectic" approach) will also be problematic. With a mixed bag of approaches, teachers lack a unifying set of principles to guide their practice. Different curricula may offer competing ideas, making it confusing for teachers to decide on the best course of action — which can result in contradictory messages being sent to young children about how and what to learn. For supplementary materials to work, it is preferable that they be specifically designed for, or approved for use with, the program's unified curriculum model.

Using a single curriculum does not mean that education is rigid and inflexible. In fact, a good curriculum allows you to change it to fit the children and community you serve, much as you might follow a basic recipe but change the seasoning to meet your personal tastes. So, for example, you can use the curriculum approach to teach reading but choose books that reflect local language and customs. The HighScope Curriculum permits this flexibility while maintaining the standards and practices that guarantee the curriculum will achieve positive and lasting results. Ideally, this is the goal of the curriculum and the programs that choose to use it.

Try These Ideas Yourself

1. Think of a product or technique you tried because you heard (from someone you know, from an advertisement, or from another source) that it "really works!" Did it? Write a brief description of this experience and what you learned from it. How might you relate what you learned to the process of choosing a classroom curriculum?

2. Think of things you learned to do as a child or an adult — for example, riding a bike, tying shoelaces, doing long division, driving a car, or using a computer program. Pick one where the learning went well and another that was difficult or frustrating. Briefly describe what you think accounts for differences in your rate or ease of learning. Did you figure out what to do on your own and/or did you have someone or something to guide you (such as a person, book, or videotape)? If you learned all or part on your own, what helped or interfered with your discoveries? If you received guidance, did it make learning easier or harder? Why?

(Variation: Think of a situation in which you taught something to another person where you considered yourself an "expert." Think of another situation in which you taught something, where you knew more than the other person but did not consider yourself an expert. Describe how your teaching style differed in the two situations. Was one more effective than the other, or were they equally effective in helping the learner?)

Components of High-Quality Early Childhood Programs

High-quality early childhood programs have the following components:

❖ *Child development curriculum* with active participatory learning
❖ *Low-enrollment limits* so adults can give individualized attention to children
❖ *Staff trained in early childhood development* so they can observe, understand, and support children's learning in all areas
❖ *Supervisory support and inservice training* so staff can understand and carry out the curriculum

❖ *Involvement of parents as partners* because they are children's first and most lasting teachers
❖ *Sensitivity to the noneducational needs of children* because preschool is just one component of children's early experiences
❖ *Developmentally appropriate evaluation procedures* to accurately measure what children know and to plan effective ways to extend their learning

Adapted from *A School Administrator's Guide to Early Childhood Programs* (Schweinhart, 2004, p. 15)

Chapter 2

What Is the HighScope Preschool Curriculum?

 Think About It

"It's easy. Let me show you!"

You have just installed the Draw-A-Lot program on your computer. A coworker, who has been using the program for a year, is eager to show you all the neat things it can do. Pulling up a chair next to you, she takes the mouse. "There are all these templates to get you started. Those are in this pull-down menu. The second and fifth ones are especially pretty." She opens and closes them so quickly you barely get a look. Then she continues, "But it's easy to start your own designs from scratch. Just go up here and choose this command. Then you scoot over to this column and pick a color and a line. After that you kind of jigger the texture icon into place like this, and then you can rotate it or flip it and ..." Your chair has gradually been shoved to the side as your colleague sits front and center at the monitor. When she's finished creating her "Still Life With Draw-A-Lot" and gets up to leave, you don't remember a thing she said. You thank her for the help, close the program, and click open Solitaire.

Early the next day, two hours before anyone else gets to the office, you open Draw-A-Lot. You read the "Get Started" pages in the manual and go through the step-by-step tutorial. Then you begin to play with program. At first, your designs and colors are limited. At one point you accidentally delete the entire image, and another time you somehow flip it upside down and can't figure out how to turn it right-side-up again. You laugh at yourself and start over. By the time your coworkers arrive, you've finished a simple but colorful poster advertising the agency's upcoming fundraiser. The colleague from yesterday stops by to admire your work. "I'm glad I was able to help you," she says.

We've all had an experience where someone has told or shown us how to do something. Usually their intent is to be helpful. Often, they know more about the subject than we do. Sometimes, in their eagerness to share, they overload us with information. But while they are active teachers, we are passive learners. As a result, we learn little or nothing. By contrast, when we have the time and materials to experiment independently, we can learn a great deal. As shown above, the best situation is when we have enough guidance to get started — whether it comes from a person or a publication — and then continue to explore on our own. Once we master the basics, we may turn back to the "expert" for advanced pointers, or even share some of our own discoveries.

In the latter type of educational relationship, both the teacher and the learner play an active role. And because the learner is an active participant in the educational process, the lessons are meaningful and lasting. This shared approach to education is what HighScope is all about. In this chapter we will explore the active learning approach HighScope uses in its curriculum.

❖

Chapter Learning Objectives

By the end of this chapter, you will be able to

❖ Define the ingredients of active participatory learning and use them to analyze children's educational experiences

❖ Explain why active learning is effective for all age groups

❖ See how the content of the HighScope Preschool Curriculum addresses all areas of school readiness

❖ Appreciate the important and diverse roles teachers play in early learning

❖ Understand how assessment and training fit within the HighScope Curriculum

The Components of HighScope

The HighScope Preschool Curriculum is a complete system of early childhood education, based on child development theory, research, and proven instructional practices. The curriculum has a set of *teaching practices* for adults, *curriculum content* in all school readiness areas with key developmental indicators (KDIs) for children, *assessment tools* to measure teaching behaviors and children's progress, and a *training model* to help adults use the curriculum to support children's development. We will discuss each of these items further in the remainder of this chapter.

The HighScope Philosophy

In the HighScope Preschool Curriculum, fully described in *Educating Young Children* by Mary Hohmann and David P. Weikart (2002), young children build or "construct" their knowledge of

the world. That means learning is not simply a process of adults giving information to children. Rather, children participate actively in the learning process. They discover things through direct experience with people, objects, events, and ideas. Preschoolers also make plans and follow through on their interests and intentions.

HighScope teachers are as active and involved as children in the classroom. They thoughtfully provide materials, plan activities, and talk with (not at) children in ways that both support and challenge what children are observing and thinking. Activities are both child initiated — built upon children's natural curiosity — and developmentally appropriate, that is, matched to children's current and emerging abilities. HighScope calls this approach **active participatory learning** — a process in which teachers and students are partners in shaping the learning experience.

This educational approach, in which children and adults share responsibility for learning, builds essential school-readiness skills. In addition to addressing traditional academic subjects, the HighScope Curriculum promotes independence, curiosity, decision making, cooperation, persistence, creativity, and problem solving in young children.

The principles that guide the HighScope Preschool Curriculum are illustrated in the "Wheel of Learning" on page 9. *Active learning* is at the center to highlight the importance of children's initiative and HighScope's comprehensive attention to educational content in its key developmental indicators (formerly called key experiences)[1]. The four quadrants represent teachers' responsibilities as they work with children: engaging in supportive *adult-child interactions,* creating a challenging *learning environment,* establishing a consistent *daily routine,* and doing ongoing *assessment* to make plans and meet children's educational needs. After reading this book, you will have a complete picture of how these parts of the HighScope Curriculum fit together in a unified whole.

Terms Used in This Chapter

• active participatory learning • materials • manipulation • choice • child language and thought • adult scaffolding • curriculum content • five dimensions of school readiness • National Education Goals Panel • key developmental indicators (KDIs) • plan-do-review sequence • comprehensive assessment tools • professional development

[1]See the HighScope Web site, *www.highscope.org,* for the alignment of key developmental indicators and key experiences.

The HighScope Preschool Wheel of Learning

ASSESSMENT
- Teamwork
- Daily Anecdotal Notes
- Daily Planning
- Child Assessment

ADULT-CHILD INTERACTION
- Interaction Strategies
- Encouragement
- Problem-Solving Approach to Conflict

ACTIVE LEARNING
Initiative
Key Developmental Indicators

DAILY ROUTINE
- Plan-Do-Review
- Small-Group Time
- Large-Group Times

LEARNING ENVIRONMENT
- Areas
- Materials
- Storage

Active Participatory Learning

The National Education Goals Panel (Kagan et al., 1995) says school readiness is enhanced when children are provided with play-oriented, exploratory activities that allow them to interact, make choices, and participate at their own developmental level. This vision is echoed in the High-Scope concept of *active participatory learning,* which has five ingredients:

1. Materials — Programs offer abundant supplies of diverse, age-appropriate materials. Materials are appealing to all the senses and are open ended — that is, they lend themselves to being used in a variety of ways and help expand children's experiences and stimulate their thought.

2. Manipulation — Children handle, examine, combine, and transform materials and ideas. They make discoveries through direct hands-on and "minds-on" contact with these resources.

3. Choice — Children choose materials and play partners, change and build on their play ideas, and plan activities according to their interests and needs.

4. Child language and thought — Children describe what they are doing and understanding. They communicate verbally and nonverbally as they think about their actions and modify their thinking to take new learning into account.

5. Adult scaffolding — "Scaffolding" means adults support children's current level of thinking and challenge them to advance to the next stage. In this way, adults help children gain knowledge and develop creative problem-solving skills.

HighScope Preschool Curriculum Content

A comprehensive curriculum model, HighScope addresses all areas of development. To organize the **content** of children's learning, the HighScope Curriculum parallels the **five dimensions of school readiness** identified by the **National Education Goals Panel** (NEGP; Kagan et al., 1995) and widely accepted as the standard in the early childhood community: *approaches to learning; language, literacy, and communication; social and emotional development; physical development, health, and well-being;* and *arts and sciences.*[2] HighScope further subdivides arts and sciences into the subjects of mathematics, science and technology, social studies, and the arts.

The NEGP emphasizes that these five dimensions are related to one another; that is, a child's development in one area affects his or her growth in all the others. Therefore, all five dimensions are equally important. It is also important to note that children's development varies widely within each age range. No two preschoolers are alike, and any individual child may be more or less advanced in each area. The objective of early childhood programs is to provide the kinds of experiences that support and nurture all these areas of learning and development in every child. HighScope agrees with all these points and therefore finds the Panel's readiness model appropriate for organizing its curriculum as well as for formulating the standards adopted by many states and school districts.

---

[2]The National Education Goals Panel uses slightly different wording to label the second, fourth, and fifth dimensions, namely: language and communication; physical well-being and motor development; and cognition and general knowledge.

Applying the Five Ingredients of Active Participatory Learning

Below is an example of how the ingredients of active participatory learning helped Erin learn to write. Her teacher recorded the following anecdote (in *italics*), which happened at work time.

Materials. The classroom has a wide range of writing materials (see Chapter 11).

At work time in the art area, Erin brought a box of markers, a stack of plain white paper, and several sheets of yellow construction paper to the table.

Manipulation. Children use writing materials in many ways, including making real letters and letterlike forms. They use, or pretend to use, writing in the same ways as adults.

Erin used a black marker to make lines, circles, and X's on plain white paper. She wrote them in rows, like lines of print. Then she said, "I want to make invitations for my birthday party."

Choice. Children are free to use materials however they want during child-initiated parts of the day (such as plan-do-review) and also during adult-initiated activities (such as small- and large-group or outside time). The teacher asked how Erin was going to carry out her plan to make invitations.

I asked Erin, "How will you make the invitations?" Erin replied, "I'm going to use the yellow paper and a red marker." She selected these materials from the array she'd set in front of her.

Child language and thought. As children work, teachers talk naturally to them about what they are doing. Adults expand children's vocabulary without dominating the conversation.

Erin folded the paper in half and drew a pink flower with blue and green leaves on top. She said, "I have to decorate the cards first." I commented, "You're making a decoration on the outside before you write the invitation on the inside." Erin replied, "It's like the card my grandma gave me for Halloween. It has pictures and words."

Adult scaffolding. Preschoolers learn to write letters and words in many different ways, for example, by tracing, copying, or writing letters as an adult spells out a word. Erin's teacher allowed her to use a combination of strategies, based on what Erin was ready for.

Erin said she needed help to write the words birthday party. I asked, "Do you want me to tell you the letters or write them for you to copy?" She asked me to write them. I wrote the word birthday and Erin copied the letters on her invitation. Then she said, "Just tell me the letters for 'party' because I can write them." I said them one at a time and Erin wrote them down. Then she said, "I can spell my name all by myself" and she wrote ERIN.

HighScope further sees development as taking place in all five areas *throughout life.* That is, individuals continue to learn from infancy through adulthood when they actively engage with objects, people, events, and ideas. The early childhood "readiness" framework thus applies equally well to the Foundation's work with elementary-age students, youth, and training for adults. Readiness to learn, extended into youth and adulthood, becomes readiness to work. It is a widely held notion in early childhood that children learn through play and that play is a child's work. Adults also learn through playful exploration of ideas, and they work most effectively when they integrate and apply all the areas of their knowledge. HighScope thus sees play, learning, and work as recurring along a lifelong continuum of personal and professional development.

Key Developmental Indicators (KDIs)

Within each of the readiness content areas, HighScope identifies 58 **key developmental indicators** that are appropriate to each age range. (See the sidebar on p. 11.) KDIs are the building blocks of thinking and reasoning at each stage of development. They pave the way for later

HighScope Preschool Curriculum Content

Approaches to Learning

❖ Making and expressing choices, plans, and decisions

❖ Solving problems encountered in play

Language, Literacy, and Communication

❖ Talking with others about personally meaningful experiences

❖ Describing objects, events, and relations

❖ Having fun with language: listening to stories and poems, making up stories and rhymes

❖ Writing in various ways: drawing, scribbling, and using letterlike forms, invented spelling, and conventional forms

❖ Reading in various ways: reading storybooks, signs and symbols, and one's own writing

❖ Dictating stories

Social and Emotional Development

❖ Taking care of one's own needs

❖ Expressing feelings in words

❖ Building relationships with children and adults

❖ Creating and experiencing collaborative play

❖ Dealing with social conflict

Physical Development, Health, and Well-Being

❖ Moving in nonlocomotor ways (anchored movement: bending, twisting, rocking, swinging one's arms)

❖ Moving in locomotor ways (nonanchored movement: running, jumping, hopping, skipping, marching, climbing)

❖ Moving with objects

❖ Expressing creativity in movement

❖ Describing movement

❖ Acting upon movement directions

❖ Feeling and expressing steady beat

❖ Moving in sequences to a common beat

Arts and Sciences

Mathematics

Seriation

❖ Comparing attributes (longer/shorter, bigger/smaller)

❖ Arranging several things one after another in a series or pattern and describing the relationships (big/bigger/biggest, red/blue/red/blue)

❖ Fitting one ordered set of objects to another through trial and error (small cup and small saucer; medium cup and medium saucer; big cup and big saucer)

Number

❖ Comparing the numbers of things in two sets to determine "more," "fewer," "same number"

❖ Arranging two sets of objects in one-to-one correspondence

❖ Counting objects

Space

❖ Filling and emptying

❖ Fitting things together and taking them apart

❖ Changing the shape and arrangement of objects (wrapping, twisting, stretching, stacking, enclosing)

❖ Observing people, places, and things from different spatial viewpoints

❖ Experiencing and describing positions, directions, and distances in the play space, building, and neighborhood

❖ Interpreting spatial relations in drawings, pictures, and photographs

Science and Technology

Classification

❖ Recognizing objects by sight, sound, touch, taste, and smell

❖ Exploring and describing similarities, differences, and the attributes of things

❖ Distinguishing and describing shapes

❖ Sorting and matching

❖ Using and describing something in several ways

❖ Holding more than one attribute in mind at a time

❖ Distinguishing between "some" and "all"

❖ Describing characteristics something does not possess or what class it does not belong to

Time

❖ Starting and stopping an action on signal

❖ Experiencing and describing rates of movement

❖ Experiencing and comparing time intervals

❖ Anticipating, remembering, and describing sequences of events

Social Studies

❖ Participating in group routines

❖ Being sensitive to the feelings, interests, and needs of others

The Arts

Visual Art

❖ Relating models, pictures, and photographs to real places and things

❖ Making models out of clay, blocks, and other materials

❖ Drawing and painting

Dramatic Art

❖ Imitating actions and sounds

❖ Pretending and role playing

Music

❖ Moving to music

❖ Exploring and identifying sounds

❖ Exploring the singing voice

❖ Developing melody

❖ Singing songs

❖ Playing simple musical instruments

 Key developmental indicators (KDIs) are the building blocks of thinking and reasoning at each stage of development. HighScope identifies 58 preschool KDIs organized under five content areas.

12

schooling and eventual entry into the adult world. In terms of the two major types of learning objectives used by many educational theorists, these indicators include both "knowledge" and the application of this knowledge in "thinking." For example, preschoolers need to know color names (knowledge) in order to sort objects (thinking) by color. (For further information on these terms, see *Designing a New Taxonomy of Educational Objectives* by educational psychologist Robert Marzano, 2001.) Now let's take a look at the components of the term *key developmental indicators*.

The word *key* refers to the fact that these are the meaningful ideas children should learn and experience. HighScope acknowledges that young children need to master a wide range of specific knowledge and thinking skills — the list could be almost endless in scope and detail. To avoid losing sight of the forest for the trees, the content captured in the individual KDIs stresses the broader areas of knowledge and skills that lay the foundation for further learning.

The second part of the term, *developmental,* conveys the idea that learning is gradual and cumulative. Learning follows a sequence, generally moving from simple to more complex knowledge and skills. Moreover, *developmental* emphasizes that it is inappropriate, not to mention futile, to expect preschoolers to behave and learn as kindergarten or first-grade students do. Whatever level we are addressing, from infancy through youth, the curriculum must be consistent with what we know about human development in that age range.

Finally, *indicators* was chosen to emphasize that educators need evidence that children are developing the knowledge, skills, and understanding considered important for school and life readiness. To plan appropriately for students and to evaluate program effectiveness, we need observable indicators of our impact on children. Further, by defin-

HighScope's key developmental indicators (KDIs) in every content area are the building blocks of thinking and reasoning.

ing these child outcomes in measurable terms, we can develop assessment tools that are consistent with the curriculum. In other words, the assessment system "indicates" whether the program is meeting its goals.

The continuity across content areas and KDIs allows for the fact that development occurs along a continuum and children of different ages and abilities cannot be pigeonholed into a single age-based category. This book focuses on the 58 KDIs that make up the HighScope Curriculum content for preschoolers, that is, children aged three to five. However, children in this age range may exhibit behaviors characteristic of older toddlers or early elementary students. Hence, the preschool indicators were developed with the entire early childhood spectrum, ages 0–8, in mind. Furthermore, children with special needs can fall at different points along the continuum, without regard to age, so this flexible system for organizing content helps practitioners understand and plan for their development.

For children to learn the content contained in the KDIs, it is not enough for adults to simply pass along information. Children must experience the world firsthand. Adults can then support and help extend children's thinking, scaffolding their learning as the children progress to each new level of insight and knowledge. Moreover, true learning takes time and repeated exposure. It is not a one-shot affair.

The HighScope KDIs are based on the latest child development research and decades of classroom practice. They are periodically updated as early childhood research reveals more about how preschoolers learn and how adults best support their development. To give an example, emerging statistics on the prevalence of childhood obesity is causing a reevaluation of how to promote healthy physical development in young children. As information accumulates in this and other areas, High-Scope will revise its content accordingly in future publications.

The KDIs are also written to be universal. Teachers and caregivers from different cultures in the United States and countries all over the world report that they see children engaging in these developmentally important experiences. Researchers confirm these commonalities among children of all backgrounds. For example, children everywhere sort objects into containers and take things apart and put them together. The exact materials used may vary from culture to culture, but the activity and the resulting learning about the nature of things is essentially the same.

Teachers use the KDIs to guide all aspects of their program. They set up the classroom, plan the day, observe children and extend their thinking, and measure children's progress based on the general principles of active learning and the specific content in the indicators. These HighScope teaching practices are described in the next section of this chapter. Part 3 of this book presents an in-depth look at the KDIs in all areas of children's learning and explains the thoughtful and practical strategies High-Scope teachers use to promote them.

HighScope Teaching Practices

HighScope teachers arrange and label classroom interest areas and stock diverse materials to give children a broad range of experience and help them begin to understand how the world can be organized. To promote initiative and independence, teachers make sure the materials are easy for children to get and put away on their own. Teachers also make sure materials reflect children's interests and their home culture so the children are both comfortable and excited about learning.

The daily routine provides a balanced variety of experiences. Children engage in both individual and social play, participate in small and large groups, assist with cleanup, socialize during meals, develop self-care skills, and exercise their small and large muscles. Some parts of the routine revolve around children's plans and choices: children are free to choose where to go in the classroom (or outdoor space) and what toys or materials to work with. Other parts of the routine are

planned and set in motion by adults. Even in these adult-led activities, however, children contribute their own ideas and choose how to use the materials supplied by the teacher.

The heart of the HighScope daily routine is the **plan-do-review sequence,** in which children make choices about what they will do, carry out their ideas, and reflect on their activities with adults and peers. We call these parts of the day *planning time, work time,* and *recall (or review) time*. By participating in the plan-do-review sequence, children gain confidence as thinkers, problem-solvers, and decision makers. They learn how to act with intention and reflect on the consequences of their actions. These are abilities that will serve them well in school and throughout their lives.

HighScope Assessment Tools

According to studies, the best programs constantly measure how well teachers teach and how much children learn. They use the results to continue what is working and improve what is not; for example, to provide more teacher training or fill gaps in children's experiences.

HighScope has developed two **comprehensive assessment tools** to carry out this review and enhancement process. The Preschool Program Quality Assessment (PQA) evaluates whether teachers and agencies are using the most effective program practices. Every area of classroom teaching and program operations is rated to identify strengths and areas for improvement. The Preschool Child Observation Record (COR) assesses children's learning in every content area. Each day, teachers and caregivers generate brief written descriptions, or anecdotes, that objectively describe children's behavior. They use these notes to evaluate children's development and then plan activities to help individual children and the classroom as a whole progress.

In addition, HighScope has developed and validated a specialized tool for literacy, the *Early Literacy Skills Assessment (ELSA)*. Other measures for specific content areas are also under development, for example, in mathematics and visual art.

Because all these instruments reflect best practices in the classroom and basic child development

14

principles and research, they are suitable for use in all developmentally based programs, not just those using the HighScope Curriculum. You can find more information on these tools at the HighScope Web site.

HighScope Training

A curriculum works only if it is used consistently and properly. We know from over 40 years of research that HighScope offers significant benefits to young children. However, to get those benefits, children must receive the same program that was proven in the research. To guarantee these optimal conditions, the HighScope Foundation has an extensive training program of **professional development** courses for supervisors, teachers, and caregivers.

In delivering training to adults, HighScope employs the same principles of active participatory learning that it uses with children. That means people in training do not just read theory and research, they also practice using HighScope teaching strategies in the classroom. They reflect on what is and is not working and discuss their experiences and observations with colleagues. Certified HighScope trainers provide feedback and support as training participants learn about the curriculum and how to use it with children.

By using the suggestions at the end of each chapter in this book, (under "Try These Ideas Yourself"), you too can "actively" learn as you read about the HighScope Curriculum. Depending on your situation, you can practice parts of the curriculum with children in your program, share your thoughts with other students and colleagues, mentor those you supervise, and even try some of the exercises with family and friends at home. Most important, you can apply the information to your personal and professional life and reflect on what you learn in the process. In exploring these ideas, and inventing your own, you will experience the HighScope way of teaching and learning.

 **Try These Ideas Yourself**

1. Draw a line down the middle of a piece of paper to create two columns. Fold it in half so only one column shows. Pick an everyday object such as an apple, a book, or a chair. Read a description of the object in the dictionary or encyclopedia, or ask someone you know to describe the object to you. In the first column, write down what you remember from reading or hearing about the object's description. Turn the paper over so the other column is showing. Now explore the same object for at least five minutes on your own, using all your senses. Write down what you learned about it in the second column. Open the paper and compare the two lists. Which method of learning produced more knowledge about the object? Why? Write down your answers along with any other thoughts you have about these different methods of learning.

2. Observe a setting with at least one adult and one child where there is an opportunity for the child(ren) to learn something. For example, it might be a preschool or day care facility where children are doing an art activity or learning about numbers and letters. It could be a kitchen where a parent and child are cooking together, or it could be a supermarket where an adult and child are doing the week's grocery shopping.

Next, review the list of active learning ingredients: materials, manipulation, choice, child language and thought, and adult scaffolding. Answer the following questions: Which of the ingredients of active learning are present in the situation you are observing? How does the adult set things up so they do (or do not) occur? What type of learning does (or does not) take place for the child(ren)? How would you change the situation to increase the amount of active learning?

3. Look at the diagram of the preschool "Wheel of Learning" on page 9. Observe in your own or another early childhood program. (It does not have to be a HighScope program.) Make a written note of each activity or situation you observe and where you think it fits on the wheel.

What Is the Theory Behind the HighScope Curriculum?

Think About It

Have you ever walked by a construction site day after day and watched a building go up, especially a tall office complex or even a skyscraper? The first thing the construction workers do is pour the foundation. They follow careful specifications, accurate to a fraction of an inch, to make sure the building has a solid base that will hold up under the most extreme conditions. Then they build the structure, one floor at a time. At each level, they construct a scaffold to stand on while they work on the floor above.

Once the basic structure, roof, and outer walls are in place, they put in the "mechanicals," including the plumbing, the electricity, and the heating and cooling system. With these essentials in place, the structure can now be divided by adding floors, ceilings, and interior walls. This organization is followed by the installation of permanent fixtures in the bathrooms, kitchens, and so on. At last, the building is ready for the occupants to move in and add the details that personalize their space, such as window and floor treatments, paint or wallpaper, and furnishings. Over time, fixtures are occasionally updated as old ones wear out or improved models come on the market. Personal furnishings may be changed more often, as new tenants replace old ones or current tenants alter the use or appearance of their rooms.

The methods teachers use to support children's development are a lot like building a skyscraper. Learning begins with a firm foundation based on a trusting relationship between the child and one or more adults. Growth then proceeds one step at a time. In order for children to advance to the next, more accurate, way of thinking, adults need to provide a **scaffold** that is grounded at children's current level and allows them to climb one level up. Bit by bit, through experience, children begin to fill in the structure with essential "divisions," or concepts. Then they add more details, based on personal experience and preferences. As with the developments in a building, the learning process never really stops. Adults, as well as children, continue to modify parts of the structure and many details throughout their lives.

The HighScope Curriculum is founded on developmental theories that see learning as an interactive growth process. In the remainder of this chapter we discuss the theoretical perspectives that underlie HighScope's basic philosophy and approach, particularly active learning and the plan-do-review sequence.

The Theory Behind Active Learning

The HighScope Curriculum is grounded in child development theory and research. It originally drew extensively on the cognitive-developmental work pioneered by **Jean Piaget** (1969) and his colleagues, and the progressive educational philosophy of John Dewey (1938/1963). Since then, the curriculum has been updated according to the

16

Chapter Learning Objectives

By the end of this chapter, you will be able to

❖ Describe the development of thinking (ways of knowing) from infancy through adulthood

❖ Understand how the thinking of young children differs from that of adults

❖ Relate the development of thinking to the use of "active learning" in the High-Scope Curriculum

❖ Understand the developmental importance of and theory behind the High-Scope plan-do-review sequence

results of ongoing cognitive-developmental research (Clements, 2004; Gelman & Baillargeon, 1983; Gelman & Brenneman, 2004; Gelman & Gallistel, 1978/1986; Goswami, 2002; National Research Council, 2005; Necombe, 2002; Smith, 2002). Brain research also supports these findings (Shore, 1997; Thompson & Nelson, 2001).

The teaching practices, particularly the notion that development occurs within sociocultural settings where adults scaffold children's learning, was first derived from the work of developmental psychologist and educator **Lev Vygotsky** (1934/1962). These educational practices in the HighScope teaching model also continue to be updated, based on the theory and research of those who have followed Vygotsky's lead (Rowe & Wertsch, 2002).

Ways of Knowing

To explain how children's thinking develops over time, Piaget described several general **ways of knowing:**

▲ From birth onward, children gain knowledge through **sensorimotor** exploration of the world, that is, by using their senses and their direct physical actions on objects.

▲ Later, children also gain knowledge through their ability to represent actions with symbols such as words and drawings. With the beginning of language, thought becomes possible. It is **preconceptual and intuitive thought** (also called **preoperational**) because the child is still tied to perceptual characteristics rather than underlying concepts.

▲ **Concrete operations** comes next as children begin to think more logically, draw conclusions, and solve problems based on the direct evidence of their observations. As they are tied to the actual or "concrete" things they see and do, however, children at this point in their development are unable to analyze the processes behind their observations. Thus, their conclusions about the world are sometimes "wrong" according to adult logic and understanding. Young children also tend to see things from their own perspective and cannot "decenter" from themselves to understand the world from other points of view.

▲ Finally, knowledge built through **formal operations** allows older children and adults to consider all possibilities in a situation, form hypotheses and make observations or conduct experiments to test them, and use deductive logic for problem solving. These abilities are also referred to as "abstract thinking." Formal operations are the basis of higher mathematics and controlled scientific experimentation.

Although Piaget tied these ways of experiencing and interacting with the world to particular ages, we now know that in some situations, Piaget underrated children's understanding, portraying them as less competent than they actually are. For example, in mathematics, "under certain conditions, preschoolers can and do use a principle of one-to-one correspondence to reason about number. And they do this with set sizes they cannot count accurately" (Gelman & Baillargeon, 1983, p. 215).

Terms Used in This Chapter

• scaffolding • Jean Piaget • Lev Vygotsky • ways of knowing • sensorimotor • preconceptual or preoperational • concrete operations • formal operations • cognitive-developmental • learning pathways/developmental trajectories • interaction • knowledge construction • developmental change • assimilation • accommodation • active learning • zone of proximal development • plan-do-review • purposeful play

Cognitive-Developmental Research

Today's cognitive-developmental researchers no longer focus on these broad age-related ways of knowing described by Piaget. Instead they study children's **learning pathways or developmental trajectories** related to specific content and tasks (for example, vocabulary and counting). These current perspectives are consistent with High-Scope's observations of children's learning. They also guide HighScope's ongoing curriculum development work in all content areas. Goswami (2002) sums up current cognitive-developmental theory this way:

> *Children's cognitive development depends on a developing understanding of what makes something happen in the physical or social world, a developing understanding that derives from socially meaningful activity, that is representational from the outset, and that is shaped by language. Children, the universal novices, are apprenticed to the "expert" adults around them, and learn from them to operate with the physical, symbolic, and cognitive tools of their culture (p. 514).*

These ideas are also supported by current brain research, which validates the idea that learning depends on **interaction.** By interaction, scientists mean a child's encounters with people, objects, events, or activities, and later, ideas: "Neuroscientists stress the fact that interaction with the environment is not simply an interesting feature of brain development; it is an absolute requirement" (Shore, 1997, p. 15). Put another way, without experiences, the brain has nothing to work with.

Some brain researchers suggest that the brain's initial overproduction of nerve cell connections captures the mass of early experiences and that these connections are later organized and pruned down through use. At the same time, researchers find that these connections are not rigidly locked in place after a certain point in development. There is evidence of the brain's continuing ability to change and form new connections (called "plasticity") throughout the life span (Black, Jones, Nelson, & Greenough, 1998; Greenough & Black, 1992). Active engagement thus plays a critical role in learning from cradle to grave!

Knowledge Construction

Children attending HighScope preschools actively build their ideas about reality through their direct experiences with people, materials, events, and ideas. Vygotsky saw the social or cultural environment as being particularly crucial in how language and thinking develop. We see in adults, for example, that the regional or national character of a people is shaped by how those in their community express themselves and the values and beliefs they grow up with. With children, this idea is supported by the study of early vocabulary development in home settings (Hart & Risley, 1995, 1999) as well as by research on the role of gesture in early language development (Goodwyn, Acredolo, & Brown, 2000; Iverson & Goldin-Meadow, 2005; Namy, Acredolo, & Goodwyn, 2000).

In a cognitive-developmental model, learning is seen as a process of **developmental change —** that is, a process in which we learn by relating and adding new information to what we already know and, if necessary, even changing the way we thought before. For example, if we know how to care for a pet guinea pig — to give it certain kinds of food and clean water — then we have a knowledge base to care for other pets, such as a cat or dog. However, we will still have to learn new things as conscientious pet owners — such as what cats and dogs eat and drink that is different from what guinea pigs eat and drink. This ongoing process of developmental change, first identified by Piaget and upheld by current research, is called **assimilation** (using our existing knowledge and behaviors to explore new things) and **accommodation** (changing our mental models — our ideas about how the world works — to take new and sometimes contradictory information into account). It often takes many experiences involving assimilation and accommodation before changes in thinking are fully formed and consistently applied in our actions.

Active Learning

HighScope adopted the term "active learning" to describe this interactive process between the learner and the environment. Learning that reflects a true change in thinking does not take place when children are simply told something. They must see and do it for themselves, with adults present to encourage and challenge their thinking.

18

Vygotsky referred to the **zone of proximal development** as the area between what children can accomplish on their own and what they can do with the help of an adult or another child who is more developmentally advanced. HighScope teachers observe children carefully so they know when and how to enter this zone to scaffold learning to the next level. Children must be secure and confident in what they already know before they are ready to move to the next level. When High-Scope says adults support and extend children's learning, it means that the adults first validate, or *support,* what children already know, and then challenge them to *extend* their thinking to the next level.

Because young children are actively constructing knowledge as they engage with the world, their thinking does not always make sense in terms of "adult" ways of thinking, but it has its own logic.

▲ **It's alive!** Children are better at distinguishing between living and nonliving things than we once believed. In their minds, something that moves may be alive; for example, a raindrop sliding down the windowpane. At the same time, three- and four-year-olds begin to use features such as animation to identify what is not real on television (Fitch, Huston, & Wright, 1993). Moreover, building on what they know about animals, toys, and objects, preschoolers can successfully distinguish between real animals that can cause themselves to move and change, and nonreal animals that cannot because their feet are "not real" — that is, not made of living matter — and, therefore, can only be moved by forces external to themselves (Subrahmanyam, Gelman, & Lafosse, 2002).

▲ **Literal definitions.** Children are very literal in the way they interpret words. For example, when four-year-old Becky was cautioned to be careful because "Big kids play rough," she asked her mother, "Do little kids play smooth?" At the same time, children continue to learn new words directly connected to their experiences, even "big" words like *observe, respiration,* and *nutrients* (Gelman & Brenneman, 2004).

▲ **Blending intuitive and scientific thought.** Children make observations about the world, just as scientists do. However, their explanations for what they see are framed in terms of what they know from past experience. For example, when there was a strong wind with clouds rushing by, Jason said, "The clouds are making it windy. The wind will stop when the clouds are gone." Thus, even preschoolers engage in causal thinking: the rushing clouds create a wind, Jason reasons, just as a truck creates a wind when it speeds by. Eventually, children's thinking will be reshaped and reorganized — in this case, by further experience with wind and air pressure.

▲ **One thing at a time.** Young children tend to focus on one thing at a time and usually do not connect events or see multiple similarities. This means they may not apply or "generalize" a lesson to related objects or happenings or think in terms of cause and effect ("If X, then Y"). For example, Zack is pressing hard to glue Styrofoam bits to his picture. As he bears down and forward on the paper, it moves and the sequins he has piled up next to it are pushed to the floor. Zack picks them up and puts them in the same place. When it happens a second time, he yells, "Stop jumping to the floor!" He does not connect his pressing on the paper to the sequins falling.

▲ **Judging by appearances and counting.** Young children tend to judge "how much" and "how many" by the way things look. For example, they judge that 15 candies spread out on the table are more than 15 candies bunched together because the row takes up more horizontal space than the pile. When working with small quantities, however, counting and matching often do carry more weight than appearances (Gelman & Gallistel, 1978/1986). So, for example, children can tell that three pretzels are more than two pretzels no matter how they are arranged.

In all these ways that children think, we see them "actively" using hands-on experiences to build or construct knowledge. As they continue to have diverse and direct encounters with the real world, children's thinking expands to take new observations and interpretations into account. Active learning thus serves as the basis for preschoolers' development of thought and understanding.

The Theory Behind Plan-Do-Review

In addition to active learning, the other hallmark of the HighScope Curriculum is the **plan-do-review process** (described in detail in Chapter 7).

Young children in HighScope programs express their intentions (*make plans* involving choices about materials, actions, and people), carry out their ideas (*do things* to achieve their goals), and reflect on the experience (*review* what they did and what they learned). The plan-do-review sequence is rooted in the work of several theorists and is supported by research conducted by HighScope and others.

Children are amateur scientists. They blend observation and intuition to make sense of their investigations.

out. When they are successful in carrying out their intentions, they develop a sense of initiative. If they consistently meet with failure, or are made to feel bad in their attempts, they may feel guilty about taking the initiative. By encouraging children's initiative, exploration, and independent problem-solving, HighScope teachers give children the social-emotional support they need to become competent and confident planners.

Making Plans

Planning has both cognitive and social-emotional components. Cognitively, in order to make a plan, a child must have a mental picture in mind of what he or she wants to do. This ability to imagine or form mental images of something that has not yet happened develops along with a child's use of language. Developmental psychologists describe the mental tools children use to plan as "executive control structures" (Case, 1985) or "executive function" (Zelazo & Mueller, 2002), by which they mean the inner blueprints for framing a problem and using existing knowledge and skills to plan, try out, and evaluate a solution.

There is evidence that, over time, as children converse with adults and participate in everyday routines, their ability to talk about a plan develops along the following lines: at first they focus on the *here and now* ("Want block"); next they begin to focus on *now and not now,* with reference to past or future ("At work time, I'm gonna play with Max"); then they can relate two points in time ("I'm painting. It's wet now, but it's gonna dry in a little bit"); and finally, they can coordinate several points in time and the sequence of events across time intervals ("I'll get scissors to cut the string. Then I'm gonna tie the strings on the fence for the birds") (Weist, 1989; Benson, 1997).

From the perspective of social-emotional development, children's capacity to plan appears as they struggle with what psychoanalyst Erik Erikson (1950) calls "initiative versus guilt." Preschoolers have many ideas they want to try

Carrying Out Plans

When children work to carry out their plans (the "do" part of plan-do-review), they are being purposeful as well as playful. In fact, what often differentiates HighScope "work" time from the "free choice" time common in most preschool programs is the sense of purpose that children bring to their play. Because they are carrying out plans they have made for themselves, preschoolers approach play as a way to accomplish something important to them. Moreover, because adults play and converse with children based on the children's interests, language learning increases (Tomasello & Farrar, 1986). (For more on the role of play in language and literacy development, see Chapter 11.)

Many educators and psychologists recognize the value of **purposeful play** in young children's learning. John Dewey (1938/1963), whose theories influenced decades of American education, saw playfulness and seriousness as the ideal combination for learning. Similarly, educator Michael Ellis (1988) sees play as an important problem-solving strategy in all humans. He says play is how our species adapted in the past and will continue to deal with an unpredictable future.

Reviewing Activities

Recall time is when children make sense of their purposeful play. It involves more than simply talking about what they planned and what they did. Recall is an opportunity for children to reflect on their actions and the lessons they learned from

20

interacting with the materials and people in their environment. During recall, children actually build, or construct, memory, forming a mental representation of their experience and interpreting it based on their current way of thinking. This process is similar to when adults tell a story about something that happened to them. The narrator selects which parts of the event to build the story around, chooses words to show how he or she reacted to what happened, and often gives a punch line to sum up what he or she gained from the experience.

When children talk with others about their actions, they are also engaging in the storytelling process. Psychologist Roger Schank (1990) says, "Creating the story also creates the memory structure that will contain the gist of the story for the rest of our lives. Talking is remembering" (p. 115). Thus, the memories created when children review their activities helps to bring about permanent changes in their growing understanding of the world.

Further, memory itself involves several different thinking processes. Psychologists give each type of memory a distinct name. *Recall of facts* (What did you do?) engages the semantic memory; *recall of procedures* (How did you do that?) engages the procedural memory; *recall of events* (What did you do first?) engages the episodic memory; and *recall of path* or route (How did you get there?) engages spatial memory. Each type of memory is associated with a different brain structure (Bourtchouladze, 2002; Kagan & Kagan, 2003).

Educational theorist John Dewey (1938/1963) and psychologist Sara Smilansky (1971) also commented on the importance of planning and reflection in learning and development. Dewey said education should be based on "goal-directed activity" and that children should actively participate in directing their own learning activities. Smilansky spent a great deal of time observing children's play and was a consultant to HighScope in the early 1960s. She urged the curriculum developers to add recall to planning and work time so children could reflect on their plans and actions and thereby gain more understanding of what they had learned in the process.

❖

The insights of developmental theory and their application in the HighScope Curriculum have been borne out by decades of research showing that active learning develops initiative in young children. Planning and reflection are the two curriculum components most positively and significantly associated with children's developmental progress. The key studies justifying these conclusions are described in the next chapter.

 Try These Ideas Yourself

1. Observe an infant, a toddler, and a preschooler each encountering something for the first time. How do they approach the object or experience? What does this tell you about differences in their development?

2. Share a new experience with a young child. Compare what you notice and how you react with what the child notices and how the child reacts. What does this tell you about differences in how adults and children think about and understand the world?

3. Remember when you moved into a new house or apartment. What did you consider essentials that you needed to have first? What details did you add later? Are you the type of person who leaves things in place once they are set or do you like to rearrange them? Do you see any parallels between how you furnish your living space and how you take in new information? How might your reflections influence your work in the classroom?

4. Observe preschoolers at play in several different settings — for example, a preschool classroom, an unsupervised playground or park, a family gathering, or a children's party. In each instance, decide whether or not the children's play is "purposeful," that is, if it is (or is not) carried out with a goal in mind. Describe the differences between purposeful and nonpurposeful play. List the advantages and disadvantages of each type of play.

Chapter 4

What Is the Research-Based Evidence in Support of the HighScope Curriculum?

Many people these days have been warned by doctors that their weight and cholesterol levels are too high. These conditions put them at risk for heart disease, diabetes, and other health problems. Some doctors recommend a program of diet and exercise. Others also prescribe a medication to lower cholesterol. Because there are differing opinions on what works best for patients — and because not every patient is the same — medical researchers continue to study the effects of various treatments. New drugs regularly appear on the market.

If you are being treated for these problems, you also want to find out if what you are doing is working — for example, if you are taking medications that cost money and may even have side effects you don't like, you may be especially eager to know whether the benefits outweigh the hassles. Stepping on the scale answers the question of whether you are losing weight. However, since cholesterol levels can't be seen, the doctor will order a blood test. If the results are good, you and your doctor know the treatment is worthwhile. If the results are not good, or not good enough, the doctor may suggest further changes in the medication itself and how you are using it, as well as changes in diet or exercise.

Just like doctors and scientists, early childhood educators wonder whether their programs and practices are effective. The push for "accountability" in the field of early childhood education is

an example of people asking whether the investment in preschool makes a difference. HighScope has asked itself this question right from the start, beginning over 40 years ago with its first preschool program. HighScope accepts the importance of proving the curriculum works — and that it works with different populations under different program conditions. Moreover, since tests tell only part of the story, HighScope measures the outcomes in different ways, including what happens in the "real world." Finally, since, like diets, effects can show up and then disappear, HighScope wants to make sure the improvements are lasting.

A Commitment to Research

Since it first began developing programs for children and youth in the early 1960s, HighScope has done research and evaluation. The first objective was to see if the programs were effective in achieving their goals. Overwhelmingly, they were. The next task was to find out if some were not working and why they were not, so improvements could be made. This commitment to research has allowed HighScope to maintain its basic, proven curriculum model while continuously adding new features to address changing education policies and further enhance the development of children in today's world.

Evidence for the effectiveness of HighScope's Preschool Curriculum and training model comes

22

Chapter Learning Objectives

By the end of this chapter, you will be able to

❖ Describe the major research studies conducted by HighScope on its curriculum and training model

❖ Describe research conducted by independent investigators that confirms the findings of the HighScope research

❖ Explain how the components of high-quality preschool programs are derived from research

from three major studies carried out by the Foundation. Independent investigations have also confirmed these positive findings in the United States and abroad. We will discuss these studies and their findings in the remainder of this chapter.

Research Performed by HighScope

The HighScope Perry Preschool Study. This study, reported in *Lifetime Effects* (Schweinhart, Montie, Xiang, Barnett, Belfield, & Nores, 2005), examines the preschool curriculum's long-lasting influences on children born into poverty. The study is based on **random assignment** (assignment of participants to different conditions, based on chance) of 123 children to a program or to a no-program group. So far, the research has found the curriculum had positive effects through age 40 on school achievement and literacy, high school graduation, adult earnings, home ownership, and lifetime arrest rates. A **cost-benefit analysis** (comparison of the costs of a particular investment with the advantages it is likely to offer) shows society saves more than $16[1] for every dollar invested in this high-quality program. Of this result, Nobel Prize-winning University of Chicago economist James J. Heckman said,

This report substantially bolsters the case for early interventions in disadvantaged populations. More than 35 years after they received an enriched preschool program, the Perry Preschool participants achieve much greater success in social and economic life than their counterparts who are randomly denied treatment.

The HighScope Preschool Curriculum Comparison Study. This study, reported in *Lasting Differences* (Schweinhart & Weikart, 1997), also examines the long-term effects of preschool on children from low-income families. It compares 68 preschoolers randomly assigned to one of three different curriculum models. Some attended High-Scope (Hohmann & Weikart, 2002), a comprehensive program in which children and teachers share responsibility for the learning experience. A second group went to a program with a traditional nursery school curriculum (Sears & Dowley, 1963), where the major focus is on social development and children determine the nature and content of their own learning. The third group attended a program that used a direct instruction model (Bereiter & Engelmann, 1966), in which learning is confined to academic subjects and is directed by adults. The data, analyzed through age 23, finds no significant and lasting group differences on language, literacy, or school achievement. However, adults who attended the direct instruction program as children have had consistently higher rates of criminal activity compared to the other two groups.

The HighScope National Training of Trainers Evaluation. This study, reported in *Training for Quality* (Epstein, 1993), surveyed 203 HighScope trainers, interviewed and observed 366 teachers in HighScope and non-HighScope early childhood settings, and assessed 200 preschool children in HighScope and comparison classrooms. It found positive results at all levels — for supervisors, teachers, and children.

HighScope training resulted in significantly better supervisory and teaching practices than did other training programs. Children in HighScope

Terms Used in This Chapter

• HighScope Perry Preschool Study • random assignment • cost-benefit analysis • HighScope Preschool Curriculum Comparison Study • HighScope National Training of Trainers Evaluation • Head Start Family and Child Experiences Survey (FACES) • child-initiated learning activities • developmentally appropriate • open-ended • inservice training

---

[1]Based on constant 2000 dollars, discounted at 3%.

programs, compared to those in non-HighScope programs, were rated significantly higher on measures of development. The findings especially showcased the importance of the plan-do-review sequence in children's learning. The more teachers provided opportunities for children to *plan and review activities of their own choice* — a hallmark of the HighScope Curriculum — the higher children scored on measures of the academic and social skills needed for school success.

Research Performed by Independent Investigators

Independent studies confirm that preschool children attending well-run HighScope programs do better than those in other program settings. Studies in the United Kingdom (Sylva, 1992) and The Netherlands (Veen, Roeleveld, & Leseman, 2000) found that when children plan, carry out, and review their own learning activities, they play with more purpose and perform better on measures of language and intellectual development. The **Head Start Family and Child Experiences Survey,** known as FACES (Zill, Resnick, Kim, O'Donnell, & Sorongon, 2003) is being conducted with 2,800 Head Start children around the country. Recent findings showed that those in HighScope programs improved significantly more from fall to spring on measures of literacy and social development than did children attending classrooms using the Creative Curriculum® or other curriculum models.

Summary of Lessons Learned From Research

The sidebar on page 5 lists the seven elements of high-quality preschool programs. Based on research conducted by HighScope and other investigators, we can elaborate these components as follows (Schweinhart, 2004, pp. 15–30):

▲ **Child development curriculum.** Of all the ingredients in a high-quality program, an educational model that recognizes the value of child-initiated active learning is the most important. Research that has tested child development theory, and verified it in practice, identifies these principles:

Child-initiated learning activities acknowledge *both the developmental limits of young children and their potential for learning.* In a balanced approach, young children are neither pushed to do things more suitable for older children, nor seen as uninterested in or incapable of engaging with meaningful content.

The best early childhood learning activities are child-initiated, **developmentally appropriate,** *and* **open-ended.** This means activities build on children's natural curiosity, are matched to children's current and emerging abilities, and allow for exploration and variation rather than having to be performed a single "right way."

Open communication between teacher and child and among children broadens children's perspectives as they learn to share ideas. Research on teaching and childrearing shows the benefits of shared control over either authoritarian or permissive extremes. A democratic style allows children to see things from different perspectives, which is an important social as well as cognitive skill.

▲ **Low enrollment limits.** Studies have found that the fewer children per adult, the better the adult-child interaction. In addition to favorable staff-child ratios, the total group size should be limited based on standards recommended by the National Association for the Education of Young Children (NAEYC) for the ages of the children served (Bredekamp & Copple, 1997).

▲ **Staff trained in early childhood development.** Adults who provide care and education for young children need specialized training in child development and early childhood education. Research also shows that the higher the level of teachers' formal education, the more developmentally appropriate their teaching practices. Current efforts within the field to raise the educational levels and credentials of teachers and caregivers stems from these research findings.

▲ **Supervisory support and inservice training.** In addition to hiring well-qualified staff, program administrators play a central role in arranging for their ongoing and appropriate inservice training. Training should occur at least once a month and help teachers implement the program's child development curriculum. (See Chapter 9 for more information on adult training and supervision.)

24

▲ **Involvement of parents as partners.** Parent involvement is essential to good education throughout their children's school years. Although there are often many obstacles to such involvement (for example, working-parent schedules and multiple demands on the family), high-quality programs are creative in overcoming these barriers. They offer many options for inviting family participation. For ideas on how HighScope programs involve families, see Chapter 8.

▲ **Sensitivity to the noneducational needs of children and their families.** Today's families cope with many demands and stresses. In addition to being concerned about the education of their children, many parents must also contend with financial, medical, social, or legal issues. Early childhood programs cannot be expected to meet all these needs directly. However, as part of a community network, high-quality programs are aware of the services available and help families obtain the assistance they need. The smoother the family's functioning, the better the child's adjustment.

▲ **Developmentally appropriate evaluation procedures.** The two main objectives of early childhood evaluation are to assess program quality and to assess children's development. Administrators use program evaluation to make decisions about agency policies and staff development. Teachers use child evaluation to plan appropriate educational activities for individual children and the class as a whole.

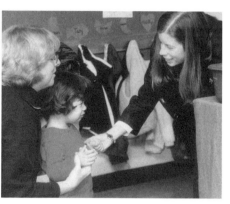

Research shows that training staff creates a pathway to quality. HighScope teachers are trained in child development and family relationships.

For evaluation results to be accurate and useful, they should be based on objective and observable behavior. Moreover, they should examine the elements of curriculum implementation and child development that are consistent with the program's philosophy and goals. (For more on child and program assessment, see Chapters 18 and 19, respectively.)

In order to achieve the lifetime effects demonstrated in the HighScope Perry Preschool Study and other research, preschools must provide the same range and quality of educational services offered by HighScope and comparable curriculum programs. First and foremost, this means adopting a child development curriculum that fosters active learning. It also means hiring and supporting qualified staff, involving families and meeting their needs, and conducting ongoing and authentic assessment of teaching practices and children.

Try These Ideas Yourself

1. First, look at the list of the seven elements of high-quality preschool programs shown on page 5. Next, write down answers to the following questions: What does it mean to include each of these elements in an early childhood setting? Think of your own program or one you have observed. What would you like to change to improve its quality? (Variation: You and a friend or colleague observe the same program and write down the extent to which you think it has each of the seven elements of quality. Compare and discuss your notes.)

2. Practice writing a grant proposal to get funding for your early childhood program. (If you don't have a program, think of one you would like to start in your community.) What information about your program do you think will persuade a funding agency that your program is worth investing in? Cover the following areas: the need or problem your program addresses, the number and characteristics of the clients it serves, the range of services it provides, the features that distinguish it from other programs, and the outcomes or benefits it gives to clients. Do you have this information collected and tabulated? How can you best present it? If you do not have the information, how could you get it and organize it for your proposal? Can you use the HighScope research findings to support your program? Why or why not? If you feel you can, on what basis can you claim that the proven benefits of HighScope will also apply to your early childhood program?

HighScope Teaching Practices

This part of the book discusses how the program's interaction strategies, environment, and schedule promote active learning.

Chapter 5 looks at adult-child interaction and how to develop a supportive climate for children.

Chapter 6 deals with setting up the physical learning environment so that it is comfortable and well-organized to engage children in active learning.

Chapter 7 discusses how to set up a consistent daily routine that provides diverse learning opportunities.

Chapter 8 describes how to work with parents so they can better understand and promote their child's education.

Chapter 9 looks at how to work well as part of a teaching team, with the plan-do-review process as a core part of the teamwork.

Chapter 5

What Does Adult-Child Interaction Look Like in a HighScope Program?

? ... Think About It

Remember a time as a child when an adult asked your opinion or let you help make an important decision. For example, your parents might have called a "family council" to solve the problem of undone household chores or to decide where to go on vacation. Perhaps you recall a teacher who let students choose their own seats or who asked the class to help make up rules for playing safely on the playground. HighScope teachers call this "sharing control."

Thinking back, how did it feel to be a partner with adults? Did you worry that grown-ups didn't have the answers themselves and think, "How should I know? I'm just a kid!"? Or did it make you feel more grown-up to be asked your opinion or advice? Do you remember whether you saw the situation as an opportunity to suggest or request something you knew was out of bounds but figured you might get away with? Or did you think seriously about something that you'd be responsible for helping to carry out?

Now think about reversing roles and remember a time when you shared control with children. Maybe you let a child choose what to order at a restaurant or decide whether or not to share a toy with a sibling. Perhaps you let children mix their own paints in the classroom or suggest a way they thought was fair for deciding who would pass out snacks. How did you feel as an adult in these situations? Were you afraid children would get out

of hand and test the limits? Did you offer real choices, or did you restrict the options to two or three that you felt comfortable with? Were you genuinely interested in children's input and prepared to consider and carry out their suggestions (with reasonable modifications, if necessary)? Were their ideas predictable, or were you surprised — maybe even impressed — by their thoughtfulness and creativity?

Sharing control can be both scary and exciting, for children and adults alike. Because most of us are used to grown-ups being in command, the idea of solving problems or making decisions jointly can make us uneasy. For that reason, most programs put teachers firmly in charge or else give "lip service" (that is, limited choice) to the idea of children taking responsibility for themselves and others. In the HighScope Curriculum, however, **shared control** is central to how adults and children interact. The curriculum includes many specific strategies for accomplishing this goal so the fear is taken out of it. In fact, when both sides know what to expect and what their respective roles are, they feel in control of the sharing. Children rise to the occasion and meet the learning challenge. And adults are often amazed by what they learn from and about young children's capacity to think. In this chapter, we will discuss what a supportive climate for learning means for adults and children in the early childhood classroom.

28

Chapter Learning Objectives

By the end of this chapter, you will be able to

❖ Explain the difference between supportive and restrictive learning environments and how each affects children's behavior

❖ Participate as a real partner in children's play and conversations

❖ Recognize and plan learning experiences that build on children's interests and strengths

❖ Understand how to support children's development by using encouragement rather than praise

❖ Help children use a problem-solving approach to resolving interpersonal conflicts

In a supportive climate, adults and children share control of the learning process. Adults provide materials and experiences that build on and extend children's interests.

Creating a Supportive Climate for Learning

Early childhood programs are sometimes described according to two extremes — the **laissez-faire climate** and the **directive climate.** In a laissez-faire, or "permissive," climate, children are in control. There is little structure to the classroom or daily routine. Adults make sure children are safe and take care of the children's basic needs, but otherwise they leave children free to play as they wish.

At the other end, a directive or adult-controlled climate is one where teachers take charge of all the activities and learning. They tell children what to do and when to do it, often using scripted lessons to teach specific academic skills and concepts. Some programs combine the two approaches. That is, part of the day is devoted to lessons — such as reading and mathematics — and the rest of the day, children are permitted to play with very little adult supervision or involvement.

A third type of program, which the High-Scope Curriculum is organized to provide, offers a **supportive climate.** In this type of setting, adults and children share control of the learning process. Adults balance the freedom children need to explore with the limits children need to feel secure. The adults provide materials and experiences that both build on children's interests and promote learning. In a supportive climate, children initiate many of their own learning experiences. Even when adults plan an activity, as for a small- or large-group time, they consider the objects, actions, and ideas children are interested in.

In a supportive learning environment, adults and children are partners throughout the day. Learning is its own reward and children know adults are there to encourage their initiative. When conflicts arise, adults understand that children are not deliberately acting "bad" or "naughty." Rather, the adults know that children need to learn how to handle their feelings appropriately. Therefore, social conflicts are seen as another opportunity for social and

---

Terms Used in This Chapter

• shared control • laissez-faire climate • directive climate • supportive climate • authentic relationship
• close-ended question • open-ended question • exploratory play • constructive play • dramatic play
• games with rules • encouragement versus praise • problem-solving approach to conflict

cognitive learning. Adults and children work together to solve problems. (See the problem-solving approach to conflict resolution on pp. 33–36.)

Active participatory learning thrives in supportive settings like these, where children are comfortable with themselves and with others, have the freedom to explore materials, and interact with people from a place of security. In the opposite approach, children are limited in their exploration or even punished for expressing feelings and trying out ideas. These conditions can inhibit learning and turn education into a negative experience.

A major goal of the HighScope Curriculum, therefore, is to create an environment where children can work and play free of fear, anxiety, and boredom. In HighScope settings, adults value and appreciate children and work to create a supportive climate in which children are given the intellectual challenges they need to grow, and learning is a positive, exciting, and natural experience.

The Effects of a Supportive Climate

The partnership that children and adults share in a supportive environment brings intellectual and social benefits to both of them. (See the sidebar below for a comparison of the effects of different types of classroom climates.)

▲ **Children and adults are free to learn.** Children are encouraged to pursue subjects and ideas that interest them. While carefully observing what children say and do, teachers develop an understanding of how the children think and the further learning experiences they need.

▲ **Children form positive relationships.** When teachers are patient and respectful, they model positive behavior. Children then learn to act this way with others and develop a positive attitude toward schooling.

▲ **Adults see children's behavior in terms of development.** By understanding that children are carrying out their own intentions in ways that are consistent with their knowledge and development, adults can teach rather than judge them.

▲ **Children become trusting and independent.** In a supportive climate, children trust adults to take care of their needs, but they also gain confidence in their own abilities to help themselves and others.

The Effects of Different Types of Classroom Environments

Positive Effects of Supportive Climates

- ❖ Allow children to pursue their own interests and ideas and to learn from them
- ❖ Help children develop independence and initiative
- ❖ Increase children's confidence in their own abilities
- ❖ Teach children to trust others, which carries over into primary grades
- ❖ Develop children's sense of empathy and caring behavior
- ❖ Teach children to solve social problems by talking and trying solutions
- ❖ Continually increase adults' understanding of children's development
- ❖ Encourage adults to interpret children's behavior positively in terms of development, not as stubborn, naughty, mean, or otherwise negatively motivated

Negative Effects of Restrictive or Punitive Climates

- ❖ Increase children's dependence on adults
- ❖ Address adults' short-term need for authority rather than children's long-term need for self-control
- ❖ Promote compliance and conformity
- ❖ Promote fear, aggression, and resentment
- ❖ Encourage mindless obedience rather than a desire to act constructively
- ❖ Teach a desire to avoid being caught
- ❖ Inhibit children's ability to express strong emotions appropriately
- ❖ Model physical punishment as an acceptable way of expressing anger and demonstrate that if you are bigger, you are allowed to hurt others
- ❖ Decrease initiative by making children "other-directed" rather than "inner-directed"
- ❖ Increase guilt by focusing on children's "badness" rather than the problem or action

The Elements of Supportive Interactions

To establish a positive climate for early learning, HighScope identifies six critical elements of supportive adult-child interactions. Strategies you can use to create these conditions in your classroom are listed below.

1. Sharing Control Between Adults and Children

Sharing control in a supportive climate means children and adults take turns being the leader and the follower, the speaker and the listener, the teacher and the learner. Everyone gets a chance to be heard and to try things.

You can use the following teaching strategies for sharing control:

▲ **Participate with children on their terms.** In play and conversation, take cues from the children. Share in children's interests, take pleasure in the things that capture their imagination, and appreciate children's creative ideas and actions. When entering children's play, take on the roles children assign to you and follow their directions.

> *Shirley, the teacher, went to the house area where several children were playing. Janey said to her, "I'm the doctor and everyone has the flu. You better get a shot, too." Shirley said, "I don't feel well, doctor. What should I do?" Janey replied, "Lie on this mat and roll up your sleeve." Shirley got on the mat and Janey gave her a "shot" using a capped marker as a needle.*

▲ **Learn from children.** Rather than viewing yourself as an all-knowing authority figure, see yourself as a learner, too. Sometimes, young children have skills to teach us. For example, they may be more comfortable using the computer than we are. At other times, they can tell us things about their needs and feelings that we could not have figured out on our own.

▲ **Consciously give control to children.** Plan ways and times to put children in charge so they can feel the power of their own ideas. Examples include asking children to suggest a song to

Learning From Children

Mrs. Walters, a volunteer parent, had a very loud laugh and played boisterously with the children. They all seemed to gather around her whenever she visited the classroom. One day she called to Jimmy, a new child, to ask if he wanted a turn with the swinging game they were all playing. Jimmy shook his head and went to the other side of the yard, where he dug in the dirt. Later, Mrs. Walters went over to him and said in a booming voice, "What's the matter, Jimmy? Don't you like to swing?" "Too loud," said Jimmy. Puzzled, Mrs. Walters asked, "What's too loud?" Jimmy said, "You." Mrs. Walters said in a quieter voice, "Is it better if I talk like this?" Jimmy smiled and nodded his head. From then on, whenever Mrs. Walters approached Jimmy, she lowered the volume of her voice. She also found he preferred to do things with her one-on-one instead of with the whole group.

sing at large-group time or the rotation system for passing out snacks.

2. Focusing on Children's Strengths

Learning occurs best when children are motivated by their own goals and interests. HighScope differs from "deficit models" in which adults focus on what children *can't do* and try to correct those weaknesses. The more pressure children feel, the more anxious they become. Nervousness can actually interfere with learning. By instead beginning with what children *can do* and what they are interested in, the motivation to learn is built in.

You can do the following to focus on children's strengths:

▲ **Pay close attention to children's interests.** Children are more willing to try something new if it builds on what they already know. Sometimes we think children are doing the same thing over and over, but if we look closely, we discover over time that they vary it or add to the activity. By providing new materials or information of interest to children, you increase the possibilities for additional learning to occur.

As they work alongside children, adults engage in authentic and natural conversations with them.

▲ **See situations from children's point of view.** Think of a baby learning how to feed himself. More food may get in the baby's hair than in his mouth, and it may be inconvenient for you to clean up the mess. However, knowing that he can feed himself is very satisfying for the baby. By openly acknowledging this, you can encourage him to make further attempts at independence.

▲ **Share children's interests with parents and staff.** When talking with parents or coworkers, focus on children's strengths. For example, instead of reporting that "Tommy still hardly played with the other children today," you might comment on his progress: "Tommy enjoyed playing with the trucks today. He even gave one to Mark to push down the ramp he built." If problems do arise, share what the child actually did, and work together with other adults to find a solution all can agree on.

▲ **Plan around children's strengths and interests.** Since each child's interests and abilities are unique, focusing on strengths is the main way the HighScope Curriculum allows you to *individualize* your program for children. Teachers in HighScope programs take anecdotal notes each day on what children do and then use these observations in their daily planning (see Chapter 9). That means teachers are consciously thinking about how to support the learning of every individual in the classroom. Likewise, each child is assured of finding things of interest and things to learn every day at school.

3. Forming Authentic Relationships With Children

Authenticity in this context means being genuine in your relationships with children. Because learning is such a social activity, children must trust their teachers to be honest and open — then teaching and learning can be a two-way activity. Because adults, like children, are unique, each adult must find his or her own way to be genuine with children. Below are strategies you can use to create meaningful interactions.

▲ **Share your own interests with children.** Joelle, a preschool teacher, loved to play the guitar and sing. She made singing a regular feature of greeting time, which made transitioning into the program day easy and fun. The children in her class taught the songs they learned to their parents and often brought in new songs to share with Joelle.

▲ **Respond attentively to children's interests.** Give your full attention to what children are doing and saying. Children can sense when teachers have their minds elsewhere or are just going through the motions of listening and looking. By contrast, when an adult is eager to share in a child's excitement, it communicates that the activity and learning are important.

▲ **Give each child specific feedback.** Statements that are generalizations suggest an adult is not paying attention to what is happening for the child at that moment or that the adult does not consider what the child is doing to be important. Specific comments, by contrast, show that the adult is focused on and involved with the child, and values his or her work. For example, suppose a child shows you a painting. Instead of making a vague comment about how colorful it is, you might say, "You made a wide red stripe at the top and two skinny green ones at the bottom. I see you also used blue and yellow in this corner."

▲ **Ask and respond to questions honestly.** An honest question is one in which the asker does not know the answer. Too often, teachers ask **close-ended questions** — those for which they seek the "right" answer. By contrast, an **open-ended question** can have many possible answers. And just as adults should only ask questions when they are honestly interested in learning the answer, so too should they answer children's questions with thoughtfulness.

32

Here are some examples of honest questions: "Jeremy, how did you get this block to balance on top of the pile?" and "Salima, what materials will you use to make your rocket ship?" Here is an example of an honest answer to a child's question: When Brenda asked if she had to wear boots to the pumpkin farm, Mrs. Taylor said, "We won't know until we hear the weather report tonight, so bring them just in case."

▲ **Limit questioning.** In addition to taking a position about the *type* of question to ask, both practice and research indicate that the *amount* of questioning should be limited (Wood, McMahon, & Cranstoun, 1980; Sawyer, 2004). When adults ask so many questions that children feel they are being quizzed, children may stop talking altogether. It is better to make comments when conversing with a child, just as one would when talking naturally to another adult. A HighScope teacher modeled this behavior for a parent, with a happy result:

> *When Mrs. M. came to pick up her son Jonathan at the end of each day, she would pepper him with questions about what he'd done in school. Because she was genuinely interested in hearing how he'd spent his time, she was frustrated that he'd clam up after answering the first question. Jonathan's teacher stood by them one day and when Mrs. M. asked, "What did you do today" and he answered, "Made a tower," his teacher joined in with a comment: "I saw you building that tower with Veronica." Jonathan elaborated: "I used the blue blocks and she added red ones." Mrs. M. listened as his teacher made more comments and Jonathan offered more details. While Jonathan went to get his coat, his mother asked the teacher, "How come he talked to you so much? He never does that with me." The teacher answered, "Sometimes I find that if I just comment on what they say, children open up more than if I ask a lot of questions." Over the next few days, Jonathan's teacher noticed Mrs. M. making a conscious attempt to limit her questioning and talk to her son in a more conversational way. Jonathan became increasingly eager to share his day with his mother, and two weeks later, Mrs. M. said to the teacher, "Thanks for the*

> *tip. I'm using it with my older son, too — at the dinner table — and it's amazing how much both boys share with us now!"*

4. Supporting Children's Play

HighScope agrees with the idea that play is a child's work. Children play because it is pleasurable and rewarding. Play is an activity in which they are free to make choices and discover new things. The play may be noisy or quiet, messy or orderly, silly or serious, and effortful or easy. Whatever form it takes, play is a time when a great deal of learning takes place. Use the following strategies to make sure that play encourages children's initiative and learning:

▲ **Observe and understand children's play.** Children tell us a great deal about themselves when they play. So it is important to understand what play, in all its complexity, means. Young children engage in many types of play. In **exploratory play,** they use materials just to learn about them, not to make something with them — for example, squeezing and pounding on play dough. **Constructive play** involves building things, such as a block house, while **dramatic play** is pretending and acting out roles. Older children play **games with rules,** although at the beginning of this stage, the rules may keep changing.

▲ **Be playful with children.** Join enthusiastically in children's play. Get down on the floor, climb to the top of the slide, and let yourself be "locked up in jail," get "shots" from the doctor, or lap up "milk" with the other "kitties." While play comes naturally to children, most adults must make a conscious choice to be playful. Once they do, they can experience great satisfaction in sharing this important learning activity with young children. Adults can also gain insight into children's thoughts and needs by becoming part of the action.

5. Using Encouragement Instead of Praise

Many adults use praise because they think it helps children feel good about themselves and their work. They may also use praise as a behavior management tool, that is, to help children settle down and "act like good boys and girls."

However, research shows praise can be damaging (Kohn, 1993). When adults use praise, children learn to depend on adults for figuring out what is right or wrong, instead of developing this ability themselves. Use of praise can also invite children to perform for external rewards rather than to embrace learning because it is self-rewarding. Children may become afraid to try something new for fear they will not be complimented, or worse, that they will be criticized. Some children may even come to view the absence of praise as criticism.

HighScope trains teachers to use **encouragement** rather than praise. By encouraging children, adults acknowledge their efforts and accomplishments. The focus is on children's actions and what they are learning, not on whether the children have pleased the adult. Try using the strategies listed below to encourage rather than praise young children.

▲ **Participate in children's play.** Joining in children's play is a form of encouragement because it lets the children know their activities and ideas are important and meaningful. It also provides opportunities for the adults to introduce new experiences and expand on children's knowledge and skills. Consider this example:

> *Ellen, a teacher, sat down at a table in the house area where several children were playing "restaurant." She asked what was on the menu and they replied, "We're cooking soup." Ellen said she wondered if they could make "tomato and rice soup." The children then put red blocks and Styrofoam pellets in a pan, stirred it up, and dished it out in a bowl. Ellen said she'd like some crackers to dunk in her soup, and one of the children cut up pieces of construction paper to use as crackers. Soon other children sat at the table and began to ask for different types of soup, including "monster chunk" and "chocolate-peanut-crayon." The cooks used materials from all over the classroom to respond to these requests. The role play continued the next day. When the table was full of customers, one child decided to write down their orders and asked the teacher for help recording the type of soup each person wanted and the price.*

In this example, the teacher could have said, "Yum, you cook good soup" when she first sat down. If she had, the play probably would not have taken off in so many creative directions, nor would it have been as likely to continue and expand the next day. But by entering fully into the children's play, the teacher inspired the children's problem-solving, involved others in the role play, and created an opportunity to develop literacy and math skills.

▲ **Encourage children to describe their efforts, ideas, and products.** Instead of telling children that they have done a "good job" or made something "beautiful," make specific comments that encourage them to talk about what they are doing, how they are doing it, and anything else about the process that is important to them. Focus on children's actions, not just the end result. For example, rather than saying to a child "That's a lovely painting," you might point and say, "I wonder how you made all the layers of color in this corner." Such a statement shows that you are interested and encourages the child to reflect on and describe what he or she did. It also leads to a natural conversation about the activity and helps you to build an authentic relationship with the child.

▲ **Repeat and restate children's words.** By repeating and restating what children say, you let the children know you're truly listening and that you acknowledge their activities and efforts. These strategies can also help you clarify what a child has said, create opportunities to introduce new words, and rephrase or model pronunciation of words children are just learning. It also prevents you from asking too many questions. Consider the following example:

> *Armondo, the teacher, observes Linda using the stapler and paper in the art area. Linda says, "It won't work. The tapler is broke." Armondo replies, "The stapler is broken?" Linda nods her head yes. She has heard the correct pronunciation and grammar without being corrected. Meanwhile, Armondo has clarified what the problem is with the material.*

6. Adopting a Problem-Solving Approach to Conflict

Conflicts are a natural part of young children's play. To give some examples, two children may each want to be the daddy in a pretend scenario,

34

four may want to use three swings, and an entire small group may want to sit next to the teacher while she reads a story. In a supportive climate, teachers see such conflicts as learning opportunities and approach them in a matter-of-fact manner. They know that disagreements arise from children's normal development and desires, not because they are being "bad" or "stubborn." The children are not the problem and should not be punished. Rather, the problem is the behavior, and it is a problem that can be solved. Children need to learn social skills just as they need to learn to read and write. Part of this learning is identifying that there is a problem, and understanding that people can solve such problems together.

In training, HighScope teachers learn to use six steps to solve interpersonal problems in the classroom. Each step is listed below, followed by a short example. (For more on children's development of social problem-solving skills, see Chapter 12.)

▲ **Step 1. Approach calmly, stopping any hurtful actions.** Children should always feel safe and secure, perhaps especially in the midst of a conflict. When you remain calm, it helps children regain control. Therefore, place yourself between the children, physically get down on their level, use a calm voice and gentle touch, and do not take sides. If an object (such as a toy) is involved in the dispute, hold it yourself. This "neutralizes" the object so children can become engaged during the rest of the problem-solving steps.

▲ **Step 2. Acknowledge children's feelings.** Emotions often run high during a conflict because children feel strongly about their desires. Helping children express their feelings — and accepting their feelings without judgment — allows children to let go of their emotions. Only then can children begin to identify and solve the problem. Use simple words to help children label their feelings, for example, "You look really upset."

▲ **Step 3. Gather information.** It is important for all the children involved in the conflict to express their point of view. You and other adults need the information, the children need to have their say, and everyone can benefit from listening to the others state what they need in the situation. You might start by asking an open-ended question such as, "What's the problem?" Do not ask "why"

Working With Children's Social Conflicts

Conflicts escalate when you...

- ❖ Use "you" statements ("You took the ball from Tommy.")
- ❖ Use intense body language (shake a finger, grab a child)
- ❖ Make accusations or blame children ("You made Yolanda cry.")
- ❖ Focus on the past ("You fought over the truck yesterday, too.")
- ❖ Focus on the person rather than the problem ("Joanne, you're hogging the drill.")
- ❖ Focus on your position ("I can't have you running across the room and knocking things over.")
- ❖ Make assumptions ("It looks like Jenny spilled water on Sammy's puzzle.")

Conflicts de-escalate when you...

- ❖ Use "I" statements ("I see you and Tommy are both upset.")
- ❖ Use gentle body language (kneel next to child, relax shoulders)
- ❖ Are specific about the source of the problem ("Yolanda says she's unhappy because she wants to use the computer.")
- ❖ Focus on present and future ("You both want to play with the truck. How can we solve this problem?")
- ❖ Focus on the problem ("We have one drill and three children who want to use it.")
- ❖ Focus on children's needs and interests ("You want to get to the other side fast. How can you do that without knocking over Sandy's block tower?")
- ❖ Listen carefully to both sides of the issue (Ask each child, in a neutral voice, "Can you tell me what happened?")

Adapted with permission from *Mediator Training Manual*, Franklin Mediation Services, Greenfield, MA, 1989. *[Editor's Note: Examples added by Ann S. Epstein.]*

questions. Preschoolers think concretely — about what they see, hear, touch, and do — and are not yet capable of analyzing the reasons behind the problem or their feelings.

▲ **Step 4. Restate the problem.** Restating the problem — "So the problem is..." — without taking sides or jumping in with your own solution, lets children know you are truly listening. Repeat the children's words, or rephrase them if the words are hurtful or unclear. For example, if a child says, "He's a dummy. He took my block," you might say, "You're upset because Vic took the block off the top of your tower." Check with the children to make sure you have stated the problem correctly, and allow them to add more information, if necessary.

▲ **Step 5. Ask for ideas for solutions and choose one together.** You might begin by asking "What can we do to solve this problem?" Encourage *children* to propose a solution, and give them ample time to think and respond. Accept all the ideas children offer, even if some do not seem realistic. If the children draw a blank, you might offer an idea or two to get them started. Help children think through the consequences of implementing their ideas and encourage *them* to pick one. Sometimes, an idea that adults think is unworkable or unfair may end up working just fine for the children. Once the children choose a solution, make sure that each child is comfortable with it.

▲ **Step 6. Give follow-up support as needed.** Acknowledge that the *children* have found a solution to the problem. ("You solved the problem!") As children return to their play, stay nearby to make sure the solution is working and everyone is satisfied. You may help carry out the solution. If a problem remains, repeat the process with the children to find another approach.

A conflict resolution example. Shari is feeding her doll a bottle. Daniella grabs the bottle away and says, "I need that." When Shari takes it back, Daniella punches her in the arm and says, "I hate you, you stupid baby!" Their teacher, Tom, comes over and kneels down between the two girls.

Tom (to Daniella, and gently putting his hands on her): Hitting and name-calling need to stop. I see that you're really angry.

Tom (to Shari): Let me hold the bottle while we talk about this problem (he takes the bottle to "neutralize" it during their discussion).

Preventing Classroom Conflicts

The following characteristics of the HighScope Curriculum help prevent problems and conflicts from happening in the classroom:

❖ Spacious work areas with enough materials for all children

❖ Predictable daily routine

❖ Children carrying out their own plans during work time

❖ Children having choices during group times and transitions

❖ Group activities being planned around children's interests

❖ Little or no waiting before getting started on activities

❖ Adults helping children identify and express their feelings

❖ Adults making daily observations and anecdotal notes about children

HighScope teachers use a problem-solving approach to help young children resolve the conflicts that are a natural and normal part of their play.

Shari: I had it first. She took it.

Tom (to Shari): You're very upset. The problem is that you were using the bottle and Daniella took it away from you.

Shari: (Nods yes)

Daniella: I need it!

Tom (to Daniella): You're upset because you need the bottle for your doll, too.

Daniella: (Also nods yes) My baby doll is very hungry!

Tom (to Shari and Daniella): So you both want to feed this bottle to your dolls. How can we solve this problem?

Shari: I could feed the bottle to both dolls.

Tom (to Daniella): Is that okay with you?

Daniella: No. I want to feed my own doll.

Tom (to both): What else could you do to solve this problem?

Daniella: We could get another bottle.

Shari: I know! We could make one.

Tom (looks at Daniella): (Daniella nods her head in agreement) So the two of you are going to make another bottle and then you'll each have one (both girls nod).

Tom (to both): What will you use to make the bottle?

Shari: A block.

Daniella: And those (she points to the Legos; the girls each get the materials they mentioned and bring them to the house area).

Tom: Who will use this bottle (he holds up the one in his hand) and who will use the one you're making?

Shari: I want that one (points to the one in Tom's hand).

Tom: Is that okay with you, Daniella?

Daniella: (Nods yes)

Shari holds a block while Daniella tapes on a red Lego "nipple." Shari uses the original bottle while Daniella uses the one they made together. When Tom checks back in a little while, the dolls are taking a nap in the carriage and Shari and Daniella are building a cradle out of blocks.

Strategies for Creating Supportive Climates: A Summary

1. Sharing control between adults and children
___ Participate with children on their terms.

___ Learn from children.

___ Consciously give control to children.

2. Focusing on children's strengths
___ Pay close attention to children's interests.

___ See situations from children's point of view.

___ Share children's interests with parents and staff.

___ Plan around children's strengths and interests.

3. Forming authentic relationships with children
___ Share your own interests with children.

___ Respond attentively to children's interests.

___ Give each child specific feedback.

___ Ask and respond to questions honestly.

___ Limit questioning.

4. Supporting children's play
___ Observe and understand children's play.

___ Be playful with children.

5. Using encouragement instead of praise
___ Participate in children's play.

___ Encourage children to describe their efforts, ideas, and products.

___ Repeat and restate children's words.

6. Adopting a problem-solving approach to social conflict
___ Step 1: Approach calmly, stopping any hurtful actions.

___ Step 2: Acknowledge children's feelings.

___ Step 3: Gather information.

___ Step 4: Restate the problem.

___ Step 5: Ask for ideas for solutions and choose one together.

___ Step 6: Give follow-up support as needed.

Try These Ideas Yourself

1. Describe an interaction you recently had with a child (in your class, at home, or elsewhere). What interaction strategies did you use? How did the child respond?

2. Read the following scenarios from a preschool classroom. Using the six elements of adult support (sharing control; focusing on children's strengths; forming authentic relationships; supporting children's play; using encouragement instead of praise; and adopting a problem-solving approach), describe how you would handle each situation.

a. At cleanup time, Sasha runs from one area of the room to another.

b. Roger and Jack are sitting on the couch, looking at a tool catalog. Bella sits down next to Jack and asks, "Can I see too?" "No girls allowed," says Roger, and Jack pushes her off.

c. After greeting circle, the children go to their small-group tables for planning time. Emily walks directly to the art area and begins to paint. Frank, who is in Emily's group, says, "She can't do that! She has to make a plan first." Emily drops the paintbrush on the floor and walks to the block area, where she proceeds to build a tower.

3. Divide a piece of paper into two columns. At the top of one column write "Praise," and at the top of the other, write "Encouragement." In the first column, write down the things you say or do to praise children (or adults). For each one, in the second column, make a list of alternative things you could say and do to provide encouragement.

4. Children can say hurtful or untrue things when they are angry or frustrated. Below are some typical statements made by preschoolers. How would you, as the adult mediator, restate their comments to acknowledge their feelings but help them communicate more effectively?

I can too get on the swing if I want to. I hate you, you big dummy!

I'm never going to play with you again.

You can't tell me what to do. I'm older and bigger than you.

Tim and John can come to my birthday party, but not Sam.

You have to have pink to come in this house. Not you — go away!

That's a stupid hat. Only stupids wear yellow hats.

I wanted to pass out the cups. I hate you (to the teacher).

If I can't play with the ball, I'm not coming back. I'll tell my mommy this school stinks!

How come Sarah always gets to sit in your lap? You like her better than me.

What Does the Learning Environment Look Like in a HighScope Program?

? ₒₒ Think About It

Think of your favorite place to shop. What makes it appealing? For example, suppose your favorite store is a supermarket. Perhaps you like it because it is not so big that you feel lost, yet not so small that your choices are limited. Aisles are wide enough that shoppers do not bump into one another with their carts. The store offers a wide selection and almost never runs out of items. Fruits and vegetables are not prepackaged, so you can check whether they're fresh and buy only as much as you need.

Good lighting lets you see what is on the shelves, read prices and labels, and there are signs over each aisle that are large and easy to read. You can reach all the items, even those on the top shelves.

In addition, the store offers weekly specials, the cashiers are friendly and efficient, and the service department answers your questions and invites your suggestions.

The environments where we carry out our activities affect what we do and how we feel. If a place is attractive, comfortable, well-organized, and interesting, we are likely to want to spend time there. Depending on our mood, we may visit the place on our own, we may go with others, or we may mix solitary and social times there. The more we get to know the setting and the people in it, the safer we feel about taking risks and exploring.

In many ways, an early **learning environment** is like the settings in which we work or perform the daily chores of living. Children need to have their basic needs for health, safety, and comfort met. Beyond that, they are like adults in needing a balance of organization and variety, of doing things on their own and with others, and of opportunities to practice existing skills while mastering new ones. An optimal environment stirs a child's sense of adventure while providing the security of knowing help is there when needed. In this chapter, we will take a look at how the indoor and outdoor spaces in HighScope programs take

A well organized environment with lots of interesting materials promotes learning in all areas of development.

40

Chapter Learning Objectives

By the end of this chapter, you will be able to

❖ Explain how a well-designed learning environment contributes to children's growth in all areas of development

❖ Organize a learning environment that accommodates a wide range of activities and types of play, is inviting to children, and is easy for children and adults to navigate

❖ Choose appropriate equipment and materials for all the indoor and outdoor learning areas of a preschool program

HighScope classrooms are divided into interest areas with simple names and clear labels. At planning time, children indicate the interest area they will work in.

all these needs into account while creating active learning environments for young children and the adults who care for them.

Why the Learning Environment Is Important

Most young children spend a significant part of their day in a preschool classroom or day care center. We want children to feel comfortable and secure in that place. Every type of early learning occurs in the preschool setting, from recognizing letter sounds to painting pictures to solving a social conflict with another child. Therefore, when you create a well-organized environment full of interesting materials, you make it possible for active participatory learning to occur in all areas of development.

▲ **Intellectual development.** When the space is logically divided into interest areas, each with its associated equipment and materials, children develop ideas about how the world as a whole is organized. For example, they find printed materials (such as books and magazines) and writing supplies in the "reading area" or measuring

tools and magnifying glasses in the "math and science area." Further, having areas based on children's natural interests lets them know their ideas and discoveries are important. This message sets the stage for them to eagerly anticipate academic and other learning when they begin formal schooling.

▲ **Emotional development.** Having a consistent play space, with things always stored in the same location, gives children a sense of security and control over their environment. This can be especially important for children whose home lives do not provide such predictability. Labels for each area and the materials in it allow children to find and use the materials they need to carry out

Terms Used in This Chapter

• indoor and outdoor learning environment • interest areas, or learning centers • labels, labeling
• open-ended materials • find-use-return cycle

their plans, then return the materials to their storage spaces. Children do not have to wait for, or depend on, teachers in order to achieve their goals. The materials they enjoy using are available every day, rather than being set out only on certain days. A constant and regular arrangement of materials and equipment promotes self-confidence and independent problem-solving.

▲ **Social development.** Space arrangements can also foster social interactions by encouraging children to gather in pairs and groups. Because HighScope does not limit the number of children who can play in each area, the children are free to socialize in small and large groups. Program settings also provide intimate or cozy places where children can curl up with a teacher or one or two classmates to read, tell stories, pretend, or just talk and be together.

▲ **Physical development.** A classroom and a spacious outdoor area that are easy to get around in are important for children's physical development. In such settings, children can move freely without fear of falling, bumping into things, or colliding with others. The predictable layout of the classroom and playground also helps young children build "cognitive maps" in their minds. Being able to create this "internal picture" of the shape, size, and relative position of things is important to the development of later mathematical skills, such as geometry.

▲ **Artistic development.** HighScope classrooms and outdoor spaces deliberately provide an array of colors, textures, natural materials, types of lighting, and sounds. Varied and attractive design, lighting, and furnishings help young children develop aesthetic principles and encourage their own creative pursuits.

The classroom is also the early childhood educator's primary workspace, so it is essential that teachers feel comfortable in the classroom, too. The environment should allow them to perform their jobs; that is, to meet the needs of children and families in ways that are compatible with their philosophy and curriculum training. With a goal of observing children and building on children's interests to extend and scaffold learning, arrange the classroom environment so you can see and hear what children are doing, so children have ample space and materials for exploring and creating and so you are able to work and play alongside the children.

Organizing the Learning Space 41

It is easy to recognize a HighScope classroom as soon as you walk into it. The room is clearly divided into **interest areas** or **learning centers.** Each area has a simple name such as the "house area" or "art area," and these names are indicated with a **label** made of words, pictures, or objects. Classroom equipment and materials, also labeled, are logically organized and grouped by function or type within these areas. (See pp. 47–50 for a checklist of areas and materials often found in HighScope settings.)

The following principles can help guide you in arranging the indoor play space. Later sections in this chapter provide guidelines for choosing materials and equipment and for setting up the outdoor play space.

1. The Space Is Divided Into Interest Areas

Young children enjoy many types of play, including exploring with all their senses, building and creating things, pretending and role playing, reading and writing, drawing and sculpting, and playing simple games. HighScope settings are divided into areas to support these activities. Areas have simple names that make sense to children; for example, "toy area" rather than "manipulatives."

The areas are chosen to reflect young children's natural interests. Areas typically seen in HighScope classrooms include the block area, house area, art area, toy area, reading and writing area, sand and water area, woodworking area, movement and music area, mathematics and science area, computer area, and outdoor area. If certain types of materials or activities are of common interest to children in a particular culture or community, these can also be reflected in a HighScope program. For example, in one northern community, the children renamed the water table the "snow area" during the winter months and brought in a fresh supply of snow at the beginning of each day. In another preschool, after the children visited the studio of a local artist, they set up a special "bead area" next to the art area to explore their interests in this activity.

The areas are *defined* by low boundaries (see #4, below) and the materials that are logically stored in them. Each area is *labeled* with a large sign that may display an actual object found there, a picture of the materials or activities typical of the area (represented with a drawing, tracing, photo, catalog picture, or photocopy), and the written name of the area. For example, children might see a real paintbrush or a large drawing of a crayon and the words "Art Area" on a sign labeling that part of the room. This system allows children at various stages of literacy development to comprehend the labels and practice literacy skills. Cover labels on both sides with clear contact paper or clear tape. This makes them easy to attach to shelves or containers — for example, with loops of masking tape — and easy to move when it is time to make room for new materials. Although materials are arranged by area, children are free to carry materials from one area to another to support their play.

There are no hard and fast rules for the number of areas to have in your program. For example, if children are engaged in sorting and matching small blocks or counting and comparing sets of plastic animals in the "toy area," there may not be a need for a separate "math area." As a general consideration, however, it is better to have fewer areas, each stocked with diverse materials that can be used in many ways, than many areas supplied with a limited number of items. Too many areas can overwhelm young children, and arbitrarily assigning materials to each one does not allow children to discover that materials are grouped together because their uses are related or to explore creative ways of using the materials.

If your program is in a small space it will likely have fewer areas, but you can compensate by changing the areas now and then, as long as such changes are made infrequently. For example, you may have permanent house, art, block, sand and water, and toy areas but add a sixth area that rotates, such as woodworking, mathematics and science, or even another category that captures children's current interests. Some programs begin with fewer areas to make it easier for children to learn them. Once these become familiar, one or two areas are added. The children can then work with the teachers to decide which materials should be moved from the existing areas to the new ones.

Where you decide to locate areas also depends on your program's facilities and how each

The location of interest areas is determined by their use. For example, the water table or art area is often located near a sink.

area is used. For example, putting the art area near a sink or other water supply enables children to mix paints and clean up easily. You might put the book area near a window to make use of natural light for reading. Or you can make the book area part of the house area, with the bookcase next to a comfortable couch or beanbag chairs. If the room is sectioned or divided, putting the block area in the biggest space gives children ample room to carry materials and build large structures. Since children often use materials from the block area to role-play in the house area, and vice versa, it makes sense to locate these two areas next to or near one another.

Each area should have enough space for materials and as many children as want to play there. Avoid limiting the number of children who can use a given area at any time — doing so restricts their freedom to make choices, pursue their interests, and learn to resolve conflicts over space and materials.

Most important, to ensure adequate space for children's play, locate other nonplay equipment, supplies, and functions elsewhere. This means situating teachers' desks, custodial supplies, adult meeting areas, and so on, outside the classroom. The classroom is for children and the activities that adults share with them.

2. The Space Is Inviting to Children

The hours children spend in preschool or day care are an important, and sometimes a large, part of their day. They should therefore anticipate and enjoy their time in this setting. The following characteristics make a play space comfortable and welcoming to children:

▲ **Softness.** Just as in a home, softness in the classroom creates a sense of warmth and safety. Carpets and throw rugs, stuffed chairs and beanbag chairs, cushions and pillows, mattresses and futons, curtains, and fabric wall hangings all add softness to a setting. They also help to absorb sound, which is important in a room full of active, noisy children.

▲ **Pleasing colors and textures.** Bright colors and soft pastel shades can all appeal to children. Harsh and garish hues can be off-putting, however, just as they are with adults. Too many colors jumbled together can also be overwhelming and make it difficult for children to focus and concentrate. The same principle holds true for patterns and textures. Some variety is important, but avoid glaring extremes that can lead to sensory overload.

▲ **Natural building materials and light.** Natural building materials, such as wood and stone, provide variety and a contrast to our society's overuse of plastic and other artificial materials. While all programs depend on artificial light, it is also good to use natural light whenever possible. Sources of natural light include windows, skylights, and Plexiglass panes in doors.

▲ **Coziness.** Even the most active and social children occasionally need a quiet place to be alone or to curl up with one or two other people. HighScope classrooms always include one or more cozy spots, such as an easy chair, couch, pile of pillows, loft, window seat, or nook. These spaces are especially inviting for reading and are often part of the book area.

3. The Space Accommodates Activities and Storage Needs

Because the HighScope daily routine includes activities that can be done alone, in pairs, in small groups, and in large groups, all these possibilities must be accommodated in the same setting. Many programs also include a snack or meal, and full-day programs may include naptime. Be sure to take these activities into account when arranging the classroom or center.

In a large space, it is helpful to locate interest areas around the outer edges (perimeter) of the room. This keeps the central space open for group activities and easy movement from one area to another. If the overall space is small, has odd angles, or is divided into several rooms (such as in a family day care home), one area may serve multiple purposes. For example, a spacious block area can also be used for large-group times, and snacks and meals can be eaten at the same tables where children do planning and small-group activities.

Individual storage space is also important because each child needs an area to call his or her own. The space might be a locker, cubby, shelf, tub, box, or basket — any surface area or container where children can put their things. Its location should be easy for children to reach so they can store and retrieve things on their own. Individual storage spaces allow children to keep track of personal belongings, such as clothing or a painting they want to take home. Each storage space in a HighScope classroom is also labeled with the "letter link" picture and name of the child who uses the space (for more on letter links, see Chapter 11). Since the first letters children learn are often those in their own name, the label on a personal storage site is important for literacy learning as well as developing a sense of ownership and responsibility for one's things.

4. The Space Is Open and Accessible

Children should be able to see all the areas from different parts of the room. This allows them to consider all the possibilities available to them when they plan and to see what's happening around the room as they play. To permit children to see everywhere, define and separate areas by using low boundary separators. These might include low shelves, carpeting, floor lanes (spaces or aisles), and tape on the floor. In multiroom settings — such as day care homes — open doors, interior windows, and mirrors can help children see from one part of the space into another.

Ease of movement between areas is also important, for several reasons. One reason is

An open space allows children to move freely and create large structures with blocks and other equipment. It also encourages children to work together and collaborate in their play.

safety. The boundaries between areas should not pose any danger to children, such as sharp edges or something that could cause them to trip and fall. Second, children's play should not be interrupted by classmates going through one space to reach another. If children do have to pass through an area, they should be able to do so quickly and easily so as to minimize disruption to others. Third, ease of movement from one area of the room to another encourages children to explore and expand their play. They feel free to elaborate on their ideas when they are able to carry materials between areas. Finally, free movement between areas promotes social interaction. Individuals and groups of children can readily join one another when something in a nearby area catches their attention. This fluidity often results in more complex play across curriculum content areas, especially among older preschoolers. For example:

Janelle and Frieda were playing in the house area. Their baby dolls were sick and they had to bring them to the doctor for shots. Frieda went to the nearby block area to get a dowel to use as a hypodermic needle. Mario, Orin, and Alex were in the block area. Mario said, "You need an ambulance to get to the hospital." Mario and Orin used some large hollow blocks to make an ambulance and then built a road from the block area to the house area with long flat blocks.

Janelle and Frieda brought their dolls to the block area and put them in the ambulance. As they were getting ready to "drive" back to the house area, Alex said, "Wait! There's going to be an accident. We better get the cops." He went to the art area to make a badge, which he cut out of yellow construction paper and clothespinned to his shirt pocket. Alex also made a stop sign by writing the letters "STP" on a piece of cardboard. Liza, who had just finished a painting in the art area, brought a large paintbrush to the block area and announced, "This is the flashlight to direct the traffic." Alex and Liza directed traffic, Mario and Orin drove the ambulance to the house area, and Janelle gave the babies their shots while Frieda rocked and soothed them by saying, "There, there, baby. Don't cry."

Being able to see and move easily between all the areas is also important for adults. A good view and easy access can help you keep tabs on what is happening throughout the room. This lets you monitor children's safety and be alert to conflicts you may need to help mediate. Seeing and hearing everything that is going on also allows you to take advantage of opportunities to join children's play and scaffold their learning.

Choosing Equipment and Materials

The "raw materials" of learning are the physical objects and the social interactions we provide young children. Therefore, a great deal of thought must go into the equipment and materials we select. Choosing them involves making decisions about the type and amount of each, as well as where and how to organize and store them.

Children need to be able to use materials wherever they choose and in whatever way they need to carry out their plans and solve the problems they encounter in play. However, it is equally important that where and how the materials are stored be consistent. When you add new materials to the classroom, or when you occasionally must move something, do so with thought and, as often as possible, with input from the children. (*Consistency with flexibility* is also a hallmark of the daily routine, covered in the next chapter.)

As you make important decisions about equipment and materials, keep in mind the following guidelines used by teachers in HighScope programs.

1. Materials Are Varied and Plentiful

45

Because their interests are varied, children need a wide range of materials to support their play and learning. It is therefore important to have many different types of equipment and materials available in each area of the classroom. (See pp. 47–50 for a list of material types and specific examples for each area; also see Part 3 for ideas on how to use these materials to support development in each content area. Stock **open-ended materials** — that is, items that can be used in many different ways. In addition to items made specifically for preschoolers (such as toys, puzzles, or climbing equipment), it is important to include actual, everyday items such as telephones, hammers, uniforms, order pads, measuring tapes, and so on. Children enjoy imitating adults by using such real items in their play. They also investigate and learn about these objects as they incorporate them in role playing, building, problem solving, and other activities.

Also be sure to stock the classroom and outdoor play space with natural, found, and recycled items. Materials of this type are often low-cost or free. For example, on neighborhood walks children can collect natural and found objects such as shells, twigs, rocks, and fallen leaves. Materials gathered in this way provide a useful contrast in texture and color to purchased items, which tend to be made of plastic or a limited range of other materials. Children need opportunities to explore and discover the properties of wood, stone, fiber, shells, leaves, and other natural materials. Discovering and contrasting the properties of such items is an important foundation for mathematics, science, art, and other areas of learning.

Families can also contribute many items to your classroom — for example, recyclable paper and containers, old clothes, small appliances that no longer work, and tools and equipment for the house and yard. Donations brought in by family members offer several advantages. One is financial, since the items are free. Second is the opportunity to involve families in your program. Even parents whose work schedules may not permit them to volunteer in the classroom feel they can play an important role by donating play items. Finally, it is important for classroom materials to reflect children's home lives. Familiar objects help

46

children feel comfortable in the classroom. Using such objects in the classroom also validates children's family and cultural experiences. (See #2, below, for more information on how materials can reflect children's home lives.)

Having plentiful materials means there are enough materials in each area so that several children can play in any particular area at the same time. For example, if several children want to paint, it is useful to have a couple of easels, table or floor space, multiple paint containers, several brushes in different widths, and a number of smocks. Having enough materials means that each child can carry out his or her plans without having to wait, as waiting is difficult for young children. It also means children can make many choices in terms of materials they can use and combine to achieve their goals.

> *Six children in Miss Peggy's small group decided to send her get-well cards. Since there were four complete sets of markers, each child was able to find the colors he or she needed to draw or write a message.*

> *After completing a puzzle, Bing announced his next plan was to paint. He wanted to work at one of the two easels, but Cheryl and Yvonne were already there. Marcus, Bing's teacher, wondered what he could do instead. Bing got a piece of paper and asked Marcus to hold it against the wall by the table while he used masking tape to attach it. Yvonne said Bing should put newspaper under it in case he dripped, and she brought him a piece. Bing pumped red, blue, and white paint into an ice cube tray. He set the tray on the table and began to paint.*

Having ample materials also helps minimize the number of conflicts children have over who gets to use what and when. While a certain number of conflicts are inevitable — and provide young children with valuable learning experiences — constant fighting over materials cuts into the time available for other types of play and exploration.

Finally, children need materials that support a wide range of play experiences in order to increase their knowledge and abilities in each area

When the learning environment is organized and labeled, children can independently find, use, and return the materials they need to carry out their plans.

of development. Provide equipment and materials for sensory exploration, building, making things, pretending, and playing simple games. When children are free to use even simple materials that support their interests, they often combine them in unique and complex ways.

2. Materials Reflect Children's Family Lives

The materials in the classroom send children a message about what adults think is important. In order to show that you value children's home and family life, include many items found in homes, such as books, magazines, photographs, dolls, clothing, music, and food containers that accurately reflect the cultural and linguistic diversity of the children in your program.

Equipment and materials can also portray such realities as disabilities and differences in family makeup. So, for example, there might be weaving supplies, recordings of folk or traditional music popular in the local community, stuffed or plastic "house pets," books in different languages, crutches, eyeglasses with the lenses removed, and work clothes from jobs held by the children's parents.

Sample Materials List for a HighScope Classroom

Art Area Materials

Materials for mixing and painting	Tempera paint, liquid starch for finger paint, soap flakes, water-color paints, easels, plastic squeeze bottles, jars with lids for storing paints, paintbrushes of different sizes, muffin and frozen food tins, saucers for painting and printing, sponges, paper towels, smocks or paint shirts, toothbrushes, screening
Materials for holding things together and taking them apart	Scissors, yarn, shoelaces, string, rubber bands, paperclips, cellophane tape, masking tape, white glue, paste, paper punch, staplers
Materials for two-dimensional representation	Pencils, colored pencils, crayons, chalk and chalkboard, markers, ink pads and stamps, magazines and catalogs, paper of different sizes and colors and textures, newsprint, aluminum foil, wax paper, tissue paper, cotton balls, paper scraps, paper plates, shoe boxes, wallpaper samples, cardboard pieces
Materials for three-dimensional representation	Clay, play dough and accessories, buttons, straws, egg cartons, ice cream tubs, empty thread spools, pipe cleaners, clothespins, bits of wood, sequins, cardboard tubes, paper bags, scraps (cloth, felt, rug, vinyl), feathers, Styrofoam bits

House Area Materials

Materials children see at home	Telephones, old clocks, one-step ladder, tool box, child-size iron and ironing board, soft chair, small vacuum cleaner, broom and dustpan, toaster, nonworking microwave, luggage, cooler or ice chest, desk, blankets, used keyboard, telephone
Materials for pretend play	Props for pretend play (e.g., pretend barbershop, farm, fire station, doctor's office, restaurant, gas station), dolls, stuffed animals, doll beds, baby equipment (rattles, bibs, bottles), clothes and hats, mirror, sleeping bag
Kitchen equipment 	Child-size appliances (stove, refrigerator, sink), pots and pans, cooking utensils, large and small spoons, large and small spatulas, egg beater, timer, teapot, coffee maker, ladle, ice cube trays, hamburger press, cake and pie tins, mixing bowls, measuring cups and spoons, canister set, sifter, potholders, dishes (plates, cups, bowls), cleanup equipment (sponges, dish clothes, towels), table linens (napkins, placemats), plastic fruits and vegetables, small items to use as pretend food items (e.g., poker chips, bottle caps, Styrofoam bits, acorns), empty food boxes and plastic containers, jars, produce and trash bags

Sample Materials List for a HighScope Classroom

Block Area Materials

Materials for building	Large hollow blocks, unit blocks, small blocks, cardboard blocks, blocks made from shoeboxes, milk cartons, carpet pieces, fabric (bedspreads, old sheets, blankets), large and small boxes, wood scraps, tubes, string, rope
Materials for representing	Steering wheel, small trucks, small cars and people, Tinkertoys, interlocking boards, wooden train set and track, barn and farm animals

Toy Area Materials

Materials for sorting	Marble games, nesting and stacking toys (cups, boxes, blocks, rings, cans), Cuisenaire rods, beads and strings, attribute blocks, natural materials (shells, stones, pine cones, seed pods), buttons
Materials for taking apart and putting together	Legos, washers, nuts and bolts, pegs and pegboards, magnets, interlocking blocks
Materials for pretend play	Puppets, counting bears, miniature animals, small people, wooden village (city, farm)
Games	Puzzles, marbles, picture dominoes, simple card games (*Go Fish, Snap, Old Maid*), simple board games

Reading and Writing Area Materials

Materials for writing	Pencils, crayons, erasers, old keyboard, markers, typewriter, rubber stamps and ink pads, paperclips, tape, rulers, different kinds of paper (with and without lines), envelopes, stamps or stickers
Materials for reading	Assorted published books (picture books, wordless books, predictable format books, poetry books, alphabet books, information books, folktale books), homemade and child-made books, photo albums (including pictures of children, their families, the classroom, field trips, special events), recorded stories and earphones for listening, beanbag chair, pillows

Sample Materials List for a HighScope Classroom

Mathematics and Science Area Materials

Materials for identifying and comparing attributes (making collections, matching and sorting)	Blocks of different sizes and shapes and colors, boxes, lids, plates, shape sorters, carpet squares, wallpaper samples, rings, dominoes, attribute blocks, Cuisenaire rods, shaving cream, foil, paper with different textures (sandpaper, crepe paper, tissue paper), natural items (leaves, pebbles, shells), magnets, containers for collecting and sorting (boxes, bags, egg cartons, buckets, plastic containers)
Materials for making series and patterns	Nesting blocks, stacking rings, measuring cups and spoons, pegs and pegboards, beads and string, cardboard and felt pieces in different colors and graduated sizes
Materials for making ordered sets	Three or four sizes of flower pots and saucers, plastic containers and cans with lids, cups and saucers, squeeze bottles and tops, cards and envelopes, nuts and bolts, boxes and covers
Materials for counting, measuring, and comparing quantities	Beads, blocks, toy vehicles, toy animals, buttons, rocks, shells, leaves, acorns, bottle caps, materials with numerals (adding machine, typewriter, calculator, playing cards, play money, number stamps, number stickers), board games and dice, devices for conventional and unconventional measuring (rulers, tape measures, balance scales and weights, lengths of string)
Materials for exploring space (filling and emptying; putting together and taking apart; shaping and arranging)	Continuous materials to pour (sand, water, salt, flour, birdseed), discrete materials (small plastic animals, beads, poker chips, nuts, shells, pea gravel, buttons), inch cubes (plastic cubes that can be snapped together), bottle caps, various scoops and containers, toys and blocks with interlocking parts, beads and string, keys and key rings, paper and cloth, clay and dough, yarn and ribbon, pipe cleaners
Materials for observing things from different perspectives	Print materials depicting various viewpoints (picture and photo books, magazines, art prints), stools, steps, ramps, outdoor equipment with different levels and viewpoints (climber, ladder, trampoline, seesaw), natural variations in elevation (hills and tree stumps, holes and pits in the ground), magnifying glasses
Materials for exploring time (stopping and starting; setting in motion)	Timers (egg, sand, water, kitchen), wind-up clocks, musical instruments, objects with wheels, objects that move in different ways (rock, roll, spin, and drip)

Sand and Water Area Materials

Materials for a water table	Plastic cars and trucks, kitchenware (pans, dishes, silverware), plastic tubing, squeeze bottles, siphon and pump, funnels, measuring cups and spoons, smocks, snow, ice cubes, shaving cream
Materials for a sand table	Materials also found in water table, shovels, spoons, sifters and strainers, Styrofoam packing peanuts, sawdust, wood shavings, pine needles, birdseed

Sample Materials List for a HighScope Classroom

Movement and Music Area Materials

Equipment	Tape player, CD player, recordings representing a variety of musical styles and cultures, microphone, earphones
Instruments	Percussion instruments (e.g., drums, tambourines, triangles, maracas, sandpaper blocks, cymbals, bells, xylophones), wind instruments (e.g., whistles, slide whistles, kazoos, harmonicas)
Props for dancing	Scarves, ribbons, hoops, sticks

Woodworking Area Materials

Tools	Claw hammers, saws, hand drills, screwdrivers, pliers, vises, C-clamps, sandpaper, safety goggles
Fasteners	Nails, golf tees, screws, nuts, bolts, washers, wire, wood glue
Wood and building materials	Wood pieces and scraps, Styrofoam pieces, bottle caps and jar lids (for wheels), dowel-rod pieces

Outdoor Area Materials

Stationary structures	Climbers, raised areas (platforms, hills, boulders, tree stumps, snow and dirt piles), swings, slides, balances (balance beam, railroad ties, rows of bricks in different patterns)
Wheeled toys	Tricycles, scooters, wagons, wheelbarrow, push vehicles with steering wheels, strollers, carriages
Loose materials	Jumping equipment (inner tubes, leaf piles, ropes to jump over), throwing and kicking equipment (balls, beanbags, low basketball hoop and net, pails, bull's eye or other targets), building materials (boards, cardboard boxes, twine, old sheets and blankets, small sawhorses, tires and inner tubes, workbench and tools), sand materials (sand pit or table), water materials (water table, spigot, hose, flexible tubing), gardening equipment, role-play props, musical instruments, art materials (Note: Many materials for the art, house, sand and water, and movement and music areas can be used outdoors)

Sources: *The HighScope Approach to Indoor and Outdoor Learning Environments* (HighScope Educational Research Foundation, 1996) and *Educating Young Children: Active Learning Practices for Preschool and Child Care Programs* (Hohmann & Weikart, 2002)

Family Diversity Classroom Checklist

To evaluate how well a classroom reflects the diversity of children's home cultures, HighScope teachers use the following checklist to examine the different areas of the classroom.

Art Area

__ Paint, crayons, and paper mirror the skin colors of people in the school and community.

__ Other art materials reflect the arts and crafts found in the community.

Block Area

__ Toy people are multiracial and without sex-role stereotyping.

__ Animal figures represent house pets and farm animals found in the local area.

__ Toy vehicles represent real vehicles found in the community.

Reading and Writing Area

__ There are books that include writing in children's home language(s).

__ Books depict a variety of racial, ethnic, and cultural groups.

__ References to color in books are not stereotypical and negative. (For example, avoid books that associate black with evil or white with goodness.)

__ Books represent a variety of family situations, including single-parent families, two-parent families, biracial couples, gay couples and parents, stepparents, multigenerational families, and children cared for by extended family members.

__ Books portray women and men in realistic situations, playing nonstereotyped roles.

__ Books show children and adults with various disabilities. Disabled characters are portrayed as real people who happen to have handicaps, not as objects of pity.

House Area

__ There are multiracial boy and girl dolls with appropriate skin color, hair texture and styles, and facial features.

__ Style and content of house area items mirror homes in the community. (For example, a house area in the Southwestern United States may include a patio area, whereas an urban program may divide the house area into two "apartments.")

__ Kitchen utensils and empty food containers reflect the food preparation and eating habits of children and their family members.

__ Dress-up clothing reflects the tastes and occupations of children and their parents.

__ Equipment used by handicapped people, preferably child-sized, is available for role play (such as wheelchairs, crutches, and eyeglasses with the lenses taken out).

Movement and Music Area

__ Musical recordings and instruments reflect children's cultures.

__ Movement games and dance steps reflect children's cultures.

Toy Area

__ Puzzles depict the community setting (for example, urban or rural scenes and activities).

__ Puzzles represent the occupations of children's parents and other community members.

__ Toy figures and puzzles depict multiracial people and avoid sex-role stereotypes.

Adapted from *Educating Young Children: Active Learning Practices for Preschool and Child Care Programs* (Hohmann & Weikart, 2002, p. 121)

3. Storage Promotes the Find-Use-Return Cycle

Perhaps the most important principle of the HighScope learning environment is that children should be able to find, use, and return the materials they need on their own. Interest areas, organized by function, help children figure out where these materials are likely to be located. Labels on areas and materials further help children to find what they need and to return materials when they are done using them.

This basic feature of all HighScope classrooms lets children take the initiative in carrying out their plans, act with independence, and develop competence in meeting their own needs. The organization and labeling of the stored materials also helps children develop concepts about how materials are grouped by appearance, function, and other features. To help children in these ways, use the following guidelines to store and label materials:

▲ **Store similar items together.** Storing things that go together in the same area helps children find and return the things they need in their play. So, for example, a program would have painting, drawing, and sculpting supplies in the art area. When similar materials are located near one another (for example, markers, tape, and string kept on adjacent shelves), children can think about different alternatives for carrying out their ideas or solving problems.

▲ **Use containers children can see into and handle.** Containers that have open tops or see-through sides make it easy for children to find what they need. Choose containers of a size and shape that small hands can manage. Place containers on low shelves or on the floor so children can reach them easily. Some materials, such as blocks, can be stacked or stored directly on floors or shelves.

▲ **Label containers in ways that make sense to children.** As with classroom areas, name materials with labels that are simple and easy for children to understand. Also, as with areas, label materials and their containers in a variety of ways that reflect different stages of children's literacy development. For example, include words, drawings, tracings, photographs, and examples of the actual objects. Young children enjoy

Labeling Areas and Materials

Labels or signs help children find what they need to carry out their plans and solve the problems they encounter in play. When they are done, labels help them know where to return things. The ability to find and put things away on their own helps young children take the initiative and develop a sense of independence and confidence. When children can take care of these needs for themselves, it also frees teachers to spend their time in more meaningful interactions with their students. Below are some pointers for making labels (or signs) for areas and materials.

❖ Use names and labels that make sense to young children, for example, "toys" rather than "manipulatives."

❖ Involve children in making labels for new materials. This encourages them to focus on the properties of the materials as they draw, trace, or represent them in other ways. Children who are writing can make the word label for an area or material.

❖ Write words in large, clear letters.

❖ Labels that children can understand include the material itself (for example, a paintbrush taped to a piece of cardboard); tracings of the material; drawings; catalog pictures; photographs; and photocopies.

❖ Cover labels on both sides with clear contact paper or clear tape. This makes them easy to attach to shelves or containers, for example, with loops of masking tape. They can also be moved easily when it is time to make room for new materials.

deciding where new materials should go and making labels for them. Involving children in making labels for new materials encourages the children to focus on the features of the materials as they draw, trace, or represent them in other ways. Invite children who are writing words to make the labels that use words.

The outdoor learning environment allows children to use big equipment, exercise their large muscles and "big" voices, and explore nature, all in a safe setting.

The Outdoor Learning Environment

Young children like and need to be outdoors, where they are freer to move and make noise than they are indoors. In addition to helping them develop large-motor skills such as climbing and running, being outdoors gives children opportunities to design and build things on a larger scale than is possible indoors. Further, the outdoor environment is a place for children to appreciate the beauty and wonder of nature and to experience variations in light, temperature, and wind, as well as different sights, sounds, smells, and textures. Children with one or more sensory disabilities may especially appreciate the heightened experience of other senses while they are outdoors.

Outdoor play spaces are best located on open land or in a yard next to the school building. This allows children to go in and out quickly and safely and to move appropriate materials from one loca-

tion to another (for example, when working with clay on pallets outdoors). If your program is located in a city, you may not have this option, in which case a nearby park or field will do. Sometimes a rooftop area is suitable for an outdoor space, provided it has high walls and smooth surfaces that make it safe for young children to play.

Your program's outdoor space, just like its indoor space, should have separate areas for different types of play. There should be areas for vigorous activities such as running, riding wheeled toys, climbing, and sliding. There should also be places for quieter, focused play, such as building things, drawing with chalk or water on pavement, or telling or acting out stories. There are several ways that you can mark and separate these areas using low barriers or different surface materials. For example, the area for wheeled toys needs a hard surface, while pea gravel or wood chips work well under swings and slides. You can also use naturally occurring boundaries, such as trees, shrubs, flower beds, or low stone walls to differentiate outdoor spaces.

Outdoor materials also need storage space. A locked outdoor shed is preferable for wheeled toys. You can store smaller materials in portable containers with handles, such as plastic tubs or baskets, that children can easily carry back and forth from the classroom to the outdoor play space.

Finally, safety is always an important consideration in outdoor play spaces. HighScope identifies four key factors in keeping children safe when they play outdoors: adult supervision; equipment that is age- and size-appropriate (and accommodates children with special needs); impact-absorbing surfaces; and well-maintained equipment. You can find more information on outdoor play spaces and safety guidelines in the HighScope publication *Let's Go Outside: Designing the Early Childhood Playground* (Theemes, 1999).

Try These Ideas Yourself

1. Look at your early childhood classroom (or arrange to observe in one). If possible, take photos. How would you rearrange the room to better promote active learning? Draw a diagram of the modified room arrangement and briefly describe how or why it improves on the original setup.

54

Guidelines for the Learning Environment: A Summary

Arranging the Play Space

1. Divide the space into well-defined interest areas that allow for many different types of play.

2. Choose names for the interest areas that children can understand (for example, "toy area" instead of "manipulatives area").

3. Create visual boundaries between the areas (but don't prevent movement between them).

4. Consider the fixed parts of the room (such as doors and windows, the sink, inside walls) and how traffic will flow within and between areas.

5. Change the areas throughout the year.

Choosing Materials

1. Choose materials that reflect children's interests.

2. Choose materials that are appropriate for children's developmental and ability levels.

3. Provide items that children can use in many different ways.

4. Choose materials that young children typically like to play with.

5. Choose materials that show the diversity of the children and families in your program.

6. Make sure the materials are safe, clean, and well-maintained.

Storing and Labeling Materials

1. Store materials where children can reach them.

2. Store materials in see-through containers in plain view to children.

3. Store materials in the same place so children know where to find them.

4. Label shelves and materials so children can find and put away materials on their own.

2. Go into an early childhood classroom when the children are not there. Spend an hour playing with different toys and materials. (Remember to clean up afterward!) Think about what you did and did not enjoy playing with, and why. (Variation: Do this activity with one or more friends. Talk about similarities and differences in the materials you each enjoyed playing with. Which materials lent themselves to solitary, parallel, or cooperative play? What were the benefits of each type of play?)

3. Pretend you just received a $15,000 grant to design and furnish a new preschool classroom and outdoor space. Draw a diagram of the new room and the outdoor play space. List the materials you will use to furnish each area, including open-ended, found, and real-life materials. Identify which items you will buy (look at school supply catalogs but don't forget garage sales and thrift shops) and those you can build, collect, or recycle from existing supplies and donations.

4. Visit a neighborhood playground and observe children's play; focus on children in the age range of three to five years. What equipment and activities are they most engaged with? What are they doing? What do you think makes that particular equipment or activity appealing to them? What are they learning as they play?

Chapter 7

What Is the HighScope Daily Routine?

 **Think About It**

You have an early morning weekday routine. You get up at 6:00, put on your exercise clothes, take a 45-minute walk, shower at 7:00 and get dressed, eat breakfast at 7:20 while you read the newspaper, pack lunch at 7:50, and leave for work at 8:00 when you can tune in your favorite news and talk show on the car radio.

A houseguest arrives on Sunday evening to spend the week. Monday morning when you return from your walk, your guest is in the shower. The newspaper has been taken into the bathroom and is now behind the locked door. You discover the yogurt you were planning to have for breakfast has been eaten, as has the fruit you were going to pack for lunch. When you finally leave the house half an hour behind schedule, you discover your guest's car is blocking yours in the driveway. Although you are looking forward to a planned change in routine tonight — the appreciative guest is taking you out to dinner — right now you feel totally discombobulated.

Routines serve several purposes in our lives. They allow us to be organized and efficient. When we follow a routine we feel a sense of control and are less likely to forget things or make careless errors. Routines are also comforting. We know what to expect and we worry less about unwanted "surprises." Children need routines for the same reasons adults do, especially since so many of the events in their daily lives are beyond their control. When chil-

dren can predict the order and content of the day's events, they feel both reassured and empowered.

Of course children, like adults, also run the risk of being overly scheduled. There may be too many events crammed into the day. The timetable may be so rigid that enjoyable or complex activities cannot be extended, while boring or easy ones cannot be eliminated or cut short. Thus, schedules and routines require careful planning and must take into account the full range of our physical, intellectual, personal, and interpersonal needs.

Daily routines in HighScope programs are designed to provide the consistency and predictability that children and adults need. At the same time, there is enough flexibility that children feel neither rushed nor slowed down in carrying out their activities. Most important, children make choices — within reasonable limits — during each part of the day. Because activities build on their interests and

A daily routine provides children and adults with consistency and predictability. Flexibility and child choice within each part of the routine gives children a sense of program ownership.

56

Chapter Learning Objectives

By the end of this chapter, you will be able to

❖ Explain the importance of routine in the lives of children as well as adults

❖ Identify the basic components of the HighScope daily routine (plan-do-review, small- and large-group times) and how to support young children as they plan, carry out, and review their activities (use the plan-do-review cycle)

abilities, and because they know they have a say in the learning experience, children in HighScope programs feel that the daily routine belongs to them. They enjoy learning it and following it. In fact, when visitors or new children come to the classroom, children who are "old hands" and eager to show them the ropes often begin by leading them through each part of the day's schedule.

Overview of the HighScope Daily Routine

The HighScope **daily routine** is the order of the day's events, each with a specified amount of time. This schedule is the same every day, which is what makes it "routine," although time periods are occasionally altered to accommodate children's interests and there are exceptions for field trips, celebrations, or other special activities. Just as the HighScope learning environment organizes space, the daily routine organizes time. In addition to giving children a sense of control and allowing them to act independently, the regular organization of the day's events helps them develop important concepts about sequence (the order of events) and duration (how long something lasts). These concepts play a central role in early mathematics and scientific thinking.

The largest part of the HighScope day, generally over an hour in total, is devoted to a *planning time, work time,* and *recall time* sequence called **plan-do-review.** Meeting in a small group, each child decides what to do during work time — what area to play in, what materials to use, and who else will be involved — and shares this plan with an adult and possibly other children in his or her group. Work time is when children carry out their plans, alone and/or with others, and then clean up. At recall time, they meet with the same adult and small group of children with whom they planned to share and discuss what they did and learned during work time.

A HighScope program day also includes **large-group times** — those times when the entire class does something together. These occur not only during large-group time itself but also during other daily routine segments such as greeting time, **outside time,** and **transitions. Small-group times** (in addition to planning and recall) that take place outside small-group time include meals or snacks.

HighScope Preschool Daily Routine* Components

Greeting time (variable)

Planning time (10–15 minutes)

Work time (45–60 minutes)

Cleanup time (10 minutes)

Recall time (10–15 minutes)

Large-group time (10–15 minutes)

Small-group time (15–20 minutes)

Outside time (30–40 minutes)

Transition times, including arrival and departure (variable)

Eating and resting times (variable)

*The order of components may vary, depending on the hours and structure of the program. However, planning time, work time, cleanup time, and recall time always occur in that order. In half-day programs, each component typically happens once. In full-day programs, one or more components may be repeated.

Terms Used in This Chapter
• daily routine • plan-do-review (planning time, work time, recall time) • large-group times • outside time • transitions • small-group times

Sample Daily Routines

Arrival & Departure Pattern

Children arrive and depart at the same time

Children arrive and/or depart at different times

Half-Day Program

▷ Greeting time
▷ Planning, work, cleanup, and recall time
▷ Snack
▷ Large-group time
▷ Small-group time
▷ Outside time
▷ Departure

Morning arrival group:

▷ Greeting time
▷ Planning, work, cleanup, and recall time
▷ Small-group time
▷ Large-group time
▷ Outdoor time
▷ Lunch
▷ Departure

Afternoon arrival group:

▷ Lunch
▷ Greeting time
▷ Large-group time
▷ Planning, work, cleanup, and recall time
▷ Small-group time
▷ Snack
▷ Outdoor time
▷ Departure

Full-Day Program

▷ Breakfast
▷ Greeting time
▷ Large-group time
▷ Planning, work, cleanup, and recall time
▷ Small-group time
▷ Outside time
▷ Lunch
▷ Books and rest
▷ Snack
▷ Outside time
▷ Departure

Staggered arrivals and departures through the day:

▷ Free play
▷ Breakfast
▷ Greeting time
▷ Planning, work, cleanup, and recall time
▷ Small-group time
▷ Large-group time
▷ Outside time
▷ Lunch
▷ Books, nap
▷ Snack
▷ Small-group time
▷ Planning, work, and cleanup, and recall time with parents

Small-group activities involve the whole class but are carried out in smaller groups. Children meet with the same adult and set of classmates for all small-group activities. This arrangement provides continuity and security for the children and also allows the adult to develop a thorough knowledge of each child in his or her group over time.

In part-day programs, each segment of the daily routine typically happens once, except for transitions, which happen between each segment. Full-day programs may repeat one or more segments and include additional meals and naptime. (See the sidebar on this page for sample daily routines for part-day and full-day programs.) In the remainder of this chapter, we'll take a look at each of these program components and how you can support children's initiative and learning during them.

The Importance of the Daily Routine

A predictable sequence of events, with room to make choices within that routine, offers the following benefits to children and adults in HighScope programs:

58

The HighScope Daily Routine

Greeting Time

Plan ⟹ Do ⟹ Review

Planning Time

Work Time

Cleanup Time

Recall Time

Large-Group Time

Small-Group Time

Outside Time

Snacks and Meals

Transitions

60

▲ **Creates a sense of security and control.** A consistent routine means children know what to expect each day. Since child care or preschool is generally a young child's first separation from family and home, predictability provides comfort during this physical and emotional transition. Children come to school confident that there will be no unwelcome surprises or arbitrary demands. If there are occasional changes in the routine, children know they will be told ahead of time what the reasons for the changes are and why they are taking place, so they can prepare for these exceptions to the rule.

▲ **Supports initiative.** Although a routine defines the type of activity in each segment of the day, it does not dictate or limit what children can do during that time. Within this set framework, children know they will have choices. These options are most obvious during plan-do-review, when children carry out their intentions. However, even during adult-planned group times, children have many choices and can follow their individual interests at their own developmental levels.

▲ **Provides a social community.** When people do the same thing at the same time, it creates a bond between them. Even though children pursue the same activity in individual ways, they are still sharing a common experience. As an example, think of eating at a restaurant with family and friends. People often order different dishes from the menu, although they may sample one another's choices and discover something new they like. Conversations sometimes involve the whole group, and at other times, pairs and small groups. While each person's dining experience is somewhat different, everyone shares the sense of adventure and togetherness.

▲ **Provides a framework for adults to observe and plan.** In addition to the benefits listed above for children, a consistent daily routine also helps adults understand and meet children's needs. Teachers observe children and think about their needs and interests during each part of the day, every day. Since each segment of the daily routine is unique — with its own content, tempo, and social patterns — adults can plan for many types of learning to occur.

Plan-Do-Review

The plan-do-review process is both a critical and unique part of the HighScope Curriculum. It involves all the elements of active participatory learning. The abilities children develop as they take initiative, solve problems independently, work with others, and build knowledge and skills carry over into their subsequent schooling and even their lifetime patterns of thought and action.

Planning Time

Planning time, which takes about 10–15 minutes, begins the plan-do-review sequence. When young children plan, they begin with an intention or purpose. Depending on their age and ability to communicate, they express their plan in actions (picking up a paintbrush), gestures (pointing to the art area), or words ("I'm going to make a painting of my house").

In order to plan, children must be able to hold in mind a picture of something that is not actually present or that has not yet happened. Planning is different from simply making a choice, because it involves children in developing specific ideas about what they want to do and how they will do it. In other words, planning involves more purpose and intentionality than choosing. For that reason, we describe infants and young toddlers as

When School Can Provide the Consistency Not Found at Home

Consistency is especially important for children whose home lives may not be stable or organized. A Seattle teacher put it this way:

The child who comes from a chaotic home environment may have very little understanding of routine. The low self-esteem that comes from this kind of powerlessness is exactly the reason why elements of High-Scope, such as giving choices and planning one's own activities, are so important for our children. Gradually the child will discover in himself the ability to make a plan and will begin to get satisfaction from the things he can accomplish through his own planning and exploration.

At planning time, children express their intentions about the materials, actions, people, and ideas they want to include in their work time activities.

> ❝*The plan-do-review routine creates more interdependent relationships between adults and children in our setting, compared to last year. Plan-do-review sets up a required child-adult interaction which establishes patterns of reflection, critical to long-term successful learning and living. Merely selecting and playing without recall lacks a vital element for growth and development.*❞ (Dayton, Ohio, Teacher)

making choices, while planning begins in the late toddler or preschool years.

It is also important to remember that young children can quickly change their plans. In fact, children often do this as they carry out their ideas or get interested in what someone else is doing. This is similar to the flexibility of adults who might alter their plans depending on how a sequence of events unfolds. Therefore, in HighScope programs, children are not required to stick to their initial plans or criticized for not completing them. Instead, adults follow up with children at work time and help them express a new plan. Children may also complete their initial plan and then, often with the teacher's encouragement, come up with a next plan to continue their work-time activity.

HighScope was the first comprehensive curriculum model to include planning by children as a major component. Today, planning is recognized as an important activity in the Head Start Performance Standards and the best practices advocated by the National Association for the Education of Young Children (NΛEYC) and other professional

organizations. Planning provides the following developmental benefits to young children:

▲ **Encourages children to communicate their ideas, choices, and decisions.** Because adults value their plans, children are eager and motivated to share them.

▲ **Promotes children's self-confidence and sense of control.** Children come to rely on their own capacity to make decisions, solve problems, and turn their ideas into reality.

▲ **Leads to involvement in and concentration on play.** Common sense, also supported by research, says people are more committed to the things they choose to do than things imposed by others. Researchers Carla Berry and Kathy Sylva (1987), studying HighScope programs in Britain, found that children who planned were engaged in more purposeful play and concentrated for longer periods of time than those who did not plan.

▲ **Supports the development of increasingly complex play.** Planned play contrasts with ordinary play, which tends to be repetitive, random, and aimless. When children carry out their plans, they play with "more imagination, concentration, and intellectual complexity" than when they engage in ordinary, unplanned play (Berry & Sylva, 1987, p. 34). Children are also more likely to set goals and learn new knowledge and skills when they plan and become involved in complex play.

It's important to remember that children's planning will change over time. Although each child handles the planning process differently, it is useful to keep in mind these basic principles:

▲ **Children's plans become more complex and detailed as children develop.** Younger children and new planners may simply point to an area or express a plan in one or two words. Older

Supporting Children at Planning Time

Consider This..

Think about your own ideas about child planning.

Many adults are enthusiastic about child planning because they understand that children learn best by carrying out their own ideas. Others are skeptical. A common fear is that adults will lose control and children will run around doing whatever they like — including making a mess, "wasting time," or even endangering themselves and others. Or teachers worry that some children will do the same simple thing over and over and never learn the basics necessary for school entry. Research shows these fears are not borne out (Sylva, Smith, & Moore, 1986). In fact, children who plan become more purposeful in their play and increasingly responsible for the consequences of their actions. Further, because individual adults and children bring up so many different ideas during the process of planning, children are more likely to have a wide range of learning experiences than they would in a highly controlled setting.

HighScope teachers learn during their training to use many **strategies to support planning** in young children. These include the following:

❖ *Plan with children in an intimate setting.* Planning can occur at a table, in an interest area, on the floor, curled up on the reading couch, or any place where children feel comfortable sharing their ideas with an adult. It helps children focus on the act of planning if it occurs in the same place every day, although an occasional variation (such as planning outside at the picnic table on a summer day) keeps the activity fresh. The smaller the number of children in the planning group — ideally, one adult with 6–8 children in a stable group — the more detailed their plans tend to be. (**Note:** Children also stay with the same adult and group of children for recall, snacks, and other small-group activities.) To make planning a relaxed and intimate process, be patient and plan where people and materials are easily visible.

❖ *Provide materials and experiences to maintain children's interest in planning time.* Use props, partners, playfulness, and novelty so planning does not become mechanical and so children

stay engaged until it is their turn. It can also help to let children take charge. As children get used to planning, they introduce their own games or variations. Over time, children also begin to plan with each other. In fact, sometimes children make more detailed plans with another child than they do with an adult.

❖ *Converse with individual children about their plans.* While the overall tone is set with the group, it is important that each child gets to express his or her plan. Therefore, put equal time and effort into eliciting each child's ideas, whether these are communicated verbally or nonverbally. There are several things you can do to encourage communication.

Providing Special Planning Games and Experiences

Ideas for planning time might include

- Taking a tour around the room or making a "train" that goes from one interest area to another, allowing children to make plans when they arrive at an area where they want to play
- Passing a hula hoop with a spot on it until a song stops and the one whose hands are on the spot takes a turn planning
- Rolling a ball from child to child as each one plans
- Making up rhymes with children's names to indicate who plans next
- Using props such as telephones or puppets to initiate planning
- Drawing pictures of materials, actions, people, and other things involved in the plan
- Taking dictation from children
- Having children write down letters and words in their plans

Whatever the strategy, it is important that every child be able to understand and perform it in some way, consistent with their developmental abilities. Planning strategies are never used as a "test" of children's knowledge.

Supporting Children at Planning Time (Cont.)

First, ask "what" questions that are simple and open ended — for example, "What would you like to do today?"

Second, talk to children about what might be making them reluctant to plan. When children are reluctant to express plans, be sensitive to figuring out why. For example, a child may want to play with another but is afraid of not being accepted. Or a child may be both curious and nervous about using a new material. By not pushing a child to voice a plan quickly, an adult can often get the child to open up. Then they can problem-solve together to overcome any barriers to planning.

Third, listen attentively to children's comments while a plan emerges. Although some children respond directly to questions or games, others plan more indirectly. For example, at planning time, Janice told her teacher about the new baby in her family. By listening carefully to Janice talk about the hospital, her new brother, and her daddy making breakfast, the teacher helped Janice describe a plan to bathe dolls in the house area, cook sand pancakes, and put the dolls to bed.

Finally, offer alternatives when children do not respond. You may be able to offer a nonverbal child choices that reflect his or her interests. For example, if you knew that a child had worked in the art area the last few days, you might say, "Yesterday, you made a painting." If the child nods, you might follow up by asking "Would you like to work in the art area again today or in a different area?" The child might nod again or point to a different area. Based on the child's response, you might comment, "So your plan is to work in the art area" or "Today you're going to the book area."

children and experienced planners can create very elaborate plans.

▲ **Planning is an adult-child partnership.** The child supplies ideas and intentions, and the adult encourages the child to think about how he or she will carry them out. Through give-and-take communication, the adult helps the child express plans in gestures and words, depending on the child's capabilities. Thus, planning is a shared process that involves cooperation.

▲ **Planning is just the beginning.** A child's plan is just the starting point. Once he or she expresses a set of intentions, the next step is to carry them out during work time with adult support and encouragement.

Work Time

Work time — the "do" of plan-do-review — is when children carry out their plans. This part of the daily routine generally lasts 45–60 minutes. The expression "play is a child's work" is consistent with the HighScope Curriculum, and calling this segment "work time" captures this philosophy. Many early childhood programs have a similar period they call "free-choice time." However, work time is often more purposeful because children have thought about and described their intentions ahead of time. They encounter interesting challenges and set about solving problems in the course of their play. Based

on their developmental level and interests, preschoolers typically engage in four types of play: *exploratory play, constructive play, pretend play,* and *games.* (See p. 32 in Chapter 5 for more about these different types of play.) Exploratory play usually develops first, followed by constructive and pretend play, and finally games (Bergen, 1988). However, any child at any point, may be involved in one or more types of play.

Work time provides the following benefits to young children:

▲ **Allows children to carry out intentions and play with purpose.** Work time is when

At work time, children carry out their plans with interest and a sense of purpose. They learn through hands-on experience and by solving the problems that arise during their play.

64

Supporting Children at Work Time

Consider This..

Think about your own ideas about how children learn.

In HighScope programs, the learning that happens during work time depends on both adults and children being active. That is, teachers neither direct the learning with children passively taking in the information nor do teachers withdraw and let children take all the responsibility for their own education. Instead, children pursue self-initiated interests and plans while adults become involved in their play and scaffold their learning, using the adult-child interaction strategies described in Chapter 5.

To make sure work time is a satisfying and educational experience for young children, use the following support strategies.

Provide work places and materials based on children's interests. Because work time generally occurs in the program's various interest areas, make sure these areas are easily accessible and contain a wide range of age-appropriate materials (see Chapter 6).

Offer children comfort and contact as needed. Sometimes children need adult reassurance about their feelings or ideas. Be alert to signs indicating that children need immediate attention before they can proceed with their plans. A child may express anxiety through gestures (shaking the head "no"), actions (withdrawing to a corner), or words (saying "No one wants to play with me"). In these instances, you might offer reassuring physical contact (for example, sit next to the child, rock or stroke, hold the child on your lap). Offer whatever type of reassurance you know that particular child will find comforting.

Acknowledge children's actions and accomplishments. Sometimes children need adults to simply take notice of what they did. You might offer a simple acknowledgment by looking at something a child has done, imitating a child's actions (moving in the same way to a song), or repeating a child's comment ("Yes, I see you made a tall tower with those blocks").

Participate in children's play. Joining in children's play lets them know that you think their interests and intentions are important. However, adults need to participate without taking over. Here are some strategies to use as you participate as a partner in children's play:

❖ *Look for natural play openings.* For example, you can explore materials alongside the child, take on a role assigned by a child in pretend play — for instance, if the child says he or she wants someone to be "the puppy" — or take a turn in a game invented or directed by the child.

❖ *Play as a partner with children.* Being a partner means acting as a follower and equal, not as a director. Therefore, adjust your speech and actions to the ideas and pace of the play, take directions from children, and follow the rules set by the group of players.

❖ *Join play on the children's level.* By seeing things from children's perspective, adults are less likely to take over the play situation. For example, if you are playing with children who are mixing Legos in a bowl to make "soup," you might begin by getting another spoon and stirring the pot, rather than adding new ingredients to the mixture. Or sit on the floor to see the tower they are building from the children's point of view.

❖ *Play in parallel.* This strategy is especially effective in joining exploratory play. Playing in parallel means playing near a child, using the same materials in the same or a similar manner; for example, rolling out play dough or filling and emptying containers with sand.

❖ *Suggest ideas within the play situation.* While being careful not to raise the level of complexity of children's play, you may offer suggestions to extend it. However, this strategy can be difficult to carry out, as there is a fine line between offering a new idea and directing the course of play. Based on her experiences with dramatic play, Sara Smilansky (1971) suggests that teachers offer suggestions within the theme of the play rather than introduce a new theme. For example, an adult could join the other "mothers" bringing babies to the doctor for a checkup rather than pretend there is a medical emergency.

Converse with children. Conversations help children express their ideas, build vocabulary, and develop the other language skills that are important in early literacy development. The strategies for

Supporting Children at Work Time (Cont.)

talking naturally with children are similar to those for entering into their play. Adults need to take their cues from children and be sensitive to times when conversation is welcome; for example, when a child eagerly talks about a painting he or she is making. At other times, talking may interfere with a child's activities — for example, if the child is concentrating on adding specific details to the picture.

To help children develop their thinking and language skills without inhibiting their actions,

❖ Look for natural opportunities for conversation

❖ Talk at the children's physical level

❖ Give children a chance to begin conversations

❖ Converse in a give-and-take manner

❖ Limit questions

See Chapter 5 for more on these strategies.

Encourage children's problem solving. Sometimes adults mistakenly believe that children should exist in a smooth-running and problem-free environment. However, solving problems is one of the most important experiences children can have during work time. In fact, children enjoy posing and solving problems. You can help children encounter these developmentally important experiences by waiting patiently for children to do things for themselves (such as putting on their winter coats), referring children to one another for help ("Tracy, can you show Jared how you got the two pieces of clay to stick together?"), and seeing yourself as a partner rather than as a "manager" ("So you both want to use the rowboat. How can we solve this problem?").

Observe and record what children do. Adults in HighScope programs make plans to support and extend learning based on what children do and say. With so much going on at work time — and the classroom is a very busy and active place! — it is often difficult to remember everything that went on for each child. Therefore, as you work and play with children, also jot down notes or use other simple reminders to help you recall details later during team planning (see Chapter 9).

Bring work time to an end with cleanup time. Teachers sometimes dread cleanup time. If they see it as an unpleasant chore, however, children are likely to pick up a negative and resistant attitude. But if you approach cleanup time as an opportunity to solve problems ("I wonder where we can hang this to dry?"), learn something (such as how materials are organized and arranged), and even have fun (inventing put-away games, using mops and sponges, reciting rhymes and chants), then children learn that this last part of work time is a natural step in carrying out one's plans.

Adults can also make cleanup time easier on everyone if their expectations for children are realistic. Children can do things to the best of their ability, but that is not the same as meeting adult standards for health and equipment maintenance. Teachers, janitorial staff, and/or other staff will need to finish the process between program sessions. Rather than emphasizing perfection, help children complete cleanup quickly so they can immediately proceed to reviewing and evaluating their work-time activities. (Also see the discussion of "transitions" later in this chapter.)

children put their ideas into action. They see themselves as "doers," capable of following through on a plan and achieving their goals.

▲ **Enables children to participate in a social setting.** As they work, children naturally come together in pairs and groups of different sizes. Even children who choose to work alone are aware of the presence and activities of those around them.

▲ **Provides many opportunities to solve problems.** Because children are engaged in activities they have defined for themselves, they are

likely to meet up with unexpected problems — for example, a piece of paper may be too big to fit in the envelope, or two children may want the same truck. As children develop solutions, either alone or with assistance from adults and playmates, they come to see themselves as competent problem-solvers.

▲ **Enables children to construct their own knowledge and build new skills.** As children carry out their plans and solve problems, they develop a new understanding of the world of things and people; they expand their knowledge and skills in literacy, math, science, art, music, and so on (see the HighScope key developmental indicators listed on p. 11 and discussed in Chapters 10–17).

▲ **Allows adults to observe, learn from, and support children's play.** By observing, supporting, and entering into children's play, adults gain insight into each child's development.

Recall Time

HighScope programs have a designated "recall time," which lasts 10–15 minutes. Children are encouraged to reflect on their actions and what they are learning throughout the day. For preschoolers, it is easiest to remember what happened when recall is as close as possible to the actual event. Younger preschoolers will often recall the last

Supporting Children at Recall Time

Consider This..

Think about your own ideas about children recalling.

Recall is successful when children tell their own stories in their own words, gestures, and drawings. The experience can be fun and social and can take many creative forms. If, however, teachers see recall as another time of day to be "gotten through," it can become rote and mechanical. Or, if they mistakenly think recall is a time when children should be held accountable for their plans, it can take on a punitive tone.

The adult's role at recall time is similar to his or her role at planning time. It grows out of observations of, and interactions with, children, based on the children's interests and the principles of active participatory learning. During recall time, use the following strategies to help young children think about and learn from their work-time activities.

Recall with children in a calm, cozy setting. As with child planning, recalling with the same familiar group of people in a consistent place creates a comfortable and trusting situation. The fewer distractions around, the more that children will be able to focus on recalling.

Provide materials and experiences to maintain children's interest in recall. As with planning, props and games keep recall interesting and help children wait their turn. For example, you might "tour" the room to the areas where children played, ask each child to bring an item he or she played with to the recall table, or use instant photos taken at work time to spark conversations about what children did. The materials or activity should be kept simple. Otherwise, children may become so interested in the prop or game (for example, spinning

the hula hoop or calling the next child on the toy telephone), that the purpose of recall is lost.

Converse with children about their work-time experiences. Again, the process of talking to children during recall is similar to that used in planning. Be patient, pay careful attention, and let the ideas unfold naturally from each child. A simple opening question may help, but avoid making the child dependent on adult prompting. Instead, you can make comments and observations to keep the conversation going. For example:

Child: I played in the house area.

Teacher: I saw you with the dolls.

Child: They was taking a bath. I filled the tub with water.

Teacher: You brought water from the sink to the house area.

Child: I took a bucket and filled it up and then I carried it to the bathtub.

Teacher: It looked like you carried lots of water.

Child: About ten-hundred-eight buckets of water. And I didn't spill any!

Teacher: You didn't spill any water. How did you keep from doing that?

Child: I only filled it up to here (gestures) so it wouldn't go over the top.

With development and experience, children become more skillful at recall. As you implement various strategies to support children at recall time, remember to stay flexible and observant. As you will also notice at planning time, children will gradually include more detail during recall, tell longer stories, listen to and contribute to the recall of others, and make plans for subsequent days based on what happened that day. The recall process helps them bring closure to their experiences.

thing they did, since it is freshest in their minds. As children become able to hold images and ideas in mind for longer periods and in greater detail, they are more apt to recall the sequence of what they did at work time, or they may even recall their original plans. Recall time should always immediately follow the work time-cleanup time sequence.

The above discussion of planning noted that planning time differs from ordinary "free choice" because, when making plans, children act with purpose and intention to develop specific ideas about what they want to do and how they will do it. Similarly, recall is different from simple "remembering." During recall, children take time to think not only about what they did but also about what they learned. Further, they are encouraged to share these observations with the teacher and the same small group of children with whom they planned, which supports the development of thinking and language. If children draw or write down what they did, they are also representing their activities in ways that helps develop their literacy skills. Finally, as the last step in the plan-do-review process, recall makes it more likely that the lessons children are learning will be lasting and applied to future actions and interactions. These benefits can be summarized as follows:

▲ **Exercises children's capacities to form and talk about mental images.** Recall encourages children to mentally picture and express their ideas about past events.

▲ **Consolidates children's understanding of experiences and events.** Recall helps children examine their choices and actions and the effects these had on objects and people (themselves and others).

▲ **Extends children's consciousness beyond the present.** Preschoolers live in the present. By helping them think about past events and how they were affected by them, we enable them to build on what they've already learned and apply it to new experiences and subject matter.

▲ **Makes children's experiences public.** Recall is a form of social interaction. During recall, children are narrators, telling a "story" about what happened to them at work time — which means they are also the stars. As preschoolers mature, they become more open to other children adding details to their recollections, and they begin to enhance the "stories" told by others as well. In these ways, recall becomes a shared undertaking that

helps children develop a sense of trust in their small community.

Group Times

Although plan-do-review is a major and unique part of the HighScope daily routine, children also benefit from a variety of other regular group experiences. These scheduled parts of the day include *small-group time, large-group time, outside time,* and *transition times.*

Small- and large-group times for preschoolers each generally last about 15 minutes. During these times, adults introduce children to new materials, ideas, and activities, which the children can then continue to explore at work time. Group experiences also offer many opportunities for social interaction. At outside time, which runs at least 30 minutes, children work with equipment and enjoy a range of physical activity that is not possible indoors. Transitions are the times in between the other activities. In HighScope programs, transitions are not seen as incidental but as planned opportunities for children to make choices, move in different ways, and learn important concepts.

Group Time
Planning Sheet
(The same sheet is used for small- and large-group time)

Originating idea: _____
_____

(Note the concept, local event, particular material, and/or what you observed children say or do that led to the idea.)

Materials: _____
_____

(List the materials you will need, including what and how many.)

Curriculum content: _____
_____

(List the main key developmental indicators the activity focuses on and any others that might occur.)

Beginning: _____
_____

(Describe how you will introduce the activity to the children, including your opening statement and/or action.)

Middle: _____
_____

(Describe what children might do during the activity and how you will support them.)

End: _____
_____

(Describe how you will bring the activity to a close.)

Follow-up: _____
_____

(Describe the materials and activities you can provide on subsequent days to build on the children's experience with this activity.)

Supporting Children at Small-Group Time

Consider This..

Think about your own ideas about how children learn at small-group time.

Some non-HighScope programs use small-group time to drill children in skills and concepts such as writing letters of the alphabet or learning color names. Adult-directed activities, ditto sheets, or children copying a craft project from an adult-made example are not part of the HighScope approach. While HighScope adults take the lead planning the small-group activity and providing materials, they realize that each child will respond to the experience differently.

The role of the adult is to support and extend each child's learning, based on the child's developmental level and interests. In fact, to verify that a small-group experience is appropriate for every child, HighScope teachers make sure that all the ingredients of active participatory learning (see Chapter 2) are present. As one HighScope trainer says,

"I wanted my trainees to understand that small-group time does not mean . . . all the children sitting and doing the same thing, using the same materials, and listening to the teacher talk." (Lincoln, Nebr., Teacher-Trainer)

As with other parts of the daily routine, it is important to use a variety of support strategies to make sure children enjoy and learn from small-group experiences. Here are some you can try:

Plan small-group experiences ahead of time. Successful small-group times appeal to children's interests, allow them to engage with materials and ideas at their own developmental level, and promote learning. The following sources will give you a wealth of small-group-time ideas.

❖ *Children's interests.* Many inspirations come from observing children at work time. For example, if children working in the art area become fascinated with mixing paints, you might plan a small-group time in which each child is given two cups of paint (one primary color — red, yellow, or blue — and white), paper, and a brush. Additional cups could be set out so children could pump another primary color or more white from big plastic jars. You could also set out extra paper and other painting tools (sticks, sponges, kitchen utensils) to explore.

❖ *Curriculum content.* Perhaps the members of your teaching team look back through their anecdotal notes and realize children are rarely engaging in certain curriculum content areas (described in Part 3 of this book). Or you and your coteachers may decide to ensure that every child receives planned and equal opportunities for learning in each area. In either case, you can use small-group time to engage children with materials and activities related to that content area. For example, to focus attention on patterns (an important area of early mathematics), you could provide each child with a cardboard grid and set out piles of small squares in different colors. After demonstrating a pattern on your board, you might say, "I wonder what patterns you can make with these pieces."

❖ *New, unexplored, underused, or favorite materials.* Small-group time lets you introduce new materials (such as computer programs) or call children's attention to existing materials that are being overlooked (for example, puzzles in the toy area). It is also a chance to encourage children to approach familiar or favorite materials in new ways; for example, using toy-truck tires to make impressions in play dough.

❖ *Local traditions and community events.* Children often bring ideas and experiences from outside the classroom into the program. These may originate in their families or the wider community and are a rich source of small-group-time ideas. For example, if several children were to talk about going to the farmer's market with their parents, you might plan a small-group activity to explore the color, shape, smell, texture, taste, and other properties of locally grown fruits and vegetables.

❖ *Teacher idea books and other curriculum materials.* To get started with small-group activities, some teachers turn to plans that have been designed and tested by experienced HighScope teachers. For example, they might use or adapt activities from *The Teacher's Idea Book: 100 Small-Group Experiences* (Graves, 1997). They may also refer to small-group activities in

Supporting Children at Small-Group Time (Cont.)

publications about literacy (*Growing Readers Early Literacy Curriculum;* Hohmann, 2005), mathematics (*"I'm Older Than You. I'm Five!" Math in the Preschool Classroom;* Epstein & Gainsley, 2005), visual art (*Supporting Young Artists: The Development of the Visual Arts in Young Children;* Epstein & Trimis, 2002), or movement (*Movement in Steady Beat, Second Edition;* Weikart, 2003). (See the HighScope Web site, *www.highscope.org,* for HighScope resources in each curriculum content area.)

Prepare for small-group time before children arrive. With a plan clearly in mind, High-Scope teachers get ready for small-group activities ahead of time, often in the morning before children arrive. This way, children do not have to wait to get started and can make good and interesting use of every minute. Getting ready means two things: First is gathering the necessary materials, often one set for each child. Second is storing materials in a place where the adult can get them easily and quickly as soon as small-group time begins. This is particularly important since groups generally meet in an area that is also used for other activities.

What to do during each part of small-group time. Use the following steps to guide children through small-group time. (Also see the sidebar on p. 70.)

❖ *Beginning.* Engage children as soon as they arrive at the gathering place. Make a brief introductory statement or offer a simple challenge, such as, "Today we have boxes in different sizes and some small, medium, and large bears. I wonder what we can do with them" or "Let's see what we can find out about this book by looking at the picture on the cover."

❖ *Middle.* Once children have begun to work with the materials, the teacher's role is to pay attention to their actions and ideas, scaffold further learning, and encourage them to interact with and learn from one another. You can do this by closely attending to each child, physically getting down on his or her level, watching and listening to the child, imitating and building on his or her actions, conversing with the child while following his or her leads, asking questions sparingly, and encouraging the child to solve problems both individually and with assistance from other children.

Teachers also support children's highly individual use of materials and their observations about what they are doing and learning. In fact, one indication of an effective small-group time is the sheer variety of ideas the children come up with. For example, in the small-group time one teacher planned with dinosaurs and carpet squares, children used the materials in the following ways: sorting dinosaurs and squares by size and/or color; making "dinosaur houses" with the carpet squares; grouping the dinosaurs into families; piling the carpet squares into towers; finding carpet squares big enough to hide different sized dinosaurs under; making patterns with the carpet squares; and lining up dinosaurs — and then themselves — by size.

❖ *End.* Letting children know when small-group time is about to end (a two- or three-minute warning) gives them control over how to bring the session to closure. Some may be ready to stop, and others may want to store their projects and materials to continue at work time the following day. Also, although small-group time has a set length, children will nevertheless finish at different times. On any given day, some will finish with the materials and activity quickly, while others will want to linger. Teachers therefore schedule the day so children can move to the next segment as they are ready (for example, getting ready for snack or outside time).

70

During all these other parts of the day, the principles of active participatory learning continue to apply. So, even though adults plan large- and small-group times around specific content, they base them on children's wide-ranging interests, encourage children to make choices about how they use the materials, and talk with children about what they are doing and learning. Group times also offer all children the chance to interact with others. This can be especially important for those who choose to work alone during the plan-do-review sequence. Group times in HighScope programs are unpressured, so even shy or solitary children can participate in ways that feel comfortable to them.

HighScope teachers put thought and effort into planning group times. They use their daily observations to see what children are interested in and how they can further their explorations in these areas. Group times are also the parts of the day when learning that needs to be systematic and sequenced — such as specific skills and concepts in literacy or mathematics — can be guaranteed

for all children. To make sure group times provide the maximum intellectual, social, and physical benefit to children, teachers complete a Group Time Planning Sheet with the information shown on page 67.

Small-Group Time

During small-group time the group is divided into smaller groups according to the number of teachers. Each small group meets for 15–20 minutes each day with the same adult. The same groupings are used for planning and recall time. These stable groups help teachers get to know each child and help the children feel comfortable with one another. (*Note:* In many programs, children also eat with the members of their small group. Snack or mealtime is discussed briefly on p. 78.)

After the teacher briefly introduces the activity, children are generally given their own set of materials to work with, sometimes with additional materials or tools in large enough quantity for

---

Small-Group Time: A Summary

Sources of Ideas for Small-Group Time

1. Children's interests.

2. Curriculum content.

3. New, unexplored, underused, or favorite materials.

4. Local traditions and community events.

5. Teacher idea books and other curriculum materials.

Small-Group Time: Beginning

1. Have materials or equipment organized and ready.

2. Briefly introduce materials, equipment, or action; for example, by

   • Handing out the materials or calling attention to the equipment

   • Playing a game with children

   • Telling a story using the materials or equipment

   • Posing a problem: "Let's see what would happen if…"

3. Let children begin working immediately.

Small-Group Time: Middle

1. Observe how children use or examine materials and equipment; listen to what they say.

2. Use and examine materials and equipment yourself, imitating children.

3. Move from child to child and engage in conversations. If gathered around one item (such as a book or the computer), attend closely to each child and support his or her contribution to the conversation.

4. Refer children to each other for problem solving.

5. Use a variety of adult-child interaction strategies.

Small-Group Time: End

1. Give children a warning signal that the activity time is coming to an end.

2. Make cleaning up materials part of the activity.

3. Start the next activity (see transition strategies later in this chapter).

everyone to share. For example, each child may get a peg board and a basket of pegs, with a large tub of additional pegs in the center of the table for all the children in the group to use as needed. If the activity is something like reading a book or introducing a new piece of computer software, the teacher places or uses the one shared copy where all the children can see, hear, touch, talk about their discoveries, and so on.

As they work with the materials, children make choices about how to use and talk about them. They talk with one another and the adult about what they are doing and seeing. The adult observes and comments on the children's actions and thoughts, refers them to one another for ideas and help, acknowledges and encourages each child's efforts, promotes independent problem-solving, and assists children in carrying out their intentions, if necessary. Children often work with the materials or extend their ideas during work time on subsequent days.

All children and adults participate together at large-group time. Whether it is vigorous (moving to music) or quiet (discussing a class problem), all the ingredients of active learning are present.

Small groups gather at a consistent, designated place each day. That way children know where to go on their own when this part of the daily routine begins. Small-group gathering places might be a table (perhaps the same one used for planning, recall, or snacktime), the floor in one area of the room, or the couch and chairs in the reading area.

Large-Group Time

Large-group time is when all children and adults participate in an activity together. There are several whole-class activities throughout the day. In this section, we specifically discuss the segment called "large-group time" (sometimes referred to as "circle time"). Greeting time, including the use of a message board, is also conducted with the entire class and is covered briefly at the end of the chapter.

Large-group time, which lasts 10–15 minutes, contributes to the sense of community in the classroom. It is a time when everyone comes together to participate in music and movement

---

Large-Group Time: A Summary

Sources of Ideas for Large-Group Time

1. Children's interests.
2. Curriculum content in physical development and the arts.
3. Cooperative play and projects.
4. Events currently meaningful to the children.
5. Teacher idea books and other curriculum materials.

Large-Group Time: Opener

1. Draw children in with an easy-to-join activity.
2. Start right away.

Large-Group Time: Activity

1. For each activity, provide a brief introduction.
2. Participate on the children's level.
3. Give props to the children.
4. Observe and listen.
5. Ask for children's ideas; use their language.
6. Let children lead; imitate their actions.

Large-Group Time: Transition

1. Give children a warning that the activity is coming to an end.
2. Make the final activity a transition to the next activity.
3. Put materials away.

Supporting Children at Large-Group Time

Consider This...

Think about your own ideas about how children learn at large-group time.

In HighScope programs, large-group time is a segment of the day when adults and children share an experience as *partners*. It is not a time for the teacher to lecture children, for example, about the weather, the calendar, or the "letter of the week." Preschoolers will generally not sit still for such instruction, and such abstract methods are not appropriate for them. Some teachers may see large-group time as a chance to be the "star," leading the children in a song or entertaining them with a story. However, HighScope's active learning approach recognizes that children need to move and sing and talk, not listen passively to someone else perform these activities. Children and adults both play important and equal roles.

The adult's role at large-group time is similar to his or her role at small-group time. Adults provide ideas and/or materials to get things started, then support children's explorations and encourage their ideas. Use the following strategies to help children learn from their activities:

Plan large-group experiences ahead of time. The following sources of ideas will help you plan:

❖ *Children's interests.* Children will be enthusiastic about large-group time if they are already interested in its focus. Use your observations of what children do at other times of the day to come up with ideas for large-group activities. For example, when the Olympic games are being broadcast, perhaps you notice at outside time that several children are using the railroad ties in the yard as "balance beams." You might then plan a large-group time in which several objects — a long block, a rubber mat, a strip of masking tape on the floor, and a row of carpet squares — can serve as balance beams for the children to walk across.

❖ *Curriculum content in physical development and the arts.* The HighScope key developmental indicators in physical development (see Chapter 13) and the arts, particularly drama and music (see Chapter 17), are fruitful sources of ideas. For example, "moving with objects" might inspire an activity in which children move their bodies in different ways using scarves, batons, sheets of newspaper, or other portable items. Building on the KDI "playing musical instruments" could lead to a large-group time in which children play various percussion instruments while listening to different types of music.

❖ *Cooperative play and projects.* Whole-group storytelling, dancing, and singing are all good ways to get the classroom community involved. To keep all the children focused, however, make sure that each child has an active role to play. You can encourage this level of involvement by giving everyone an object to manipulate, an individual space in which to move, words to sing, and so on. For example, in making up a group story about a dog and a cat, one teacher gave children two different color socks to put over their hands. Whenever they wanted the dog in the story to say or do something, they would move their red sock, while the cat was represented by the blue sock. Children moved their sock-covered hands in all kinds of ways, inventing roles for the two characters in the story.

❖ *Events currently meaningful to the children.* Large-group activities built around holidays or other topical events will only work if the children find them meaningful. If they are based on what adults find current — such as Ground Hog Day or summer vacation — children may not relate to them. Therefore, it is important to first observe what engages children before planning large-group time.

For example, in one classroom, children were not caught up in Christmas gifts or decorations. However, twins who spent time with their grandmother were interested in her seasonal baking and got other children involved in role playing in the house area. On a field trip, the class visited a bakery where children saw these activities on a large scale and tried them out with their own pieces of dough. Then the teachers planned a large-group time in which children sang a bakery song while they rolled, kneaded, folded, and made other baking-related motions with their bodies.

Supporting Children at Large-Group Time (Cont.)

❖ *Teacher idea books and other curriculum materials.* Teachers sometimes try out proven large-group activities and adapt them for use with the children in their own classroom. This strategy is useful for new teachers developing confidence in their planning skills, as well as experienced teachers seeking new ideas. Resources include publications such as *The Teacher's Idea Book: 50 Large-Group Activities for Active Learners* (Boisvert & Gainsley, 2006). Adults may also try the large-group activities suggested in various curriculum publications focusing on literacy, mathematics, and other content areas. (See the HighScope Web site, *www.highscope.org,* for HighScope resources in each curriculum content area.)

Prepare for large-group time before children arrive. As with small groups, it is important for large-group activities to begin right away. Prepare materials beforehand to avoid having children wait. If you plan to use songs or stories, practice them in advance — both for a smoother performance and also so children aren't distracted by false starts or mistakes that make them lose interest. Equipment, such as a CD player, should also be checked for proper functioning ahead of time.

What to do during each part of large-group time. Use the following steps to guide children through large-group time. (Also see the sidebar on p. 71.)

❖ *Opener.* Draw the group together with a "starter" activity that children can join as soon as they come to the gathering area; for example, singing the "run-around-the-circle song" and running around the circle, or singing a familiar song and doing the hand motions that go with it. Once everyone is assembled, the rest of the planned activity can begin.

❖ *Activity.* Briefly explain the activity — for example, "Today let's see how we can move in and out of the tires." Give props and materials (in this case, inflatable inner tubes) to children immediately and show interest in what they do with them. Encourage children to come up with ideas, ask children who would like a turn as leader, and repeat and follow up on children's suggestions. For example, you might say something like, "Tim says we should curl up inside our tires, then pop out like space ships!" (then everyone tries this action).

❖ *Transition.* Most of the time you will end large-group time with a transition to the next activity. If the session has been quite physically active, something quieter can help children settle down. The transition can also build on the learning that took place during the large-group time. For example, after children have figured out ways to move in and out of their tires, you might ask them move to their tables for planning time with just one part of their body inside the tire.

74

activities, storytelling, or a discussion about something important to the children, such as the first snowfall of the season. Like every other part of the HighScope day, the five ingredients of active participatory learning are present at large-group time. There are *materials* for children to *manipulate* (such as props for storytelling, scarves for dancing, or their voices for singing); *children make choices* about how to use the materials or move their bodies; *children talk* about their ideas and actions; and *adults scaffold learning* by building on children's interests and knowledge.

> *Ursula, a teacher, begins to tell a story about a raft journey, then pauses to invite children to board this imaginary raft with her. Some children decide to gather materials they want to bring — cooking utensils from the house area to prepare meals, boards from the block area to build a rain shelter, books to read at bedtime, and stationery and markers to write letters home to their parents. When everyone is "on board," Ursula opens her bag of spyglasses (empty paper towel tubes). As they "drift out to sea," the rafters call out the sights they "spy." Some are literal ("I see an easel") while others are imaginary ("There's a whale!"). Ursula acknowledges and supports each child's observations. After escaping some "hungry sharks" and weathering a "bad storm," Ursula says, "I see land. We're almost home." They "dock" the raft and return the items they brought aboard to their appropriate areas. Ursula then says, "That was a long trip — I'm hungry," and children move in different ways to their snack tables.*

Large-group meetings require a space that can handle either vigorous activity (moving to music, acting out a story) or quiet intimacy (a cozy setting to share ideas or hold a discussion). Programs with enough space may have a permanent gathering area, such as a rug in the middle of the room. In smaller facilities, they may have to move equipment aside to create this space. In warm climates or seasons, the class may gather outside under a tree or on a patio.

The formation of the group depends on the experience planned for that day. In fact, one way teachers can provide enough variety in the large-group experiences they plan is to make sure they don't all start from the same position. For example, certain games take place in a circle; a movement activity may involve children going from one carpet square to another in different ways; and the use of various props, such as hula hoops, may require children to spread out widely so they don't bump into one another. And discussion, such as setting class rules for cleanup, is best done with all children sitting near an easel pad where the teacher writes down the children's suggestions.

As with small-group activities, large-group time is planned and initiated by adults, but children have many choices. For example, children decide how to move their bodies as they listen to music of different moods and tempos. They can make various motions for others to imitate or suggest a favorite song or rhyme for everyone to sing or recite. During large-group time, adults also encourage children to offer suggestions and generate solutions to problems. It is also a time of day when children can take turns being leaders. For example, if the group is singing "Hokey Pokey," each child who wants to can choose which body part everyone will put in and take out. Children are never forced to be leaders, but most are eager to have everyone's attention. In fact, children who are otherwise shy or withdrawn may welcome a situation where others naturally listen to them because it is their turn to lead.

At outside time, children exercise their large muscles, see their school as part of a campus or neighborhood, enjoy nature, and collaborate with others to operate big equipment.

Supporting Children at Outside Time

Consider This...

Think about your own ideas about how children learn at outside time.

To guarantee that children learn actively outside as well as inside, HighScope teachers act as partners in the outdoor setting. Children take the initiative and adults follow their lead with enthusiasm and energy. Adults don't see this part of the day as their time to relax and chat with one another. Nor do they direct children in sports or rule-bound games that are inappropriate for young children.

Outside time presents many opportunities for learning, not only in the area of physical growth, but in all the other domains of development as well. There are signs in and around the playground to read, leaves and rocks to arrange by color or size, insects and clouds to study, and social conflicts to resolve about who has the next turn on the slide. To support development in each of these areas, use the following strategies at outside time:

Help children get the materials they need. Playgrounds have permanent structures, and other materials can be stored in an adjacent shed or brought outside from the classroom (see Chapter 6 for a list of outdoor area equipment and materials). Together with the other members of your teaching team, think of ways to store and easily transport materials (for example, you might use milk crates, buckets, plastic baskets with handles), to involve children (and sometimes parents) in gathering materials at the end of the day, and to ensure children can get the things they need independently or with minimal assistance.

Use work-time support strategies. The same interaction strategies adults use to support children's indoor play apply to their outdoor play. Teachers participate as partners, talk to children, and encourage them to solve problems. (See "Work Time" above and see Chapter 5.)

Observe nature with children. The outdoors presents children with a whole new environment to explore. Share their discoveries enthusiastically and call their attention to such natural features as the wind, clouds, changing light, air temperature, mud and dirt, snow and ice, different smells and textures, and the wide diversity of plant and animal life. Keep in mind that walks in the neighborhood, field trips to farms and ranches, and strolls along city streets with houses and businesses also increase children's experiences with the outdoors.

Bring outside time to a close. As with other activities, give children a warning when outside time is almost over so they can bring their play to an end. For example, you might announce, "In three minutes, parents will begin to arrive and we'll have to put away the bikes and other toys." Encourage children to help with cleanup, storing portable equipment in the shed or bringing items such as scarves and chalk back into the classroom. When outside time is at the end of the day, parents may assist with cleanup, too. If children are reluctant to end their play, you can help them make a plan to continue it the next day.

Outside Time

During outside time, which lasts 30–40 minutes, children can enjoy physical, noisy, and vigorous play. Rather than standing to the side and just observing, HighScope teachers join children in their outdoor exertions. Being outside also lets children and adults alike connect to the school campus and/or neighborhood community and use all their senses to appreciate nature.

The outdoors is a place where young children can run, jump, throw, kick, swing, climb, dig, and ride. Their pretend play ranges over a wider area than is possible indoors and can incorporate props not found inside — for example, a tree, the flowerbed, a climber, or a slide. Outdoor surfaces also provide larger areas for artwork: for example, children can make chalk drawings or water paintings on the pavement and weave yarn and twigs through the lattice of a fence. Additionally, outdoor equipment promotes social play. For example, children face one another through the openings in the climber, and they dig next to one another in the sand box. Discoveries are also eagerly shared ("Look at the shiny green bug I found!").

In most cases, outside time takes place in a play area on the grounds of the school or center where the program is located. This space is specifically designed for use by young children, with size and safety taken into account. When

Supporting Children During Transitions

Consider This...

Think about your own ideas about how children learn during transitions

Teachers often dread transitions, those times between activities. At best, they are seen as periods to get through quickly so the class can begin the next "real" activity in the daily routine. At worst, transitions become power struggles between children resisting a shift and adults eager to move them along without losing momentum or throwing off the day's schedule. In HighScope programs, by contrast, transitions are seen as real and meaningful activities in themselves. When viewed as educational opportunities — for example, how to solve the problem of storing a "work in progress" so a child can continue with it the next day — transitions incorporate all the aspects of active participatory learning. Approached with this positive attitude, transitions not only go more smoothly, they allow children and adults to enter into the next activity calmly and eagerly.

To ensure that transitions go as smoothly as possible, and to also make them positive learning experiences, use the strategies listed below.

Adjust transition times to suit children's developmental needs. As a general rule, the fewer the number of transitions, the better. Preschoolers can more easily remember a daily routine that has fewer components. They can quickly derive comfort and control from its predictability. It also helps to keep changes in location to a minimum. For example, if children begin the day with breakfast, they might then plan at the same table. Within this consistent framework, use your creativity to make transitions fun — for example, with varied movements, songs, rhymes, and chants. Children can act as leaders at these times. Finally, keep the amount of waiting between activities to a minimum. This helps children transition smoothly. For example, having materials ready for small- and large-group time keeps transitions short and simple.

Plan for transitions with individual children in mind. While the above strategies work well for the group as a whole, there may be individual children who still find any change, or perhaps certain times of the day, difficult. In these cases, giving ample warning, maximizing choices, and providing extra support can be very helpful. For example, if a child has trouble with cleanup, you might say, "Work time is almost over. You played in the house and block areas today. Which area would you like to clean up first?" If transitions are a time when a child might hide or act aggressively toward a classmate, adults can position themselves nearby at that point. For example, Timmy hid under the table whenever the lights were flicked for cleanup time. Rachel, his teacher, joined his activity near the end of work time and was able to engage him in cleaning up.

Plan for cleanup time, the longest transition. Cleanup time is the longest and often the most stressful transition of the day. Adults know it must be done before moving on to the next activity, but a child's natural inclination is to continue playing. To help cleanup time go more smoothly, teachers first need to realize that children are not being bad or resistant (negative) when they want to keep playing but, rather, that they are motivated and engaged in purposeful activity (positive). Adults also need to keep their expectations realistic and view cleanup time as another learning opportunity. Children will not clean up as thoroughly as adults, nor should they (program staff can do this at the end of the day).

It can also help to clean up as work time goes along, provided it does not interrupt purposeful play. (Think of cleaning up the kitchen as you cook, instead of leaving all the pots and pans until after dinner.) Finally, use children's individual and group interests to make cleanup time fun. For example, if children were "writing" grocery lists at work time, they might write down, in order, the areas or materials they will clean up. (For more cleanup ideas, see pp. 63–66, "Work Time.")

Other Large- and Small-Group Times: A Summary

Outside Time:

1. Children enjoy physical, noisy, and vigorous play.

2. Adults join as partners in children's play.

3. Equipment promotes physical and social development.

4. Environment provides an opportunity to appreciate nature.

5. Outside time takes place on school ground or nearby outdoor area; indoor space (such as a gym) substitutes only when weather is extreme or a safe outdoor area is not available.

Transitions:

1. Adults view the time between scheduled activities as learning opportunities in themselves.

2. Adults plan transitions to account for individual and developmental differences.

3. Cleanup, the longest transition of the day, presents adults and children with many problem-solving situations.

Meals and Snacks:

1. Adults and children eat together, usually in the same small group used for planning, recall, and small-group time.

2. Emphasis is on social interaction.

3. Children have many opportunities for developing self-help skills (pouring liquids, wiping up spills) as well as skills in literacy (writing turn-taking lists), mathematics (matching napkins to the number of people at the table), and other content areas.

Greetings and Departures:

1. Teachers welcome and say goodbye to each child (and any accompanying adults) individually.

2. Adults help children enter into the program day and bring closure to ongoing activities when it is time to leave.

Message Board:

1. Messages are "written" using pictures and words so children of all literacy levels can "read" them.

2. Adults share announcements and let children know about upcoming special events, new materials, visitors, and so on.

3. Class may engage briefly in group problem-solving discussion.

4. Time at the message board creates a sense of "community" in the classroom.

---

programs do not have their own playgrounds, they may use a neighborhood park. If possible, the teachers and children bring loose or free-standing equipment (balls, scarves, bikes, or wagons) to add to the fixtures that are there. Occasionally, especially in inner cities, there may not be a nearby park or one that can be reached safely. In such cases, a rooftop or similar area made safe for young children may suffice. If no outdoor area is available, or the weather is extreme, a gym or other large indoor space can substitute.

Transitions

Although transitions happen "between" other activities, they are important enough to treat as activities in themselves. Transitions include arrivals and departures (also discussed below), and the intervals between each of the daily routine components described above. In addition to involving a change in activity, transitions may also include a shift in location (for example, from the greeting circle to a work-time area), materials (such as crackers at snacktime to pipe cleaners at small-group time), clothing (adding or removing outdoor wear), caregiver (if there is a shift change), or playmates (for example, when groupings change between small-group time and large-group time).

Some children take transitions in stride, while others find them stressful. Transitions are often most difficult when children are first getting used to the routine. For example, a child may cry and cling to a parent when beginning school. Or a child may not want work time to end, not yet realizing the same play materials will be available every day thereafter. Generally, once children experience the sense of comfort and inner control that develops from following a consistent routine, transitions are no longer stressful. However, for any child at any time, a transition may be hard. This could be due to fatigue, an ongoing home situation (divorce; a new sibling), or something that happened in school that day (such as a conflict with another child or even dissatisfaction with the morning snack).

Other Group Times

The HighScope daily routine also includes other group times, discussed below.

Meal and snacktimes. In most part-day programs, children and adults share a snack, while full-day programs have both meal- and snack-times. Eating together is generally done in small groups, preferably with the same adult and children who gather together for planning, recall, and small-group time.

The emphasis during snacks and meals is on social interaction. It is important for adults to eat with children, both as a natural social situation and as an opportunity to share relaxed conversation and to support children's ideas. Teachers should not have a hidden agenda for teaching specific academic skills during mealtimes, although opportunities for teaching and learning often occur naturally. For example, a list indicating whose turn it is to set out the plates and cups can help children develop literacy skills, and children taking a turn will be involved in one-to-one matching of utensils and people who will be eating, which helps develop mathematics skills. Snack- and mealtime are also occasions when children enjoy practicing self-help skills such as pouring their own juice, cutting things into portions (with plastic child-safety knives), folding napkins, wiping up spills, and so on.

Greeting and departure times. You will find that elements of both individual and group activities are characteristic of greeting and departure times. These periods are also transitions, and you can use the transition strategies described above to help children make the shift from home to school and back again. For arrivals, it is important that each child be welcomed every day by a teacher. When an adult brings a child to school (as opposed to the child's arriving by van or bus), that adult should also receive a personal *hello* from a staff member. The same holds true for saying *goodbye* on a daily basis.

If arrival and departure times are staggered, the teacher helps each child enter into or finish up whatever part of the routine is underway. For example, you may plan with a child so he or she can begin working, or you may help a child put things away and get dressed shortly before a parent is due to pick up the child. If children arrive at the same time, greeting takes on more of the character of a group event; however, it also may happen in various pairings and small groups. For example, children, along with parents who can stay a while, may look at books until the rest of the children arrive. When most of the children depart from the program at the same time, departure is still likely to be more individualized since parents rarely come at the same moment. Nevertheless, since a child is leaving the group as well as the current activity, teachers help the child bring his or her day to a close with a sense of completion.

Message board. Gathering at the message board is a large-group activity that generally takes place once everyone has arrived. This is a time to share announcements and let children know about things that are happening that day or that are coming up soon. For example, visitors may be expected (such as a local artist or a prospective student and parent), perhaps new material or equipment introduced the day before can now be found in a specific area of the room, or perhaps a field trip is planned for the next day. You can also use this time as an opportunity for the whole class to solve a problem that affects everyone. For example, if running through the classroom poses a safety hazard, the children might brainstorm possible solutions and choose one or two to try out. A few days later, during message board time, they may review the situation and decide if the problem is solved or whether they need to try a different approach.

Teachers "write" these messages — on a dry-erase board, easel pad, chalk board, or similar surface — using pictures and words. Writing messages in various ways allows children of all literacy levels to "read" them, know what to expect, and participate in the discussion. It is also an opportunity for children to recognize letters and words (especially their own and others' names) and for adults to introduce language and literacy games, such as rhyming and alliteration. Finally, the message board helps to create a sense of community before children proceed to the next part of the day.

Throughout the daily routine, HighScope teachers are continually aware of what children are experiencing and learning. To guide their planning and interactions with children, teachers keep in mind the key developmental indicators that are important in the early years. These essential indicators — in all content domains of learning — are described next, in Part 3 of this book.

Whether activities during the daily routine are child- or adult-initiated, they always build on children's interests and offer children genuine choices.

Try These Ideas Yourself

1. On Friday, make a plan for the weekend. Write down what you will do, the materials or information you will need, who else is involved, how long each activity will take, and so on. On Sunday evening, review your plan. Think about what happened the way you planned it and what got changed. What did you learn about planning similar activities in the future? How does reflecting on this plan-do-review process help you think about the importance of plan-do-review to children?

2. Think about a young child from a chaotic, disorganized household. Think about a child from a rigid, overly scheduled household. How might they each react to a consistent daily routine at preschool?

3. How would you help a child who does not speak English learn the daily routine?

4. Think about the daily routine in your classroom (or observe the daily routine in someone else's classroom). Write down the parts of the day in order and how much time is spent on each. Note whether the day has an appropriate number of segments and transitions, or whether parts need to be added, omitted, or combined. Next to each part of the day, note whether its place in the order makes sense. Is it too short, too long, or just right? Based on your comments, revise the daily routine. How will you introduce children to the new routine? Will you make the changes all at once or gradually? Why?

5. List five strategies you can use to encourage children to plan. List five different strategies you can use to encourage children to recall. Remember to identify strategies that can be used with children of different ages and ability levels (for example, from nontalkers to highly verbal children). Try out your ideas (or ask a teacher you know to try them out while you observe). Write down what happened and reflect on what did (or did not) work. How would you modify your original ideas based on your observations? (*Note:* The same strategies can often be used for both planning and recall, so think of different ones for each to end up with a total of ten ideas.)

6. Divide a piece of paper into two columns, one headed "Child-Initiated" and the other, "Adult-Initiated." Observe a small-group activity in an early childhood program. Whenever children contribute an idea, use materials in their own way, make a spontaneous comment, and so on, make a check mark in the "child-initiated" column. When adults introduce materials, model behavior, ask questions, and so on, make a check mark in the "adult-initiated" column. At the end, add up the number of check marks in each column. What is the balance of child- and adult-initiated activity? If it is predominantly adult-initiated, what would encourage more child initiation? If it is mostly child-initiated, did adults miss opportunities to extend and scaffold children's learning?

7. Plan a small-group activity for eight preschool children, based on something you have observed them to be interested in. Include each of the features listed in the Group-Time Planning Sheet on page 67.

8. Plan a large-group activity for sixteen preschool children, based on something you have observed them to be interested in. Include each of the features listed in the Group-Time Planning Sheet on page 67.

9. Think of a specific transition that is a problem in your classroom or one you have observed (for example, the children take so long to clean up after snack that they only have 10 minutes left to play outside). Make a plan for this transition based on one or more key developmental indicators, and be sure to incorporate the five ingredients of active learning. Try out the plan. Did the transition go more smoothly? Did you feel it was valuable time instead of wasted time? Why (or why not)? If necessary, what else could you do to make this transition a positive learning experience for the children?

Throughout the daily routine, children engage in all the diverse learning experiences encompassed by the HighScope key developmental indicators.

Chapter 8

How Do HighScope Programs Work With Parents?

Think About It

How were your parents involved in your education? For example, did one or both of them help you with your regular homework? Help you with special projects? Look over schoolwork your teachers sent home? Send treats for you to share with classmates on your birthday or holidays? Encourage you to practice or rehearse certain skills? Attend school performances and sporting events? Volunteer as a classroom assistant? Go on field trips? Share their own skills or interests with your class or school? Attend parent-teacher conferences, open-school nights, or similar events? Telephone or e-mail your teachers? Read class or school information you brought home in your backpack? Read newsletters or other information that arrived in the mail? Go to PTO or PTA meetings or serve as an officer? Attend meetings or serve as a member of the school board? Discuss your report card or grades with you? Get involved in other ways? How did you feel about each of the ways in which your parent(s) did — or did not — participate in your education?

The term **parent involvement** means many things. As the list above shows, it can include participating in activities at school or encouraging a child at home. Parents can communicate with adults that include teachers, principals, and other parents. They can work directly with their own child or help the child's classmates. Family contributions can also take many forms, including time (such as volunteering in the classroom or on a school committee), resources (for example, providing food and supplies; sharing skills), and ideas (for example, offering suggestions and helping to shape school policies).

HighScope programs provide varied and meaningful opportunities for families to participate in the life of the program. Staff are sensitive to other demands that might limit family members' availability, and because staff also understand that not everyone is comfortable participating in the same way, they offer choice and options. HighScope acknowledges that families are a child's first and most important source of learning and that teachers can learn from them as well as vice versa. In this chapter we'll look at how families in HighScope programs can contribute to the education of their own child, their child's classmates, the staff, and even to the program in ways that may have an effect beyond the time their child is enrolled in the program.

The Benefits of Family Involvement

Research repeatedly shows that family involvement is critical to a child's success in school. For example, the Head Start Family and Child Experiences Survey (FACES; Administration for Children and Families, U.S. Department of Health and Human Services, 2003) found that parent involvement in Head Start was associated with a number

82

Chapter Learning Objectives

By the end of this chapter, you will be able to

❖ Explain how family involvement provides benefits to children, parents, teachers, and the program as a whole

❖ Promote family involvement using diverse strategies that both respect differences and build bridges between home and school

❖ List effective ways to share information with parents about their child's development, how the program promotes it, and what parents can do to further their child's learning at home

Parents receive information about the curriculum to help them understand child development and promote learning at home.

of positive academic and social outcomes for children. To give one example, children whose parents read to them more frequently had higher scores on early literacy assessments. To give another example, the more parents participated in activities with their children, the fewer behavioral problems children had in school. Importantly, parents' involvement in Head Start moderated the negative effects of violence, depression, and other risk factors on children's school readiness and emotional well-being.

Supportive relationships between early childhood programs and families benefit children, parents, staff, and the program as a whole. Educators can foster these relationships in many ways, for example, by talking to parents who are dropping off and picking up their children each day, inviting parents to volunteer time in the program, conducting home visits, and becoming involved in the local community themselves. HighScope advocates family involvement in its programs for these reasons:

▲ **To build bridges between home and school.** Child care or preschool is often a young child's first extended experience outside the family. From that point forward, the child needs to be able to function in at least two worlds — home and school. While adults take multiple settings for granted, it is quite a challenge for toddlers and preschoolers to navigate different places, each with its own expectations and experiences. The more teachers can connect these two important places for young children, the easier it will be for the children to make the twice-daily transition between them. To help children feel comfortable, teachers can incorporate familiar materials and activities from home into the classroom and help children understand what to expect and how to adapt their behavior in the two settings.

Establishing continuity between school and home may also ease the transition from preschool to kindergarten. It sets the stage for parents to continue their involvement from one setting to the other because they will have come to think of themselves as being an important part of the school experience. And children will have established the routine of sharing educational activities with their parents.

▲ **To enhance teachers' understanding of children.** The more that staff learn about children's home life and culture, the better they can support children's development in school. An awareness of the materials, activities, and values in children's homes lets teachers plan meaningful experiences that build on the children's knowledge, interests, and skills. For example, a teacher may

---

Terms Used in This Chapter

• parent involvement, family involvement • personal filter • home visit

learn that a child is interested in insects or has a repertoire of gospel songs. Knowledge of home and family life can also help make staff aware of any circumstances that may affect a child's ability to concentrate, learn, or socialize. Staff can then provide the child and family with appropriate assistance, through services offered directly within the program or referrals in the community for medical, social, financial, or legal services.

▲ **To enhance parents' understanding of children.** Staff have many opportunities to share information with families about how young children develop. They can also help them become better observers of their own children. This information can be exchanged formally, for example, during parent-teacher conferences or parent education workshops. It can also be shared informally — for instance, while talking about what a child did and learned at school that day when the parent or other family member arrives to pick up the child.

Many parents form ideas about education based on their own school experiences, which may not reflect current research and practices. Or they may have seen products advertised to make their children "smarter" and wonder if the program uses similar techniques. As a result, teachers often find that parents do not realize the importance of play in young children's learning. By drawing parents' attention to key learning experiences, such as the math concepts involved in building with blocks, early childhood educators can help parents understand and support their child's development in appropriate ways.

In addition to enhancing childrearing knowledge and skills, involvement in their child's HighScope program can also empower parents. By becoming more effective in their parenting role, they may increase their feelings of competence as individuals and as community members as well. For example, agencies may provide them with opportunities to serve on policy councils and planning committees, continue their own education, or enroll in job training programs.

▲ **To promote child development at home.** Parents are a child's first teacher, and children spend more time at home than in school. Therefore, teachers play a critical role in "translating" the classroom curriculum and offering suggestions on how to apply active learning principles to everyday family situations. For example, grocery shopping can become a literacy experience in identifying letters, sorting clothes can become a mathematical exercise in classification, and both provide opportunities for parent-child conversations.

Parents realize they are already providing learning experiences for their children during the normal course of the day — for example, setting the table or sorting the laundry. They are allowing their children greater independence in self-care, and some have provided child-manageable storage containers in their bedrooms. Parents are more accepting of letting children explore and are not so concerned about "mess." (Sacramento, Calif., Parent Involvement Coordinator)

> **❝** Parents have seen how HighScope deals with many conceptual skills that are prerequisite to academics. The comment "All they do is play" is becoming a thing of the past as parents gain insights into the developmental appropriateness of HighScope. **❞**
> (Houghton, Mich., Teacher)

▲ **To enrich the program.** Parents can contribute to programs in many concrete ways. For example, they can volunteer in the classroom, assist on field trips, and serve on committees. Parents who cannot volunteer on a regular basis may have interests and talents to share during occasional visits or may be able to invite children to visit their workplace or studio. Even busy parents can donate materials, such as old clothes for the dress-up area, empty food containers and cooking utensils for the house area, and other items that would otherwise be recycled or discarded.

Parents play a real part in the choice of materials. Very often they will not only send them in with their children, but will make an effort to bring in the materials themselves. Parents feel appreciated when the children react and choose what area to put the materials in. (Battle Creek, Mich., Teacher)

The HighScope Approach to Working With Family Members

The HighScope approach

❖ **Focuses on the family** — Teachers learn about the family's background and culture, discover their strengths, and identify what they can contribute to their child's education and the program as a whole. They support and encourage family initiative. Staff are also sensitive to issues that affect child and family well-being, and assist families in obtaining the assistance they need.

❖ **Promotes partnerships** — Information is shared in both directions. Parents educate teachers about their children. Teachers offer parents insights into child development and how the curriculum supports their child's learning. The relationship is characterized by mutual respect.

❖ **Is guided by the plan-do-review process** — Teachers and parents discuss their goals for a child and how active learning both at home and school can help the child achieve them. As they carry out their respective roles, teachers and parents periodically review the child's progress and make adjustments if needed.

❖ **Shares child observations** — Teachers share anecdotal information from the Child Observation Record (COR) with parents to help them understand and support their child's development. Parents are encouraged to record and share observations about what the child does and says at home.

❖ **Incorporates home-based materials and activities** — Teachers include real and familiar objects from the home in the classroom. They plan activities that reflect the home and community environment. Parents are encouraged to share materials, experiences, interests, and skills with all the children in the program.

❖ **Emphasizes adult-child interaction** — Staff help parents become better observers of their children so the parents can scaffold learning at home. Parent volunteers are also given meaningful roles in the classroom so they can interact with children and become partners in the active learning process.

When parents do volunteer their time, it is important for them to be given meaningful roles in the classroom. Assigning them custodial chores, such as mixing paints, may help teachers, but it does not allow parents to interact directly with children and learn about their development. With appropriate orientation and ongoing support from staff, parents can play an active role in children's learning in the classroom. Moreover, when parents understand the goals and methods of the program, they can become its strongest advocates.

Strategies to Promote Family Involvement

HighScope promotes diverse strategies to encourage family involvement in children's programs. Many of these ideas are not unique to High-Scope, and are recommended as part of general "best practices." However, as you carry out these strategies, continually review their effectiveness from the perspective of the curriculum's *five ingredients of active participatory learning*. Emphasize the use of familiar *materials* from home that children can *manipulate* as they investigate ideas, acquire knowledge, and practice skills. Give children *choices* that reflect family life, and explain to parents how they can offer children many choices in their daily activities at home. Encourage *language from children* in many ways, such as welcoming children's talk about their home experiences, hiring staff who speak the children's home languages, and, if you do not speak these languages, taking the time to learn important words and phrases so children (and family members) feel comfortable communicating with you. Finally, *scaffold children's learning* by building on the experiences the children bring from home and by helping parents extend education from the classroom to the family environment.

Parents are welcomed into the classroom and encouraged to help their children transition into the program day.

Four Elements of Family Involvement

Below are the four main elements of involving families in HighScope programs, along with suggestions for carrying them out. The sidebar on page 87 lists 50 strategies for connecting with parents, generated by teachers and parent involvement specialists attending HighScope training sessions.

1. Examine Your Own Family Roots, Beliefs, and Attitudes

To understand the beliefs and practices of the children and families you serve, first reflect on how your own background influences your perception of others. The following strategies can help you better understand yourself so you do not unintentionally judge or misinterpret others.

▲ **List your family origins and living arrangements.** You may be surprised by the diversity within your own family, going back two or three generations. For instance, family members may have moved from one part of the country to another and found creative ways of adapting their language, clothing, food, home furnishings, and so on to local conditions.

Living situations also change within a society or family over time. For example, multigenerational families living under one roof are more or less common in certain cultures or periods of

history. Similarly, children may be raised by people other than their parents — not just today, but in past times of economic hardship or migration. Discovering this type of diversity in your own family tree can help you realize that, in most instances, there is not one right way to do things.

▲ **Examine your "whats, hows, and whys."** Examine what is important to you and what makes you feel comfortable and "at home" — such as certain types of food, art, music, or humor; particular topics of conversation, or different levels of affection or reserve. Think about your behavior as a parent, family member, friend, and colleague. Reflect on why you behave in certain ways and what it says about your beliefs and attitudes. When you and your coworkers share these things about yourselves, it can help the staff to become more open to — and respectful of — individual differences.

▲ **Be aware of personal filters.** One's personal filter is that combination of beliefs, attitudes, and lifetime experiences that affect one's impressions of people and events. Once you see the roots of your own beliefs and practices, you can separate your views from those of the families in your program. It is then easier for you to say, "I may not do it this way but I can see and appreciate why this family does." Owning up to one's personal beliefs makes it easier to see things from another perspective.

2. Learn From Children and Families About Their Traditions

Knowing ourselves is the first step; learning about others comes next. The following can help you learn about children and their families:

▲ **Conduct home visits.** Home visits are occasions when teachers go to families, instead of families coming to the program. At a minimum, HighScope teachers visit each child's family before the children begin the program. A visit later in the program year or at the end of the program (for those programs that close over the summer) also wraps up and personalizes the home-school relationship. When you visit families, especially when children are entering the program, you see and hear firsthand what children are like on their own turf, surrounded by familiar people, sights, and sounds. Children are often eager to show their teachers where they sleep, eat, keep their toys, or engage in favorite activities. Making an

86

effort to visit with family members in their own surroundings also shows parents that you are genuine in your invitation to have them partner with you in educating their child. Moreover, by keeping the focus of the visit on a shared interest in the child, parents are reassured that teachers are not there to judge them or their home.

▲ **Participate in community life.** This strategy is especially important if you do not live in or near the community in which you teach. Joining local events and visiting neighborhood places demonstrates to families that you are eager to connect with them as citizens and community members. It is also one of the ways you can make sense of the experiences and expectations children bring to school. Examples of community participation include shopping at the local markets, attending street fairs and festivals, and getting to know community leaders and services.

▲ **Observe children every day.** Home visits and community events, while important, are infrequent occurrences. On the other hand, staff observe children on a daily basis. The conversations and activities initiated by children provide a window into their interests, thoughts, and experiences outside of school. So, for example, when a teacher in one program saw a child "weaving" strips of paper in a collage, she learned that the child's mother had a small loom at home. The teacher invited this parent to demonstrate weaving to the children. After the demonstration, children wove with simple frame looms made of wooden canvas stretchers using a variety of materials. Several laced yarn and twigs through the fence.

▲ **Reach out to families.** You and your coworkers can welcome families into your program in many ways. See the sidebar on page 87 for a list of 50 ways to connect with parents.

3. Share Information About Child Development With Parents

When parents understand how children learn and how the curriculum supports active learning, they are in a better position to be partners in the educational process. Teachers in HighScope programs share information with parents using several proven strategies (Brand, 1996; DiNatale, 2002):

▲ **Parent orientation.** During recruitment and enrollment, you have many opportunities to present family members with information about

Children are eager to show and tell parents about their daily activities in a HighScope classroom.

the HighScope Curriculum and the types of experiences their child will have in the program. Also encourage family members to visit during program hours so they can see the curriculum in action and allow their child to start becoming familiar with the setting and the people in it. Once parents have signed up, provide them with a parent handbook that includes program policies and procedures and a brief description of the curriculum.

▲ **Parent workshops.** Many HighScope teachers conduct monthly workshops about the curriculum and how to use its key elements at home. You can also encourage parents to suggest workshop topics of interest to them — for example, how to choose appropriate books for preschoolers or what to do when siblings fight. (*Note: The Teacher's Idea Book: The Essential Parent Workshop Resource,* by Graves, 2000, has step-by-step plans and handouts for 30 popular topics.) To carry out lively and effective workshops, apply the same principles of active participatory learning you use with children to working with adults.

▲ **Newsletters.** Each HighScope program is encouraged to produce a newsletter on a regular basis (for example, once a month). Newsletters provide general information about the program, including policies, procedures, and upcoming events such as a family potluck. Your program's newsletter might introduce a new staff member, report on a field trip, describe an activity the children especially enjoyed, or include frequently asked questions (FAQs). With digital cameras and scanners, it is easy to include photos as well as anecdotes about the children. You can also encourage parents to contribute their own articles and photos.

50 Ways of Connecting With Parents

1. Newsletters
2. Parent meetings
3. Parent workshops
4. Personal notes
5. Phone calls
6. E-mails
7. Activity calendars
8. Home visits
9. Parent networks
10. Field trips
11. Orientation visits
12. Parent handbooks
13. Classroom volunteer opportunities
14. Parent bulletin board
15. Parent library
16. Toy lending library
17. Parents' room
18. Parent support groups
19. Continuing education (such as GED)[1]
20. Family literacy program[1]
21. Job training[1]

22. CDA training[1]
23. Links with agencies of interest to parents
24. Invitations to professional meetings
25. Visits to other early childhood programs
26. Child activity logs for each part of the daily routine
27. Parent-teacher conferences
28. Child, family, and classroom photos posted in the classroom
29. Donations of materials from home
30. Advisory board or policy committee
31. Book study group
32. Family night
33. Potlucks and picnics
34. Suggestion box
35. Discount coupons for family activities

You can also connect with parents by involving them in the following:

36. Help in classroom setup
37. Fundraising
38. Making story tapes
39. Building the playground
40. Repairing classroom equipment
41. Helping children transition to kindergarten
42. Preparing special snacks
43. Sharing a talent
44. Making furniture or materials
45. Getting books from library
46. Sharing observations of children
47. Completing child assessment together
48. Conducting playground assessment
49. Completing program assessment
50. Sharing their photos or videos of the classroom

[1]Provided directly by the program or by referring parents to relevant community agencies.

Each issue of the newsletter might also highlight a particular aspect of the curriculum, discussing how it is carried out at school and what families can do to continue it at home. For example, an article on early literacy might describe the classroom's new lending library and include pointers on how to read with children at home every day.

▲ **Formal conferences.** Regular parent-teacher conferences, ideally held at least twice per year, give you another opportunity to share information with families about the program and individual children. HighScope teachers use the Family Report Form of the Child Observation Record, Second Edition (COR; HighScope Educational Research Foundation, 2003a) to summarize observations and share anecdotes with parents in each area of children's development. (See Chapter 18 for a sample page from a

COR Family Report Form and for more information on sharing anecdotal notes from the COR with parents.) Additionally, it is important to invite parents to ask questions, share information about the child and family, express concerns, and offer ideas for the program as a whole.

▲ **Informal contact.** Drop-off and pickup times provide natural opportunities for teachers to chat briefly with parents about what their child did at school that day as well as about anything noteworthy happening at home. Sending work home also creates a context for talking about the child's activities and development — for example, about how the child made a painting or dictated a story and what he or she learned in the process. You can also write notes, make phone calls, and send e-mails — strategies especially important when

88

children are transported to and from school by a bus or van, or if daily face-to-face meetings with parents are rushed. It is important to use these informal contacts to share the "good" things children do and learn, not just as a means to discuss problems.

4. Join Parents in Expecting Excellence From Each Child

Parents have high expectations for their children and want them to do well in school. They also want teachers to recognize what is special about their child and give them the individual attention they need to succeed. Because HighScope teachers are attuned to child development, they also know each child is capable of succeeding on his or her own terms. To convey this belief and confidence to parents, use the following strategies:

▲ **Avoid labeling or stereotyping children and families.** Labels set limits on who a person is and what he or she can become. Terms like "immature," "shy," "disadvantaged," or "bully" are subjective. They often say more about what the labeler sees as "weakness" than they do about the child or family being described. In HighScope programs, people are instead identified by their strengths — for example, "Ramon draws detailed pictures" or "Madison's dad asks many questions about where to find low-cost educational materials." Learning how to observe and record objective anecdotal notes (see Chapters 9 and 18) can help you focus on actual behavior, not judgmental labels. Then, even if there is a problem, you can use your observations to examine when and how the behavior occurs and devise appropriate strategies to deal with it — for example, to help a child who bites express and channel feelings in safer ways.

▲ **Assume each child will succeed.** When you regard all children as competent learners, you invest in the idea that they can and will do well in a supportive educational climate. Sometimes teachers and parents of children with special needs question whether such children can succeed in a HighScope setting. By focusing on the disability, they overlook a child's potential to make plans, explore the world with all available senses, and solve problems with materials and people. Because HighScope builds on individual strengths and interests, every child has a chance to learn and succeed.

When families join in program activities, they also learn how to extend their children's learning opportunities at home.

Try These Ideas Yourself

1. Think about how the person you are today was influenced by your family — for example, your values and beliefs, how you feel about education, your choice of career, your feelings about marriage and parenthood, your friendships, what you like to do in your spare time, your favorite foods, how you handle money, and so on. In what ways are you the same or different from other members of your family? In what ways might these insights about yourself help you appreciate the diversity in a classroom of children?

2. Divide a piece of paper into three columns. In the first column (a), list all the ways parents can become involved in their child's preschool program. In the second column (b), list all the barriers that might prevent them from this type of involvement. In the third column (c), list what you as a teacher or administrator could do to help eliminate each barrier. For example, the first row in your chart might read like this: (a) coming to a parent workshop; (b) no transportation; (c) arranging a car pool.

3. A teacher writes the following:

I teach in a center-based preschool program with a home-visit component. Some parents make it clear they expect the home visitor to teach the child letters, numbers, colors, and shapes using very directive methods. This is not our view of education. I don't know how to respond.

What suggestions do you have for this teacher?

How Do Staff in HighScope Programs Work Together?

 **Think About It**

Imagine you are a member of a group working on a new playground for your local community center. You first meet to discuss your ideas about how the playground should look and how children and families in the neighborhood will use it. You invite people from the area to share their hopes and their concerns. Through negotiation and compromise, you develop an overall plan everyone can live with and that has at least one feature each person is really excited about.

Some committee members do research on different playground designs and costs. They invite a local architect who specializes in play spaces to talk to the group. Other members look into paying for the playground through grants and charitable contributions. A few people on the committee, as well as parents in the neighborhood, are skilled carpenters who donate time to build and to supervise volunteer work crews. The project takes two years, from discussion of the original idea to the completion of the playground. There is a big party to celebrate the opening, and the city council votes to give the community center money each year to maintain the playground.

What makes a **team** experience like this one successful? How does it differ from groups where members think meetings are a waste of time and have little confidence in the outcome? What does it say about people listening to different viewpoints, handling disagreements, and learning to

trust one another? Think about the importance of gathering information before making decisions, sharing the work according to each person's abilities, and continuously taking stock of what's been accomplished and what still needs to be done. You might call it plan-do-review at the team or group level. The process is just as necessary for the work of adults as it is for children.

Based on research and practice, HighScope has created a system to apply these principles to early childhood teams. **Team members** include supervisors and teachers as well as support staff such as bus drivers, janitors, and cooks. (We discussed ways to include parents as part of the team in the previous chapter.) Why is **teamwork** important? In order for staff to serve children and families well, they must be able to work well among themselves. They must share goals for clients and have guidelines they can depend on to resolve differences. In HighScope programs, this guidance comes from the curriculum, which gives team members a common understanding of human development and practical information about how to accomplish shared goals.

Early childhood team members must maintain two important sets of relationships. One is with the children and families they serve. The other is with their coworkers. In this chapter, we'll explore how HighScope team members work together on a daily basis to observe and learn about children and plan experiences that meet their developmental needs. We'll also look at how the HighScope

Chapter Learning Objectives

By the end of this chapter, you will be able to

❖ Describe the characteristics and processes that create an effective working team

❖ Understand how to record objective anecdotal notes about children

❖ Appreciate why and how daily team planning is essential

❖ Describe what is unique about High-Scope's approach to providing staff support and supervision through observation/feedback and the Program Quality Assessment

model of supervision helps staff meet their own needs to continue growing as professionals. (For more on the principles of adult learning and High-Scope teacher-training, see Chapter 20.)

Forming the Team

A team in a HighScope program consists primarily of the staff members responsible for taking care of children and communicating with their families. This would typically include the teachers or caregivers who work with young children every day. Other team members who may also have regular contact with children or families include such staff as the center director, bus driver, cook, and parent involvement coordinator. Those who support the work of the direct service providers — for example, secretaries, curriculum specialists, or evaluators — can also be considered members of the team.

While all team members must communicate with and trust one another, it is especially important that the teaching or caregiving team observe the children and plan for them on a daily basis. It is also essential that teachers and their supervisors have a system for observing and evaluating what is hap-

pening in the classroom or center so they can work together to guarantee a high-quality developmentally based program for the children and their families.

Characteristics of Effective Teams

Effective teams establish a trusting and supportive climate for working together. You and your co-workers can create this atmosphere using the strategies described below.

▲ **Communicate openly.** Simple and honest communication is at the heart of good working relationships. Psychologist Virginia Satir (1988) calls such direct communication **leveling.** In everyday language, we may call it "being straight" with one another.

Leveling is a straightforward statement of how one sees a problem and how one feels about it and the solutions proposed to address it. If, for example, the members of your teaching team disagree on the value of a bubble-blowing activity at large-group time, a teacher might say, *"I'm sure the children will enjoy blowing through the straws to make bubbles. But how can we make sure all the ingredients of active learning are included in the activity?"* This statement can then lead to a team discussion of what other materials to provide and how children might use them, things children might be expected to do and say, how the activity relates to the **key developmental indicators (KDIs),** ways adults can support and build on children's explorations, and how teachers can document what happens in order to plan appropriate follow-up activities.

Leveling is not easy. It is human nature to feel afraid of rejection, loss of power or control, embarrassment, or any of the other emotions that make us act protectively. However, leveling allows all team members to be heard, to listen to others, to make mistakes without fear of punishment or humiliation, to arrive at a solution together, and to review the agreed-upon solution later to see if it worked or whether it needs to be revised. This open communication system not only helps staff members work together well, it maximizes the

Terms Used in This Chapter

• team, team members, teamwork • leveling • key developmental indicators (KDIs) • anecdotal notes •
• objective versus subjective anecdote • team planning • observation/feedback (O/F)
• Program Quality Assessment (PQA) • professional development

In daily team planning, teachers share objective anecdotal notes about children to plan supportive and challenging educational experiences for individuals and the group as a whole.

chances that the solution they arrive at will be in the best interests of the children.

▲ **Respect individual differences.** Team members will naturally differ in their ideas, preferences, and personalities. In the HighScope model of teamwork, these differences are seen as a source of creativity and variation rather than a cause for anger or failure to reach agreement. Looking at things from more than one perspective can help teachers understand and plan for all the ways children might respond to a situation. Tapping both personal and role differences to brainstorm alternatives can increase the choices and learning opportunities the team provides.

▲ **Have patience with the teamwork process.** As staff members get used to working in teams, and as new members are added, it is common for staff to feel frustrated or impatient with the teamwork process. Often, team members are getting to know the curriculum and one another at the same time. Support staff, such as cooks or bus drivers, often have less access to training and are more focused on applying what they do know to a different set of goals (such as feeding or transporting children) than are the classroom staff. Despite these occasional frustrations, know that teamwork does get easier.

As staff in all positions become more familiar with the curriculum, it guides them in understanding and supporting children's development. As you and your coworkers get to know each other and the different roles each team member is called on to perform, you will appreciate one another's strengths, accept one another's limitations, feel secure taking risks in front of the team, and trust

that the group process will result in a good educational experience for children.

Gathering Information About Children: Anecdotal Notes

A key characteristic of HighScope teaching teams is daily planning, and a critical input to team planning is individual teachers' **anecdotal notes** — that is, written observations about what children do and say. These notes, which teachers learn to record objectively, are not only used in daily team planning but also to complete and score the Child Observation Record (COR; HighScope Educational Research Foundation, 2003a), an assessment tool for monitoring children's developmental progress. The COR and its uses are described in Chapter 18. Anecdotal notes are also used to share meaningful information with parents (see Chapter 8 for more information on communicating with parents).

Characteristics of An Effective Team

1. **Climate:** There is a positive climate of mutual sharing and trust. Staff and administrators know what is expected of them.

2. **Goal setting:** Staff work together to set goals. The goals then drive the team.

3. **Expectations:** Expectations are clear and are based on a shared philosophy and set of goals.

4. **Decision making:** Whenever possible, staff make decisions by consensus. They discuss many alternatives. Once a decision is made, everyone commits to carrying it out.

5. **Handling conflict:** Problems are viewed as a normal part of working together. Staff use conflict-resolution strategies to solve problems effectively.

6. **Regular evaluation of teamwork:** All members work together to achieve team goals. Program evaluation is based on whether the team as a whole has achieved the group's goals.

Anecdotal Notes: A Summary

How to Use Anecdotes

Use anecdotes to

❖ Learn about and plan for individual children.

❖ Learn about and plan for groups of children.

❖ Share information about children with parents.

❖ Complete and score the Child Observation Record (COR).

How to Write Objective Anecdotes

When writing anecdotes,

❖ Focus on what the child did and said.

❖ Be factual.

❖ Be specific.

❖ Be brief.

Format for Anecdotes

Each anecdote should include the following:

❖ Date the anecdote happened.

❖ (Beginning:) When a behavior or activity took place, where it took place, and who was involved.

❖ (Middle:) What a child did and said; quotes to document the child's language.

❖ (End:) When applicable, the outcome.

Tips for Taking Anecdotes

❖ Use abbreviations. Examples: the child's initials, *HA* for house area, *SGT* for small-group time. Record just enough information to jog your memory, then elaborate the anecdote later.

❖ In each area, keep a supply of note-taking materials, such as sticky notes, index cards, mailing labels, clipboards, an instant or digital camera, a tape recorder, or a small notepad attached to the wall with string. Other options include wearing a necklace pen or a shop-type apron with several pockets.

❖ Set a realistic goal for the number of anecdotes to record each day. Begin with four or five and gradually increase the number as the process becomes routine.

Example

A teacher jotted the following information on a sticky note: *Maddy, WT, HA dressed up, asked Mike "marry, not same," "older, red hair."* Later that day, she wrote this anecdote and shared it with her team member:

> *12/07/02 — At work time, in the house area, Madeline put on a dress, hat, and beads, and then asked Michael if he would marry her because "You are not the same." When I asked what was different, she said, "He is older and has red hair."*

In Madeline's computerized COR file, the teacher entered this anecdote under Dramatic Art as an example of the key developmental indicator "pretending and role play" and copied it under Science and Technology (Classification) as an example of the indicator "describing differences." (*Note:* For programs without computers, anecdotal notes may be recorded by hand on note forms. Rather than repeating the handwritten note under other categories, the teacher makes reference to the first indicator and date, adding only the relevant indicator in the other entry or entries.)

Recording Anecdotal Notes

To record **objective anecdotes** — that is, notes that are factual and neutral — do three things:

▲ **Observe children throughout the day.** Watch and listen to children as you support them and interact with them during all parts of the daily routine. Pay attention to the ingredients of active participatory learning, noting what materials children choose, how they manipulate them, and what they say and do in their interactions with adults and other children. Use the HighScope KDIs to describe the problems children encounter in play, how children solve the problems, and the kinds of knowledge and skills the children demonstrate. Your observations can also guide you in on-the-spot interactions with children. During team planning, refer to individual team members' observations to plan individual and group experiences that will further children's learning.

▲ **Briefly note observations.** So much happens each program day that teachers cannot depend on their memories alone to recall what each child or group of children did and said. Therefore, it is important that all teachers in the program try to write brief but complete anecdotes on the spot, or jot down a few key words they can refer to later for writing more detailed anecdotes. You have many options for recording events as they happen. See the sidebar on page 92 for an overview of anecdotal note taking.

Teachers take several anecdotes a week on each child and make sure, over the course of the program, that all developmental areas are covered for individuals and for the class as a whole. (See Chapter 18 for guidelines on how often to take notes on each child and how to cover all categories of the KDIs.)

▲ **Suspend judgment.** Anecdotal notes are meant to record what happens, not to guess what a child intends or to state whether the teacher thinks the child is acting "good" or "bad." For example, an objective anecdote might say, "At work time, in the art area, John made three paintings with wide red and thin blue stripes, wide green and yellow stripes, then all four colors. He hung them up to dry." A **subjective (or judgmental) anecdote** might state, "John painted three pictures using just a few lines. He left most of each page blank. Wasted lots of paper." Objective anecdotes help teachers both value what each child does and plan according to children's needs, interests, and developmental level.

Anecdotal Notes: Benefits to Staff

Anecdotal notes offer you and your coworkers many benefits. Recording and reviewing them helps you *learn and think about how young children develop.* Because observations are organized by KDIs, note taking also helps you *become more knowledgeable about the learning content of the HighScope Curriculum.*

As you review the notes with the rest of your planning team, you may find that you have little information about particular children or few examples of learning in a particular content area. This alerts the team to the fact that teachers need to pay more attention to certain class members, plan individual and group experiences to fill in the gaps, and/or add materials that promote a particular area of development. The team may even decide to set up an *inservice training* session to learn more about early development in that domain. Finally, although note taking adds some time to each day's tasks, most teachers find this *less burdensome* than

compiling several months' worth of data at the end of each assessment period.

Daily Team Planning

Once team members have gathered information about children, their next step is deciding what it means and how to act on it. Teachers use the High-Scope KDIs to reflect on the significance of an event or activity for a child or a group of children. The teachers then generate ideas for building on individual and group interests and for scaffolding children's development (see p. 9 for more on scaffolding). Team members decide on one or more strategies, try them out, and review them the next day to see what did or did not work.

Below are the strategies you can use to make planning an effective and rewarding experience for your teaching team.

▲ **Plan together at a consistent, mutually acceptable time.** While daily team planning is recommended, it is not always possible. Planning every other day or twice a week can work, but planning should happen not less than once a week. If scheduling is an issue in your program, think creatively about when the team can plan. If you have a half-day program, the team might plan each day right after the children leave and before the adults do a final cleaning up. If you have a full-day program, the team might plan quietly in the nap area while children are resting, close enough to keep watch but far enough not to disturb children or be overheard discussing them. Occasionally, other onsite staff or parent volunteers might help watch children at naptime while the teachers plan. When team members are used to the planning process, team planning time does not take long — teachers can go over the day's notes and make plans for individual children and the group as a whole in about half an hour.

▲ **Use plan-do-review strategies to plan effectively and efficiently.** During planning time, turn the strengths and problems of one day into the plans and strategies for the next. The team can do this systematically, by reviewing what happened, developing a new work plan, deciding how to carry it out, and establishing criteria for evaluating its success. Do the following together with your team members as you plan:

A Successful Team Planning Session

Margaret told her coteacher Becky that at work time several children were moving and making noises like their pets — cats, dogs, and a parrot. Based on this observation, they decided to do a large-group time in which children would pretend to be animals and imitate animal sounds. This would let them focus on the dramatic art key developmental indicators *imitating actions and sounds* and *pretending and role playing.*

To begin, the teachers decided they would sing a favorite song — "Old MacDonald Had A Farm" — and encourage the children to name an animal, then stop singing in order to imitate the animal's actions and sounds. As a backup, however, they decided to have pictures of familiar animals and a recording of animal sounds. Margaret said she would get the pictures and Becky said she'd bring in a CD with animal sounds.

The teachers agreed Becky would introduce the activity by saying "Yesterday, I heard some of you barking like dogs and chirping like birds. I thought today we'd sing 'Old MacDonald' and

pretend to be different animals on his farm." She would begin singing the song, stopping after the words "And on his farm he had a _____." Once a child named an animal and everyone pretended to be and make a noise like that animal, Margaret would begin the song again, then stop to call on children who volunteered animal names. For children who were reluctant to name an animal, or for variety, she would bring out the animal pictures so they could choose one by pointing. If necessary, Becky would play the CD of animal sounds so children could name and imitate the animal whose sound they were hearing.

The teachers decided that, at the end of large-group time, they would tell the children that the pictures would be in the house area beginning the next day (and the CD, if they used it, would be in the music area). Becky would bring large-group time to a close by suggesting children move and make noises like an animal of their choice on their way to the snack tables.

Evaluate what did and did not work in the previous day's plan.

Pool the day's anecdotal observations; add to what each team member was able to observe children doing and saying.

Discuss what each anecdote reveals about the observed child's development and make plans about how to act on that knowledge the next day. Strive for consensus on plans.

Plan group activities based on observations, children's interests and developmental levels, and the curriculum's learning content.

Plan for individual children based on observations, children's interests and developmental levels, and the curriculum's learning content.

Set responsibilities for each team member and make sure everyone holds the same expectations for carrying out the next day's plan.

Set long-range goals for individual children based on their particular interests and development, and plan strategies for engaging children in activities and interactions to help them accomplish these goals.

Discuss and resolve any group or individual problems; for example, agreeing on when and where children can run, hop, and jump in the classroom, or how to respond to a parent's concern about the food served at snacktime. Strive for consensus on solutions to problems. If team members cannot agree on one idea, they can decide to try out alternative solutions and then review them later to see what did and did not work.

Occasionally, review the team planning process itself to identify both strengths and areas for improvement. It is useful for team members to ask themselves three questions as they plan: (1) *What do you know* (what happened today)? (2) *What does it mean* (what do you understand about children's interests, development, and learning)? and (3) *What actions will you take tomorrow* (what will you do to support children)?

▲ **Remain focused and organized during the planning session.** To keep planning manageable, team members break each task down into smaller parts. For example, as a source of

Sample Daily Planning Forms

The following two sample daily planning forms were developed by different programs. On the first one, children are divided into two groups for small-group activities. On the second form, the classroom is divided into three groups. The two forms also reflect the different order of the parts of the daily routine in each setting (although planning time, work time, cleanup time, and recall time always occur in this same consecutive sequence in all HighScope programs).

Sample HighScope Daily Planning Form for Classroom with Two Groups

Date: 1/15/07 | **Adults:** Nancy and Ben

Outside Time: New sand toys/rakes/shovels and pails for gravel. Bats & balls. Encourage interest in Hide & Seek game. PD/SE

| **Greeting Time:** Books and Sign-in on class chart — Message Board LL/AL/SS
 Door: Nancy — Greet parents, children — collect permission forms for field trip. SE
 Books: Ben — Support choosing and reading books together on blue carpet. LL/SE | **Child Messages:** 1) New cotton balls and glue sticks in Art Area
 2) New sand toys in outside sandbox
 3) List children who are absent today
 4) Three no-school days LL/M/AL |

Large-Group Time: Start with a few children as they join the circle — "Follow Follow" for easy-to-join activity.
Song book: Give clues as to who will choose the song.
Go outside as a large group — Use large, clean wastebaskets and large balls, hoops, and basketballs. Encourage tossing into receptacles, throwing and catching. PD/TA/M/SE

| **Planning Time: Ben**
 Use planning wheel. Give children clothespins with their names and symbols on them. Ask them to place the pins on the area in which they will play. Discuss details. LL/ PD/ SE/AL | **Nancy**
 Planning train. Children line up — first child leads the group to where they will play. They can get off the train after they plan. Encourage detailed descriptions. SE/PD/AL |

Work Time: Support Vishnu's first day. Encourage problem solving in the block area. Look for anecdotes. ST/LL/SE

Clean-up: Tambourine sound for 5-minute warning. Use kitchen timer for 5 minutes. Free Children cleanup but freeze when they hear the pauses in the music. M/AL/TA/PD/ST

| **Recall Time: Ben**
 Small white boards, erasers and dry-erase markers. Ask children to draw or write what they did at work time. Provide area signs and children's names and picture cards for copying. TA/AL/LL | **Nan**
 Place area to ta they LL/A |

Snack: Alphabet and oat "O" cereal mixed. Milk for cereal. Apple juice.
Books: Nancy — "Seven Silly Eaters" / Ben — "Color Dance" LL/PD

| **Small-Group Time: Ben**
 Reread (skim) the book "Color Dance" with the children. Provide watercolor sets and cups of water and brushes for all children. Large pieces of paper placed on easels and/or floor. Encourage children to describe the colors they are using and mixing. Use vocabulary words from book and others that come up as children's ideas come forth.
 Backup: Markers to write names on paintings. TA/ST/AL/PD | **Nan**
 Lette Distr clea their Poss thes Back |

| **To Remember:** Buy juice/napkins | **Pare** |

Content Area Key:

AL Approaches to Learning	**PD** Physical Development, Health, and Well-Being
LL Language, Literacy, and Communication	**M** Mathematics
SE Social-Emotional Development	**ST** Science and Technology

Sample HighScope Daily Planning Form for Classroom with Three Groups

Date: 1/20/07 | **Adults:** Chris, Sue, Beth

| **Greeting Time:** Books and Sign-in on class chart — message board SS
 Door: Chris — Greet parents, children — book and book bag returns. LL
 Books: Sue & Beth — Read with children and encourage sign-in on class chart. LL | **Child Messages:** 1) Red water in the blue water tables LL
 2) Who is absent today? SS
 3) Wash out paint brushes when finished painting AP |

| **Planning Time: Chris**
 Distribute handled paper shopping bags — ask children to think about something they may play with today and put it in the bag. Discuss details. LL/AL | **Sue**
 Use cell phones. Distribute phones to children and ask them to discuss what they plan to do at work time. LL/AL | **Beth**
 Planning sheet — Cut out area in which you will play. PD/AL |

Work Time: Support replanning. Take anecdotes on Pete and Olivia. Support cleanup as you go.

Clean-up: Play triangle as 5 minute warning sign. Sand timer for 5 minutes. Play music as we clean up. CD 2 #8. M/TA

| **Recall Time: Chris**
 Use hula hoop with green marking tape. Chant: "Fandegumbo diddy wa day, when it stops on you say what you played!" TA/AL/LL | **Beth**
 Give children a piece of foil to wrap a toy they played with. As they open it, encourage discussion. PD/ST/LL | **Sue**
 Write a recall story. As children recall, write their words on their page in the book. Give children paper and pencil. Encourage them to draw what they did or where they played — paste it on to opposite page as an illustration. LL/AL/TA |

Snack: OJ / alphabet pretzels mixed with oyster crackers / cheese LL/PD
Read book as we are finishing snack: **Sue** — "Blueberries for Sal" • **Chris** — "Ferdinand" • **Beth** — "The Snowy Day" LL

Large-Group Time: 1) Songbook choice (Alyjah's turn to pick — mark chart) LL/TA
2) Pizza Pizza (action chant with leader's ideas) TA/PD/LL/SE
3) Transition to small-group time by chanting the Pizza Pizza chant with changed words on last line…They jump back up and they go to small-group time.

| **Small-Group Time: Chris**
 Cuisinaire rods and play dough. Give each child a basket with assorted rods and a dish of play dough. Opening: "Yesterday, Evan was using the blocks and he noticed that they were all different sizes. I wonder how you will arrange these small rods in the play dough?"
 Backup: Tape (to make smaller pieces longer) M/TA/ST/AL | **Sue**
 Use Growing Readers activity: Connect to Good Night, Gorilla Level 1, Activity 2 — Try Out Flashlights and Keys
 Backup: Paper and pencil to trace keys. LL/AL | **Beth**
 Go to block area. Each child has a basket with various block shapes and some animal figures. Opening: These animals need a home. How would you make one?
 Backup: Orange spots TA/ST/AL/M |

Large-Group Time: Outside Time: Sleds / new shovels / plastic buckets. Support sledding hill and tree house area. PD/AL/SE/ST

| **To Remember:** Flyer for upcoming field trip — permission forms. | **Parent Messages:** Volunteers for field trip; due date for permission forms. |

Content Area Key:

AL Approaches to Learning	**PD** Physical Development, Health, and Well-Being	**SS** Social Studies
LL Language, Literacy, and Communication	**M** Mathematics	**TA** The Arts
SE Social-Emotional Development	**ST** Science and Technology	

ideas when planning a large-group time, each team member might first share what he or she observed children doing that day, come up with an idea for the next day's large-group time, and talk about the KDIs that could happen during the activity. Next, the team might go over the materials needed for the activity and decide which team member would be responsible for preparing which materials. After making sure they are clear about these expectations, team members might discuss who will introduce the activity and in what way, who will do what in the middle of the activity, and which team member will use which strategy for bringing the large-group time to a close.

▲ **Decide together on the form for planning and recording decisions.** A standard form serves several purposes. It highlights what needs to be reviewed and decided. It helps team members organize and focus their discussion. Finally, when information and decisions are written down for all to see, confusion or disagreements become obvious and can be resolved.

The most convenient forms are those which simply follow the order of the daily routine. Another useful tool is to put abbreviations for the relevant curriculum content areas at the bottom of the form and then use these initials to indicate the area(s) of focus for each part of the day. Your program might also include state standards, Head Start Child Outcomes, or other important categories in a legend on the form and indicate when these are being addressed in the daily plan.

Whatever form the staff in your program develops, it should be simple, convenient, and reflective of the daily schedule and content of your particular setting. See page 95 for samples.

▲ **Rotate tasks.** Take turns carrying out different parts of the plan. Dividing the labor in this way keeps each team member attuned to each part of the day. It also makes it less likely anyone will feel he or she is regularly stuck with a difficult or less desirable task. Rotation also allows team members to grow as professionals. Even if someone is unsure of his or her ability to do something, such as leading the children in a song, colleagues can provide the support and encouragement to take a risk and try something new. When teams establish trust, anything is possible!

▲ **Take advantage of each team member's strengths.** Every adult brings unique interests and talents to the team. Just as teachers acknowledge children's efforts and accomplishments, HighScope recognizes it is important to let team members know their contributions are valued. Also, as they do with children, teachers use encouragement rather than praise with one another. For example, adults feel acknowledged when other adults they work with ask them to contribute to a classroom activity, observe what they do in order to learn from them, comment on how children reacted to the experience, and suggest ways for continuing and building on the activity in the future.

Staff Support and Supervision

Just as observation is essential to teachers' learning about and supporting children, it also helps adults learn about and improve their teaching practices. In addition to being observation based, supervision in HighScope programs is also mutual and interactive. Unlike styles of supervision that go in one direction (top-down), supervisory relationships in HighScope settings are joint problem-solving endeavors. All the players are motivated to serve the best interests of children and families. Put another way, supervisors and teachers act as a team to promote professional development in the same way that teachers work together to promote child development.

HighScope uses two techniques, both based on observation and supervisor-teacher interaction, to support curriculum implementation and solve problems in the classroom. One form of support is called **Observation/Feedback (O/F).** This process may be initiated by the supervisor or teaching team and occurs in response to a specific question or concern about curriculum implementation. The supervisor writes an extensive narrative based on the focus of the observation (for example, the learning environment), makes the relevant curriculum notes (for example, how well the setup of the environment encourages children to elaborate on their play and interact with others), and then discusses these in a mutual feedback process with the teachers.

The other system for supporting and supervising teachers uses the **Preschool Program Quality Assessment** (PQA; described in Chapter 19), a tool for evaluating specific aspects of program implementation. The supervisor conducts a classroom observation using one or more PQA sections (such as the learning environment or daily routine) and shares the results with the teachers. Together they set goals for program improvement. In addition to identifying goals for individuals or teaching teams, the PQA can serve as an agency-wide needs assessment. The results can then be used to design a tailor-made **professional development** program, in which staff members can enhance existing skills and develop new ones.

Each of these observation-based procedures for providing staff support are described briefly below. To carry them out effectively, staff in supervisory positions receive extensive training and practice in the techniques during the HighScope Training of Trainers Course (see Chapter 21).

Observation/Feedback

In Observation/Feedback (O/F), supervisors observe children in the classroom and how teachers interact with them. Supervisors then provide feedback on teachers' strengths and areas for improvement (or "modifiable issues"). Teachers and supervisors together decide on the focus for the observation session. They agree on a time of day, the child(ren) to observe, and the part of the curriculum that will be the focus of the observation (for example, active learning, small-group time, adult support during work time). The observation itself lasts approximately 15–20 minutes. The observer uses a two-column Narrative/Notes Form to record a detailed narrative of what happens and makes notes about its relevance to the curriculum issue(s) in question. The supervisor and teaching team then discuss the observation, list strengths and modifiable issues, generate solutions to problems together, and make a plan for improvement that includes follow-up support.

Observation/feedback is effective for several reasons:

▲ **Supervisors and teachers share a commitment to understanding children.** Because they are interested in providing the best program possible, supervisors and teachers are able to look objectively at what is working well and what is working less well in terms of outcomes for children, rather than viewing the session as a personal critique of the teacher.

▲ **Children are the focus of the observation.** By focusing on the children, supervisors actually learn more about the quality of the pro-

---

The Elements of Team Planning: A Summary

❖ Plan daily.

❖ Plan as a team.

❖ Keep planning forms simple, based on the program's daily routine.

❖ Use anecdotes to assess children's interests and abilities.

❖ Plan by incorporating

- Children's interests

- Children's developmental abilities

- Curriculum content (key developmental indicators)

- Classroom materials

- Adult ideas

---

gram's teaching and learning than when their focus is on the adult's behavior. Supervisors can identify which elements of the curriculum are being implemented well and where the gaps might be. The process is also less anxiety-provoking for teachers since the spotlight is on the children, not on them.

▲ **The curriculum guides observation and team discussion.** By reviewing the ingredients of active learning, the elements of adult support, and other distinctive features of the curriculum, the team can see what is working and, when necessary, develop strategies for improving teaching practices.

▲ **Conversation about the observation is reciprocal.** In the dialogue that follows the observation, the supervisor and teacher talk and listen, give and take. Often O/F is initiated by teachers, rather than supervisors, because teachers want a trusted and knowledgeable "third person" to help them see and hear what is going on with a particular child or group of children during a particular part of the day. For example, a teacher might say to a supervisor, *"Large-group time isn't going well for some of the children lately. Jackson and Alyce, for example, lose interest after a few minutes and it's hard to get their attention back. Can you observe our large-group time next Tuesday? We have some ideas but would really appreciate another pair of eyes and ears."* The supervisor would then observe Tuesday's large-group time, complete the Narrative/Notes Form, and join the teachers for their daily team planning meeting.

▲ **Team discussion results in mutually agreed-upon action.** Once the team members examine what's happened in terms of the curriculum — especially the ingredients of active participatory learning and KDIs — they generate solutions and decide which one(s) to try.

Note that the work of the adult team follows the same principles as does the work of the children in the program. In O/F, the "review" discussion results in a "plan" that the teachers "do." Later, supervisors and teachers will repeat this cycle to see if the action is working or needs adjustment. Participants of all ages learn valuable lessons in the process. (See the sidebar on p. 99.)

Preschool Program Quality Assessment (PQA)

The Preschool Program Quality Assessment (PQA; HighScope Educational Research Foundation, 2003b) also uses observation as a tool for focusing team discussion — in this case, with a focus on the quality of program implementation. HighScope teaching practices, described in preceding chapters, are reflected in the 39 classroom items in the PQA. (Another 24 items focus on agency-level factors.) The PQA is organized to enable the supervisor and teachers to record objective anecdotes about what they observe in the classroom. Because supervisors and teachers are both familiar with the PQA, there is nothing hidden or surprising about the content of the observation. Teachers know what to expect during the observation and contribute as equal participants during the discussion that follows the observation.

The PQA supports teamwork and professional development in several ways. Teachers might request that the supervisor, who is knowledgeable about the curriculum, look at a specific area or set of items when the teachers have identified a concern about the classroom or the program. For example, teachers may want to know if children have adequate time in each part of the daily routine. The items on the PQA may also serve as a starting point for team discussion around such questions as, "Where do we think we are most and least effective as a classroom?" or "Room arrangement is working pretty well. Now what

Observation and feedback allows supervisors and teachers to collaborate in identifying what practices work and what needs to be changed to best support children's development.

can we do to improve adult-child interactions?" A supervisor might also initiate a complete or partial PQA observation to pinpoint strengths and areas for improvement across the agency's classrooms. The results could then lead to ideas for a series of professional development workshops, mentoring activities, and so on.

HighScope agencies typically conduct a PQA on the four classroom-level sections (Learning Environment, Daily Routine, Adult-Child Interaction, and Curriculum Planning and Assessment) two or three times per year. Agency-level sections (Parent Involvement and Family Services, Staff Qualifications and Staff Development, and Program Management) are usually completed once or twice per year and rely more on documents and interviews than on observations as the sources of information. (For more on the PQA, see Chapter 19.)

In summary, the purpose of staff supervision and support is to gather data about what teachers do in the classroom — not to pass to judgment on them but to see how well the classroom is working for the children. When the class is going well, supervisors can make teachers aware of the practices they use that are effective and supportive of children's development. If something is not going well — for example, if children are wandering away during the reading of the message board —

Observation and Feedback

Two teachers asked their supervisor to observe a large-group time. The planned activity was to have children move their bodies in different ways to slow and fast music. After the observation, the team talked about where the teachers got the idea for the activity, the KDIs featured, which elements of active learning were present or missing, the extent to which children were engaged, and what the teachers would continue or do differently the next time they planned a similar activity.

Supervisor (sharing her observations): Eleven of the 16 children — Jeremy, Dahlia, Noah, Patsy, Bing, Jacob, Dewan, Juan, Tiffany, Pilar, and Sasha — were engaged the whole time. During the slow music, Karl and Bella went to the house area and brought back scarves to move with.

Teacher A: We planned the activity to focus on "expressing creativity with movement." Karl and Bella added another key developmental indicator, "moving with objects."

Teacher B: Several children called out what they were doing, which is "describing movement." I cracked up when Jeremy wiggled his bottom and said "Lookit me shake that thing!" Others used words like *bend, turn,* and *back-and-forth.*

Supervisor: Yes, and I heard Bing say, "Twist, twisting my arms!" I also noticed Jackson, Kate, and Bethany stopped moving to the music and went to the block area about 20 seconds after you began the slow piece. You called them back to the group but they continued building with the blocks.

Teacher B: They weren't disrupting things, but it bothered me that they weren't engaged in the whole group activity. I wondered if the slow piece lasted too long to hold their attention.

Teacher A: They were "moving" in a way. They were moving blocks. I wonder if we could have encouraged them to move the blocks in time to the music.

Teacher B: We might even do an entire large-group time around that idea! Something like "building to music." Let's see what building materials the children are most interested in and use those.

Supervisor: Yes, that would certainly be following the children's lead! That leads me to ask you a question. When you were planning the large-group time, where did the idea come from?

Teacher B: Driving to work yesterday, I heard a bouncy oldies tune on the radio and found myself swaying to the music. Later, when we were planning, I thought the children would enjoy moving to music. We decided to use different tempos, not just fast ones.

Teacher A: I just realized that whole idea came from us. I wonder how we could have built it more on what we observed the children doing.

Supervisor: Do the children ever sing or move to music on their own?

Teacher A: I heard Dahlia humming tunes from that new Disney movie the other day. She kind of skated around the house area and fetched dishes while she hummed.

Teacher B: Lots of kids have been to see that movie and have the album at home. It's got a whole range of musical tempos. Maybe we could use the selection at the beginning of the CD. It plays through all the tunes and tempos, but it's instrumental — no singing, which can be distracting because the children stop moving to listen to the words.

Supervisor: So next time you do a "moving to music activity," you can use music the children are familiar with, like the tunes from the Disney movie.

Teacher A: What about Noah and Patsy? They got so excited jumping to the fast music that they began running around the room. I had to practically corral them back to the group. Any ideas on how we can support those large movements but still keep them focused on the music?

Supervisor: The children who were working with objects — whether it was the scarves or the blocks — seemed to stay focused. Can we come up with any ideas from that?

Teacher B: Maybe if we do moving to music with objects, it will work better than just moving bodies. Having something in their hands seems to help some children stay focused. Or we could start with one and give children the option of doing the other once things got underway.

Supervisor: So, let's review what you'd do next time with this type of activity.

Teacher A: We'd still use slow and fast music, but it would be music the children were already familiar with, like the Disney album or holiday tunes we heard the children singing.

Teacher B: Giving the children a choice of moving their bodies or moving with objects seems like a good idea. We'd also be focusing on several key developmental indicators that way.

Teacher A: As a variation, let's also try the "building to music" activity sometime. I don't know if all the children will get it, it may be too abstract. But I'd be interested to see what happens. I'll keep an eye on the block area and go over our anecdotal notes from the past three weeks and see which building materials are especially popular with the children these days.

Supervisor: Sounds like a plan to me. Try it and let me know how it goes.

the supervisor-teaching team will collaborate to find a more engaging way to share the messages.

This way of thinking is similar to the attitude HighScope encourages teachers to adopt with children. When children are focused on a task, teachers support and encourage their work. When children hit one another or run away during a conflict, it is not viewed as "misbehaving" but rather as children not having yet learned how to behave appropriately in that type of situation. Similarly, when a classroom situation does not go well, it is not seen as stemming from "bad" behavior by the teacher but, rather, that the teacher needs to examine his or her teaching practices — often with input from other trusted adults — to learn how to handle it better. HighScope teams assume good intentions and help teachers and supervisors achieve them. The children are the ultimate beneficiaries.

Try These Ideas Yourself

1. Think of a good experience you had as a member of a team or committee. What made it a good experience? Make a list, considering such things as the group's goals, the personalities and skills of its members, the qualities of the leader (if there was one), how you gathered information and resources, the division of labor, how disagreements were handled, and so on. How might your reflections help you be a better team member?

2. On a piece of paper, make a grid of staff members and activities in your program (or one where you can observe and interview staff). Across the top (in the columns), write down the names of all the staff members. Down the left side (in the rows), list typical responsibilities. Include everything such as housekeeping chores (preparing materials and snacks, cleaning up what the children cannot do themselves), ordering supplies, communicating with parents, conducting parent meetings and workshops, making arrangements with community agencies for family services, completing children's health records, submitting licensing forms, recruiting families, taking prospective clients on a tour, leading various activities with children (such as music time), taking anecdotal notes on children, making daily activity plans, and so on. Check off who does what — that is, fill in the

boxes of the chart. Underline the items where the team is working well — for example, where tasks are getting done and labor is divided fairly based on job descriptions, interests, and skills. Circle problem areas. Think of way(s) teamwork could be improved in these areas to make the tasks more efficient or fairer, or to better take advantage of the interests and skills of team members.

3. Observe in an early childhood classroom and take anecdotal notes. Focus on one child and one small-group time. Based on your observations, make a plan for the next day that includes (a) ways to support that child at work or choice time and (b) a small-group activity.

4. The following problems might make it difficult for team members to plan together every day:

- There is no free time in the daily routine; both teachers must be with the children at all times.

- There is only a brief overlap (15 minutes) in the shifts of staff caring for the same children.

- Parents are often late picking up children so teachers cannot plan at the end of the day.

- One team member has to run to catch the last bus of the day right after work ends.

- Team members do not speak the same language.

- There are personality conflicts; some team members do not like one another.

- One team member prefers to do things on his or her own.

- The administrator does not think planning is a good use of time.

Add any other problems you can think of to the list. For each problem listed, write down how you could solve or lessen it to make it easier for team members to plan together on a daily basis.

5. Think of someone, such as a teacher or a boss, who gave you useful feedback on your work. What made it useful? Think of another person whose feedback was not helpful. Why did you not find it helpful? What was different about the two people or situations? How might your reflections apply to the relationship between a supervisor and teacher(s) in an early childhood program?

HighScope Curriculum Content

This part of the book discusses the HighScope curriculum content, with each area of child development covered in a separate chapter.

Chapter 10 discusses approaches to learning, which includes how one goes about acquiring knowledge and skills (learning styles) and attitudes toward education in general.

Chapter 11 explores language, literacy, and communication, including the four essential components of early literacy: comprehension, phonological awareness, alphabetical principle, and concepts about print.

Chapter 12 discusses social and emotional development, including taking care of one's own needs, expressing feelings, building relationships, and dealing with social conflicts.

Chapter 13 explores the content area of physical development, health, and well-being, with particular emphasis on movement education.

Chapter 14 deals with early mathematics development, including basic number sense, comparing quantities, identifying regularities, ordering things, and navigating space.

Chapter 15 discusses science and technology development, including observing, classifying, exploring materials, drawing conclusions, and communicating ideas.

Chapter 16 explores social studies, which includes the ways in which children learn about themselves as individuals and as members of a group.

Chapter 17 deals with children's development in visual arts, dramatic arts, and music, both as creators and appreciators of art.

Chapter 10

What Is the HighScope Curriculum in Approaches to Learning?

 **Think About It**

An article in The New York Times *(October 27, 2005) described a ten-year-old girl who was eager to enroll in an experimental school that was opening the following year. An avid learner, she read six books a month, played violin and piano, and "asked so many questions that her teachers sometimes got angry at her." Overjoyed at the prospect of attending the new school, the frustrated girl said, "A lot of times now, I ask three and four questions that are really complex, and the teacher stops and says, 'We're not getting into that. Let's go on to another subject.' At the [new] academy, I know I could ask whatever I wanted and the teacher wouldn't get mad."*

Imagine a preschooler in a similar situation who bounds into the room each day with all kinds of ideas and ends up spending a lot of time in the "thinking chair" for such "naughty" acts as using masking tape to "caulk up the cracks" in his block tower, building a roof for his fort out of storybooks, and jumping off the end of the slide to test his "magic cape."

Our nation's leaders, including those in the business community, often complain about the lack of creative thinkers in our society and the loss of our "competitive edge" in the world. One source of the problem becomes clear when we see how teachers sometimes respond to such able and motivated students as those described above. Eager to learn, these children are nevertheless held back by adults in educational systems who

see children's persistent curiosity and creativity as drawbacks rather than assets. For instance, think of all the children whose early educational experiences discourage them from asking questions, pursuing subjects that interest them, or using materials creatively. Picture settings where children are criticized for not doing things the teacher's way or for failing to conform to a single mode of learning. In these cases, both the individual and society suffer from the lost potential.

Although children come to school with different abilities and styles of learning, the burden is on the educational setting to create universal opportunities for success. This process can and

When teachers work alongside children, they convey the message that children's interests are valuable and important. As a result, children develop a positive attitude toward learning.

104

Chapter Learning Objectives

By the end of this chapter, you will be able to

❖ Explain why approaches to learning is an important component of all aspects of early development and school readiness

❖ Describe the influences that shape a child's approaches to learning

❖ Describe the HighScope key developmental indicators in approaches to learning

❖ Understand and begin to apply the strategies adults use to support and enhance children's approaches to learning

should begin in early childhood. Encouraging children to express and explore their own interests and take on challenging problems will establish positive lifelong **approaches to learning.**

In this chapter we will discuss approaches to learning — how one goes about acquiring knowledge and skills (learning styles or modes of learning) and attitudes toward education in general — and how teachers can support and enhance children's motivation to learn.

Why Approaches to Learning Is Important

The content area of approaches to learning is extremely important because it shapes children's educational experiences in all other content areas.

Definitions. As central as it is to development, this area is hard to define and measure. The National Education Goals Panel (NEGP; Kagan, Moore, & Bredekamp, 1995) says approaches to learning includes the following components in the early childhood years: curiosity, creativity, confidence, independence, initiative, and persistence.

On this list are what psychologists call **dispositions,** which are "enduring habits of mind and characteristic ways of responding to experiences" (Katz & McClellan, 1997). Dispositions include **styles of learning** (see the sidebar on p. 105) and attitudes toward education. Such traits are especially difficult to measure in young children who cannot describe their work style or articulate how they feel about schooling!

However, some of children's approaches to learning involve behaviors or skills that adults can more readily observe. For example, we can see whether children take the initiative to explore materials and ideas or whether they independently solve problems as they carry out their intentions. Persistence, or the motivation and ability to pursue a task or activity, is another trait that adults can see and measure. This was the case in a Seattle HighScope classroom where, after the teacher provided more choices to children she noted, "Children are staying with a task much longer because it is more open-ended and matches their interests and ability levels."

Children's approaches to learning have a bearing on their ability to *break down a task* into its components, *organize a plan* of work, and *reflect* on the meaning and success of their endeavors. In other content areas, you might observe a child's approaches to learning in whether the child engages in conversation or chooses to read a book (language and communication) or whether he or she collaborates with others (social-emotional development), thereby also building on his or her existing knowledge. Approaches to learning thus cuts across all domains of development.

🔑 HighScope Key Developmental Indicators in Approaches to Learning

❖ Making and expressing choices, plans, and decisions

❖ Solving problems encountered in play

Terms Used in This Chapter

• approaches to learning • dispositions • styles of learning • temperament • initiative

Styles of Learning

Psychologists and educators use the term "styles of learning" to describe how people go about acquiring knowledge and skills, solving problems, and generally dealing with the information and experiences the world presents. Individual differences in styles of learning appear early in childhood and persist into adulthood. These differences vary along several dimensions, including sensory mode, pace or timing, and social context.

For example, some children are visually oriented. They learn primarily through sight, observing objects, examining patterns and relationships, and watching the behavior of others. Others may be better at processing information orally and respond well to verbal descriptions and directions. Still another set of individuals needs to handle and manipulate objects to fully grasp how things work. While using this tactile mode is characteristic of young children in general, for some people, a preference for learning through touching and doing persists into adulthood.

There are also individual differences with regard to the pace of learning. Some children do well with a faster pace and can shift rapidly from one activity or experience to another. As adults, they may succeed at multitasking or they may be more comfortable with change. Other children are slower and more deliberate in the way they process information. They focus on one thing at a time and transition gradually between activities or ideas.

Finally, children and adults also differ in whether they learn best by working on their own or by interacting with others. Some thrive on independent pursuits, quietly and methodically investigating things or practicing skills. Others learn well in a group context, where the give and take of social exchange helps them consider new ideas and master new skills.

Everyone uses virtually every style of learning at some point in their ongoing education, depending on the subject matter or the situation in which they find themselves. However, a preference for certain modes predominates in their approach to learning. And while some of these differences are due to innate temperamental differences — the dispositions or tendencies we are born with — our environment and educational experiences also play a major role in shaping the ways we can and do learn.

By providing young children with a variety of options and opportunities, the HighScope Curriculum respects individual differences while also allowing children to discover and develop competence in other modes of learning. And because formal schooling, and the subjects children must master, often require them to learn in certain ways, helping them develop positive and adaptive approaches to learning prepares them for future success.

The influence of temperament. A child's approaches to learning are shaped by his or her **temperament** — that is, by the child's activity level, approach and withdrawal, adaptability, intensity of reaction, distractibility, and persistence (Thomas & Chess, 1970). Babies are born with these temperamental differences, which continue into adulthood. However, the Collaborative for the Advancement of Social and Emotional Learning (CASEL; Elias, et al., 1997) says environment also plays a significant role in determining whether such traits are expressed constructively. For example, a helpful disposition such as persistence allows a child to master new material or solve problems. But if it shows up as stubbornness, this trait can interfere with the child's ability to meet challenges and form satisfying social relationships. In such cases, a supportive environment that gives the child decision-making power

A child's approach to learning affects all areas of development. By encouraging initiative, problem-solving, and collaboration, HighScope helps set children on a path of school success.

106

and encouragement to pursue his or her own interests can channel persistence in a positive rather than a negative direction.

School readiness. The NEGP emphasizes that school readiness is enhanced when young children are encouraged to explore, ask questions, and use their imaginations. These early experiences prepare them in a positive way to venture into the world.

HighScope uses the term **initiative** to describe children's desire and ability to begin and then follow through on a task. Children *intentionally* decide to engage with the objects, people, events, and ideas they encounter — that is, they do so with a specific goal in mind. The goal can be simple (get the ball) or more complex (write my name with stones in the sand). By encouraging young children to follow their own interests, the HighScope Curriculum supports the development of initiative and intentionality. Children's play is purposeful and confident. The difference between simply making a choice (Red or blue beads?) and making a plan (What shall I do at work time?) is that planning involves thinking about and expressing intent (see "planning" in Chapter 7).

Whether children perceive learning and problem-solving situations as positive challenges, insurmountable barriers, or even threats directly affects children's ability to benefit from their educational experiences. How young children approach learning carries long past their entry into formal schooling. In fact, it will likely shape their educational careers and adult lives. Therefore, it is important to provide young children with experiences that help them develop initiative and the skills needed to solve problems with confidence, flexibility, and persistence.

Key Developmental Indicators in Approaches to Learning

HighScope has two key developmental indicators (KDIs) in approaches to learning, described below. The first reflects the curriculum's emphasis on initiative and focuses on how young children express their intentions (plans and choices) throughout various parts of the daily routine. The second looks at how children deal with the problems they encounter as they interact with materials, people, events, and ideas. Along with the description of each KDI, you will read about the strategies adults use to support its development in young children.

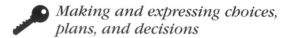

Making and expressing choices, plans, and decisions

To play an active role in their own learning, children must think of themselves as doers. That is, they must have confidence in their ability to make plans and purposefully carry them out. At the same time, they need to see others as respecting their choices and, when necessary, providing assistance to achieve them.

You can use the following **support strategies** to help children confidently and successfully formulate and express their intentions.

▲ **Create an environment and consistent daily routine that encourage making choices.** As detailed in Part 2 of this book (HighScope Teaching Practices — see Chapters 6 and 7), it is important to set up a classroom environment and create a predictable schedule within which children can make plans and carry them out every day. A classroom that is well-designed for active learning allows children to do many things on their own so that they gain confidence in their ability to act on their intentions. The daily plan-do-review sequence is centered on children making choices based on their interests, expressing their intentions, and following through on their ideas. Because young children quickly learn that interesting materials and the opportunity to carry out their ideas will be available every day, they often make plans even before they get to school.

On the way here this morning, Lisa said she was going to play in the house area with Margaret. They were going to make pizza with lots of cheese and butterscotch chips. She knew exactly what she was going to use to make it, too. She told me you gathered small brown pebbles on the walk yesterday and those would be the butterscotch pieces. The Styrofoam pellets I brought in last week (used to wrap the family's new dishes) were going to be the cheese, "But not too much," Lisa told me. (Parent talking to a teacher at drop-off)

▲ **Provide opportunities for choice throughout the day.** In addition to your work with children at planning time, encourage them to make choices and decisions throughout the day. For example, although you or other adults select and give materials to children at small-group time, encourage the children to explore them in their own way. Similarly, children can invent their own variations for moving their bodies or making up rhymes and verses at large-group time and during transitions, even though adults plan these experiences. Outside time is another segment of the day when children make choices, by deciding what equipment they want to play with and with whom they want to play.

▲ **Show interest in the choices children make.** Children are not used to being planners, decision makers, and leaders. Simply because they are children, it is natural and often necessary that adults make decisions for them, particularly with regard to basic matters of health and safety. That is why it is so important for children to set their own agenda at those times when they can appropriately do so. Making choices about playing and learning is an example of such a time. Children can do this at school, and you can also share ideas with parents on how to encourage child choice at home. Because planning is a new experience for young children, it is particularly critical that adults support them in this process. As detailed in Chapter 5, you can support children's initiative by commenting on their ideas, repeating and extending their thoughts, imitating their actions, accepting their suggestions, and letting them be the leaders.

🔑 *Solving problems encountered in play*

As they carry out their plans, children (like adults) inevitably run into problems. You can encourage children to come up with their own solutions, rather than jumping in to resolve the situation for them. Allowing children to work through problems serves two purposes. First, it helps them see themselves as competent individuals who can handle situations independently. Children also then

---

107

Strategies for Supporting Approaches to Learning: A Summary

Making and expressing choices, plans, and decisions

__ Create an environment and consistent daily routine that encourage making choices.

__ Provide opportunities for choice throughout the day.

__ Show interest in the choices children make.

Solving problems encountered in play

__ Encourage children to describe the problems they encounter.

__ Give children time to come up with their own solutions.

__ Assist children who are frustrated.

---

form the "problem-solving habit," a trait that will help them successfully meet challenges throughout their school years and into adulthood.

Use the following **support strategies** to encourage children's independent problem-solving:

▲ **Encourage children to describe the problems they encounter.** When you see a child having a problem, hold back to let the child recognize and describe it. This is an essential first step for the child to be able to arrive at a solution.

Children may not see problems in the same way adults do; in viewing and describing the problem in their own words, children begin to trust their skills as observers and analyzers. Not only is this process central to positive emotional development, it also lies at the heart of scientific thinking and reasoning.

Cole came to his teacher, Jackie, and said, "The computer's not working." She asked him to tell her how it wasn't working and followed him back to the computer. Cole said, "See, it keeps going back to where I started." When Jackie asked Cole what he wanted the computer to do, he said, "Go to the next part of the game." She pointed to the arrow keys and encouraged Cole to try each of them and see what happened.

108

When he touched the right arrow key (→) and the game advanced, Cole said, "Now I got it working!"

▲ **Give children time to come up with their own solutions.** Just as it is important to wait patiently for children to identify problems, it is equally important to hold back so children can figure out how to solve them. While your solution may be more efficient or effective, simply giving it to the children would deprive them of an opportunity to learn and develop confidence in their problem-solving abilities.

▲ **Assist children who are frustrated.** Sometimes children do need adult help, especially when their inability to solve a problem keeps them from moving forward with their plans. Be alert to situations in which children have tried to solve a problem and run into roadblocks they cannot get past on their own. This is an appropriate point to step in to provide just enough assistance for children to either continue working through a solution on their own or proceed to carry out their intentions. When you provide a brief explanation in such cases, the children are able to learn from the experience and perhaps use the information independently at a later time.

While Ashlyn was in the woodworking area, the drill bit came off the manual drill she was using. She put it back in place, but it kept falling out. She brought it to her teacher, Chris, and asked her to "fix it." Chris tightened the bit in the drill and said, "Sometimes I have to tighten it like this for it to stay." Ashlyn proceeded with her plan to make a dinosaur bed.

Try These Ideas Yourself

1. What were your early school experiences like? For example,

- What made you feel confident or insecure about your abilities as a learner?

- To what extent did teachers encourage or discourage your initiative and independence?

- How did these early experiences affect your later attitudes toward school and your behavior as a student?

- How do you approach learning now?

- How might you apply your own early school experiences to working with young children?

2. Think about an important decision you have made, then answer the following:

- How did you gather the information you needed to make the decision?

- What roles did thought, impulse, or intuition play?

- How satisfied are you with the way you go about making decisions now?

- How might you change your approach to decision making?

- How might you apply your experiences and insights about decision making to working with young children?

3. Think of a recent problem you faced at home, school, or work (for example, juggling several deadlines at once, repairing or replacing broken equipment, or trying to accommodate conflicting needs or viewpoints).

- How did you approach solving this problem?

- To what extent did your approach involve anger, a feeling of challenge or intrigue, deliberation, organization, or moment-by-moment responses?

- How does your approach to problem situations vary? What determines your response in each case?

- What might you do to make your approach to solving problems more satisfying?

- How might you apply your experiences and insights about problem solving to working with young children?

4. Observe children in a preschool setting. Look for and write down examples of children making choices, plans, and decisions and solving problems they encounter in play. What do your observations tell you about children's development and about supportive teaching practices?

Chapter 11

What Is the HighScope Curriculum in Language, Literacy, and Communication?

❓ Think About It

Imagine you are traveling in a foreign country named Paminiland. Not only do residents speak another language — Pamini — they also use a different written alphabet. At first, you depend on your tour guide for everything. She makes the arrangements at your hotel, orders food, and hires transportation to and from the sites you want to visit. She translates signs at the market so you can sample the local delicacies and buy gifts to take back home. Once you decide on a purchase, she plucks the correct amount of money from your open palm. A word that keeps coming up in these transactions is kindalay, *so you figure out this is the name of the local currency. By mid-week, you notice all the signs in the marketplace have a number followed by the same set of marks. What at first looked like a bunch of squiggles now appears to you as three distinct shapes — a square with a dot in the middle, a left-facing half-moon, and a vertical line with a curlicue on top. You realize this must be the written word for Paminiland currency, and the three marks stand, respectively, for the sounds in kin/da/lay. On the fifth day, you walk up to a stall and buy a piece of mellani, the local pastry, on your own. You ask your tour guide to write the letters for mellani on the corner of your map, and later that day you copy them on the postcard to your family. You vow not to leave Paminiland before getting the recipe for this wonderful confection.*

The connection between language and literacy is powerful. In the above anecdote, the "aha" moment connecting the spoken and written word for *kindalay* came only after you had heard and then seen it many times. You recognized this particular word because of its importance to you — it allowed you to get the services, and especially, that delicious pastry you wanted. Later in your travels, you would probably pick up other words and phrases that were especially useful as you journeyed around Paminiland, such as words corresponding to *bath room, too expensive,* and *stop and rest*.

The development of literacy in young children follows a similar course. Before they can read, children need many rich experiences speaking the language represented in print. The first letters and

Literacy is an important school readiness skill because so much learning depends on reading. Being able to read in turn depends on developing language skills, especially vocabulary.

Chapter Learning Objectives

By the end of this chapter, you will be able to

❖ Explain why language, literacy, and communication are important in children's early development

❖ Describe and discuss the four essential components of early literacy emphasized by the National Reading Panel and National Early Literacy Panel

❖ Describe the HighScope key developmental indicators in language, literacy, and communication

❖ Understand and begin to apply the strategies adults use to support early learning in language, literacy, and communication

❖ Understand the Growing Readers Early Literacy Curriculum and how it can be used in an early childhood program

words they read and write are the ones most personally meaningful to them and are usually their own names. The HighScope Curriculum honors and promotes this connection between language (listening and speaking) and literacy (reading and writing). In this chapter, you will learn about HighScope's overall approach to enhancing these essential skills in language, literacy, and communication, as well as the Foundation's in-depth curriculum in early literacy.

Why Language, Literacy, and Communication Is Important

Early literacy is often cited as the most important academic skill in school readiness because most school learning depends on knowing how to read. Knowing how to read, in turn, is highly depend-

ent on language skills, particularly vocabulary. Put another way, understanding and using oral language (listening and speaking) is the first step in mastering printed language (reading and writing). Communication in all its forms — oral, written, and gestural — is also central to establishing the human relationships through which we exchange information.

In choosing the term "language development and communication," the National Education Goals Panel (NEGP; Kagan et al., 1995) also emphasized that this area of school readiness should not be limited to learning how to read. The Panel noted that language is the means by which children convey their needs, describe events, interact with others, and express their thoughts and feelings. Language and communication are therefore intertwined with all areas of individual development, as well as also being essential to children's becoming members of their classroom and other groups.

Language and Literacy Development

The development of language and literacy begins at birth. Older infants and toddlers talk to communicate their needs and relate to the people around them. During preschool there is a significant increase in the use of language to establish and maintain relationships. Three- and four-year-olds interact with others, ask questions, consider what they hear, refer to things that are not present in their immediate environment, and talk about desires and imaginary situations. Their vocabularies are growing and they are mastering the basic rules of grammar. These young children are also beginning to read and write. They do this in unconventional ways at first (such as "reading" pictures — that is, narrating a story based on the images and drawing horizontal lines of scribbles) but are eager to learn how to read and write in conventional ways.

Terms Used in This Chapter

• comprehension • phonological awareness • alphabet knowledge/alphabetic principle • concepts about print • rhyming • alliteration • phoneme/phonemic awareness • segmenting • blending • letter links • dictation • Growing Readers Early Literacy Curriculum (GRC)

During the past three decades, researchers such as Catherine Snow, Susan Burns, and Peg Griffin (1998) have learned a great deal about how language and literacy develop in young children. Before the results of their research became known, reading instruction often began in first grade. However, as studies showed the connection between spoken and written language, literacy was no longer seen as something children were suddenly ready for at age six. Instead, we now know that literacy "emerges" gradually in the early years. Reading and writing begin with learning language and looking at books in infancy. The preschool years continue (and in some cases fill the gaps in) this process. An effective early literacy curriculum enables children to make the most of the literacy instruction they receive in their elementary years.

HighScope teacher-educator Linda Weikel Ranweiler, in her book *Preschool Readers and Writers: Early Literacy Strategies for Teachers* (2004), summarizes the lessons learned from recent research on language development, literacy, and early communication:

▲ Language and literacy are connected from infancy onward. Speaking, listening, reading, and writing develop concurrently (together) rather than sequentially (one after the other).

▲ The acquisition of language and literacy skills is social. It happens because young children want to interact and communicate with others.

▲ Literacy learning occurs during meaningful interactions, experiences, and activities.

▲ Children differ in how — and how fast — they learn. For example, some pick up the sounds of language (phonological awareness) easily while others need more time and formal lessons.

▲ Some language and literacy learning happens naturally during play and everyday experiences, and some depends on explicit instruction from observant and sensitive adults.

▲ Differences in children's home language and culture can affect literacy development. An effective program of instruction in the language used in the classroom, together with support for the language and culture of the home, allows for and values these differences.

The HighScope Preschool Curriculum takes all these findings into account, particularly the strong association between language and literacy development. This connection is reflected in HighScope's key developmental indicators (KDIs) for this area, as well as its Growing Readers Early Literacy Curriculum (GRC; HighScope Educational Research Foundation, 2005), a set of small-group activities and other daily learning experiences. The KDIs and the GRC are both described in this chapter.

Four Essential Components of Early Literacy

Widespread concern over early literacy development is reflected in the workings of numerous governmental bodies and educational legislation, such as the federal No Child Left Behind Act (08 January 2002). The National Reading Panel (2000) and National Early Literacy Panel (Strickland & Shanahan, 2004) have emphasized four essential components of early literacy: comprehension, phonological awareness, alphabet knowledge, and concepts about print.

Comprehension is the process of deriving meaning from action, speech, and text by connecting what one is learning to what one already knows.

Phonological awareness is recognizing the sounds that make up words.

Alphabetic principle is the relationship between letters and sounds in oral and written language.

Concepts about print is knowing how print is organized on the page and how it is used for reading and writing.

You can find examples of each of these research-based components on pages 122–124. They are embedded in the six language, literacy, and communication KDIs and are also addressed in the GRC and the Early Literacy Skills Assessment (ELSA; HighScope Educational Research Foundation, 2004), a standardized literacy measure described in Chapter 18. Both the GRC and ELSA can be used by any developmentally based program, not just those implementing the HighScope Preschool Curriculum.

❖

112

The next part of this chapter describes the HighScope Curriculum's six KDIs in language, literacy, and communication. A later section of the chapter describes the GRC.

Key Developmental Indicators in Language, Literacy, and Communication

HighScope has six KDIs in language, literacy, and communication. The first three focus on *speaking and listening*. The remaining three focus on *reading and writing*. Each is described below, along with the strategies adults use to support their development in young children.

> *We had this curriculum in place last year. I have been getting feedback about our "graduates" who are in kindergarten and first grade. HighScope's integrated approach to reading and writing during the*

planning and review times helped to give them a purpose for these activities. The experiences were there when they were ready. This allowed their language abilities to flourish and help them to succeed in school. (Fresno, Calif., Teacher)

 Talking with others about personally meaningful experiences

Young children talk because they want to make sense of what is happening in their world, and they want to tell those they trust about their experiences. This desire to communicate means preschoolers are naturally motivated to talk. Conversing with others creates opportunities to expand their vocabularies and convey meaning through language, essential in developing their comprehension skills. As with other activities, preschoolers' motivation to communicate is strongest when it stems from their own interests and concerns.

To create an environment in which children's natural inclination to talk can flourish, use the

 HighScope Key Developmental Indicators in Language, Literacy, and Communication

Key Developmental Indicators	Related components of early literacy development
Talking with others about personally meaningful experiences	Comprehension
Describing objects, events, and relations	Comprehension
Having fun with language: Listening to stories and poems, making up stories and rhymes	Comprehension Phonological awareness
Writing in various ways: Drawing, scribbling, and using letterlike forms, invented spelling, and conventional forms	Alphabetic principle
Reading in various ways: Reading storybooks, signs and symbols, one's own writing	Comprehension Alphabetic principle Concepts about print
Dictating stories	Comprehension Alphabetic principle Concepts about print

following **support strategies** to promote early language.

▲ **Establish a climate in which children feel free to talk.** Children who talk to classmates and adults throughout the day gain skills in vocabulary, grammar, and usage. Creating a warm environment naturally leads to friendly interactions and conversations.

Spontaneous exchanges between preschoolers and teachers are especially likely to happen when adults act as partners with children, rather than assuming control of the classroom. As a teacher in Michigan's Upper Peninsula commented, "Children plan, carry out, and talk about their activities. Even shy children have become vocal!"

▲ **Be available for conversation throughout the day.** Children talk to adults when they sense that adults take pleasure in talking to them. To let children know you are eager to talk, get down on their physical level, listen to what they say, and follow their lead in the direction of the conversation. Keep children's interests in mind and, above all, be patient. Young children, and especially English language learners, sometimes struggle to find the right words to express their thoughts and may give up when rushed.

▲ **Comment on what children do.** Describe what children do when they play. For example, you might make an informational statement like, "Dwayne, you are putting lots of blocks on your tower. I wonder how you'll keep it from tipping over." Dwayne, knowing the teacher is watching and listening, feels encouraged to share his thoughts.

Observing and commenting on children's activities is also an opportunity to introduce new vocabulary words *in context,* that is, in relation to what is happening at the moment. Children are more likely to remember and use words heard in this way, and their expanded vocabulary increases their comprehension of oral and written language. For example, when a child pauses while painting, you might use words like *color, hue, shade, tint, texture, background, brush stroke,* and *artist* during the conversation.

▲ **Encourage children to talk with one another throughout the day.** Many children talk naturally with their classmates, but even the most verbal children sometimes need adult support to

do this. To encourage child-to-child conversations, you can provide materials that lend themselves to cooperative play (such as heavy items that take two children to carry), invite children to plan and recall together, and refer children to one another for help. Sometimes teachers interpret what a child is saying as a way to help other children understand and respond appropriately.

🔑 *Describing objects, events, and relations*

As children talk about personally meaningful things, they often describe the materials they work with, what they are doing with them, and who else is involved. By showing an interest in what children say, teachers can add to their vocabularies and elaborate on their sentences, both of which are key to comprehension. For example, when Tina, a toddler, said, "Me, banana," her caregiver said, "You want me to give you a banana." And when Lewis, a preschooler, said, "I'm going up and up," his teacher said, "Yes, I can see you swinging higher each time."

Use the following **support strategies** to help children develop descriptive language.

▲ **Provide children with interesting materials and experiences.** Children spontaneously describe their actions and freely share ideas when they manipulate objects with different properties and become involved in activities that interest them.

> *At small-group time, while using toothbrushes to wash the blocks, Caitlin talked about the type of toothbrush she had at home. Margaret (a teacher) conversed with Caitlin about her toothbrush and other aspects of toothbrushing. Caitlin said her toothbrush had a horse on it and that it was smaller than her mom's and dad's.*

▲ **Listen as children describe things in their own way.** In their eagerness to increase children's vocabulary, adults sometimes talk too much. Or they are too quick to correct mistakes in grammar or pronunciation, and as a result, children may grow quiet or even withdraw from an activity. HighScope teachers are taught to listen first. They do not jump in with questions or rush to suggest how children might do something dif-

114

Encouraging Children to Talk to One Another

This conversation illustrates how adults can support children's verbal interactions with one another.

Carl: *(Tries to stick golf tees into Styrofoam)* I can't get this to go in.

Mr. Ryan: Yolanda was doing it before. Maybe she can explain how she did it.

Yolanda: You have to bam it!

Carl: How do you do that?

Yolanda: You just have to bam it really hard.

Carl: Huh?

Mr. Ryan: *(To Yolanda)* Can you show us what you mean? *(Carl and Mr. Ryan watch her)*

Yolanda: See. You push it in. *(She pushes in the tee part way)* And then you bang it hard from the top. You bam it in! *(She pounds it in with a mallet and hands it to Carl)* Here, you try now.

Carl: *(Does the same with his golf tee and the mallet)* Look. I'm bamming it too!

Having fun with language: Listening to stories and poems, making up stories and rhymes

Children enjoy playing with sounds and words. In doing so, they become familiar with the sounds that make up words; that is, they develop the phonological awareness that is one of the four components of early literacy. Children play with language on their own and often join eagerly when adults initiate word-play games. Infants babble to try different sounds and listen to their own voices. Preschoolers enjoy hearing and making up stories, rhymes, and chants, which also adds to their comprehension skills. They repeat words, including big ones and even those whose meanings they do not know. Young children also enjoy making up words and combining sounds. These activities require them to use existing skills and develop new ones. Two essentials of phonological awareness are recognizing the ending sounds or syllables that are the same in two or more words (rhymes) and recognizing beginning sounds that are the same in two or more words (alliteration).

Use the following **support strategies** to encourage children's interest in language sounds and story structure.

▲ **Listen for children's spontaneous word play throughout the day.** Children often talk to themselves while they play. If you honor children's use of language, you can encourage further elaborations.

ferently or better. They repeat and restate what children say so the children know they are being listened to and heard. When children know adults respect their intentions and ideas, they are more likely to talk about them. [*Note:* In reflecting back what children say, teachers use correct grammar and pronunciation, thereby allowing children to hear correct usage without being explicitly corrected.]

▲ **Let children take the lead in games that require giving directions.** When children take the lead in a game, they have to describe what body part to use or in which direction to move. Being the leader thus encourages speaking and thinking. Familiar action games can be adapted so they are appropriate for preschoolers. For example, the game Simon says can be simplified so there are no winners or losers. Instead, a child might say, "Put your hands on your knees" or "Look behind you" and others would follow his or her instructions.

To promote early literacy skills, HighScope encourages children to have fun with language. Children enjoy telling teachers and parents about what they did and what they learned.

As Timmy was digging, he said, "I'm digging a hole, a hole for a mole." His teacher commented, "You're digging a mole hole." Timmy replied, "When I finish my mole hole, I'm making a mouse house." As his teacher repeated each of his rhymes, Timmy would add another one, such as "cuddle puddle" and "snack stack." His teacher commented, "You're saying a lot of rhyming words."

▲ **Tell stories and encourage children to make up stories.** Telling stories, in addition to reading books, is another way to have fun with language, voice inflection, and dramatic gestures. You might tell folk tales and stories you heard as a child, as well as myths and fables that are part of the local culture.

You can also invent narratives and encourage children to tell and make up their own stories. Creating stories about class events automatically grabs children's attention — for example, telling what happened during a field trip to the petting zoo. Children might suggest an idea for a story, such as the first line ("A little boy got a great big dog for his birthday") or a general theme ("Tell about a witch"). Stories can be based on real happenings or totally imaginary characters and events. Adults may use props, hand gestures, or just an interesting voice when telling stories. Likewise, children might use props, act out the tale, or just listen and picture the characters and events. If children offer comments and ideas, the adult or child narrator can incorporate these into the story. This makes storytelling an interactive process.

▲ **Play with word sounds in rhymes, chants, and alliterations.** Reciting and making up rhymes and chants is another way to explore the parts of oral — and later, written — language. Rhymes help children attend to the ending sounds or syllables two words have in common, such as the /all/ sound at the end of *call* and *ball*. Once children can identify rhyming word pairs in familiar nursery rhymes and rhyming phrases, they can use their understanding of rhyme to invent rhyming word pairs, as found in "Hickory, dickory, dee. The mouse ran up a tree."

Rhyming Games

Rhyming — generating words that end with the same sound — is fun for young children. It increases their phonological awareness, that is, the ability to pay attention to the sounds of language (apart from its meaning). Here are some ideas for rhyming games to play with young children.

Word substitution. Substitute a word at the end of a line of a familiar song, poem, or chant, and ask children to choose a rhyme for it. Here is an example:

Row, row, row your boat

Gently down the block

Merrily, merrily, merrily, merrily

Life is but a _____. (What rhymes with block*?)*

Rhyming I spy. Using an empty paper towel tube or other prop as a "spyglass," ask children to find words that rhyme with different items you "spy" around the room. Make sure they can see all the areas while you play this game. Here is an example:

❖ "I spy something in the art area that rhymes with *crush*. What do you think it is?"

❖ "I spy something in the house area that rhymes with *vroom*. Can you guess what it is?"

❖ "I spy something in the toy area that rhymes with *guzzle*. What do you suppose it could be?"

Rhyme time. Present a word and ask the children to think of words that rhyme with it. As a variation, give them a rhyming phrase and ask them to fill in the last word. Once they have the idea of the game, children can be the leaders. Accept nonsense words, conventional words, and parts of speech that do not fit, as long as they rhyme. Here are some examples:

❖ "Let's think of words that rhyme with *toe* (*bow, go, grow, hoe, Joe, voe, low, snow, no*)."

❖ "I saw a pig sitting on a _____. What rhymes with *pig* (*fig, dig, big, snig, twig, jig, rig, hig, wig*)?"

Alliteration Games

Alliteration — words that start with the same sound — offers game opportunities the same way rhyming does. Alliteration deals with the smallest unit of sound, or **phoneme,** that starts a word, such as the /b/ sound in *ball, boy, banana.* Alliteration games develop **phonemic awareness,** which is part of the more general knowledge of language sounds known as **phonological awareness.** Here are some alliteration games that are fun and promote learning in young children.

Who is it? Ask children to guess who in the group has a name beginning with a certain phoneme. You can also play this game with the names of characters in a familiar book you've just finished reading with the children. Here are some examples:

❖ "There are two people in this circle whose names begin with the /b/ sound. Who are they?"

❖ "I'm thinking of a person in this room whose name starts with /sh/. Guess who."

❖ "I'm remembering someone in the story "The Three Bears" whose name began with a /g/ sound. Who do you think it is?"

Doing the names. Combine the initial sound of children's names with the initial sound of actions for them to perform. Consider these examples:

❖ "Whose name begins with a /k/ sound?" (Pause for children to figure this out.) "Yes, Carl and Carol. Let's clap with Carl and Carol."

❖ "Whose name starts with the sound /w/?" (Pause for children to figure this out.) "Wendy and Walter, let's see you wave. Everybody wave with Wendy and Walter. Now let's see everyone wiggle."

Word starters. Ask children to think of words that begin with the same sound.

❖ "Let's think of words that start with the same sounds as *car, cat, call…*"

❖ "What words that begin with /d/ sound like *daddy* and *door?*"

❖ "How many things can you see that start with a /p/ sound?"

Letter substitution. Pick a sound and substitute it at the beginning of words during an activity such as snacktime or a transition. This game is especially good to make cleanup time silly and fun. When children get the idea, let them pick the sound.

❖ "At cleanup time, what if we started the name of each thing we picked up with the /m/ sound. So if you stacked the puzzles, you could say you were stacking the /m/ _____." (Pause to let the children work out "muzzles.")

❖ "Lee, it's your turn to pick a sound to help us get ready for outside time." (Lee says he wants /l/ like in his name.) "Okay, see if you can make whatever you're putting on — your coat, hat, mittens, boots — start with the /l/ sound like the first sound in the name Lee."

At greeting time, when listening to his teacher read Mrs. Wishy Washy and the Scrubbing Machine, *Reggie filled in the word hair to rhyme with chair.*

Alliteration games help children attend to the **phonemes** (the smallest units of sound) that begin words. Here too, as children gain awareness of beginning word sounds, they can generate their own alliterations. For example, they can substitute the /f/ sound in "fee fie, foe" with /m/ and say "me, my, moe" and so on.

As Henry was getting ready for outside time, he picked up his hat and said, "Hey, Henry and hat! They have the /h/ sound!"

To encourage children's awareness of **segmenting** and **blending** the sounds in words, you might introduce name games, for example, "I'm thinking of someone whose name begins with the /k/ sound and ends with the /arl/ sound. Who do you think it is?" Also include rhyming, alliteration, and other word activities throughout the day — for example, during transitions ("Everyone whose name starts with the /b/ sound, like *book* and *box,* go to the circle") or at the beginning of an activity (for example, speaking or singing "It's snacktime/ Everyone gets a *treat*/It's snack time/Let's see what there is to *eat*"). For more ideas on rhyming and alliteration games, see the sidebars on page 115 and above).

Writing in various ways: Drawing, scribbling, and using letterlike forms, invented spelling, and conventional forms

Through their experiences with books and print, children come to know and expect that written words are connected to spoken words and carry meaning. They want to figure out how written language works so they can use it themselves. Preschoolers begin to experiment with writing by drawing and making letterlike marks, such as lines, squiggles, and dots. With time, their writing takes on more conventional forms and they produce recognizable letters and words. As they make the connection between spoken and written letters, preschoolers are developing the alphabetic principle, one of the four components of early literacy.

HighScope teachers support children at all stages in the development of their writing. They do not demand that children copy letters by rote, nor do they correct children's early writing efforts. Force and criticism can dampen children's enthusiasm. By giving children reasons to write, and trusting in their motivation, adults can support children on the path to becoming proficient writers.

Use the following **support strategies** to encourage young children's emergent writing skills.

▲ **Provide a variety of writing and drawing materials.** The art area is a logical place for writing and drawing materials such as crayons, markers, chalk, paints and brushes, colored pencils, and different types of paper. Some programs also set up a writing area that includes office supplies such as pads, notebooks, stamps, and ink pads. (An "office area" could also include various mathematics materials such as adding machines, rulers, and postal scales.) You can also find computer programs with writing and drawing activities appropriate for preschoolers. In addition to the writing and drawing materials already located throughout the room, make sure children know they are free to carry them from one area to another (see Chapter 6).

▲ **Expect and support various forms of emergent writing.** Typically, children's efforts at writing start with horizontal lines of scribbles rather than recognizable attempts to write letters. Young children's written work may also include specific marks and symbols they see in print — for example, a circle with a line through it (the "no" sign). In general, children's writing pro-

Children have daily opportunities to write about their interests and activities, such as recording plans, making chore charts, signing and captioning artwork, or authoring stories.

gresses from *drawing,* to *printlike scribbles,* to *letterlike forms* (shapes, lines, and dots), to *actual letters* (sometimes written in different places on the page), and finally to *conventional forms* (letters written in order from left to right on the page, with increased attention to correct spelling). Knowing this progression will help you recognize and support children's earliest attempts at writing.

As they begin to write letters and combine them in words, children reflect what they hear — their oral language experience — in their written attempts. So, for example, they might write the word *open* as OPN. Over time, spelling is often self-correcting through reading and other visual experiences. When children ask how to spell a word, you might then either spell the word aloud, offer the sound and its letters ("The /m/ sound needs an *m,* the /ŏ/ sound needs an *o...*"), write the letters for the child to copy, or find the word in printed material for the child to use as an example.

> At greeting time, Breanna signed her name on the snack chart by writing lines back and forth on the paper.
>
> At recall time, Sara said, "I want to spell the word *babies.*" She identified the initial /b/ sound in the word and wrote the letter B on her dry-erase board. She wrote the other letters as Jade (a teacher) spelled the word.

▲ **Encourage children to write for a wide variety of reasons.** Provide many situations in which children will want to write. For example, they often want to add a descriptive caption to

118

their artwork. And because of their constant exposure to books, children want to be "authors," too — encourage them to record the stories they invent. Children also enjoy writing things down in the course of their play. For example, while role-playing "restaurant," they may create a menu or write down orders. They also write to one another or to their family members, creating such items as party invitations and get-well cards.

The daily routine provides many opportunities for writing. For example, children may write down their plans or draw and caption their work-time activity at recall time. Lists, such as those indicating whose turn it is to pass out snacks, are additional examples of places where children enjoy writing their names. Mathematics activities also lend themselves to writing. For example, after collecting and sorting natural objects on a field trip

(leaves, stones, and so on), children might list the names and numbers (amounts) of what they found.

> *At work time in the house area, Bethany used a pencil to write squiggly lines on a Post-it note. She said, "I'm writing my mom a note." When Claire (a teacher) asked her what the note said, Bethany replied, "I care about my dog."*

▲ **Display and send home samples of children's writing.** Children write to communicate, and they enjoy seeing and reading their own writing in a public space. Sending their writing home also lets family members appreciate their emerging abilities. When posting children's writing, it is important to put it low enough for children to see and read easily.

How to Read to Young Children

HighScope teachers read interactively with children frequently, both individually and in small groups. They also encourage parents to read interactively with their children at home every day. Here are a few simple suggestions you can share with parents to make sure reading is a good experience for both readers and listeners:

(1) Take your time. Invite children to tell you what they see on the cover. Once inside the book, have children examine and talk about the picture in front of you, before you read the accompanying text.

(2) Read clearly. Pronounce the words carefully so children can follow the story and hear and see the connection between spoken and written words.

(3) Read with interest. Make your voice expressive. If you appear to be interested in what you are reading, children will be, too.

(4) Use different voices. Give different voices or other unique qualities to the characters in the story. Let the children come up with different voices.

(5) Occasionally, follow the words with your finger. From time to time, show children the printed words you are reading, so you can help them distinguish between text and illustrations. Do this with a familiar book in which it is easy see the differ-

ence between print and pictures. Examples would be a book that displays the text by itself on one page and the illustrations themselves on the facing page, or one that has pictures on the top half of the page and text on the bottom half.

(6) Stop reading to look at and talk about the pictures, story, and characters. Invite children to examine the illustrations and talk about what they see. Support children's comments and observations. Answer children's questions. Occasionally ask them to recall what has happened. Rather than asking closed-ended questions, invite comments by saying something like "Let's see what we can remember about what happened to the little pigs so far." To encourage children's predictions, wonder about what might happen next. With a familiar book, ask children to imagine different events and endings.

(7) Extend the learning. Give children drawing materials to represent events or characters in the book. Encourage children to act out favorite parts of the book or do things the way a character might. Visit places and do things that appear in the book. Make up stories and play games with children that build on the book's characters, events, and ideas.

Adapted from *Helping Your Preschool Child Become a Reader* (Epstein, 2002, p. 28)

Reading in various ways: Reading storybooks, signs and symbols, one's own writing

Children "read" long before they can read actual letters and words. For example, they look at the pictures in a familiar book and "read" (tell) the story as they turn the pages. Or they will "read" their own scribbles. These actions demonstrate that young children are highly motivated to become readers, indicating children's natural impetus to explore and expand their abilities in three of the four early literacy components: comprehension, alphabetic principle, and concepts about print.

Use the following **support strategies** to foster children's emergent literacy.

▲ **Provide a print-rich environment.** Learning to read is part of making sense of one's world. Therefore, include printed materials in every interest area of your program. Of foremost importance is a well-stocked reading or book area. Provide a wide variety of storybooks and other types of printed materials, including wordless board books, nonfiction (information) books, nursery rhyme and poetry collections, picture dictionaries, magazines, atlases, and catalogs.

In other parts of the classroom, keep printed materials appropriate to that area. For example, you might place cartons with writing on them in the block area, plastic containers with printed labels at the sand and water table, empty food boxes and telephone books in the house area, magazines and greeting cards in the art area, magnetic letters and playing cards in the toy area, tool catalogs and instruction manuals in the woodworking area, cassette and CD holders in the music area, seed packets and bird guides outdoors, a message board by the door, or a list of titles for the lending library in the book area. Additionally, children can manipulate and talk about (and eat) alphabet pretzels at snacktime, and to supplement printed materials inside and outside the classroom, you can call attention to signs, window displays, and other forms of print on walks and field trips.

▲ **Read interactively with children every day.** There are many opportunities to read interactively with children each day. In addition to reading environmental print in the classroom (such as the daily message board, task lists, or interest area signs), read books with children during work time and other small-group times. Read and converse

Adults read interactively with children, individually and in small groups, so children can see, hear, turn pages, point, comment and ask questions, and actively engage with printed materials.

with children about books one-on-one, in pairs, and in intimate groupings and settings.

Make sure all the children are engaged with the book — that is, that they can see and point to the pictures, turn the pages, hear the story, and comment and ask questions about what they see, hear, and understand. Because this personal and active involvement is so important, HighScope does not recommend reading to children in large groups. It is also important to encourage parents to read interactively with their children at home.

▲ **Encourage children to read to adults and to one another.** Most adults enjoy reading aloud with children. It is also important for children to experience the pleasure and sense of competence that comes with reading to others. A good starting place is with wordless picture books, where children can describe the illustrations or make up a story about them. As they become familiar with the text of a book, children like to "read" it by turning the pages, looking at the pictures for clues about the story, and reciting remembered phrases or making up their own versions of the words.

Eventually, as they develop an understanding of the alphabetic principle (the relationship between letters and sounds), children begin to recognize specific letters and words and to sight-read highlighted, recurring, or familiar words. This process also gives

120

them hands-on experience developing concepts about print (how books work) and comprehension (deriving meaning or understanding from illustrations and familiar text). For more on these literacy skills, see the section at the end of the chapter on the Growing Readers Curriculum.

> *At work time in the house area, Alyjah looked at the book* Owl Babies *(by Martha Waddell and Patrick Benson), turned the pages, and "read" the story to Crystal (a teacher). He explained to Crystal that the mother owl was at work getting food for the babies.*

▲ **Provide children with nametags and letter-linked pictures.** Children begin to read by learning letters and words that are personally meaningful to them. It is therefore common for them to first read and write the letters in their names. *Letter Links: Alphabet Learning with Children's Names,* by HighScope literacy researcher Andrea DeBruin-Parecki and curriculum developer Mary Hohmann (2003), is a name-based letter-learning system that pairs a child's printed nametag with a letter-linked picture (also referred to as a **letter link**) of an object starting with the same letter and sound. A letter-linked picture for *Alice* might be the drawing of an ant with the letter *A* in each corner of the drawing. One for *Pedro* could be the drawing of a paintbrush with the letter *P* in each corner of the drawing.

You can place letter links alongside children's names on their cubbies, on the bottom of their artwork, on chore charts, and in other places throughout the classroom. Not only do children quickly recognize their own letter links and the first letters in their name and the letter-linked object, they soon learn those of other children in the program, thereby expanding their letter (alphabetic) knowledge.

> *At work time, Michael pointed to his nametag under his coat hook and next to his letter link and said, "That's my name." Then he pointed to his name on the posted small-group time chart.*

> *At snacktime, when the children were talking about their letter links, Breanna said that hers was the bridge and that Micah's was the moon. "Breanna has* B *and bridge has* B. *Micah and moon are both* M.*"*

 *Dictating stories*

While children enjoy doing their own writing, there are times when they want to dictate their ideas to adults. For example, children may want something written down that they are not yet capable of writing on their own. HighScope teachers take **dictation** at the request of children rather than requiring them to dictate something, such as a picture caption. True to the principles of active learning, children's writing skills develop as they themselves write and read their own writing. In the process of recording their ideas, children expand their comprehension and further their grasp of the alphabetic principle. They also apply concepts about print to their own writing activities.

Create dictation opportunities and use the following **support strategies** to build on children's natural interest in the process of dictation.

▲ **Write down children's personal dictations.** Children who do not yet write are still interested in having their ideas recorded. Even those who have begun writing independently may want a record of something too complex for them to write on their own. Or they may ask an adult to write down something for them so they can then copy it themselves. When taking dictation from a child, write down and read back exactly what the child says, without correcting grammar or word order. This duplication helps children establish the connection between the spoken and written word. It also lets the child know you value what he or she says.

▲ **Write down group dictations.** Taking dictation about a shared experience, such as a field trip, has many benefits. In addition to being important for language and literacy learning, it creates a social bond as children listen and add to one another's ideas. Group dictation also provides an opportunity for children to recall an experience in greater detail than they might on their own. When taking group dictation, be sure to give each child who wants to contribute a chance to do so. Also write down and read back exactly what each child in the group says.

▲ **Extend dictations into other literacy experiences.** You can build on children's dictations in many ways. For example, the dictations can be collected in a homemade book and added to the class library. If the words come first, children might choose to add their own illustrations later. Also, children enjoy acting out even the simplest dictations. As their ideas become more detailed and elaborate, they can dress up and use props, including making their own. Often this process leads to other literacy-related activities.

After several weeks of working with clay, children in one class visited a sculpture garden. Upon returning, they did a group dictation about what they saw. Children noticed that the statues were made of different materials, that some were on pedestals and others sat on the ground, and that some stood still while others had parts that moved in the wind. Each sculpture had plaques with the title, artist's name, and date the work was completed. The next day, several children made a plan to create their own sculpture garden. Some worked in clay while others made structures with blocks or created mixed-media collages. A few children collaborated on their projects. When the children had finished their pieces, the sculpture garden was set up in the art area and the house area. The children and teachers turned over unused cubbies to serve as pedestals. They spread a tarp on the floor for one child's "water sculpture." Each child attached a plaque to his or her artwork. Some made their own and others dictated them to the teacher. Whenever parents or visitors came to the classroom, the children acted as guides, showing them each piece and reading its label.

Growing Readers Early Literacy Curriculum

Overview

The Growing Readers Early Literacy Curriculum (GRC) is a comprehensive set of detailed activities for literacy instruction with preschoolers. The GRC includes a set of teacher-led small-group activities, additional short activities and teaching strategies for promoting literacy throughout the program

day, and a sample set of children's books. The activities in the GRC focus on the four essential content areas of early literacy described at the beginning of this chapter: comprehension, phonological awareness, alphabetic principle, and concepts about print.

Within each of the four content areas, the GRC includes activities for children at three levels of literacy development: *early emergent* (level 1, or "exploration"), *emergent* (level 2, or "awareness") and *competent emergent* (level 3, or "application"). See the sample GRC kit small-group activity card on this page. Since children in the same class are generally at different levels of literacy development, teachers can adapt each activity or book to provide instruction at any and all levels. The GRC also offers children books and other materials to manipulate and allows them choices about what to say and do.

During GRC activities, teachers and children engage in thoughtful conversations about the text and illustrations in the books they are reading

---

SMALL-GROUP ACTIVITY

3 Predict *Rosie's Walk:* The Next Episode!

LEVEL 3

CONTENT AREA Comprehension

TOPIC Prediction

Literacy Learning Focus
Children observe and talk about Rosie and the fox. They anticipate what the characters will do next and predict another adventure for Rosie and the fox.

Quick Plan
- Teacher and children examine and discuss pictures and predict Rosie and the fox's actions.
- Children predict another adventure for Rosie and the fox.
- Children draw and share their predictions.

Materials
☆ A copy of *Rosie's Walk* by Pat Hutchins
☆ Red, orange, yellow, green, brown, and black crayons (or markers)
☆ White paper for each child
☆ *Rosie's Walk* Vocabulary Card

Beginning
1. Gather in a comfortable spot where children can cluster close to you and *Rosie's Walk* and can easily spread out and draw. Place the book where everyone can see the cover. Prepare for a "trip" around the farm with the fox in pursuit of Rosie.
2. Begin by saying something like "Today, let's tell the story of Rosie and the fox and then think about some other adventures they may have on Rosie's farm."
3. Invite the children to look at the pictures and tell the story of Rosie and the fox. Give the children plenty of time to describe what Rosie and the fox are doing on each page. Weave their comments and observations along with some of your own into a simple story.

4. On the first page of each new episode, wonder aloud about what will happen next (that is, the first part of the rake episode, the pond episode, the haystack episode, and so forth).

Middle
5. At the end of the story, turn back to the title page and ask "**What other adventures do you think Rosie and the fox may have on the farm?**" Listen to and support the children's ideas.
6. Give the children crayons and paper and ask them to draw a picture of another adventure with Rosie and the fox.
7. Watch and listen to the children as they work. Comment on what you see them drawing and any parts of the story they reference from *Rosie's Walk*. (See the *Rosie's Walk* Vocabulary Card for words to incorporate into conversations about the children's drawings.)

End
8. As the children put away their crayons, gather their drawings. Show the drawings one at a time and ask the child whose drawing is on display to tell about the adventure he or she has drawn. Let the children know that you would like to save their pictures to put into another book about Rosie and the fox, and have the children create the title.

Follow-Up
Gather these pictures into a book and place the title the children have suggested on the cover. Put it on the shelf with *Rosie's Walk*.

Related Small-Group Times
Level 3 prediction activities 1 and 2

L3P-SG3

 SMALL-GROUP ACTIVITY 3

Sample GRC Teaching Strategies

Content Area: Alphabetic Principle

Topic: Name Writing

Level 1: Early Emergent

Strategy 1. Engage children in name writing each day.

Strategy 2. Comment positively on the up-and-down strokes, linear scribbles, and discrete symbol units children have used to write their name.

Level 2. Emergent

Strategy 1. Engage children in name writing each day.

Strategy 2. Comment positively on the symbol units, letterlike forms, and correctly formed letters children have used to write their name.

Strategy 3. Draw attention to similarities between children's signatures and their nametags.

Level 3. Competent Emergent

Strategy 1. Engage children in name writing each day.

Strategy 2. Comment positively on the letters children have used to write their name.

Strategy 3. Draw attention to similarities between children's signatures and their nametags.

Strategy 4. Draw attention to similarities between a child's name and other names that use some of the same letters.

and/or other materials they are using. Children exercise both oral language and visual literacy skills as they observe, listen, and talk about the characters, objects, actions, and ideas in the books. In all these ways, the GRC embodies the general principles and strategies of the HighScope KDIs in language, literacy, and communication. Children are encouraged to make choices about what to say and do as they work with the books and other materials. And teachers consistently support children's efforts, so Growing Readers is consistent with child development principles of active learning.

In addition to the extensive collection of small-group activities, each GRC kit contains short literacy activities that can be done at other times of the program day, along with specific teaching strategies for implementing activities at each level of development. The teaching strategies emphasize that literacy develops gradually; children need to practice earlier skills as adults scaffold them to help children master emerging ones. See the sample teaching strategies in the sidebar on page 123, which presents strategies for the content area *alphabetic principle* and the topic *name writing*.

The GRC has been piloted in 31 classrooms with 630 children, including English-language learners and children with special needs. Children in the pilot study made significant gains on the Early Literacy Skills Assessment (ELSA) in comprehension, phonological awareness, alphabetic principle, and concepts about print (Hohmann, 2005, pp. 47–48).

Growing Readers Content, Scope, and Sequence

The GRC addresses the scope of topics listed below for each of the four key literacy areas. Each topic is covered in sequence using the three developmental levels described above. (For more information on the definition and measurement of each literacy area and topic, see the description of the ELSA in Chapter 18.)

▲ **Comprehension.** GRC comprehension topics include *vocabulary* (learning new words), *prediction* (saying what will happen next in a book or story), *connection* (relating pictures and text to real life), and *retelling* (recalling actions and events from stories).

At snacktime, while looking at and listening to the book What Shall We Do with the Boo Hoo Baby? *by Cressida Cowell, Anna named the animals she saw in the pictures. When Jan (the teacher) read the words and said, "Quack went the…," Anna added "duck" and so on for other sentences the teacher started.* (vocabulary, prediction, connection)

Strategies for Supporting Early Language, Literacy, and Communication: A Summary

Talking with others about personally meaningful experiences

__ Establish a climate in which children feel free to talk.

__ Be available for conversation throughout the day.

__ Comment on what children do.

__ Encourage children to talk to one another throughout the day.

__ Converse with children about what they see, hear, and do during Growing Readers activities (see GRC).

Describing objects, events, and relations

__ Provide children with interesting materials and experiences.

__ Listen as children describe things in their own way.

__ Let children take the lead in games that require giving directions.

__ Encourage children to describe what they see and hear in illustrations during book reading (see GRC).

Having fun with language: Listening to stories and poems, making up stories and rhymes

__ Listen for children's spontaneous word play throughout the day.

__ Tell stories and encourage children to make up stories.

__ Play with word sounds in rhymes, chants, and alliterations.

__ Plan rhyming, alliteration, and segmentation activities (see GRC).

Writing in various ways: Drawing, scribbling, and using letterlike forms, invented spelling, and conventional forms

__ Provide a variety of writing and drawing materials.

__ Expect and support various forms of emergent writing.

__ Encourage children to write for a wide variety of reasons.

__ Display and send home samples of children's writing.

__ Draw children's attention to letter names and sounds as they write (see GRC).

Reading in various ways: Reading storybooks, signs and symbols, one's own writing

__ Provide a print-rich environment.

__ Read interactively with children every day.

__ Encourage children to read to adults and to one another.

__ Provide children with nametags and letter-linked pictures.

__ Plan small-group activities based on picture books (see GRC).

Dictating stories

__ Write down children's personal dictations.

__ Write down group dictations.

__ Extend dictations into other literacy experiences.

▲ **Phonological awareness.** GRC phonological awareness topics include *rhyming* (words that end with the same sounds or syllable), *alliteration* (words that begin with the same sound), and *segmentation* (breaking names and familiar words into syllables).

At the sand table, Cheryl (a teacher) asked Halley what she was making. Halley said, "Jell-O." Cheryl repeated "Jell-O" and Halley said, "Yeah, like Jordan," recognizing the /j/ sound at the beginning of Jell-O *and* Jordan. *(alliteration)*

▲ **Alphabetic principle.** GRC alphabetic principle topics include *name recognition* (identifying one's own printed name), *name writing* ("writing" one's own name), *letter recognition* (naming the letters of the alphabet), and *letter-sound correspondence* (knowing a letter's sound or a sound's letter).

124

At greeting time, as Ashlyn looked at the book Chicka, Chicka Boom Boom *by Bill Martin, Jr., she pointed out the letters* A, S, H, L, Y, *and* N *each time they appeared and said the letter was in her name.* (name recognition, letter recognition)

▲ **Concepts about print.** GRC concepts about print topics include *identifying book parts* (for example, front and back cover, title page, and story pages), *orienting books for reading* (recognizing front and back, top and bottom, and right side up), *distinguishing between pictures and words* (recognizing the differences between illustrations and text), and *understanding the direction of text* (flowing left to right, returning or "sweeping" left at the end of a line, continuing on the next page).

At greeting time, Maria chose The Z Was Zapped *by Chris Van Allsburg, for her dad to read to her. She handed it to him right side up and turned each page as they finished reading the text and talking about the picture.* (orienting books for reading, understanding the direction of text)

☀ Try These Ideas Yourself

1. Look at a series of illustrations or photographs in a book or magazine you have not read before. Make up a story from the pictures. What personal experiences did you draw on for your story? How might children draw on their interests and experiences to make up stories from pictures?

2. When Becca was three, her mother once cautioned her about big kids in the neighborhood playing "rough." Puzzled, Becca asked her mother, "Do little kids play smooth?" Below are some statements made by preschool children. What do their comments reveal about how they think about the world?

• I'm going to spread out my crackers so I'll have more to eat.

• When I put on my jacket, that will make the wind blow really cold.

• You can't have chocolate cake until you're five. If you're three or four, you only get vanilla.

• When I grow up, I'm going to have a longer name.

• I can't go to France with my parents because I don't know how to fly yet.

• You have to stand on this chair to sing up high.

How might your reflections on these statements influence your interactions with children in the classroom?

3. List the five most important things you think preschoolers need to know or be able to do in the area of literacy when they enter kindergarten. Why do you consider these abilities important? How can teachers support the development of the knowledge and skills you listed?

4. In the following scenario, identify the KDIs for language, literacy, and communication. What types of learning are occurring in other areas of development? How could a teacher support and extend the learning? (Refer to the list of key developmental indicators on p. 11.)

Jared and Evan sit next to one another, each looking at a book. Jared says to Evan, "Do you want me to read you this book about bears?" When Evan says yes, Jared moves closer to him so they can both look at the pictures. Jared turns the pages and "reads" the book to Evan, making up a story about what the bears are doing. "Now you read your book to me," says Jared. Evan knows his book, which is about a family car trip, by heart. As he recounts the tale, he occasionally points to a word as he says it. "That was a good book," says Jared when Evan is finished.

5. Think of a familiar nursery rhyme, song, or chant. Invent a rhyming game that focuses on pairs of rhyming words. Invent an alliteration game that focuses on the common beginning sound in a series of two or more words. (See sidebars on pp. 115 and 116 for examples.) How might you introduce each game to children in a preschool classroom?

6. Think of all the words you can use with young children for describing books and how books work (for example, *title, author, first page, the end*). Share your list with a colleague and ask for additional ideas. Use these words the next time you read a book with children.

Chapter 12

What Is the HighScope Curriculum in Social and Emotional Development?

Think About It

Did you ever play "school" as a child, perhaps even before you began formal schooling? An older sibling or neighbor may have been the teacher, while the other children were the students. Whoever got the coveted role of teacher would be eager to share his or her knowledge. For example, that child might have read aloud to the other children or given them arithmetic problems to solve. Occasionally, the child playing teacher would relate some interesting tidbit of history gleaned at "real" school, such as the haunting mystery that the first group of European settlers on Roanoke Island, off North Carolina, disappeared without a trace! The children playing students might have also had information or skills they wanted to demonstrate, whether these had been learned at home, in class, or in their jaunts around the neighborhood.

While playing school, you also would have picked up more than academic knowledge. A great deal of social learning would have been going on as you and the other children set out the rules for this elaborate game (debates about "how" to play school may have taken up more time than the game itself!), negotiated roles, and interacted in character. You may have practiced certain skills, such as writing or drawing. Depending on how the pretend teacher ran the class (which was often as an authoritarian), you may have been required to

sit still for long periods of time and listen to lectures or instructions. The game also would have reflected and even developed attitudes toward school, what educational psychologists call **dispositions toward learning.** *In sum, the childhood social activity of playing school was also a learning ground in many other areas of development — academic, creative, and physical.*

HighScope recognizes that early social and emotional experiences can shape the rest of a child's life. While children's first and primary social experiences take place at home, high-quality child care and preschool programs support and supple-

Early social experiences influence our relationships with family, friends, and coworkers. Because learning is social, interactions also provide the context for gaining knowledge and skills.

Chapter Learning Objectives

By the end of this chapter, you will be able to

❖ Explain why early learning in social-emotional development is important

❖ Describe the HighScope key developmental indicators in social-emotional development

❖ Understand and begin to apply the strategies adults use to support early learning in social-emotional development

Social-emotional development has always been important to early educators. HighScope creates nurturing environments to give young children a good start on schooling and life.

ment family relationships. In some instances — for example, for children living in homeless shelters or with a depressed parent — preschool programs can provide the consistent environments and trusting relationships children need to grow and thrive.

As the "playing school" example shows, early social experiences are important in their own right. In their encounters with others, children observe and try out different ways of interacting. These early experiences influence children's later ability to form satisfying relationships with family, friends, and workmates. Social exchanges also provide a context for gaining knowledge and skills in other areas. When the social context for learning is positive and supportive, children are likely to become engaged and motivated learners. When the context is harsh or punitive, children are apt to turn away from school, often without more positive or nurturing alternatives.

For these reasons, the HighScope Curriculum puts a high value on creating warm and nurturing environments in which young children can get a good start on schooling and life. In this chapter, we describe children's early social and emotional development and how educators can support it. [*Note:* Later in the book (Chapter 16) we discuss a related but distinct content area, social studies. Whereas social-emotional development deals with children's ability to regulate their feelings and behaviors, and to interact with peers and adults, social studies refers more broadly to children's ability to understand communal rules and be good citizens.]

Why Early Social-Emotional Development Is Important

Social-emotional development has always been a major concern of early childhood education. Today's practitioners face special challenges as they strive to support children confronted by changing family dynamics, unsafe neighborhoods, war, natural disasters, and academic pressures at ever younger ages. In addition to learning social norms at home and school, young children in the twenty-first century are increasingly exposed to influences from the media and technology, where they face evolving and often contradictory expectations for individual and interpersonal behavior.

For these reasons, the importance of paying attention to social as well as intellectual development is receiving renewed attention among educators and the public at large. The National Education Goals Panel (NEGP; Kagan et al., 1995) sees social development as a critical area of readiness because so much early learning takes place in a group setting. Other recent literature citing its importance includes the major report

Terms Used in This Chapter

• dispositions toward learning • social competence • supportive emotional climate • civic competence
• collaborative play • parallel play • problem-solving approach to conflict resolution

Neurons to Neighborhoods by the National Research Council (2000b) and the Society for Research in Child Development Social Policy Report *Emotions Matter: Making the Case for the Role of Young Children's Emotional Development for Early School Readiness* (Raver, Izard, & Kopp, 2002). Policymakers cite the results of the HighScope Perry Preschool Study and similar findings (see Chapter 3) to show that high-quality programs can set at-risk children on a path toward better social adjustment during their school years and into adulthood.

Social-emotional development begins at birth and continues into high school and beyond. Depending on the security of their attachments with parents and other caregivers, children may learn from their earliest experiences to view the world as a welcoming and exciting place, a place to approach with caution, or one that is empty of love and stimulation — perhaps even fraught with peril. A safe environment invites exploration, while an untrustworthy one may lead to confusion, anger, or hopelessness.

Young children are social beings. From late toddlerhood on, their desire for relationships expands from associations with adults to other children, especially those with shared interests.

The way children are treated affects how they view and feel about themselves. Their early self-image in turn determines how they approach learning and human relationships throughout their school years and, indeed, throughout their lives. In other words, their inner emotional well-being affects their outward-directed social selves. As noted early childhood researchers Lilian Katz and Diane McClellan say, "Socially competent young children are those who engage in satisfying interactions and activities with adults and peers and through such interactions further improve their own competence" (1997, p. 1).

Social-emotional growth in the early years affects, and is affected by, virtually every other aspect of children's development. Infants are born with innate temperaments and individual dispositions that affect how they approach and deal with interpersonal and educational experiences (see Chapter 10). For preschoolers, their expanding use of language (see Chapter 11) and the ability to form mental images helps them better understand their own motivations and express their wishes to others. Preschoolers' developing capacity for social relations is also characterized by the following features: a desire for friendship, a struggle to resolve the competition between "me" (an individual, and sometimes self-centered, perspective) and "we" (identification with the group) and growing **social competence.** These are each described in the sections that follow.

Desire for friendship. Children are social beings. Beginning in late toddlerhood and continuing throughout the preschool years, they expand their desire for relationships with adults to include associations with other children. In particular, they appear to seek friends who share their interests and who approach activities with the same spirit of investigation.

> *At small group time, Marissa and Lee used the blocks and the dollhouse figures together. Their figures talked to each other and Marissa and Lee built structures for them.*

Children may not always know how to create friendships. They may stand uncertainly on the sidelines or attempt to force their way into the group. Even friends often fight over toys, ideas, or who gets to be the leader. But because their desire to connect with others is strong, young children are generally very open to discovering and learning the strategies that will allow such connections to develop.

"Me" versus "we." Sometimes a child's need to do or get something conflicts with the desire for friendship. For example, a child may want to play "firefighters" with a friend but at the same time want to hold the hose the friend is carrying. The urge to be independent (the "me") does not

128

> **HighScope Key Developmental Indicators in Social-Emotional Development**
>
> ❖ Taking care of one's own needs
> ❖ Expressing feelings in words
> ❖ Building relationships with children and adults
> ❖ Creating and experiencing collaborative play
> ❖ Dealing with social conflict

always mesh with the longing to be part of the group (the "we"). Preschoolers are increasingly aware of the tensions that arise when these desires meet head-on.

Teachers play a critical role in creating a **supportive emotional climate** in which children's conflicting desires are seen as normal and problem-solving can proceed in a nonjudgmental way. To become a participating group member, children must be able to give up some individuality for the greater good. Professors Richard Jantz and Carol Seefeldt (1999) see this transition from the "me" of toddlerhood to the "us" or "we" of preschool as the beginning of **civic competence,** or the ability to participate as a responsible citizen in society, which continues to develop into the elementary and adolescent years. (See also its relationship to

the development of social studies knowledge and skills, discussed in Chapter 16.)

Social competence. Preschoolers gradually begin to sort out the types of conflicts described above, such as what to do when their intentions clash with those of others. As young children experience and understand the consequences of their actions, they become better able to choose between positive and negative social interactions. Using language to understand others and express themselves gives them a powerful tool for resolving conflicts in nonaggressive ways. And while they still focus a great deal on their own needs, young children are becoming increasingly aware of, and sensitive to, the needs and feelings of others. In fact, research shows they are more capable of empathy than scientists originally thought (Katz & McClellan, 1997).

Key Developmental Indicators in Social-Emotional Development

HighScope has five key developmental indicators in social and emotional development. The first two focus on emotional self-help and awareness, while the remaining three focus on social relations and understanding others. Each indicator and how adults support its development is described below.

🔑 *Taking care of one's own needs*

Young children enjoy doing things for themselves. Self-help includes such skills as getting dressed, using the toilet and washing up, serving food to oneself or others, retrieving and putting away materials, cutting and gluing an art project, making a tower of blocks balance, or getting emotional support and reassurance when one is upset. As children learn to take care of themselves, they also become interested in taking care of others.

Adults are sometimes amazed at how long and intently children will work at mastering a self-help skill such as zipping up their jacket. The satisfaction on children's faces when they succeed at such a task is obvious. It is also important to remember that children need only meet their own goal for "success," not an adult's standard. For example, a glue job doesn't have to be neat or precise for a child to be happy with the result.

Young children enjoy doing things for themselves and will often work intently at mastering self-help skills. HighScope encourages and supports children's desire for independence.

Below are some of the **support strategies** you can use to encourage young children to take care of their own needs.

▲ **Let children do things for themselves.** Adults are often tempted to do things for children, such as helping them clean up a spill or get dressed. It is faster and often neater. But young children cannot learn how to take care of their own needs unless they have opportunities and plenty of time to do so. HighScope teachers understand that children will not do things perfectly. Resist the temptation to improve on or correct a child's performance, such as giving the table an extra swipe with the towel or straightening the blocks on the shelf. It sends the child a message that he or she is not competent or "good enough," and the child may give up trying.

It is also important to recognize that children may take a long time carrying out skills they are just developing, such as putting on their boots or gathering supplies for an art project. Build enough time into the daily routine for children to practice self-help skills without feeling rushed.

> *At cleanup time, Juan used a butter knife to pry the dried play dough out of the toaster.*

> *Before outside time, Sophie put on her coat, zipped it, and then put on her hat and gloves by herself. "I'm all set!" she announced.*

▲ **Encourage children to use tools.** Children enjoy learning how to use simple household tools such as scissors, staplers, hole punches, hammers, screwdrivers, brooms, and shovels. They also take pleasure in performing many chores, such as washing dishes or sorting markers and their caps. These activities may provide experiences with the sense of touch (such as the feel of suds in warm, soapy water) and also opportunities for growth and learning (for example, exercising arm muscles, matching colors, or practicing eye-hand coordination).

In addition to providing tool-using opportunities at work time, plan small-group activities that allow children additional practice with these skills. Such experiences often lead children to make plans for incorporating tools into their work-time activities. Becoming aware of, and adept at using,

a wide variety of everyday tools is an important component of school readiness — indeed, of life readiness.

> *At work time in the block area, Matthew noticed a tangle of yarn looped and knotted around the handle of the Magnatile basket. When Enid (a teacher) asked him how he could fix it, Matthew said, "I know, cut it." He got scissors, then cut and cleared away the yarn.*

▲ **Support children's attempts to take care of their emotional as well as physical needs.** Being able to take care of ourselves emotionally as well as physically is important to managing our lives well. Adults can often anticipate the kinds of emotional reassurance children need. Preschoolers become increasingly able to communicate and satisfy such needs on their own as well. Typical examples include curling up with a security object at naptime (such as a blanket or stuffed animal) or seeking out and sitting on a teacher's lap for a while at arrival time before venturing out into the play group.

> *Kevin came over to his teacher, Mary, and nestled in the crook of her arm with his head down. Mary said, "You look a little sad right now," and Kevin said, "I need a hug today."*

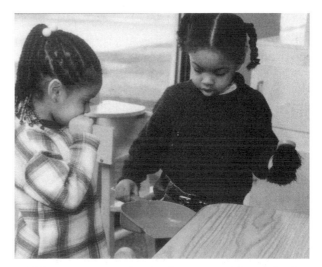

Children may not perform tasks up to "adult standards." Rather than criticize or correct them, teachers encourage children to see themselves as motivated and competent problem-solvers

Expressing feelings in words

People experience feelings from the very beginning of their lives. Infants and young toddlers depend on adults to recognize these feelings and respond accordingly. However, older toddlers and preschoolers have a new set of resources for dealing with emotions: their growing language and representational skills. They can use words to differentiate and label feelings — words such as *happy, sad, angry, excited,* and *scared.* As they hear additional feeling words used by adults, young children expand their self-expressive vocabulary, which can sometimes surprise us with its sophistication:

> *At work time in the toy area, Patrick crossed his arms and said he was mad that someone knocked over his Duplo building.*

> *At work time at the computer, Felicity called out to Andrea (a teacher), "Carol (another teacher) and I are frustrated" and explained that the computer game would not work.*

Being able to identify feelings gives children a sense of control over them. If the feelings are positive, language provides another way besides gestures or facial expressions to communicate that they are feeling good. If the feelings are negative, words also give voice to the feelings and make it easier to identify the source of a problem and take appropriate steps — alone or in interaction with others — to solve it. Use the following **support strategies** to help children develop these skills.

▲ **Establish a supportive emotional climate.** A supportive emotional climate is one in which children feel free to express emotions because adults acknowledge and accept them. Because children live so much in the present and focus on themselves, their entire world may be colored by the emotion of the moment. Encourage children to talk about and express their emotions (without harming others) and the circumstances behind them. An understanding of child development allows teachers not to think of children as being "bad" for the depth of their feeling but, rather, to expect it and to understand it as normal.

Expressing a feeling and having it acknowledged is sometimes enough for the emotion to subside and the child to regain a sense of balance and control. If necessary, help the child (or chil-

A supportive emotional climate allows children to express their feelings, both positive and negative. In addition to using words, children convey emotions through dramatic play, art, and music.

dren) deal with the problem that is causing the emotion. (See "Dealing with social conflict," the last key developmental indicator described in this section, as well as the discussion on conflict resolution on pp. 33–36 in Chapter 5.)

▲ **Help children label their feelings.** As you help a child identify his or her feelings, strive to do the following: First, encourage and enable the child to come up with his or her own words for feelings. Second, avoid imposing your own assumptions on the child. To begin this process, listen to how the child describes the situation and the name the child attaches to the emotion. If the child does not have a word for the feeling, you can help him or her by using a general term; for example, "You're upset because Tanya took the big doll and you wanted to play with it, too."

Children are often not receptive to learning new vocabulary words in the heat of emotion; therefore, introduce these terms at neutral times, such as while reading or telling a story. Adults can also use vocabulary words to describe their own feelings, for example, "I'm happy today because it's sunny" or "When my dog ate my shoe, it made me feel angry." When children learn feeling words in a calm context, it is easier for them to apply these terms to their own emotions at a later time.

> *At work time in the house area, Stevie told Barbara (a teacher) he was angry because he couldn't see the pictures in the book when Katie's hand was on the page.*

At work time, Daniel talked to Madge (a teacher) about his dad going on trips and missing him when he was gone.

▲ **Encourage children to role play and make up or illustrate stories about their experiences.** Children often express their emotions through play, stories, or pictures instead of talking about them directly. They might tell or "write" the stories themselves, or dictate them to a teacher to record (see Chapter 11 for more on dictation). Likewise, they might paint a picture and write or dictate a caption about the feelings it expresses. The story or picture is most likely to reflect the emotions of an earlier situation or experience, once children are no longer caught up in the full intensity of their feelings.

Role playing, inventing stories, and creating art can also give children practice for identifying and expressing feelings in the future. When children invent or illustrate stories that explore emotion in the context of play, and adults support their efforts, it emphasizes the idea that feelings are okay and not something to be afraid of. Further, as children act out scenarios that evoke strong emotions — such as illness and injury or stressful situations at home — it gives them confidence that they can master their feelings in the real world.

> *At work time in the toy area, Turk stacked Duplos on the Duplo table and said it was a hospital. He crashed cars into Duplo people, put the people in the hospital, and said, "The car guys just want to bash into people."*

> *At work time in the block area, Zachary made a bed out of blocks and pretended to sleep on it, along with Rhoda (a teacher) and other children. Zachary picked up his cell phone and said he had to call his "boss." He said, "I might get fired."*

🔑 *Building relationships with children and adults*

Child care or preschool is often a young child's first opportunity to establish relationships outside the home or immediate neighborhood. Most youngsters talk proudly about "going to school" and are eager to tell parents and other family members about their growing social circle.

Young children's ability to establish these relationships with adults and other children is important for several reasons. First and foremost, the program becomes a place where the child wants to spend time. Additionally, human connections provide an important context for all kinds of learning — cognitive, creative, and physical, as well as social. Early relationships also guide children's later interactions with teachers and other students when they begin formal schooling. You can use the following **support strategies** to help young children form meaningful and positive relationships.

▲ **Establish supportive relationships with children.** It seems obvious that teachers should build good relationships with children. Yet this does not happen automatically. HighScope preschool teachers learn to continuously monitor their own behavior with children to make sure positive interactions are frequent and, above all, genuine. Teachers treat children with kindness, not only because they care about them but also because they understand them and see children's "mistakes" as matters of development rather than as personality problems.

Adults in HighScope programs also have genuine conversations with children — not exchanges that are mechanical or managerial. Instead of bombarding children with questions or orders, teachers listen to what children have to say and respond appropriately, much as they would do

Adults in HighScope programs establish authentic relationships with young children by having genuine conversations with them and playing as partners.

132

naturally when having a conversation with another adult. Children sense this respect and respond in kind in their interactions with adults and other children. Finally, HighScope emphasizes that if teachers trust in their own ability to relate well to children — based on a knowledge of child development and effective teaching practices — it becomes a self-fulfilling prophecy. The adults' confidence will then be reflected in the interactions that children initiate.

> *At work time at the sand table, Mona called Hillary (a teacher) over and said, "Will you play with me?" Hillary said "Yes" and knelt down beside her. Mona then began to make sand cupcakes for Hillary and Frank (another teacher).*

HighScope encourages young children to form relationships with their peers. Friends often plan, work, and recall together as well as share other group activities and help one another.

▲ **Maintain a stable group of children and adults.** Relationship building takes time. Children, like adults, get to know others through repeated contact. They learn about another person's interests and whether that person is quiet or talkative, prefers a slow or fast pace, is someone to be silly or serious with, and so on. To give children time to form relationships, strive to maintain a consistent grouping of adults and children that the children relate to on a day-to-day basis. For example, in HighScope programs, one adult typically meets with the same small group of children for planning and recall, small-group time, and snacks.

As in all high-quality early childhood programs, adults in HighScope settings try to mini-

mize staff turnover by creating a supportive work environment. Even if the program has student interns or parent and community volunteers, these assistants supplement but never replace the teaching team members who support, teach, and care for the children every day.

▲ **Support relationships children establish with one another.** When your daily observations show children forming friendships, you can use a number of strategies to support them. For example, you might put two friends in the same planning and recall group so they can make plans to play together and jointly recall what they did. If the children's play revolves around certain themes and materials, you can make sure these materials are plentiful and easy for the friends to access. You can also encourage children to check out what their friends are doing at small-group time, to sit next to a friend during a field trip experience, and to interact in other ways.

> *At work time in the house area, Janie said to Elise, "I'm gonna ask my Mom if you can come to my house." Elise replied, "I can see what is in your bedroom," and Janie said, "I have a cat." When their mothers came to pick them up at the end of the day, their teacher mentioned having overheard this conversation and the mothers arranged a play date.*

▲ **Provide opportunities for children to interact with other children with whom they are less familiar.** For example, you might put two children who like to tell jokes in the same small group or ask the two children who were fascinated by the cider press to put the cider mill field trip photos into an album together. Friendships can blossom as children share mutual interests and skills; at the same time, new friendships give children rich exposure to classmates with backgrounds and personalities different from their own. Finally, know that it is also natural for young children to play alone. HighScope teachers don't require children to socialize, nor do they grow concerned when children choose to spend part of the day in solitary or parallel play.

▲ **Refer children to one another.** You can also support peer interactions by referring children to one another, either for help solving a problem or as a source of ideas. Here is an example of the first type of support: When Olivia was having trouble getting two pieces of clay to stick together, her teacher said, "I see Rudy attached his. Maybe he could show you how he did it." An example of the second type of support would be a teacher commenting to the table of children at small-group time, "I see that Zach is bending his pipe cleaners into the letters of his name." Some children may be inspired to look at what Zach is doing and either imitate his actions or come up with their own variations (for example, "I'm making a *C* for Christina" or "I'm bending mine into a kitty").

Such referrals serve multiple purposes. They promote social development by giving children concrete reasons to interact. Another benefit is that encouraging children to turn to one another acknowledges their competence in solving problems and taking care of their own and others' needs. Children are also then more likely to offer help on their own.

> *At outside time, when Delilah approached Katherine (a teacher) with a problem about getting a turn on the swing, Stella (another child) interjected, "I can help Delilah." Stella walked Delilah to the tire swing and talked to Ashley and Thomas about giving Delilah a turn.*

🔑 Creating and experiencing collaborative play

Playing together with one or more peers is a complex skill that develops gradually in young children. They need to be able to communicate their intentions, listen to and imagine the ideas of others, and allow the "we" to take precedence over the "me."

Because so many important abilities develop during collaborative play, HighScope programs are designed to promote it. Supports for collaborative play are built in to the curriculum's basics; in particular, the physical environment (materials and space) and the daily routine (especially allowing ample time during plan-do-review and group times). You can help to scaffold cooperative play in preschoolers by using the **support strategies** described below.

▲ **Provide materials that encourage collaborative play.** Generally, any materials that are of interest to young children will inspire collaborative play (see Chapter 6 for a list of suggested materi-

---

Collaborative Play at Work Time

Children in HighScope programs are free to explore a wide range of ideas at work time. They carry out their own intentions, rather than performing a structured activity designed by an adult. They learn from one another and build on the thoughts and actions of their classmates. Collaborative play also helps them see things from multiple perspectives. Children challenge one another's thinking, and sometimes this happens through conflict. A statement such as, "It is too more than yours!" can inspire children to devise a way of measuring the difference. Other times, they learn from differences in their experiences, such as when two children reenact Thanksgiving dinner in the house area and one says to the other, "My grandma put water chestnuts in the stuffing. They were crunchy!"

> *At work time in the block area, Evan and Quincy made a tent by putting a blanket over chairs. When Dottie asked to play, Evan said, "Sure, you can help put the blanket on."*

---

als). One child's ideas for using materials will often spark the interest of others, and each child's contributions will increase the complexity of the group's play. For example, blocks often lead to collaborative structure-building. Musical instruments encourage children to form a band.

Another strategy is to provide large-sized materials, equipment, or play items that require more than one child to operate or manage. Some examples: A rocking boat, which works best when there are at least two people, one on each side; long boards (in the block area), which require two children to carry and balance them; and couches and big beanbag chairs, which invite children to sit together while looking at a book or listening to music.

▲ **Allow enough space for collaborative play.** A basic HighScope principle is to allow enough space in each activity area for many children to play together (see Chapter 6). Spaces should be open and accessible so play in one area can spill over into another — for example, from the house area to the block area. The number of children who can play in each area is not set by

134

the teacher. So when the play "overflows," being able to extend the activity into an adjoining space allows children to continue in a natural way.

A less obvious area for collaboration is the computer area. Early mathematics researcher Doug Clements (2004) points out that working on the computer is something many children actually like to do with one another. Therefore, arranging the computer area so two or more children can sit around each keyboard and monitor can encourage interaction.

> *At work time at the computer, Davy showed Wendell which icon to click on to print his picture and story.*

It is also important to recognize that the art area is not just easels and tables but also includes floor and wall space. Children can spread out and work together on large pieces of art (such as murals or collages) or they can engage in **parallel play** (that is, work side by side) while observing and getting ideas from one another.

The program's outdoor area is another space to design for collaborative play. In addition to having outdoor equipment that children use together, HighScope settings include open spaces where children can run, roll, race, and move together freely.

▲ **Encourage children to plan, work, and recall together.** Encouraging children to plan together acknowledges the importance of their collaboration, while work time provides many opportunities for their initial ideas to evolve into complex play. When they recall as a team, each one adds richness and details to the narrative. For example, at planning time, addressing a question such as, "Linda and José, what will you need to build the engine?" to both children can result in each one adding to the list of materials they will use. Likewise, a simple teacher comment such as, "Jonah, Rafael, and Tracy, I saw you all working in the house area together," can encourage children to elaborate on their playmates' statements during recall.

▲ **Provide opportunities for collaborative play at group times.** When your teaching team plans small- and large-group times, think about what types of experiences will encourage collaborative play. Here are some ideas: You might give children balls and ask the children to think of ways to pass the balls to one another. A group might meet outdoors so the children can wash doll clothes, ground-level windows, or playground equipment — this invites the children to

Children do not intend to misbehave, rather they make social "mistakes." HighScope teachers actively involve young children in learning appropriate ways to resolve conflicts.

collaborate as they carry tubs of water or divide the tasks of washing, wringing, hanging, or drying items. Children can collaborate on an imaginary voyage, each contributing items to take onboard or suggesting sights they see on their journey. Finally, large-group movement and music activities provide many opportunities for children to take turns leading and following. This allows them to share ideas and expand on one another's input, which is the very essence of collaborative play.

Dealing with social conflict

Because the "me" often overpowers the "we," young children inevitably have conflicts as they play. These conflicts — perhaps over who uses a toy, sits next to a friend, or passes out snacks — often result in verbal or physical aggression.

> *At the snack table, Grace wanted to sit close to Tilda (another child). Tilda began to gently push her away. Grace said, "I want to sit there." Ellen (a teacher) acknowledged that Grace wanted to stay where she was and asked Grace and Tilda what they could do to solve the problem of them being too close. Grace said she could move her chair, and then moved it a bit farther away.*

Strategies for Supporting Social-Emotional Development: A Summary

Taking care of one's own needs

__ Let children do things for themselves.

__ Encourage children to use tools.

__ Support children's attempts to take care of their emotional as well as physical needs.

Expressing feelings in words

__ Establish a supportive emotional climate.

__ Help children label their feelings.

__ Encourage children to role play and make up or illustrate stories about their experiences.

Building relationships with children and adults

__ Establish supportive relationships with children.

__ Maintain a stable group of children and adults.

__ Support relationships children establish with one another.

__ Provide opportunities for children to interact with other children with whom they are less familiar.

__ Refer children to one another.

Creating and experiencing collaborative play

__ Provide materials that encourage collaborative play.

__ Allow enough space for collaborative play.

__ Encourage children to plan, work, and recall together.

__ Provide opportunities for collaborative play at group times.

Dealing with social conflict

__ Treat conflicts as a normal part of development.

__ Prevent conflicts when possible.

__ Help children resolve conflicts when they do occur.

Children tend to name-call or hit one another when they have not yet learned how to resolve conflicts appropriately. As HighScope teacher-trainer Betsy Evans says in her book *You Can't Come to My Birthday Party! Conflict Resolution With Young Children* (2002), "Children don't misbehave, they make mistakes" (p. 13). Therefore, teachers can view such occasions as learning opportunities, rather than something to be dreaded or avoided. By implementing the following **support strategies** used by HighScope teachers, you will play an active mediating role, but the emphasis should be on children devising their own solutions, rather than adults taking over.

▲ **Treat conflicts as a normal part of development.** As preschoolers are still quite self-centered, the desire to have their own needs met competes with the wish to be part of the group. At this age, children also think very concretely. Ideals such as "sharing" or "fairness" are too abstract for them. Children can describe *what* happened and *how* they feel, but they cannot analyze *why* they or others respond in a certain way. Therefore, when talking to children, focus on specific information — such as what the dispute is about and how each person feels. So, for example, instead of saying, "Jim and Carl, you have to share the truck," you might gather information from each child and then say, "Jim you want the truck because it is the same size as your other one. And Carl you want the truck because you used it yesterday and want to keep using it today. How can we solve this problem?"

▲ **Prevent conflicts when possible.** Many components of the HighScope active learning approach help to prevent conflicts. For example, by having ample and multiple sets of materials, there is less fighting over toys. Further, when children

136

have choices and pursue their own interests they are less likely to feel bored or frustrated — emotions that can lead to fighting or other "behavior management problems" (note that the HighScope approach generally considers the program, not the child, to be the problem).

A consistent daily routine also gives young children the reassurance and sense of control they need to manage their own behavior. Finally, since adults plan for transitions between activities, children do not have to wait or remain idle and so are less likely to get into conflicts. If transitions are short and playful, with reasonable choices, children quickly become engaged in the next activity.

Making their own choices and decisions has resulted in fewer behavior problems in the classroom. Because children are actively learning, there is no time for boredom. There is less crying, fighting, hitting, kicking, and "s/he has mine." (Bakersfield, Calif., Teacher)

▲ **Help children resolve conflicts when they do occur.** HighScope teachers learn in training to use a six-step **problem-solving approach to conflict resolution** (Evans, 2002). When teachers use these steps and feel confident about their ability to handle social conflicts, they not only help young children learn important social lessons, they also encourage language development, reflection, and problem-solving. (See pp. 33–36 for a summary of the steps and an example, as well as a discussion of the adult's role in helping children learn how to resolve social conflicts.)

Try These Ideas Yourself

1. List what you consider to be the five most important things preschoolers need to know or be able to do in the area of social-emotional development when they enter kindergarten. Why do you think these are the most important? How can teachers support the development of the knowledge and skills you listed?

2. In the following scenario, identify the key developmental indicators that show social and emotional development. What kinds of learning are occurring in other areas of development? What could you as a teacher do to support and extend the learning? (Refer to the list of KDIs on p. 11.)

Brenda and Mikey are pretending to be kitty cats under one of the small-group tables. "We need bowls for milk," says Brenda. "I'll get some in the house area," replies Mikey. When he brings them back, Brenda says, "Those are too small. We're really thirsty!" When Mikey says those were the only bowls he could find, they decide they will have to make their own bowls. "I know," says Mikey. "They can be square bowls. Let's make them out of the big blocks." Brenda and Mikey go to the block area and they each carry several blocks under the table. Greg comes over and asks what they are doing. "We're kitty cats and we're going to drink milk out of these big bowls," says Brenda. Greg asks if he can be a kitty cat, too. "No," says Mikey. Greg watches them for a while, then gets some more large blocks. "Bring them under here," says Brenda. "You can be the guy who pours the milk for the kitties."

3. Think of the last time you had a disagreement with someone (for example, a family member, friend, or colleague). Did the other person acknowledge your feelings? How did you respond? Did you acknowledge the other person's feelings? How did the other person respond? What ideas do your reflections give you for working with children in the classroom?

4. Think of all the words you can use with children that have to do with feelings (such as *happy, angry, sad*). Share your list with another adult and ask for additional ideas. Use these words when you help children identify and express their feelings. Write down the instances in which you used them and how children responded. Over time, notice if and under what circumstances they begin to use these words themselves.

Chapter 13

What Is the HighScope Curriculum in Physical Development, Health, and Well-Being?

❓ Think About It

"Pick me, please pick me," the child silently pleads as his or her classmates choose up sides for a game. Those who are selected first walk with pride to their place in the lineup. Posture erect, heads held high, their palms match those of their teammates perfectly as they "high five" one another. Meanwhile, the children still waiting to be chosen grow progressively more stooped and despondent. Even standing still, their bodies seem to fall apart with rejection and embarrassment. They would rather be any place other than the playing field.

Decades later, we can still remember which group we belonged to and the feelings it evoked. If we were one of the first children picked for the team, we felt it not only meant we were coordinated but also by extension popular, smart, and an all-around good student. By contrast, if we were chosen near the end, we took it as a negative reflection — not only of our athletic prowess but also of our general intelligence and likableness. This familiar ritual could also work in the opposite direction. That is, children who were not particularly talented at hitting a ball or scoring a basket but were well-regarded otherwise might be selected first for a sports team. Knowing they were well thought of, regardless of athletic ability, allowed them to play with gusto and self-confidence. They had fun!

At what point in our development does our self-image become so tied to our physical abilities? Very young children learning how to crawl or walk do not think in these terms. Their bodies are their own and they practice using them, gaining satisfaction at the same time they gain skill. No one has to be looking for an infant to roll over and over, or for a toddler to hurl himself or herself across the room in pursuit of a desired toy. "Look at me" only comes later, when the child senses that others (parents, siblings, caregivers) attach value to his or her physical accomplishments.

A curriculum that supports physical development, health, and well-being aims to recapture the sheer determination and delight of the young

Involvement with the physical world is important in HighScope programs. Children discover what their bodies can do and how they can use materials to carry out their intentions.

138

child's earliest experiences. It recognizes that physical development is not a contest or a means for gaining approval. All children need to see themselves as competent explorers, not as winners or losers. Young children love to move, and moving is one of the primary ways they learn about the world. To shake children's confidence in their ability to move with purpose and increasing skill is to discourage an important desire and pathway to learning. But to encourage children to discover what their bodies can do and how they can use materials to carry out their intentions is to give them a valuable self-image and a tool kit they will own for life. With its emphasis on "active participatory learning," the HighScope Curriculum naturally promotes children's physical involvement with the world as central to early growth and development.

Why Physical Development, Health, and Well-Being Is Important

Including physical development as a dimension of school readiness, the National Education Goals Panel (NEGP; Kagan et al., 1995) cites a strong body of research linking mothers' and children's health to children's school performance. Factors such as prenatal care and early nutrition affect brain development, which in turn impacts virtually every area of physical, mental, and social development. Maintaining good health and developing physical skills has many benefits for young children. Using their bodies to accomplish physical feats and complete tasks is gratifying to them. Physical development is also a way for children to learn other cognitive and social concepts, such as ideas about space and forming human relationships.

The proposition that children need to be "taught" how to develop physically may seem odd. We assume physical development happens on its own, provided children receive adequate nutrition and have opportunities to move around safely in the environment. However, it is a mistake to think that this is all there is to physical development. Professor Stephen Sanders, who developed one of the first preschool movement curricula in the country, says, "Movement programs enhance play, and play provides children with the opportunity to practice movement skills in a variety of contexts. Play alone, however, is not a substitute for helping children develop physical skills.… Some structuring of physical activity is necessary to help children maximize their movement experiences" (Sanders, 2002, p. 31).

Movement education is currently receiving increased national attention because of its potential health benefits. This country has seen an unprecedented rise in childhood obesity, which is in turn associated with increased risk for diabetes, heart disease, high blood pressure, colon cancer, and other health problems in adulthood. The percentage of children identified as overweight has more than doubled in the past 30 years. Along with poor diet, "physical inactivity has contributed to the 100% increase in the prevalence of childhood obesity in the United States since 1980" (Sanders, 2002, p. xiii). By contrast, children who develop basic motor skills (such as throwing, catching, skipping, galloping) and are physically active have a greater chance

Physical Education and Movement Education

The terms *physical education* and *movement education* are often used interchangeably. However, some early educators prefer the term *movement education* to emphasize its difference from the traditional physical education found in elementary and secondary grades.

Physical education typically emphasizes vigorous activity as an antidote to the time children spend sitting at their desks. It is often sports-related (involving rules) and competitive (with winners and losers). Furthermore, it is done at a specific time of day (think "gym class"), and carried out under the direction of a physical education specialist (think "gym teacher").

Movement education, while it may be vigorous, can also be less intense since young children exercise their large muscles throughout the day. Because rule-bound sports and competition are not appropriate for preschoolers, movement education focuses on developing physical skills such as balancing, kicking, galloping, throwing, and catching.

Further, although such activities are typically carried out at large-group and outside time, movement education can happen any time of the day; for example, "moving" the body in interesting ways during transitions. For that reason, planning and carrying our movement education is more often the responsibility of the regular classroom teacher rather than that of a physical education specialist.

Whichever term is used, the nature of physical or movement education is changing at the elementary level, too. The public is increasingly aware that getting children involved in regular physical activity can help to avert obesity and the other health problems that are costly to individuals and society as a whole. Programs that allow all children to be successful, are sensitive to individual differences in ability, and emphasize building skills that can be applied to a wide variety of endeavors, are likely to establish the early habits that result in lifelong fitness and the enjoyment of physical activity.

---

of participating in daily physical activity and being healthy adults (National Center for Health Statistics, 2004).

Developing and practicing basic physical abilities is also important in its own right. **Large and fine motor skills** — that is, physical movements involving larger or smaller muscles and motions — serve many functions in our lives. Physical coordination is essential to accomplishing many, if not most, everyday tasks. In addition, movement is, or should be, inherently pleasurable. There is joy in the motion of the body, whether just in feeling the freedom of using one's muscles or in expressing creativity through music and dance. Preschoolers enjoy moving their bodies to music in dance-like ways and maneuvering objects through space as they vary the direction and speed. Such freedom of expression can build young children's self-confidence and social skills.

Conversely, research shows that children who are less physically adept can have problems in other domains of development (Pica, 1997). They may lack social skills, perhaps because they are perceived by others (or themselves) as clumsy or as

Two Components of Physical Development

Broadly speaking, young children's physical development involves two components. One is their capacity to use and move their bodies in ways that are safe, satisfying, and purposeful. The other component is the ability to use objects with skill, confidence, purpose, and satisfaction. The preschool years are an especially exciting time to see both sets of capacities develop. Having mastered as toddlers the basics of locomotion (moving their bodies from place to place) and coordination (moving their limbs and handling objects with ease), preschoolers are now ready to apply these skills. HighScope programs support young children's continued physical growth and their growing ability to use their bodies and move with objects in increasingly complex ways.

---

physical "outsiders." Children's self-confidence as risk-takers may also be adversely affected, with troubling implications for their willingness to tackle

140 challenging academic and social tasks. As a result, the overall school performance and adjustment of children with undeveloped physical skills may suffer. The self-image that young children form in the early grades — positive or negative — can color their experiences for the rest of their school years and carry over into adulthood. In this chapter we discuss the importance of physical development, health, and well-being to children's overall development.

Key Developmental Indicators in Physical Development, Health, and Well-Being

HighScope has eight key developmental indicators (KDIs) in this content area, derived from the comprehensive movement curriculum developed by Phyllis Weikart (2000). Four KDIs focus on experiencing movement, two focus on observing and describing movement, and two focus on basic timing or "beat competence." Based on a framework used by many movement educators, moving the body is further divided into two categories — nonlocomotor and locomotor.

🔑 HighScope Key Developmental Indicators in Physical Development, Health, and Well-Being

❖ Moving in nonlocomotor ways (anchored movement: bending, twisting, rocking, swinging one's arms)

❖ Moving in locomotor ways (nonanchored movement: running, jumping, hopping, skipping, marching, climbing)

❖ Moving with objects

❖ Expressing creativity in movement

❖ Describing movement

❖ Acting upon movement directions

❖ Feeling and expressing steady beat

❖ Moving in sequences to a common beat

Nonlocomotor (or anchored) movements are those carried out with any part of the body while another part of the body is anchored in place. Examples include bending, twisting, stretching, swinging one leg, or raising one's arms while sitting on the floor.

Locomotor (or nonanchored) movements involve transferring weight while moving. Most locomotor movements involve traveling from place to place by such means as rolling, crawling, walking, running, galloping, jumping, hopping, and skipping. However, some locomotor movements, such as marching or jumping or hopping in place, do not involve traveling.

Below you will read about the strategies HighScope teachers use to promote young children's physical development, thereby enhancing their health, well-being, and readiness for school.

 Moving in nonlocomotor ways

Children like to try different positions as they play — for example, curling up in a ball, standing on one foot, or putting their head down between their knees to look behind them. They also like to explore various stationary movements such as swinging, bending, rocking, and twisting. These whole-body actions help them develop a sense of physical boundaries and coordination.

You can use the following **support strategies** to assist children's exploration of position and nonlocomotor movement.

▲ **Encourage children to explore a wide variety of positions.** Play position games with children. A classic one is "Statues," in which children move until asked to freeze in one position. Children also enjoy being the leader and having teachers and classmates imitate the poses they strike. They like to move their bodies in sand and snow (for example, making snow angels) and examine the visual effects created when they assume different positions and make various motions. Children can also try to make the same motion from different positions; for example, lying on their backs or their sides while lifting their legs.

▲ **Encourage children to explore different types of nonlocomotor movement.** Remaining stationary while moving their arms, legs, head, or upper body offers children many possibilities for learning what their bodies are capable of doing. For example, children might stand in place and swing their arms to music at large-group time or pretend to be trees bending in the wind or stretching their "branches" up to the sky.

Outside time also offers possibilities for nonlocomotor movement. Although we commonly think of the outdoors as a place to move vigorously from one location to another, children enjoy putting energy into stationary types of movements, too. For example, as they twist hard back and forth or bob their heads up and down, they can feel changes in air currents or observe shifts in light and shadow.

▲ **Call attention to children's nonlocomotor movements.** As children engage in various types of nonlocomotor movements, you can support their movement awareness and movement skill development in several ways: Play games that focus on one movement at a time so children can fully explore and experience each one. (For example, hokey pokey lets children repeat an action, such as shaking, with different body parts.) Make up chants, rhymes, and songs that help children explore different types of anchored movements, such as thumping, pounding, punching, dabbing, cutting, pushing, pulling, rocking, and twisting. Children enjoy playing the role of leader. They can suggest different actions for a movement game, or adults can suggest an action — such as wiggling — while children choose which body part to use in doing it.

▲ **Label nonlocomotor actions and their characteristics.** As children engage in these types of anchored (stationary) movements, label both the action (swinging, twisting, and so on) and its characteristics. For example, motions vary in *direction* (up and down, in and out), *size* (big or little movements), *level* (high or low), *intensity* (weak or strong), *shape* (bodies in a circle, straight line, bent at an angle), and *timing* (fast or slow). These variations may happen accidentally at first. But as they learn these labels, preschoolers enjoy deliberately making their bodies perform according to these different characteristics. For example, they may try twisting in slow motion or standing high on tiptoe and then crouching down as low as possible.

 Moving in locomotor ways

Young children embody the "active" in active learning! They walk, run, roll, climb, march, hop, gallop, and skip. Compared to toddlers, preschool-

ers are more skilled at balance and coordination. As a result, they are able to move with confidence, and they are proud of their emerging physical abilities.

There are a number of **support strategies** you can use to acknowledge and encourage the development of young children's locomotor skills. The idea, as noted at the beginning of this chapter, is not to praise or compare children's accomplishments but to show interest and let children know adults value these activities.

▲ **Provide space for movement.** Children need open spaces where they can move their bodies and manipulate objects freely without endangering themselves or others. Therefore, arrange your classroom with this goal in mind. Provide large, uncluttered areas where children can move their bodies without bumping into things and where they can carry or swing objects freely. The outdoors provides even more open space in which young children can run and jump, swing and climb, roll down the hill, and ride wheeled toys. Note that these learning environments allow preschoolers to safely engage in both locomotor and nonlocomotor actions.

At large-group time, the children spread out and spun around with their arms extended in different positions.

In addition to physical space, young children need psychological space in which to move. They need to know that adults will encourage and support them as they test and stretch the physical

Children like to explore the effects of moving their bodies. For example, how does moving their arms and legs leave a dent and create interesting sound effects in a pile of crunchy leaves?

142

limits of their bodies or practice using equipment and tools. For many children, school is a welcome contrast to the physical constraints of home or other settings.

▲ **Provide time for movement.** Open and flexible space should be accompanied by flexible time periods that allow children to move at their own pace. Young children like and need to practice physical skills over and over. Work time, large-group time, and outside time are all occasions when preschoolers can experiment with movement, repeat and vary their actions, and move in a manner and at a pace that is comfortable for them.

Keep in mind that transitions provide other opportunities during the daily routine for children to try moving in different ways — to reach a destination (for example, going from the sink to the table for snack) or to achieve a goal (for example, carrying blocks from the floor to a shelf across the room). Above all, because moving and doing are natural for young children, plan the daily routine in a way that minimizes the amount of time preschoolers spend waiting.

▲ **Encourage children to explore different types of locomotor movement.** Plan games that involve running, jumping, and other active movements. These can take place during small- and large-group time, outside time, and transitions. Additionally, observing and helping children extend their work-time interests may lead to further opportunities for children to hop, leap, gallop, and so on.

> *At large-group time, Alex showed how to creep across the floor so the other children could imitate his movements. Some crawled on their knees, others crept with their stomachs flat on the ground.*

▲ **Give children movement challenges.** Extend children's movements by issuing challenges that intrigue them. For example, challenges might begin with the words "I wonder what would happen if…?" or "How else could you…" or "Does someone have a different way to…?" Preschoolers enjoy trying to move higher or lower, faster or slower, and according to other contrasts or extremes. In addition to enhancing children's motor skills, these challenges help them develop important concepts about space (higher and lower, backward and forward) and time (faster and slower). Children also like to experiment with accomplishing a goal in

In addition to supporting large-motor development, HighScope programs provide materials that can be manipulated to encourage the use of small muscles and eye-hand coordination.

different ways (for example, you might say, "How can you get from the table to the sink faster?"). As with other movement games, give children the chance to be leaders as well as followers.

▲ **Label locomotor actions and their characteristics.** As children respond to these challenges and invent their own movements, comment on and label their actions. Just as you will do with nonlocomotor movements, help make children aware of the properties of the locomotor action, including its *direction* (forward and back, in and out), *size* (big and small moves), *level* (the body held high, medium, or low), *pathway* (straight, zigzag, in circles), *intensity* (weak or strong), and *timing* (fast, medium, or slow).

 Moving with objects

HighScope learning environments offer attractive equipment and materials that children can manipulate, move with, and use to carry out their plans (see Chapter 6).

Use the following **support strategies** to foster children's experiences of moving with objects. These strategies are based on several types of materials that are particularly useful for supporting movement activities.

▲ **Provide materials that encourage the use of small muscles and develop eye-hand coordination.** HighScope classrooms, like all developmentally based early childhood programs, stock small items that small hands can hold, manipulate, and combine in various ways. Typical materials for preschoolers include jigsaw puzzles, beads and string, nesting toys, small blocks, miniature animals, pegs and pegboards, writing and art materials, and woodworking tools such as hammers, nails or golf tees, and soft wood (such as pine boards) or Styrofoam. Books, notepads, and containers with different types of lids and caps also help children practice fine-motor skills. Finally, dress-up clothes with different types of fasteners encourage the use of small muscles during children's dramatic play.

> *At small-group time, Natalie held a piece of paper in one hand and cut around the individual photographs on the page. She glued the photos onto another piece of paper.*

▲ **Provide lightweight and floating materials that children can easily set in motion.** Examples of lightweight items include scarves, streamers, and ribbons that float in the air as children release or move with them. Preschoolers also enjoy dressing in capes and tying long pieces of fabric around their arms or waists to see how the materials move as they change body positions or alter their speed.

▲ **Provide novel objects to hold while moving.** Young children may feel more secure if they hold on to objects while trying out new movements. Children can also see the effects of their movements by carrying interesting items as they swing, run, slide, and so on. For example, a pinwheel, a carton of water, or a strip of paper each will behave differently as a child "skates" across the room while holding the object. Noise-making objects, such as rhythm sticks, also intrigue children as accompaniments to different types of movement. Other novel objects include paper fans, chopsticks, popsicle sticks, strips of jingling bells or shells, and closed containers filled with sound-making materials such as pebbles, beads, or dry food such as rice.

> *The children carried buckets of water from the spigot to the garden. Sean observed that when he moved "a little fast" the water "wiggled" on the surface. Wendy raced across the yard and said "Oops!" when the water splashed over the edge. After she slowed down, she looked in the bucket and commented, "Now it's not doing anything."*

▲ **Provide materials to move on and with one's feet.** Once children have mastered walking, they are free to become interested in how their feet move. Preschoolers enjoy moving on or inside different things, such as sliding their feet atop paper plates, walking with their feet in boxes or adult-size shoes, strapping tin cans underneath their feet, or rolling dowels ahead of their toes.

▲ **Provide materials for tossing, throwing, kicking, striking, and catching.** Though all children like to play with balls, preschoolers are sometimes unable to handle their speed or bounce. It is therefore good to provide additional alternative (nonrubber) materials that can be used in similar ways. Examples include pompoms, beanbags, balls of yarn, balled woolen socks, and lightweight foam balls. Many of the floating objects described above (such as scarves) also can be thrown in the air and will return to earth slowly enough for children to catch, kick, or strike. Containers that make easy targets, such as large cardboard boxes or laundry tubs, are also good for practicing these large-motor movement skills. Of course, balls can still be part of the equipment list. However, for preschoolers, these balls should include large ones made of foam, rubber, or lightweight plastic. Broad bats and boards to practice hitting such objects are also appropriate.

▲ **Provide large items for pushing and pulling.** Large equipment includes wagons, wheelbarrows, carriages, tires, and big boxes, such as the ones household appliances come in. (Appliance stores and families are often happy to donate empty cartons.) Big equipment that children can push, pull, or use to transport people and objects meets several developmental goals. Children develop strength and coordination by maneuvering them around the room. Also, because they often require more than one person to manage, such objects can help promote collaboration.

> *Kerry and Gillian were playing with the racing cars. Zeke hung around nearby, wanting to join them but not sure how to*

144

enter their play. When Kerry said, "We need the big boards to build a race track," Zeke offered, "I can help carry them." "Come on," said Gillian. Zeke and Gillian carried the boards to the center of the room, each holding one end. Kerry told them where to put the boards and lined them up as Gillian and Zeke went to fetch more.

Expressing creativity in movement

Children like to express themselves through movement, sometimes contorting their bodies in almost unimaginable ways. It is important that young children feel comfortable experimenting with all types of positions and actions, knowing they will not be criticized or ridiculed for doing so.

Use the following **support strategies** to encourage children to use their imaginations and represent their ideas through creative movement.

▲ **Watch and comment on children's actions.** Notice the spontaneous ways that children express themselves with movement throughout the day. For example, at work time, Ilana's teacher commented, "You're walking slowly so the scarf doesn't fall off your head." During large-group time, another teacher noted the movements of two children and encouraged their classmates to imitate their idea: "Jonathan and Luke are flapping their arms like birds. I wonder if we can all try that." As other children took turns moving in various ways, the teacher labeled their actions, calling special attention to each one's use of representation.

▲ **Challenge children to solve movement problems throughout the day.** As previously noted, children enjoy movement challenges. You can help inspire young children's movement imaginations by inventing interesting and unusual challenges. For example, at cleanup, large-group, and recall time, respectively, you might say,

How can we move the blocks across the room with just our feet?

I wonder how you would move if you were a cow jumping over the moon.

Show us with your hands what you did at work time today.

Moving from place to place like animals, machines, scarves, or other familiar things in their environment gives children other ways to represent their experiences, much as visual art and music allow them to express their creativity through painting and singing.

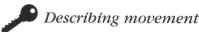 Describing movement

Preschoolers are eager and ready to learn the "vocabulary" of movement, and adults can help them learn and apply the new words and descriptions in a wide range of contexts. Use the following **support strategies** to help children learn movement words

▲ **Acknowledge and comment on children's movements.** Listen as children describe movements in their own way. Then, repeat and extend the children's language (for example, after Stevie says, "I'm stretching high!" you might say, "Stevie, you're stretching way up high to put away the small cubes and bending down low to shelve the big blocks"). As you acknowledge and comment on children's movements in this way, make your comments brief and natural. Calling too much attention to children's actions might disrupt the flow of their play. A short statement, on the other hand, invites the child to comment in return. For example, when Ruth, a teacher, commented, "Odell is turning in a circle," he replied, "I'm the mixing machine and I'm mixing up the cupcake batter."

▲ **Label movement throughout the daily routine.** Use every part of the daily routine to introduce movement terms and to encourage children to use movement vocabulary. Provide opportunities for children to plan, carry out, and recall various movements — for example, miming what they will do (or did) at work time. Invite children to move in different ways at transition times by saying things like "I can hop to the door," "I'm twirling with my napkin from the table to the sink," or "You're taking itty bitty steps carrying the chalk inside." At snacktime, a child may pass out plates and napkins using different types of movement. A sample teacher comment in this case might be, "You held the stack of plates in that hand and used this hand to put down the first one. Then you switched hands for the next place." At recall time, a teacher may ask about a child's movements

HighScope classrooms have large, uncluttered spaces where children can move their bodies and carry objects freely. They enjoy being both leaders and followers in these activities.

during work time: "Christina, can you show us how you pretended to be a snake?"

Large-group time provides many opportunities to expand children's movement vocabulary. You might begin with a single word, for example, chanting *Tap, tap, tap* as children tap their fingers on their heads to the beat of the music. Once children have the idea, you can ask them to name and show a movement for others to imitate. Preschoolers usually suggest simple movements such as shaking, waving, jiggling, bouncing, and twisting. Occasionally they come up with more complicated movements, allowing them and/or the teacher to use elaborated language. Sometimes children invent vocabulary words to describe their actions. You can acknowledge children's inventiveness by repeating the words they create.

> *"I'm squiggling my arms around and around," said Todd. "Let's all squiggle our arms," said his teacher.*

 Acting upon movement directions

Preschoolers are able to follow and describe more complex movement directions than are toddlers. For example, a toddler can respond to a simple direction, such as "Find teddy," or describe what he or she is doing by using the phrase "Get ball." A preschooler, with expanded verbal and representational powers, can follow a two-step direction

("Get the stool and bring it to the bookshelf") and also offer more complex directions ("First you put this leg in front, and then you lift the other one behind you").

The following **support strategies** will help you foster preschoolers' growing ability and interest in working with movement directions.

▲ **Encourage children to use and give movement directions.** Listen to and acknowledge children's spontaneous use of directions in their indoor and outdoor play. Comment on the directions children create and interpret, imitate their movements, and follow children's verbal and physical instructions. Group games provide many opportunities for young children to hear, understand, follow, and give directions. For example, a simplified version of Simon says, in which every instruction begins with that phrase and there are no winners or losers, is a fun way for children to follow or give movement directions.

> *Leah said, "Simon says scrunch your fingers." When no one seemed to understand, she said, "Like this, see. You scrunch 'em" and showed the other children what she wanted them to do. They imitated her movement and Leah smiled.*

▲ **Separate verbal and physical movement directions.** It is easier for preschoolers to understand movement instructions if words and actions are communicated separately. For example, a simple verbal direction at the beginning of large-group time will help get a movement activity started. You might *say without the accompanying motion,* "Pat your hands on your head." Allow a pause to give children time to listen, comprehend, and carry out the movement. After children are performing the action, you might ask a question such as, "Where else can you pat?" This gives each child who wants to take a turn an opportunity to state a movement direction and experience the pleasure and power of being the leader. Other times that verbal instructions are effective include planning time and transitions. For example, during some transitions you might say something like, "Jump to the area where you plan to play," or "Think of a 'low' way to move to the coat rack."

You can also show children how to *move without using words.* For example, you might begin large-group time by standing in the circle and tapping a foot in front of your body. Children

146

will quickly imitate your action. After a while, you might change the movement, for example, switching to the other foot or tapping to the side. Again, children will follow what you demonstrate. Once they have the idea, the children will be eager to act as leaders, too, and to show a movement for you and the other children to imitate.

🔑 *Feeling and expressing steady beat*

Infants first feel a steady beat[1] when they are rocked by an adult who is singing, playing music, or saying a rhyme to them. Toddlers and preschoolers enjoy swaying from side to side, tapping a hand or foot, or patting with an object as they listen to music. They also create their own steady beat, for example, when they pump on the swings or bang two blocks together. As adults, we, too, find ourselves nodding or tapping to music or an inner beat as we work around the house, take a walk, or pound a nail. A steady beat is naturally pleasing. It can energize us and offer comfort.

Being able to keep a steady beat also prepares preschoolers to coordinate their actions with others as they enter school and mature into adulthood. For example, a feeling for steady beat is essential to singing in a choir, playing with a band or orchestra, rowing with a crew team, or twirling around the dance floor with a partner.

You can use multiple **support strategies** to help young children internalize steady beat and to help prepare them for later experiences that rely on it.

▲ **Provide equipment with steady, predictable motions and sounds.** Equipment that allows and encourages young children to feel and express steady beat includes rocking chairs and rocking horses, swings, pedal toys and scooters, metronomes, and wind-up clocks or kitchen timers.

▲ **Provide opportunities for steady-beat experiences throughout the day.** At large-group time, many activities incorporate a steady beat, such as moving in nonlocomotor ways (swaying or rocking to music) and locomotor ways (marching in place or around the circle to music). Preschool-ers still enjoy being rocked and rocking themselves to music or steady tapping. A steady beat can help to calm a particularly boisterous group or provide comfort to an individual child who is upset.

Patting and rocking a beat can also underpin music and language experiences during various parts of the day. As you sing or chant rhymes with children, pat the beat on your knees, shoulders, or head, or rock your body to the steady beat and have children do the same (children often do this spontaneously, imitating the adult's actions). Then add the song, rhyme, or chant to the beat. Once children become familiar with this practice, they may add the song or chant themselves. You can also try tapping a beat when children play musical instruments, swing, or engage in other steady actions. Once the beat is set up physically, syllables (such as *la, la, la, la*) or words (such as *pat, pat* or *up, down, up, down,* or *side, side*) may then be added.

▲ **Acknowledge when children move to a steady beat as they play.** Children make beat-related movements during a wide range of outdoor, construction, role-playing, and art-making activities. Motions made while swinging or propelling a scooter are among the more obvious examples you will see in preschool, but remain alert to other instances and variations that you can acknowledge, comment on, and even imitate. For example, if a child makes a steady "chugging" sound while pretending to be a train going around the track, you might say something like, "Olya, you are chug-chug-chugging like a train!"

Other actions you might observe and comment on could include children steadily pounding a ball of clay into a flat circle, shuffling steadily across the room to carry dirty napkins to the trash, or clapping under water to set up regular fountains of splashing.

> *Odin pounded golf tees into Styrofoam with a steady beat. "Bang, bang, bang," he said each time his hammer hit. Marta, his teacher, began to chant "bang, bang, bang" with him. When Odin changed his chant to "Boom, boom, boom," Marta took up the new chant.*

---

[1]**Beat** is not the same as **rhythm.** Beat is a steady sequence of pulses in which each pulse has the same length or duration. Rhythm is a variation in the division between beats for shorter or longer duration. For example, the phrase *"**Ma**-ry **bad** a **lit**-tle **lamb**"* has four "marching" beats (**in bold**) and two "organizational" or "rocking" beats (the first and second half of the phrase, indicated by underline). It has seven pulses in rhythm (in *italics*). Because beat is steady, consistent, organized, and predictable, beat (not rhythm) is appropriate to emphasize with young children.

Strategies for Supporting Physical Development, Health, and Well-Being: A Summary

Moving in nonlocomotor ways

__ Encourage children to explore a wide variety of positions.

__ Encourage children to explore different types of nonlocomotor movement.

__ Call attention to children's nonlocomotor movements.

__ Label nonlocomotor actions and their characteristics.

Moving in locomotor ways

__ Provide space for movement.

__ Provide time for movement.

__ Encourage children to explore different types of locomotor movement.

__ Give children movement challenges.

__ Label locomotor actions and their characteristics.

Moving with objects

__ Provide materials that encourage the use of small muscles and develop eye-hand coordination.

__ Provide lightweight and floating materials that children can easily set in motion.

__ Provide novel objects to hold while moving.

__ Provide materials to move on and with one's feet.

__ Provide materials for tossing, throwing, kicking, striking, and catching.

__ Provide large items for pushing and pulling.

Expressing creativity in movement

__ Watch and comment on children's actions.

__ Challenge children to solve movement problems throughout the day.

Describing movement

__ Acknowledge and comment on children's movements.

__ Label movement throughout the daily routine.

Acting upon movement directions

__ Encourage children to use and give movement directions.

__ Separate verbal and physical movement directions.

Feeling and expressing steady beat

__ Provide equipment with steady, predictable motions and sounds.

__ Provide opportunities for steady-beat experiences throughout the day.

__ Acknowledge when children move to a steady beat as they play.

Moving in sequences to a common beat

__ Provide opportunities for moving in sequences throughout the day.

__ Include two-part movement sequences in action songs.

🔑 *Moving in sequences to a common beat*

Moving in sequences to a common beat is difficult for many preschoolers, who tend to focus on one movement at a time. Yet those who have mastered feeling and expressing steady beat may enjoy the challenge of doing two steady movements in succession, together with others.

You can employ several **support strategies** to give children who are able and interested an opportunity to explore moving in sequences to a common beat.

▲ **Provide opportunities for moving in sequences throughout the day.** You can initiate movement sequences at group times and stay alert to other opportunities that arise spontaneously during play. For example, at one preschool, when Rachel was pumping on the swings and started to chant, "Up, down, up, down," her teacher, Lena, picked up the chant. Soon other children began to chant, and Lena wondered what other up-down motions they could make. Some children alternated squatting and standing, others raised and lowered their arms, and still others nodded their heads up and down. Lena kept up the chant, which helped the children coordinate their movements.

▲ **Include two-part movement sequences in action songs.** Familiar action songs present many opportunities to build in two-movement sequences. For example, as children at one preschool chanted "Five little monkeys jumping on the bed," they tried jumping forward and then backward to the rhyme's steady beat.

💡 Try These Ideas Yourself

1. List the five most important things you think preschoolers need to know or be able to do in the area of physical development, health, and well-being when they enter kindergarten. Why do you think these are the most critical? How can teachers support the development of the knowledge and skills you listed?

2. What health concerns do you think confront young children today? How can a program of movement education help to address these problems? What would you say to a school board to convince them to fund such a program?

3. Keep a written record of all the ways you move your body in the course of one weekend. Divide the list into two columns, one for nonlocomotor movements and the other for locomotor movements. Before you begin the list, estimate how many items will appear in each column. At the end of the weekend, see whether the lists include more or fewer items than you predicted. What did you learn? How might you use this awareness in the classroom?

4. In the following scenario, identify the key developmental indicators that show physical development, health, and well-being taking place. What indicators suggest other areas of development? What could you as a teacher do to support and extend the learning?

Melanie and Liza are playing a game in which they dig a small hole under one tree, run to a second tree, put both hands on the trunk and say "dino bobo," and run back to the first tree. Then they repeat all four steps. After Melanie takes a turn, Liza says, "You didn't use both hands. You have to do it all over again." Melanie repeats the part where she runs to the second tree and says "dino bobo," this time putting both hands on the tree trunk. Liza says, "No, you have to do the whole thing again!" Melanie refuses.

5. List all the words you can think of to use with children that have to do with the position of the body relative to other things (for example, *above, underneath, next to,* and so on). Share your list with a coworker, classmate, or friend and ask for additional ideas. Make a plan for how you will use these words the next time you are involved in a movement experience with children.

Chapter 14

What Is the HighScope Curriculum in Mathematics?

 **Think About It**

Have you ever heard someone say, "Let's look at the numbers!" They may be referring to sports statistics, the household budget, ticket sales, polling numbers, or a guest list. Whether you love numbers or they fill you with anxiety, it is important to realize that mathematics involves much more than numbers. In fact, we use mathematics routinely and comfortably in our everyday lives, often without being aware of doing so.

For example, have you ever rearranged a room to make all the furniture fit? Working with shapes and space involves geometry. Dividing a problem into steps and working through each one methodically involves logic and ordering, similar to solving a series of algebra equations. Mathematics is also involved in adapting a recipe to serve a smaller or larger number of people or figuring how much mulch to buy for your garden. There are different ways of approaching the latter problem. You might measure the length, width, and depth of the flower bed and divide it by the number of cubic feet listed on the bag of mulch. Or, based on your gardening experience, you could "eyeball" the planting area and estimate the amount you need. All these activities draw on the ability to work with the mathematical properties of common objects and events.

For children as for adults, mathematics is about numbers, putting things in order, comparing quantities, discovering patterns, and maneuvering ourselves and our belongings safely from one place to another. Recognizing how basic these operations are to carrying out our intentions each day, HighScope sees all children and adults as capable mathematicians. Research and experience also show that early childhood teachers can and should include mathematics as a vital part of the curriculum.

While understanding that some adults may shy away from mathematics, the HighScope Curriculum gives teachers the reassurance and practical strategies they need to offer young children meaningful and age-appropriate learning experiences. Children are then prepared to engage in mathematics with interest, confidence, and ability in their subsequent schooling.

Why Early Mathematics Development Is Important

If there is any question about whether preschoolers are ready to learn mathematics, observing their play shows how interested they are in this subject. Here are some comments made by young mathematicians:

Add more water to the other glass to make them even.

150

Chapter Learning Objectives

By the end of this chapter, you will be able to

❖ Explain why early learning in mathematics is important

❖ Describe the HighScope key developmental indicators in mathematics

❖ Understand and begin to apply the strategies adults use to support early learning in mathematics

Six children and six napkins. And a mud-soup spoon on top of each one.

I won't be five until after José. But then it will be my turn to be the oldest.

My new shoes cost my mom eleventy-eight-one dollars.

I'm running faster. I bet I get to the top of the hill before you!

When the big hand points down at the six, I'm going to clap my hands for cleanup.

You be the daddy kitty because you're the tallest. She's the baby because she's the littlest. And I'll be the mommy so I can sit in the middle.

Research findings. During the past 25 years, researchers have come to appreciate how much young children enjoy and are capable of mathematical investigation and reasoning. For example, when Herbert Ginsburg and his colleagues observed children's free play, they were amazed not only by how much the children used mathematical ideas but also by how advanced their thinking was (Ginsburg, Inou, & Seo, 1999). Professor Arthur Baroody (2000) says preschoolers actively construct basic mathematical concepts and use them to solve problems. In fact, researcher and curriculum developer Douglas Clements (2004) named his technology-based math program "Building Blocks" to emphasize that young children do not "receive" such knowledge but build it from experience.

The field has further discovered that early mathematics is more than just **numeracy,** or reciting numerals or rote counting. It also includes investigations into patterns, size and quantity, and **spatial relations** (the position and movement of people and objects in space relative to one another). Many people in the field therefore prefer to talk about **mathematical literacy** rather than numeracy. In fact, observations of preschoolers' spontaneous activities shows that number exploration accounts for the lowest percentage of mathematical investigation. Young children are much more interested in patterns and shapes and the transformations brought about by processes like adding and subtracting (Ginsburg et al., 1999).

Curriculum components. Based on this research, HighScope describes its mathematics curriculum as "numbers plus" and groups the key developmental indicators (KDIs) in mathematics into three areas: **seriation, number,** and **space** (defined and discussed in the remainder of this chapter). Child development researchers, testing the ideas of Jean Piaget and other theorists (see Chapter 4), refer to these as **logical operations** because they underlie the development of logical thought and problem-solving abilities. These curriculum components also parallel three of the categories listed by the **National Council of Teachers of Mathematics** (NCTM, 2000) in its early childhood stan-

---

Terms Used in This Chapter

• numeracy • spatial relations • mathematical literacy • seriation • number • space • logical operations
• National Council of Teachers of Mathematics (NCTM) • repeating sequence or pattern • number sense
• one-to-one correspondence • conservation • matched sets • sense of perspective

Early Mathematics Development

Preschool children are developing understanding and skills in the following mathematical components:

Basic number sense — Intuiting amounts and the concepts of addition and subtraction (precounting); understanding that numerals represent numbers of objects; grasping one-to-one correspondence; counting; knowing that a quantity stays the same even if the shape of the container or arrangement of objects changes **(conservation)**

Comparing quantities — Recognizing what is bigger or smaller, has more or less, and so on; estimating and/or calculating differences in quantity; comparing amounts in continuous materials (such as sand and water) and discrete objects (such as blocks and beads)

Identifying regularities — Recognizing and creating patterns; identifying the core unit of a pattern; identifying regularity and repetition in objects and events; making predictions based on observed patterns

Ordering things — Putting things in order according to some graduated attribute on which they differ, such as size, age, loudness, and color intensity

Navigating space — Arranging objects in the physical environment; understanding how one's body relates to the objects and spaces around it; figuring out how things fit together and come apart; understanding direction (for example, up, down) and position (for example, near, far)

---

dards — namely, algebra, number and operations, and geometry. The other two NCTM standards — measurement and data analysis — involve not only mathematics but also science, and they are therefore described in the next chapter. (See Epstein & Gainsley, 2005, for the alignment between HighScope KDIs and NCTM early childhood standards.)

Key Developmental Indicators in Mathematics

This section describes the HighScope KDIs in three areas of early mathematics — seriation, number, and space — and the strategies teachers use to support their development in young children.

Seriation

Seriation is ordering items by *differences* (for example, from the smallest to the largest) or according to a **repeating sequence or pattern** (for example, alternating red and blue beads). With their growing ability to hold images in mind, preschoolers can identify and describe variations — exemplified by a child who says, "I have lots more hair than my dad. He's bald." Preschoolers can also make decisions based on variations, a skill evidenced by a child who insists, "I want the *biggest*

piece of cake." Arranging things in series or patterns is also satisfying for young children, although they may change the rules after one or two repetitions. Finally, preschoolers enjoy matching ordered sets; for example, the small doll with the small doll bed, the medium doll with the medium bed, and so on.

HighScope has three key developmental indicators in seriation (see the sidebar below). The first focuses on fundamental differences and the other two involve the ability to explore finer distinctions and create patterns.

Opportunities for seriation experiences arise from using materials and solving problems. Adults

🔑 HighScope Mathematics Key Developmental Indicators in Seriation

❖ Comparing attributes (longer/shorter, bigger/smaller)

❖ Arranging several things one after another in a series or pattern and describing the relationships (big/bigger/biggest, red/blue/red/blue)

❖ Fitting one ordered set of objects to another through trial and error (small cup and small saucer/medium cup and medium saucer/big cup and big saucer)

152

in HighScope classrooms therefore provide children with appropriate materials, opportunities, and challenges that encourage youngsters to create and comment on serial comparisons and patterns. The following **support strategie**s can help you foster these experiences for children.

▲ **Provide materials and experiences whose attributes can be easily compared.** For adults, creating a pattern or organizing materials by size is relatively easy. We often do such tasks without giving them much thought; for young children, however, these activities involve deliberate study. To involve children with these key learning experiences, provide sets of materials in different sizes (for example, nesting blocks or measuring spoons), materials children can use to make their own series and patterns (for example, beads or collage materials), computer programs that involve recognizing and creating series and patterns, and ordered sets of materials that go together (for example, nuts with thick, medium, and thin shafts together with bolts that fit each shaft size).

If you take time to observe the serial qualities in common objects, you are likely to find yourself generating many creative ideas for acquiring, storing, and labeling materials with these qualities.

> *At planning time, Celia said, "I am going to play with the big dinosaurs and the small dinosaurs and the horses.*
>
> *At small-group time, while building with blocks of different sizes, Doug picked up the smallest block and said, "This one is smaller than those."*

Foster opportunities for children to create and observe differences in the quality of their experiences. These might include differences in height, speed, satisfaction, position, and so on.

> *At outside time, Charlotte asked to be pushed as high as Lacey was swinging. Charlotte then said she was going "higher" than Lacey.*
>
> *At greeting time, Vance observed that he was happier than his big brother because "Mark was bad and my daddy got angry at him."*

▲ **Ask children to make or do things that involve series and patterns.** You can offer

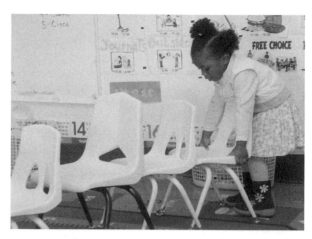

Seriation involves ordering things by differences (such as the smallest to the largest) or making repeating patterns (such as alternating chairs with one or two openings in the back).

diverse materials, such as those listed above, to provide many opportunities for seriation experiences during small- and large-group times and other parts of the daily routine. For example, during small-group time, you could initiate activities in which children string a repeating sequence of colored beads, use clay to sculpt family members of different sizes, or create a pattern on a pegboard. During large-group time, you might invite children to experience seriation with their bodies by successively lying, sitting, and standing. You might label their body movements and positions with words such as *low, middle,* and *high.*

> *At work time at the computers, Patricia helped Jared, Lila, and herself take turns by repeating the sequence, "Jared, me, Lila, Jared, me Lila" each time the timer stopped.*

▲ **Read and act out stories that feature graduated qualities.** A classic example that you might use is *The Three Bears.* After reading the story, you might ask children to model play dough beds in three sizes for the three different-sized bears. Another option would be for children to choose instruments varying in pitch or loudness to represent the papa, mama, and baby bears, respectively.

▲ **Validate and extend children's attempts to compare things.** *Repeat* children's comments as a way of acknowledging their awareness of seriation.

When Latoya said, "These giants are hungrier because they have bigger teeth," her teacher agreed: "Those bigger teeth will help the giants eat lots and lots of food — more food than the people with the smaller teeth."

Also look for ways to *extend* children's comments and elaborate their ideas to focus attention on seriation.

Josh was washing his hands at one sink when his teacher, Beth, turned on the water in the next sink full blast. Josh said, "Mine is running slow." Beth turned down her water and said, "I made my water run slower like yours."

Number

Preschoolers begin understanding the concept of number as they sort materials into groups and collections. Young children begin to see that counting involves equalities — for example, each toy car in a set of toy cars is counted as one car equal to each of the others, even though the cars themselves may differ in color, size, or shape. In this way, an understanding of number develops along with classification (see Chapter 15 for a discussion of the classification KDIs). At the same time, preschoolers see that there are ordered distinctions among the cars or items they are counting — for example, there is a first car, a second car, and so on. In this respect, their understanding of number develops in parallel with seriation.

As children explore these similarities and differences in quantity, they begin to construct what mathematicians call **number sense** (Baroody, 2000). That is, they develop a basic understanding of what numbers are and how they work. Numbers become "real" things that can be manipulated and transformed, not just abstractions to which we apply mechanical rules. Children need varied and everyday experiences working with quantity to construct this number sense, which in turn is the foundation for all later mathematical thinking and operations.

The idea of number also emerges along with awareness of **one-to-one correspondence** — for example, one driver for each car and, ultimately, one number (*one, two, three* or *first, second, third,*

HighScope Mathematics Key Developmental Indicators in Number

❖ Comparing the numbers of things in two sets to determine "more," "fewer," and "same number"

❖ Arranging two sets of objects in one-to-one correspondence

❖ Counting objects

and so on) for each car or item counted. Finally, an understanding of number develops along with **conservation** — the understanding that quantity remains fixed regardless of shape or spatial arrangement (for example, whether you line up four cars or toss them in a basket, there are still four cars in the set). This realization is still hard for preschoolers, who might wonder whether a line of four marbles really does have the same number of items as a line of four frisbees. For preschoolers, generally, the larger the quantities, the more appearance wins out over truth. With small quantities, however, counting and matching carry more weight.

To develop number concepts, children work from their current level of understanding. Even if their conclusions are flawed according to adult reasoning, they reflect a kind of logic on the part of the child. For example, Becky was the last child in her preschool to turn five. On her fifth birthday, she said, "Now I'm finally the oldest in my class!" She was demonstrating her knowledge that the number five is greater than four, even if she missed the idea that she would always be the youngest on the age continuum. Only by making their own observations and drawing their own "logical" conclusions can children build a base for later mathematical and scientific thinking.

HighScope has three key developmental indicators in number (see the sidebar above). In the first, children are often influenced by appearances in evaluating quantity. In the other two, children apply more advanced logical strategies to reach numerical conclusions.

For preschoolers, number understanding comes from handling objects, exploring and

Number sense develops when children work with discrete materials, count and compare real objects, see what happens when they add to or subtract items from collections, and so on.

pretending, and solving problems with materials and social relationships. You can use the **support strategies** given below to help young children develop basic concepts about number.

▲ **Provide materials that encourage counting and comparing.** Materials that lend themselves to exploring number include small items that children can easily handle, such as beads, shells, and bottle caps. Art materials also work well. For example, children enjoy comparing the number of colors in their paintings or the number of items in their collages. Also stock your classroom with materials that have numbers on them, including calculators, playing cards, wooden numbers to copy and trace, and simple board games with dice or spinners. (Remember, rules are less important to young children than counting spaces as they move around the board!) Finally, provide materials that fit together in one-to-one correspondence (for example, pegs and peg boards; colored markers and their tops).

At small-group time, after stringing wooden beads, Audrey counted hers. She pointed to each bead and counted to 11.

▲ **Encourage children to gather and distribute materials.** Collecting and distributing materials engages children with the concepts behind addition and division. You can support children's awareness of these foundational math skills at snacktime, cleanup time, small-group time, and other parts of the day. For example, children are eager to set the table for meals. As they distribute one place setting per person, they practice the one-to-one correspondence that underlies numbers and counting. Some storage systems, such as one hook for each tool in the woodworking area, also help children develop number concepts as they play with and put away materials. Group activities often involve multiple numbers of the same items, such as small toys, blocks, or pebbles and shells the children have collected on a nature walk. As children gather and distribute these items, they gain a concrete understanding of how numbers work.

At snacktime, Danny counted four graham crackers. He put one on each corner of his napkin.

▲ **Think of fun and unusual things to count.** Howard Gardner says, "Preschoolers see the world as an arena for counting. Children want to count everything" (1991, p. 75). To support children's love of counting, encourage them to count both typical things (such as blocks in a tower) and unexpected or even silly things (for example, mosquito bites on their ankles). Mathematics researcher Herbert Ginsburg and his colleagues found that children also love to count to big numbers, even if they don't always get them correct (Ginsburg, Greenes, & Balfanz, 2003). Therefore, provide materials and experiences that allow children to work with large quantities, such as counting the number of pebbles or leaves they collect on a walk, or guessing the number of food pellets in the guinea pig's dish.

▲ **Listen for and build on the number comparisons children make.** Children commonly make comparisons, such as those involving materials ("My tower has more blocks than yours") and ages ("My cousin is older than us. She's seven").

At work time in the block area, Nathan stacked cylinder blocks to make two towers. He added another block to one tower and said, "One more to make this tower taller."

Paying attention to children's observations about number will help you get additional ideas for number-related classroom materials and experiences. If a child comments, "My farm has more animals than yours," you might respond by saying "Show me how you know that!" and by stocking the toy area with more sets of plastic animals. A remark about birthday parties might suggest a small-group activity where children represent their ages in different ways on play dough birthday cakes. In one classroom, a group of children was very interested in how many birds came to the bird feeder. With the teacher's help, they made a chart and kept a record of the birds they saw at the bird feeder each day during snacktime.

▲ **Show interest in the matched sets children create.** Children will use almost anything to create their own matched sets. These may be conventional, for example, one place setting per child or one hat per doll. Often they are creative and unconventional, for example, each bear on a square of colored paper representing a "sleeping bag" or one pizza for each plastic fish.

At work time, Kristin matched big, middle-sized, and small items (dishes, Legos, paper squares) for big, middle-sized, and small plastic people. When she put a small item on a big character, she said, "that's too small." Debbie (a teacher) commented, "You want a bigger Lego for the bigger doll."

Matched sets arise naturally out of children's play ideas, even though children may not be consciously aware of the numerical roots of their ideas. To help raise children's awareness, comment on and attach numbers to the sets they generate ("Jason, I see you put one bear on each block. You have five bears on five blocks"). This labeling not only supplies children with a number word, it draws their attention to the one-to-one correspondences they have created.

▲ **Use written numerals and encourage children to use them.** If adults use and write numerals, children will show an interest and begin to

use written numerals themselves when they are ready. Young children read and write numerals in the same way they explore letters. For example, they may take orders and write down prices when playing "restaurant," or they may write their age on a birthday party invitation. When you take part in such pretend play, model the use of numerals; for example, by saying "A hamburger will be three dollars" (writing down the numeral 3). You can also use numerals on sign-up sheets. For example, one teacher helped her preschoolers make a list for taking turns with a new camera. Once the children problem-solved the order of turn-taking, each child wrote the appropriate numeral in front of his or her name. Several children also made hatch marks or wrote numerals after their names to indicate the number of turns they wanted.

🔑 **HighScope Mathematics Key Developmental Indicators in Space**

❖ Filling and emptying

❖ Fitting things together and taking them apart

❖ Changing the shape and arrangement of objects (wrapping, twisting, stretching, stacking, enclosing)

❖ Observing people, places, and things from different spatial viewpoints

❖ Experiencing and describing positions, directions, and distances in the play space, building, and neighborhood

❖ Interpreting spatial relations in drawings, pictures, and photographs

---

Space

By the time they reach preschool, children move about the physical world with confidence. They climb, run, cycle, and find their way along familiar routes. Young children work on puzzles, fill up two-dimensional space by drawing and writing, and build with clay, blocks, and other materials in three-dimensional space. Preschoolers also solve spatial problems with people and materials, such as deciding whose chair can be nearest the teacher's or figuring out to how to rewind a hose so it goes back inside its basket. As their

156

command of language increases, children also talk about their spatial interactions ("More of us can fit if we sit close together"). They form mental images of objects in space and use these inner pictures to remember location and position, solve problems, give directions, or accomplish other goals ("I left it at the front of my cubby so I won't forget to show it to my mom" or "Bring the scissors and tape. They're on the top shelf").

There are six KDIs (see the sidebar on p. 155) describing how preschoolers construct an understanding of spatial relationships. The first three involve actions on objects. The other three involve not only actions but also observations and interpretations about space.

Young children need to move freely and safely about the classroom as they carry out their plans with materials and people. Organize the room and its contents to create ample space without significantly reducing the amount or variety of materials. (See Chapter 6 for ideas on organizing and labeling the classroom.) Within this open environment, use the following **support strategies** to encourage young children to think about and apply their understanding of spatial relations.

▲ **Engage children in spatial exploration with materials and experiences.** HighScope programs provide varied materials and activities to raise children's spatial awareness. All classrooms include materials that children can

Fill and empty (materials for continuous pouring and scooping, such as water and birdseed; discrete materials that can be held, such as shells and small toys)

Fit together and take apart (commercial products such as Legos and Tinkertoys; household items such as boxes and lids)

Set in motion (things with wheels; things that roll, spin, and drip).

Additionally, group activities call children's attention to where they stand or sit relative to their classmates. So, as children handle materials and engage in group experiences on a daily basis, they become increasingly aware of spatial concepts.

At work time in the art area, Freddie said, "I'm painting inside this box."

At snacktime, Brittany said she wanted to sit in the middle seat.

Also make sure the outdoor learning environment contains equipment and materials that children can explore with their bodies in various ways. Such items might include wheeled toys, slides and climbers, low and high ground, pathways, open and enclosed areas, and so on. In addition, neighborhood walks help children get a sense of their school building in relation to other local landmarks. These excursions allow children to see the same things from different viewpoints (from above and below, front and back, next to, near and far) and to develop a **sense of perspective,** or how they fit into the world around them.

▲ **Allow time for children to explore and work with materials on their own.** Be aware that spatial exploration takes time and practice. Provide extended opportunities throughout the daily schedule for children to explore and work with materials on their own and in collaboration with others. For example, in one classroom, a group of children spent nearly all of a one-hour work time building an elaborate set of ramps and straightaways for racing their cars. Rather than dismantling it at the end of the day, they put up a "work-in-progress" sign and continued adding to the structure over the following two weeks. Different children joined the core group on any given day, and many eagerly showed their parents which part of the structure they had worked on.

▲ **Encourage children to talk about how they made things.** To call children's attention to spatial aspects of their experiences, encourage them to talk about how they made things. For example, at work time or recall time, you might ask children to describe the locations and positions of the objects and people involved in their activities ("How did you make this part on the bottom?" or "Where were you when you threw the ball? Where did the others in the game stand?").

▲ **Encourage children to explore movement.** Children like to challenge their bodies to assume different poses. They often try out different ways of walking or crawling, they twist their torsos and limbs into various shapes and positions, and so on. To show that you value these explorations, imitate children's actions and copy their positions. Encourage young children to crawl, roll, bounce, and lie on their backs to view the world from various angles and describe what they see.

Strategies for Supporting Early Mathematics Development: A Summary

Seriation

__ Provide materials and experiences whose attributes can be easily compared.

__ Ask children to make or do things that involve series and patterns.

__ Read and act out stories that feature graduated qualities.

__ Validate and extend children's attempts to compare things.

Number

__ Provide materials that encourage counting and comparing.

__ Encourage children to gather and distribute materials.

__ Think of fun and unusual things to count.

__ Listen for and build on the number comparisons children make.

__ Show interest in the matched sets children create.

__ Use written numerals and encourage children to use them.

Space

__ Engage children in spatial exploration with materials and experiences.

__ Allow time for children to explore and work with materials on their own.

__ Encourage children to talk about how they made things.

__ Encourage children to explore movement.

__ Provide pictorial representations.

__ Encourage children to make two- and three-dimensional representations of real places and things.

__ Allow children to solve spatial problems their own way.

__ Take instructions from children.

At work time in the house area, Dana lifted her feet off the floor by propping herself up on the table with her arms. This made her appear taller. She said, "Now I'm high." She let herself down and said, "Now I'm not." When Jill (a teacher) asked her how she did that, Dana responded, "I lift myself up."

▲ **Provide pictorial representations.** Children enjoy depictions of familiar situations, and looking at them supports their development of spatial concepts. HighScope teachers use instant or digital cameras to document the stages in which children transform something — for example, as they build a block structure or paint a group mural. Teachers photograph objects or events from different angles and ask children to comment on the location and relative positions of what they see. This encourages an awareness of perspective. (The sequence of images also sup-

ports development of *time concepts,* which are discussed in Chapter 15.)

▲ **Encourage children to make two- and three-dimensional representations of real places and things.** When children make drawings, paintings, and models of real places, people, and objects, it encourages them to consider where things are in relation to one another. For example, if they are drawing their house, will they put a window next to or above the door? If they are building a house with blocks, will the garage be at the front, back, or on the side? (Also see Chapter 17 for what and how children learn by representing their world through the arts.)

▲ **Allow children to solve spatial problems their own way.** Instead of jumping in to help children, encourage them to figure out how to attach things, make something balance, or solve other spatial problems. Children learn more by inventing their own methods rather than turning the

158

problem over to, or imitating, an adult. For example, when the roof of Erica's block structure kept falling down, she built an interior wall to hold it up instead of pushing the outer walls closer together. Her teacher was tempted to tell Erica to just get a longer block, but Erica learned something by solving the problem her own way. The teacher also learned that spatial problems have many possible solutions and that one is not more "correct" than another.

▲ **Take instructions from children.** Children love to be leaders. A natural time to invite children to lead is large-group time, when children can take turns demonstrating and describing how others should move their bodies to a chant or song. When children give instructions, it encourages them to use words related to position, direction, and distance. At first, teachers might supply the appropriate words ("Michael wants us to lift our arms over our heads"), but as children's language and spatial skills improve, they can give the instructions ("Everybody walk backward around the circle").

Opportunities to take direction from children also arise during work time and small-group time, especially when partnering adults follow children's leads. Teachers might ask how a child did something so they can do it, too. And children may spontaneously use position words to direct a teacher to do something. Additionally, adults may refer one child to another for an idea or help solving a problem ("Gregory, I think Michelle can tell you how to get the hair rollers to stay closed").

At work time in the toy area, Caitlin was using the small people figures and the doll house. She put the cook in the house near the stove and said to Francine (a teacher), "I put him inside here." She looked at the doll Francine was using and said, "Put it on top."

Try These Ideas Yourself

1. List the five most important things you think preschoolers need to know or be able to do in the area of mathematics when they enter kindergarten. Briefly note alongside each why you think it is important. How can teachers support the development of the knowledge and skills you listed?

2. In the following scenario, identify the mathematics KDIs taking place. What learning is occurring in other areas of development? What could you as a teacher do to support and extend the learning? (See the sidebar on p. 11 for a full list of HighScope KDIs.)

Mark and Jennifer are building a race track with blocks for their toy cars. "Let's make it really long," says Jennifer. "All the way from one end of the room to another." Their teacher says, "I wonder how many blocks you'll need to reach from the door to the back wall." Mark answers, "A hundred!" Jennifer says she isn't sure. They decide to build their track and then count the number of blocks. They carry the big blocks together, each child holding up an end. When they run out of big blocks, they finish with small ones. "Good," says Mark. "Now our track will have even more blocks."

3. Write down all the things you do in a week that involve mathematics — for example, balancing your checkbook, adapting a recipe to feed half or twice the number of people, calculating your car's gas mileage when you fill up the tank, figuring out how to fit everything in your suitcase. Next, think about how children use simple mathematics in their daily lives.

4. Make a list of all the words you can use with children that have to do with number, other than actual numbers (for example, *some, many, large amount, fewer than, as much as, for each person,* and so on). Share your list with a colleague and ask for additional ideas. Plan ways to use these words the next time you are involved in a number experience with children.

5. Take a walk around your house or in a park. Make a list of all the things you see that have patterns (for example, curtains, linoleum tile, leaves, a mural). Now think about what happens during a typical week in your life. Make a list of all the patterns or repeated sequences you can identify in these events (for example, your morning routine, errands done in a particular order). Next, make a list of the patterns young children are likely to come across in their belongings, surroundings, and day-to-day activities. Think of the ways in which you can enhance children's awareness of, and involvement with, patterns and repeated sequences.

Chapter 15

What Is the HighScope Curriculum in Science and Technology?

 Think About It

"I wonder what would happen if…? " "They're kind of the same, but did you also notice their differences?" "Let's try it both ways and see which one works better." These typical statements indicate how much we use the principles and methods of science in our everyday activities. Without even realizing it, we often think and act scientifically with knowledge, skill, and confidence.

For example, we sort laundry according to how items of different colors and fabrics should be washed. Likewise, biologists observe and sort nature when they develop classification systems for plants and animals. Cooking involves chemistry — knowing how different ingredients interact and are "transformed" by processes such as heating or chilling, adding liquids or solids, or stirring or shaking. When we play sports and position or pace our bodies to score points, we make judgments about energy, force, and matter — concepts involved in physics. Carpentry and sewing involve gathering information about the amount and type of materials and equipment needed to carry out a project. Laboratory research involves the same thing — that is, collecting data to solve a problem.

In all these instances, we are being scientists. We gather information and form hypotheses, sometimes intuitively, about objects, people, and events in our lives. We rule out certain ideas and settle on others as likely explanations for what we observe. For example, we speculate about why one candi-

date won an election or why the car is making a funny noise. Our behavior is based on how we analyze the past and what we predict will happen as a consequence of specific actions.

The types of pursuits described above are rooted in curiosity, which young children possess in abundance. Preschoolers pose questions about how the world works, they make observations, and they then use the information (data) they collect to answer their questions. In this way, they **construct knowledge** about the principles and systems that govern daily life and the universe at large. Children are thus natural scientists, even if their conclusions represent early stages of thinking and will change with time and increasingly sophisticated observations. In this chapter we will discuss how the HighScope Curriculum encourages child scientists, and the adult scientists who teach them, to engage in this ongoing process of investigation and discovery.

Young children are natural scientists. They pose questions, investigate materials and actions, make observations, and construct ideas about how the world works.

160

Chapter Learning Objectives

By the end of this chapter, you will be able to

❖ Explain why early learning in science and technology is important

❖ Describe the HighScope key developmental indicators in science and technology

❖ Understand and begin to apply the strategies adults use to support early learning in science and technology

Why Early Science and Technology Development Is Important

A hundred or more years ago, science was primarily the study and classification of nature. As chemistry and physics took their place alongside biology, science became increasingly concerned with how things change when acted upon in different ways, a process sometimes called **transformation.** Read the following comments from preschool-age scientists and you will see that they, too, are interested in observing and sorting objects and in understanding how things are changed by what happens to them:

> *Big yellow rings in this box and small ones there. Same for the big and little green squares.*

> *Make this end (of the ramp) higher so the cars will go down faster.*

> *This spot is still light (pointing to the dry dirt under the slide after it has rained).*

❖

> *I made two kinds of orange. This one has lots of yellow and this one has lots of red.*

> *These worms are all curled up. But those are flat, 'cause they're still asleep.*

> *Just put one seed in each hole so they don't fight over the rain!*

> *(Looking at a bug under a magnifying glass) It's got hairs on its feet! Does it tickle when it walks?*

Comments like these make it clear that early science is more than memorizing information about the biological and physical world. Curriculum developers and researchers Rochel Gelman and Kimberly Brenneman point out that "to do science is to predict, test, measure, count, record, date one's work, collaborate and communicate" (2004, p. 156). In other words, science is as much about the investigative process as it is about knowing facts and formulas. And science also uses math, literacy, and social skills.

Educators are increasingly recognizing the appropriateness of introducing science as a distinct content area in the early childhood curriculum. Israeli professors Haim Eshach and Michael Fried (2005) argue that young children should be exposed to science for the following six reasons:

▲ Children naturally enjoy observing and thinking about nature

▲ Early exposure develops positive attitudes toward science

▲ Early scientific experiences form the basis for later formal education

▲ Using scientific language at a young age helps to develop scientific concepts

---

Terms Used in This Chapter

• knowledge construction • transformation • classification • duration • pacing • sequence
• spatial awareness • temporal awareness

Early Science and Technology Development

Preschool children are developing the following science and technology-related skills:

Observing — Discovering knowledge about the physical world through all the senses (for example, looking at, smelling, touching, and tasting vegetables in the garden)

Classifying — Organizing information, fitting new information into existing categories or changing categories to fit the new information (for example, from thinking of all four-legged pets as "dogs" to differentiating dogs and cats; distinguishing living and nonliving things)

Exploring materials — Discovering properties of objects and how things work, seeing how things change when they are acted upon by people or events (for example, seeing what happens when two colors of paint are mixed together; observing what happens on the screen after hitting different computer keys)

Drawing conclusions — Offering explanations for what one observes, predicting — accurately or not — what will happen (for example, deciding the cat likes wet food more than dry food because it eats more of it; guessing someone is older because she is taller)

Communicating ideas — Sharing thoughts about the world with others through talking, drawing, writing, or other means of representation (for example, giving directions to a friend on how to build a tall block tower that will not fall down; sharing how to make a computer program work)

▲ Young children are beginning to reason scientifically

▲ Science experiences help to develop scientific thinking about the world.

Using computers. Discussions about science education also raise issues about the appropriate use of computers in the early childhood classroom. Educators today agree preschoolers need to be familiar with and knowledgeable about basic technology as part of getting ready for school. Computers can also play a vital role in learning about other content areas, but only *if* the technology is used correctly (Hyson, 2003). Software should be age-appropriate and, rather than emphasizing rote drill and practice, should be open-ended and designed to promote discovery. Good programs pose a problem, ask children to solve it, and provide feedback (Clements, 1999). Problems for which there is a "correct" answer are acceptable if the program provides feedback that causes children to reflect on where their reasoning was off track and how to solve the problem differently. If the program does not provide this type of feedback, then an adult working alongside the children can.

Clements further points out that technology can also increase children's manual flexibility and use of handheld objects. Because most children work well with the keyboard and mouse, they can often move objects on the screen more easily than they do actual objects. This is *not* to say objects in computer programs should replace real objects, which provide other sensory feedback and foster motor skills. Rather, computers extend the range of materials children use and the possibilities for manipulating and transforming materials.

Finally, as one researcher puts it, "Contrary to initial fears, computers do not isolate children. Rather they serve as potential catalysts for social interaction" (Clements, 1999, p. 122). Children working at the computer solve problems together, talk about what they are doing, help and teach friends, and create rules for cooperation. In fact, many children prefer working on the computer with a friend to doing it alone.

Key Developmental Indicators in Science and Technology

HighScope groups its key developmental indicators (KDIs) in science and technology into two areas: classification and time. Many of these indicators parallel the National Council of Teachers of Mathematics (NCTM) early childhood standards in measurement and data analysis (NCTM, 2000). Each area, and the strategies teachers use to support its development, is discussed below. As researchers learn more about how young children

162

**HighScope
Science Key Developmental
Indicators in Classification**

❖ Recognizing objects by sight, sound, touch, taste, and smell[1]

❖ Exploring and describing similarities, differences, and the attributes of things

❖ Distinguishing and describing shapes

❖ Sorting and matching

❖ Using and describing something in several ways

❖ Holding more than one attribute in mind at a time

❖ Distinguishing between "some" and "all"

❖ Describing characteristics something does not possess or what class it does not belong to

[1]This key developmental indicator was formerly a key experience under creative representation.

construct scientific principles and engage with the latest technology, HighScope is continuing to update its curriculum content in this emerging area.

Classification

Classification means grouping things according to their common attributes, or traits. Children, like adults, classify things to help organize their lives. They develop rules for treating things the same or differently, based on their characteristics. In learning about and sorting things, children use all their senses to attend to a wide range of properties. They may therefore sort things conventionally (for example, "hard" and "soft" textures) but also with surprisingly imaginative categories (for example, "tinkly" and "bong-bong" sounds). HighScope identifies eight KDIs in classification (see the sidebar on this page). The first five are readily seen in the behavior of younger preschoolers, and the other three are beginning to be seen in older preschoolers.

To help children develop knowledge and skills in classification, use the following **support strategies** when setting up the learning environment, scheduling the daily routine, and interacting with children.

▲ **Provide and label diverse materials in the classroom.** A HighScope classroom contains many types of materials that children can sort according to a wide range of attributes. These materials include household and natural items with appealing characteristics (baby oil, sandpaper, shells); items with moving parts (kitchen utensils, musical instruments, cameras); materials that change through manipulation or on their own (clay, computer drawing programs, sand, water, real animals); and items that invite sorting by *two* attributes (large and small counting bears in different colors).

At snacktime, Sadie put away her dishes and threw her trash in the wastebasket. She held up a plastic knife and asked Laura (a teacher) where it went. Laura said, "See if you can find the container with the other knives." Sadie looked and said, "All the knives go in the white one." After putting the knife inside, she observed, "Pink for forks and spoons go in the blue."

▲ **Provide materials with a wide range of sensory features.** To ensure children have opportunities to explore with all their senses, provide the following: items that create light and shadow (flashlights, adjustable blinds and shades, cellophane papers), items that can be covered up or buried (hidden under blankets, felt for beneath sand, pea gravel, or Styrofoam pellets), materials with distinctive textures (bark, sandpaper, slippery and coarse fabrics, feathers, metal screens), things that are aromatic (indoor and outdoor plants, neighborhood smells carried by the wind, spices, pet food), items that make noise (musical instruments, timers that tick and ring, computers with appropriate software, workbench tools, running water), and foods with a variety of tastes and textures for children to sample at snacks and meals (fruits and vegetables, seeds and grains, raw and cooked foods, and spices, herbs, and condiments).

▲ **Ask children to make things that are the same and things that are different.** HighScope teachers encourage children to make and describe things with similarities and differences. For example, after reading a favorite book at a small-group time, the teacher might give children art materials and say, "How could we make monsters that are the same in some way as those Max saw in *Where the Wild Things Are* [by Maurice Sendak]?" Another day she might say, "I wonder how we

*Classification involves knowing what something is —
and what it is not. HighScope encourages children to use
the concepts of "no" and "not," such as this sign that
means "Do not touch!"*

could make monsters that are different in some
way from the ones in *Where the Wild Things Are.*"

▲ **Encourage children to collect and sort
things throughout the day.** Children love to collect things. Plan time to make collections in the
classroom, on the playground, and during walks.
Provide a variety of containers so children can sort
their collections based on the different attributes
of the items they collect. You are also likely to
find that cleanup time is a natural occasion for
matching and sorting. These activities challenge
children to group items according to specific characteristics (for example, after an activity with
markers, you might ask children to recap the blue
markers with the blue caps, the red markers with
the red caps, and so on).

You can also invite children to choose the location for storing books, magazines, and other
printed materials related to different areas of the
classroom (such as putting a cookbook in the
house area). The labeled storage containers and
shelves in each area promote sorting and matching as children find and return materials independently at work time and cleanup time.

> *At the end of small-group time, when it
> was time to put things away, Rosie sorted
> all of her materials into five piles: one pile
> of wooden pieces, another of magnet balls,
> one of paper clips, one of paper, and one
> of Duplos. She put each pile into the prop-
> er basket that Ted (a teacher) had set out
> for collecting them.*

▲ **Encourage children to sort things by two
attributes.** This is what the teachers in one class-

room did: When the teachers noticed that children
were interested in dinosaurs, they added a plastic
set to the toy area. The dinosaurs came in two sizes
(which the children called "mommies" and "babies") and four colors (blue, green, yellow, and
purple). At first, teachers stored all the dinosaurs in
one basket, but after hearing the children referring
to them by size *and* color, they made a new storage box with four large storage cubicles on one
side and four small ones on the other. The inside of
each cubicle was lined in blue, green, yellow, or
purple. Depending on their developmental level,
children progressed from not sorting the dinosaurs
at all to sorting them by size *or* color (one attribute)
to sorting by size *and* color (two attributes).

▲ **Encourage children to respond to and
use "no" language.** Classification also involves
knowing when something does not possess a particular attribute. HighScope teachers therefore help
children acquire an understanding of the terms *no*
and *not.* For example, as children dress to go outside, teachers might ask all the children to look
around and identify whose jackets do *not* have
hoods. They also encourage children to use the
universal symbol for the "no" concept (a circle
and diagonal line superimposed on an image of
the object or word at issue).

> *At the end of small-group time one day,
> Hector announced his plan to continue
> with his wooden sculpture at work time the
> next day. He carried it to the art area shelf
> and put a "work-in-progress" sign in front
> of it. The sign had a picture of hands with
> a line through them below the words.
> Pointing to the picture, Hector said em-
> phatically, "That means DO NOT TOUCH!"*

▲ **Play guessing games that require children to hold more than one attribute in mind.**
Older preschoolers can identify objects by two or
more traits. You might therefore say to them, "I
see something in the house area that is red and it
rings. What can you see in the house area that
rings and is red?" Transitions and group movement
or music activities are excellent times to try the
two-trait strategy. For example, during a transition
you might say something like, "I spy someone
who has on shoes that are blue *and* they have
laces. (Pause for children to figure this out.) Greta,
your shoes have laces and they are blue! You can
go get your coat."

Time

164

Though time is an abstract concept, preschoolers experience it in concrete and sensory ways. To a young child, a week is a long time for a friend to be absent; and an hour can be a really long time to ride the bus but a really short time to build with blocks. Adults measure time objectively, using clocks and calendars. Preschoolers begin by measuring time subjectively, but as they form mental representations, they are increasingly able to see time in symbolic ways, too. They become able to remember the past and anticipate the future. They become aware of **duration** (how long things last), **pacing** (the speed of events), and **sequence** (the order in which things happen).

Four KDIs describe preschoolers' emerging understanding of time (see the sidebar on this page). The first three deal with duration and pacing, while the last one deals with sequence.

The most important way HighScope teachers help children appreciate the order and regularity of time is by *creating a consistent daily routine*. Within that routine, they respect children's pace and, whenever possible, their desire to continue working for however long on something that interests them. The following **support strategies** can help you foster children's concepts about time.

▲ **Provide materials that children can use for exploring time concepts.** Offer materials that children can use to *signal stopping and starting* (timers, stop signs, musical instruments) and things they can *set in motion* (wheeled toys, metronomes, balls, tops). Objects that help children develop spatial awareness (those which spin, drip, and rock) can also be used to explore time concepts such as "fast" and "slow." Each movement becomes a concrete way for children to measure the units and passage of time.

> *At work time, Lonnie described the salt timer. She said, "The salt goes up and goes down and then it stops. Then it's time for someone else to have a turn."*

▲ **Call attention to the daily routine and its occasional exceptions.** Young children quickly learn and become comfortable with the daily routine in a HighScope program. You can use several strategies to raise children's awareness of the daily routine and its various parts. For

> ### 🔑 HighScope Science Key Developmental Indicators in Time
>
> ❖ Starting and stopping an action on signal
> ❖ Experiencing and describing rates of movement
> ❖ Experiencing and comparing time intervals
> ❖ Anticipating, remembering, and describing sequences of events

example, you might post an illustrated schedule at children's eye level to show the order and length of each daily routine segment.

> *At snacktime, Ariel glanced at the daily routine chart in the block area and noticed that the arrow needed to point to the snack-time symbol. She moved the arrow and said, "After snack is small group, then outside time. That's when my mommy comes to get me!"*

To help children anticipate each part of the day, signal the beginning and end of time periods — for instance, you might flick the lights or sing a chant. Later in the program year, children enjoy taking on this role. If there is to be a change in routine (such as a field trip), inform children ahead of time. This kind of notification serves a dual purpose: First, an exception calls attention to the rule. That is, labeling something as "different" highlights what is "typical." Second, preparing children for a shift in routine helps avoid the anxiety that can be caused by unexpected changes. Knowing what will happen helps children retain a sense of power and control over their environment.

▲ **Encourage children to describe intentions and activities in time-related language.** Part of learning about time is understanding and using its vocabulary. It is therefore important to encourage children to use time-related language. For example, you might inquire about the sequence in which a child plans to do something ("What will you add next?"). You might ask about the timing or speed of children's actions ("I wonder if it took longer to carry the blocks or to stack them"). Adults also comment on the rate or speed with which things happen ("When you added another block to hold up the ramp and make it steeper, the cars rolled down faster").

> *At planning time, Chen-wei described how he was going to make a picture. He said, "First put glue on paper. Then put beans on the glue."*

> *At work time in the house area, Jackson glued paper letters on a piece of paper. When he spilled glue on the table, he said, "I'll clean it up after."*

▲ **Relate lengths of time to familiar actions or events.** As noted above, preschoolers, especially young ones, deal with time in real-world and personal ways. Adults therefore give them concrete references with which to mark and measure time ("It will be cleanup time when all the sand falls to the bottom of the glass" or "Your daddy will be here to get you when the big hand points straight down"). As adults refer to these concrete indicators, they simultaneously help children become familiar with conventional and unconventional ways to measure time as well as more abstract time indicators.

▲ **Encourage children to move at different rates of speed throughout the day.** Just as children enjoy adopting different body positions **(spatial awareness)**, they enjoy moving at various speeds **(temporal awareness)**. Adults can make transitions fun by encouraging preschoolers to move at different rates — for example, suggesting children move "as slow as a snail" or as "fast as a rocket" from the large-group area to the snack table. Children also like to suggest the speed at which the class can travel between places or activities. As with other activities in which they act as leaders, children may begin by demonstrating the action while the teacher supplies the words. Later, children can provide the time-related words on their own.

▲ **Celebrate special occasions if and when they are meaningful to children.** Holidays are abstractions to young children, who cannot connect what's on a calendar to real time and often do not know the significance of a special event. Holidays and other celebrations only have meaning if and when they relate to the events and people in young children's lives. So, for example, a birthday or the arrival of a new sister or brother takes on significance to them, while New Year's Day or the Fourth of July may mean very little.

Therefore, take your cues from children about the special occasions in their lives and whether and for how long to celebrate them.

Also keep in mind that just because a date has passed on the calendar, it doesn't mean children are ready to let it go. For example, the excitement children feel about Halloween may mean they still want to play "trick or treat" at Thanksgiving. Similarly, a child may continue to reenact her fourth birthday party for several weeks after the event. These child-chosen celebrations offer many opportunities for teachers to scaffold more elaborate role playing and add to children's vocabularies.

▲ **Call attention to time in nature.** Objects and experiences in the natural world offer many opportunities to enhance children's awareness of the passage of time and changes that occur over time. Include living things indoors and use those found outdoors to show young children the natural cycles of plant and animal life. Comment on seasonal changes, and take photographs to help children describe and reflect on changes over time.

Other nature-based activities might include planting a garden (with both fast- and slow-growing plants), comparing the time it takes a wet doll shirt to dry in the sun with the time it takes a similar doll shirt to dry in the shade, or inviting a parent to periodically bring in a younger sibling as the child grows from an infant to a toddler.

Try These Ideas Yourself

1. List the five most important things you think preschoolers need to know or be able to do in the area of science when they enter kindergarten. For each, briefly note why you think these are the most important. How can teachers support the development of the knowledge and skills you listed?

2. Write down all the things you do in a week that involve science and scientific reasoning (examples: looking at the sky to anticipate the weather, packing a grocery bag to protect fragile items, thinking about why the shelf fell down or the souffle collapsed and trying different solutions to address the problem). How do you think children use simple scientific thinking in their daily lives?

3. Design and make timers for a preschool classroom (attach two containers using glue or

Strategies for Supporting Early Science and Technology Development: A Summary

Classification

___ Provide and label diverse materials in the classroom.

___ Provide materials with a wide range of sensory features.

___ Ask children to make things that are the same and things that are different.

___ Encourage children to collect and sort things throughout the day.

___ Encourage children to sort things by two attributes.

___ Encourage children to respond to and use "no" language.

___ Play guessing games that require children to hold more than one attribute in mind.

Time

___ Provide materials that children can use for exploring time concepts.

___ Call attention to the daily routine and its occasional exceptions.

___ Encourage children to describe intentions and activities in time-related language.

___ Relate lengths of time to familiar actions or events.

___ Encourage children to move at different rates of speed throughout the day.

___ Celebrate special occasions if and when they are meaningful to children.

___ Call attention to time in nature.

---

tape with a material that flows between them). Make them work for different amounts of time by choosing different materials for each one. For the containers, choose see-through plastic bottles of different sizes, shapes, and colors. Fill them with a variety of materials such as sand, water, rice, beans, pebbles, or sequins. Use different size openings through which the filling can flow. Give the finished timers to children to explore; record their reactions. How do children investigate the timers and how they work? How do they use them in games or other activities?

4. In the following scenario, identify the key developmental indicators taking place in science and technology. What types of learning are occurring in other areas of development? How could you as a teacher support and extend the learning? (Refer to the list of key developmental indicators on p. 11.)

At outside time, Heidi made a campfire with sticks. She sorted them into short, medium, and long lengths and said, "You have to start with the littlest ones so they catch fire. That's how my daddy does it." She said she would light the fire at midnight and invited George, Ben, and Fae (a teacher) to sit by the fire. Heidi pretended to make s'mores by putting one small twig

between two big, flat stones. She made four s'mores, one for each person (including herself) at the campfire. Then she filled a bucket and put water on the fire, explaining that "water makes the fire go down."

5. Here are some typical "why" and "how" questions children might ask about their world and how it works:

Why does water make bubbles when you blow through a straw?

How do you make glue?

Why don't the wheels on the toy car turn in the mud?

How come we're not the same size if we're the same age?

Choose one of these questions, or another one you've heard a young child ask, and decide how you would help children be "scientists" and answer their own questions.

What Is the HighScope Curriculum in Social Studies?

 **Think About It**

A preschool child went to his older brother's wrestling matches and got several classmates interested in playing "wrestling" at work time. They used an area rug as their mat, pushed up their sleeves, and got down to wrestle. The game went on for several days, becoming more elaborate. The children gave themselves wrestlers' names and developed a scoring system.

In the second week, however, a few children complained that the play was too rough. The teachers also worried about children getting hurt but did not want to stop a game that many children clearly enjoyed and that promoted learning in many areas — counting, spatial awareness, moving in various ways, direction and position vocabulary, relating to other children, engaging in complex play, resolving conflict, and generating and discussing action sequences. So one day, when the wrestlers were setting up their game, a teacher voiced her concern. She said, "What rules can we make up so children will not get hurt?" She wrote down children's ideas and posted them on the wall above the mat. Here are the rules the children came up with:

1. Take off your shoes (but not your socks).

2. No hitting.

3. No punching. (The children debated whether punching was the same as hitting, but decided it deserved its own rule.)

4. No pinching.

5. You can't call someone a bad name.

6. No spitting.

7. No head butts.

8. ~~Only boys can play.~~ (Several girls protested this rule and it was dropped.)

9. At least three people have to play so one can be the referee and make sure the fight is fair.

10. The referee has to be able to count to ten. (After a count of ten, the match is declared over.)

11. You can't wrestle if you don't have a wrestler name.

12. You can't have the same wrestler name as someone else.

Young children's capacity to consider the needs, feelings, and safety of others sometimes surprises adults. This girl tied her friend's shoe because she didn't want her to "trip and get hurt."

168

Chapter Learning Objectives

By the end of this chapter, you will be able to

❖ Explain why early learning in social studies is important

❖ Describe the HighScope key developmental indicators in social studies

❖ Understand and begin to apply the strategies adults use to support early learning in social studies

13. Everyone who wants to wrestle gets a turn. The referee decides who goes next.

14. People who want to watch have to stand behind the line. (After some debate, they decided the edge of the block shelf would mark the "watching line.")

The children referred to the rules in subsequent weeks as their interest in wrestling continued. If one of them broke a rule, the other children were quick to point out the infraction. Later in the year, when some children wanted to "box" in the sandbox, it was their idea to set up rules for alternating use of the space with those who wanted to play in the sand and also to guarantee safety when the space was used as a boxing ring.

The above anecdote shows young children participating in a democracy. While preschoolers are often self-centered, their capacity to consider others can sometimes seem quite amazing! In this instance, the teachers played a vital role in bringing potential problems to the children's attention. But once they were aware of them, the children demonstrated genuine sensitivity to the safety and feelings of others. Their creative solutions balanced their personal enthusiasm for the wrestling game with a keen desire to preserve the sense of community in their classroom.

HighScope views the preschool classroom as an important and meaningful community for the children and adults who share it every day. It is a place where children form their identities as both individuals and members of a group. They learn

that one part of being themselves is being connected to a network of people who share their interests and care about their feelings. While those in the school community may differ from one another in significant ways, they still find commonalities that let them bond with and respect one another. Everyone gets a voice, regardless of their age, size, knowledge, or ability level. In short, classrooms aim to operate according to the principles upon which a participatory democracy is founded. Experiencing and learning these basic principles defines the content of social studies at this age.

Why Social Studies Is Important

The Standards of the National Council for the Social Studies (NCSS) says social studies is "designed to promote civic competence…and integrates knowledge from several disciplines including history and geography" (1994, p. 3). There are no standards specific to the pre-kindergarten years, explained by the fact that history and geography are too abstract for preschoolers. Although young children do develop concepts about time and space, these subjects are more appropriately dealt with in the content areas of science and mathematics, respectively (Jantz & Seefeldt, 1999).

However, if one focuses on the notion that the ultimate goal of social studies is to foster **civic competence,** or the ability to be a good citizen, then it is clear that early childhood programs do a great deal toward accomplishing this end. Certainly, efforts to foster empathy, promote tolerance for diversity, and encourage collaboration meet this criterion. Moreover, even preschoolers are developing rudimentary ideas about community, justice, and democracy. In fact, the promotion of these traits is included in the National Association for the Education of Young Children (NAEYC) accreditation criteria for "understanding ourselves, our communities, and the world" (NAEYC, 2005, 2.63 to 2.75).

It is noteworthy that NAEYC, the National Education Goals Panel (NEGP), and state standards all treat social studies as a distinct curriculum content area, whereas before it was often seen as a subset

---

Terms Used in This Chapter

• civic competence • socialization • social skills

of social-emotional development (covered in Chapter 12). Social-emotional development continues to refer to children's ability to regulate their feelings and behaviors, and negotiate everyday interactions with adults and peers. Social studies refers more broadly to understanding and applying the rules and sensitivities that govern interactions among members of groups, communities, and society as a whole. Given the complexity of today's society, the field recognizes the importance of helping children develop the knowledge and skills they will need to negotiate multiple roles in a rapidly changing world.

Two Components of Social Development

The following two components of young children's social development are particularly important to their ability to engage in the subject matter of social studies.

Social knowledge and understanding. Social knowledge is defined as knowledge of social norms and customs. Acquiring this knowledge in the early years is called **socialization** or becoming a "member of the community." The emphasis on the classroom as a community, and the teacher's role in establishing a supportive group environment, is central in early childhood practice (as is establishing ties with families and the community beyond the school). To become a participating member of the group, children must be able to give up some individuality for the greater good, transitioning from the "me" of toddlerhood to the "us" of preschool (for more on this, see Chapter 12). This shift is also the underpinning of civic competence (Jantz & Seefeldt, 1999).

Social skills. The range of appropriate strategies for interacting with others form an individual's social skills. Cognitive development, especially perspective-taking and empathy, facilitates the development of these skills. Emerging classification skills — understanding similarities and differences and concepts such as "some" versus "all" — also means preschoolers are becoming aware of how they are both "like" and "not like" others. Teachers can play a crucial role in helping young children respect the differences they observe in gender, ethnicity, language, ability, and ideas. While attention to diversity is very concrete in preschoolers (for example, being aware of differences in appearance or diet), their early attitudes

169

For preschoolers, social studies means developing a sense of community. The classroom is a community in which they share common experiences, routines, interests, and conversations.

about accepting or rejecting those who are different form the basis for later ideas about tolerance, fairness, and the principles of democracy.

Curriculum components. Core components of the HighScope Curriculum contribute to young children's growth in the area of social studies. An important element is the shared and consistent daily routine, which creates a sense of community among all members of the classroom. Practices in other content areas also help preschoolers become aware of multiple viewpoints. For example, the emphasis on language development and communication (Chapter 11) develops listening as well as speaking skills. In learning how to solve social conflicts (Chapter 12), preschoolers become increasingly adept at seeing things from others' perspective. Even art appreciation (Chapter 17) enhances young children's awareness of cultural diversity and differences in the way people perceive and represent the world. All of these experiences help to build the civic competence that is seen as the goal of social studies education.

HighScope Key Developmental Indicators in Social Studies

HighScope has two key developmental indicators in social studies. One focuses on children's emerging sense of community, and the other, on their

> **HighScope Key Developmental Indicators in Social Studies**
>
> ❖ Participating in group routines
> ❖ Being sensitive to the feelings, interests, and needs of others

Following group routines, such as reading the message board, is an important form of social participation. Children know what to expect each day and make choices about how to join in.

ability to feel empathy and take another's perspective. These indicators, and the strategies adults use to support their development, are discussed below.

Participating in group routines

Belonging to a group and sharing group activities is consistent with the social nature of preschool children. Whether acting alone, in parallel, or interacting with others, they enjoy taking part in the daily routine. At the same time, programs must acknowledge children's individuality and desire to engage in activities that are personally meaningful to them. Therefore, group activities that offer choices and opportunities for active participatory learning are most effective in encouraging young children's social participation.

The following **support strategies** are effective for encouraging children to become active members of the classroom community and its routines.

▲ **Establish a consistent daily routine with clear expectations.** As discussed in Chapter 7, a consistent routine means children know what to expect and how they fit in. Routines give them a sense of control over their lives. This is especially true when they play an active role in shaping their own experiences. Therefore, provide many opportunities for children to play meaningful roles. For example, children like to do "adult" things such as passing out utensils and silverware, cleaning up, choosing a song, or signaling transitions. Hold reasonable expectations for how children carry out these behaviors — expect children to imitate, but not to be like or perform at the same level as, adults.

▲ **Make active learning part of group routines.** To encourage young children to participate with ease and enthusiasm, make sure routines build on their interests and acknowledge their developmental abilities. That means all parts of the day should include the five ingredients of active participatory learning: materials, manipulation, choice, child language and thought, and adult scaffolding (see Chapter 2).

▲ **Understand and support if, when, and how children choose to participate in group routines.** Children's reluctance to participate from time to time tells adults something about the children or the activity. For example, a child may still be upset about a conflict that happened at work time and refuse to participate in large-group time. In such cases, a sensitive adult might be able to talk to the child and resolve the problem while another teacher carries out the planned activity with the rest of the group. If the problem is with the activity itself, the teachers would analyze it in terms of the ingredients of active learning and modify it to encourage children's participation.

Like adults, children also have their own preferences for how they do things. For example, one child may choose to pass out the napkins by circulating around the table with a basket and having each child take one. Another child may prefer to place a napkin at the place setting in front of each child. Yet a third child may wait until everyone is seated and then put a napkin on each child's lap. Accept each child's way of participating as a valid expression of his or her individuality within the shared routines of the group.

Being sensitive to the feelings, interests, and needs of others

Young children can sometimes surprise adults with their insights and empathy. Preschoolers are increasingly able to understand and respond to the needs and feelings of others — a result of several trends in their development. First, their growing language abilities allow them to grasp and communicate the emotional meaning of an event. For example, when Collette saw Michael crying at greeting time, she asked, "Do you miss your mommy?"

Second, because children can hold mental images (or representations) in mind, they can imagine what someone else is feeling. So Frank, remembering how upset he was when his dog ran away, said to his teacher, "I bet Jimmy is sad because Sport (his cat) died."

Finally, preschoolers are learning to see things from the perspective of others. They do this with varying degrees of success when they give directions to another person on how to do something or how to move from one point to another. A child's ability to see another's person's viewpoint is also central to understanding how that person reacts to a situation, especially if the other person's feelings are different from the child's.

Adults acknowledge when children are sensitive and caring, for example, when a child takes the hand of a friend who is having trouble saying goodbye to a parent at the beginning of the day.

The following **support strategies** are effective for encouraging an emerging social awareness and sensitivity in young children.

▲ **Treat children with sensitivity and care.** When adults respond thoughtfully to children's feelings, interests, and needs, they serve as role models, communicating that such behavior is valuable. Further, if children know they are in a safe and secure environment, it is easier for them to pay attention to the needs of others. They do not worry about competing for care when there is clearly enough to go around.

One day Kim saw her teacher rocking and singing to Tyler, who was upset after his grandfather dropped him off at school. The next morning, when Tyler sat by himself, Kim went over, stroked his arm, and hummed "Row, row, row your boat." Tyler began to hum with her. Then they went to the book area together and chose a book to look at until it was time for the message board.

▲ **Recognize and comment when children are sensitive and caring.** Reminders to "be kind" or "share" generally do not work with young children. They are too abstract and do not account for how children may be feeling at the moment. However, when children do show caring and sensitivity, adults can acknowledge and encourage such behavior by commenting on the specific incident. For example, when Kim and Tyler's teacher saw the incident described under the strategy listed immediately above, she said, "Kim, you saw that Tyler was sad after his grandpa left. Singing to Tyler made him feel better."

Try These Ideas Yourself

1. Think about what it means to create a "community" in the home, the workplace, and the classroom.

   a. How do people build community in each of these settings?

   b. How long does it take?

   c. What supports the process of community-building? What threatens it?

172

> ## Strategies for Supporting Social Studies: A Summary
>
> **Participating in group routines**
>
> ___ Establish a consistent daily routine with clear expectations.
>
> ___ Make active learning part of group routines.
>
> ___ Understand and support if, when, and how children choose to participate in group routines.
>
> **Being sensitive to the feelings, interests, and needs of others**
>
> ___ Treat children with sensitivity and care.
>
> ___ Recognize and comment when children are sensitive and caring.

2. Think about the routines and procedures you participate in at home, school, or work.

   a. How long did it take you to learn these routines and feel you were part of them?

   b. When have you ever had to help someone else learn these routines?

   c. What did you do to help them understand the policies and become part of the routine in that setting?

   d. How might your reflections help you work with children in the classroom?

3. In the following scenario, identify the key developmental indicators taking place in social studies. What types of learning are occurring in other areas of development? How could you as a teacher support and extend the learning? (Refer to the list of KDIs on p. 11.)

On the message board, Nell (a teacher) drew a female stick figure with a line through it, wrote the letters P-O-L-L-Y below it, and told the children that Polly (another teacher) would not be there today because she was sick. At planning time Maureen said she was going to make a picture for Polly, and at work time she drew a house with a big sun and flowers "so Polly will get better and come back tomorrow." Then Maureen went to the mes-

sage board and copied the letters of Polly's name on the top of her picture. She folded the paper in half, drew a stamp on the outside. and said "I'll mail it on the way home from school."

4. Consider what the phrase "tolerance for diversity" means to you.

   a. How did your early experiences at home and school help to make you more or less tolerant of others?

   b. When have you ever done something to purposely put yourself in contact with people whose backgrounds or beliefs differ from yours? Why and how did you do that? What did you learn from the experience?

   c. How might your reflections help you understand and work with children in the classroom?

Active learning provides many opportunities for children to be part of the classroom community. They work together and help one another, and experience being both leaders and followers.

Chapter 17

What Is the HighScope Curriculum in the Arts?

 **Think About It**

After attending a parent workshop on young children and art, a parent offered this recollection:

[The session] brought back some less-than-happy memories of my own art experiences in school. Not that overall I had a bad time in school — quite the contrary. But music and art were far less than they could or should have been. I remember going through a voice "audition" one year whose ostensible purpose was to determine our voice range for the class chorus. I was one of several people whose singing was so below the music teacher's standards that we were told we would be "listeners." We sat in the back of the room to appreciate what everyone else did with their voices. Another time, we took an art placement exam. The results would determine whether we got to take art class. The teacher played the musical composition "Ebbtide," and we were told to paint whatever came to mind. My work must have gotten totally washed away by the tide because I don't remember ever having an art class that year.

Another parent shared a very different memory:

My oldest sister was considered the artist in the family. She won prizes at school and my parents signed her up for special lessons. Compared to her, the rest of us children never even tried to make art. Then in fourth grade I had a teacher who told us we were all artists. First thing every morning, we'd spend 15 minutes playing with the materials on the art table. One wall of the classroom was a big collage, and children would often add things to it. Well, playing with art was a great way to begin the day because every child succeeded and felt confident tackling math or reading or whatever subject came next. I never had much artistic talent by conventional standards, but I still think of myself as an artist today. Whether I'm just choosing clip art for a report or rearranging the living room, I keep that sense of playfulness. My teacher taught me that if you approach life as an artist, then that's what you are!

When teachers work on art projects alongside children, children stay with the activity longer, are more creative in their use of materials, and talk spontaneously about what they are doing.

174

Chapter Learning Objectives

By the end of this chapter, you will be able to

❖ Explain why early learning in the arts is important

❖ Describe the HighScope key developmental indicators in the arts

❖ Understand and begin to apply the strategies adults use to support early learning in the arts

From these two examples, it is clear that early experiences shape how we see our artistic abilities. We put ourselves in the "talented" or "untalented" column, and act according to what we think that label does or does not allow us to do. Some of us feel confident decorating our homes or landscaping the garden. Others say, "I have no idea what I like" and rely on decorators or magazine photos to make choices for us. We express — or silence — the artistic voice within.

Like the second parent's teacher, HighScope believes that an artist lives inside each of us and that age and talent do not matter. Adults often marvel at the wonderful pictures, dramas, dances, and songs that children create. But too often we fail to give ourselves credit for applying aesthetic judgment to our everyday actions. Because we do not see ourselves as creative people, we may be inhibited from offering children a wide range of artistic experiences. We are especially uneasy about including art appreciation in the curriculum, lacking confidence in our artistic opinions. But the arts are a type of language. And just like any other form of literacy, once we learn how to "speak" this language, there is no limit to our ability to create and converse. By helping teachers learn the "vocabulary" of art, HighScope encourages artists of all ages to express themselves. Moreover, the arts in their many forms can become a means of exploring other content areas.

Why the Arts Are Important

Art has been a standard feature of early childhood programs since their beginning. Researcher Carol Seefeldt (1999) says that even during periods when educators are pressured to focus on other academic skills, such as reading, most continue to believe art should remain an essential component of the curriculum in preschool and the early grades. Research supports this enduring belief, showing that experiences in the arts benefit children throughout their school years.

The value of artistic instruction for students is both emotional and intellectual. Art is **intrinsically rewarding,** that is, studying art is important for its own sake. We learn to value artistic expression in ourselves and others and derive inner satisfaction from appreciating its beauty or wrestling with its challenges.

Stephen Dobbs, professor of arts and humanities at San Francisco State University, says that through art education, "Students begin to see the rich mosaic of the world from many perspectives" (Dobbs, 1998, p. 12). For young children in particular, art provides an inner sense of competence and control. The Task Force on Children's Learning and the Arts notes that "As they engage in the artistic process, children learn that they can observe, organize, and interpret their experiences. They can make decisions, take actions, and monitor the effect of those actions" (Arts Education Partnership, 1998, p. 2).

Art is also **extrinsically valuable** in that it promotes other areas of development. Experiences with art engage our minds and bodies in ways that promote learning in nonart domains — for example, analyzing the spatial relationships among a group of dancers or developing the eye-hand coordination to weave a scarf. Noted art educator Rudolph Arnheim (1989) emphasizes that art is as much an intellectual activity as an intuitive one. And, as emphasized by the Arts Education Partnership, art education contributes to the development of many social and academic skills. "For all children, at all ability levels, the arts play a central

---

Terms Used in This Chapter

• intrinsic reward or value • extrinsic reward or value • artistic representation • pliable materials
• fixed or rigid materials • imitation • pretending and role play • action dialogue • pitch-matching • environmental music

role in cognitive, motor, language, and social-emotional development. The arts motivate and engage children in learning, stimulate memory and facilitate understanding, enhance symbolic communication, promote relationships, and provide an avenue for building competence" (Arts Education Partnership, 1998, p. v).

The developmental changes that occur during the preschool years make young children especially open to enjoying and learning from the opportunities that art education presents. Preschoolers, as distinct from infants and toddlers, are able to form mental images. They convey these through various forms of **artistic representation,** such as drawing a picture of their family, pretending to be a favorite character in a book, or making up a song about the birthday party they are planning. That is, preschoolers are able to *represent* their experiences, feelings, and ideas through these various art forms.

At the same time that young children are developing their language skills, art also opens up new avenues for expression and communication. As their expanding cognitive capacities combine with their growing physical and social abilities, preschoolers have a wide array of options for appreciating and creating art. They can make drawings and build models, imitate and pretend, sing and invent the words to songs, and do many of the things that adult artists do. However, they do this in ways that are consistent with their developmental levels and abilities.

Four Developmental Principles

Keeping the above points in mind, HighScope is guided by four developmental principles in its approach to early art education:

1. Representation grows out of children's real experiences. To form mental images, young children first need hands-on experiences with objects, people, and events. For example, when they play "mommy" and "baby," children carry out the roles they typically see in their own families. Their drawings, clay models, and other representations reflect the people, animals, furniture, and so on that they see in their everyday lives, as well as in books, television shows, and computer games. Similarly, children's melodies, rhythms, and song topics arise from their musical experiences at home and school.

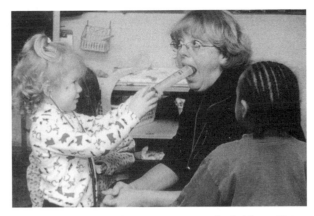

HighScope teachers play as partners with children. This partnership encourages children to represent their experiences and ideas through dramatic role play, visual art, and music.

At work time in the block area, Eva sat in the "car" built by Kyle. She said, "My baby threw up." She called Shannon [a teacher], the doctor, to give her baby a "check up."

2. Children's representations develop from the simple to the complex. Whatever the medium (painting, acting, singing), children's representations begin simply and evolve in complexity with time and practice. Initially, children hold only one or two characteristics of an object, person, or event in mind. Later, as they are able to mentally store images with more attributes and become better at using materials, their representations also become more detailed.

At recall time, Bridget drew in her Recall Journal. She made some marks with crayons and said they were the things she was using in the toy area (the widgets).

(One year later.) At recall time, Bridget drew three people and the widgets she used at work time. She drew the people with legs, arms, bodies, eyes, ears, noses, and hair.

Remember, however, that children do not move neatly through stages of artistic development (Taunton & Colbert, 2000). Rather, they shift within levels, especially as they discover an unfamiliar medium or explore a new means of expression. In this respect, young children are like adult artists. At all ages, creativity means giving oneself

176

over to play and exploration and enjoying both the simplicity and complexity that an artistic medium has to offer.

3. Each child's representations are unique. Children express themselves in ways that make sense to them and reflect their interests, experiences, and personalities. For example, children's behavior may be silly or intense; their manner of working, slapdash or painstakingly slow; and their attitude, one of indifference or one of concern for their audience. Adults should therefore view each child's artwork as a one-of-a-kind creation. Children, like adult artists, need the emotional and physical space to create freely in a supportive environment.

> *Since the introduction of more "found" and open-ended materials in the classroom, I have seen children blossom into their own creativity. Their artwork is more imaginative. There is a definite increase in the amount of dramatic play, especially in the house and block areas.* (Salt Lake City, Utah, Teacher)

4. Young children are capable of appreciating as well as making art. Educators often think that art appreciation is too abstract or analytical for preschoolers. But because young children are so observant and in-tune with all their senses, they are ideal candidates for appreciating the world of art. In fact, they are often eager to share their reactions to a picture, song, or story. The key, says art educator Marjorie Schiller, is that "talking about art should spring from the interests of the children and be initiated, for the most part, by them" (1995, p. 34). HighScope therefore includes appreciating as well as making art in its curriculum, grounding both in the experiences that young children relate to and find meaningful in their own lives.

> *Preschoolers looked at reproductions of fine artwork on postcards and in books. Then they discussed what they saw and thought about the paintings. They found out that Michelangelo painted on the ceiling, noticed the cracks in old paintings, compared Georgia O'Keefe's canvases to the flowers in their science area, and were*

> *surprised to hear that the names of Ninja Turtles were those of real artists. "The children instantly recognized that Matisse had a very different style than the realism of Michelangelo and da Vinci"* (Schiller, 1995, p. 37).

In this chapter, we will discuss how High-Scope teachers foster active learning in visual art, dramatic art, and music.

HighScope Key Developmental Indicators in the Arts

The HighScope arts curriculum includes key developmental indicators (KDIs) in visual art, dramatic art, and music.[1] As noted above, experiences to support artistic development include both making art and appreciating art. HighScope also encourages young children, and those who teach them, to enjoy the arts for the pleasure they bring as well as for their potential to enhance learning in a wide range of perceptual-motor, social-emotional, and academic content areas.

Visual Art

HighScope has three KDIs in visual art. They help children connect visual art objects and experiences with their everyday lives. Looking at a representation, such as a sculpture or drawing, and understanding that it stands for a real object or event, is a precursor of reading in young children.

> 🔑 **HighScope Key Developmental Indicators in Visual Art**
>
> ❖ Relating models, pictures, and photographs to real places and things
> ❖ Making models out of clay, blocks, and other materials
> ❖ Drawing and painting

---

[1]Visual art and dramatic art (KDIs) were formerly included under creative representation key experiences. The music category remains the same.

After realizing that visual images can represent concrete things, a next step in literacy is seeing that written words can stand for spoken words.

In the HighScope visual arts curriculum, children also work directly with two- and three-dimensional materials to create their own representations of people, objects, events, and ideas. Children exercise cognitive skills in these acts of turning mental images into physical ones. To promote art appreciation, adults talk with children about the process of making their own art and also reflect on the artwork created by others. Use the following **support strategies** to foster this process of aesthetic discovery and development in visual art.

▲ **Provide models, photographs, and pictures.** Interest areas in HighScope classrooms are full of models of the people, places, and things young children encounter every day. Models of real objects include dollhouses and furnishings, child-size furniture and kitchen appliances, plastic fruits and vegetables, toy vehicles of all kinds, and scaled-down tools. Model animals include those made of wood, rubber, or plastic as well as stuffed animals and

HighScope emphasizes "process" over "product" in the arts. Children are encouraged to explore the properties of materials and tools rather than copy or make something to please an adult.

puppets. There are nesting dolls, model people to use in the dollhouse, and dolls and puppets reflecting human diversity.

In addition to these scale models, provide pictures and photographs of familiar items and activities from the following sources:

Magazines and catalogs. Children look at them, cut them up and sort them, paste them into collages, or use them in other ways to support their play.

Instant or digital cameras. Teachers take pictures of children during different parts of the daily routine. They capture the sequence of activities as children build things, and teachers also use photographs to create a record of a special event such as a field trip or a visitor to the classroom. Photographs (and other kinds of pictures) are displayed at children's eye-level, as well as in albums.

Illustrated storybooks and art reproductions. Children can "read" books by looking at the pictures and providing their own story line, whether they are remembering the words read by the teacher or creating their own stories. Postcards, prints, and posters, and books with illustrations

Taking an Architectural Tour

One way you can help young children to develop their visual literacy skills is to go on a field trip to look at architectural features in the neighborhood. Adults can invite children to look at and talk about doors, windows, gates, ornamental details, and so on. In addition to pointing out these features, adults can initiate discussion by talking about the size, shape, and color of different architectural elements. You may be surprised at the comments and artistic connections children make!

As the group started out, the children stopped in front of a garage door [that was] a grid of square panels. "It has lots and lots of squares," one marveled. The next day, the children had pretzel squares at snacktime and one of them observed, "These pretzels look just like the garage door!"

You can also follow up these experiences with related activities that you plan with your coteachers. For example, you might have children represent in various art media what they saw on their walk. Or, you might put together a notebook of architectural features clipped from magazines or scanned from books that children can compare to photographs they bring in of their homes and neighborhoods.

— From "Walking and Talking About Art" (Epstein, Marshall, Lucier, Delcamp, & Gainsley, *Supporting Young Learners 3*, 2001, pp. 195–197

178

encourage children to talk about what they see and what they think the artist was trying to convey. Used greeting cards often have pictures of familiar objects and scenes that children can connect to real items and events in their own lives.

> *After reading the book* Where the Wild Things Are *by Maurice Sendak, the children talked about what they would do if they were sent to their rooms for being bad. Most agreed they enjoyed spending time in their rooms. At small-group time the next day, their teacher set out paper, colored pencils, and markers and asked children to draw their rooms. Eric drew two beds, a small cage, and a big box in the middle. He explained, "One bed is for me and the other is for Grampa Johns. That's for the gerbil and this big box is for my toys and books and Grampa's books and extra blankets and a flashlight." After looking at his picture, Eric made another rectangle in the corner. "I almost forgot the closet," he said. "Grampa Johns keeps his squishy smelly galoshes in there!" Then he drew a pair of big black boots. "Now it's done!" he announced.*

▲ **Encourage children to compare models and illustrations with the real things they represent.** Encourage preschoolers to make comparisons between two- and three-dimensional representations and the real objects or events they portray. Not only do children become aware of what the model signifies, they eventually notice details that are the same as or different from those they encounter in real life. To help children make these connections and comparisons, avoid drilling them with close-ended questions (for example, "What's the girl in the painting holding?"). Instead, invite children to discuss the associations they make with objects and activities in visual representations by commenting on similarities *they* see (for example, "The watering can the girl in the painting is holding is like the one we have in our sandbox"). Such a comment opens the door for a natural conversation about things that are meaningful to the child.

▲ **Provide a variety of model-making materials.** Young children make three-dimensional models with both **pliable materials** (things that can be shaped and molded) and **fixed or rigid materials** (things that keep their structure and

---

Benefits of Exploring Art Materials

Young children benefit in many areas of development when they explore art materials. Handling materials, planning and reflecting on what they create, and collaborating with classmates contributes to their perceptual-motor, cognitive, and social growth. HighScope teachers therefore provide ample time throughout the day for preschoolers to explore art materials and processes.

Model-making materials. Working with three-dimensional materials gives children the satisfaction of creating something with their hands while helping them develop knowledge about space, including notions about the relative size and shape of objects and how things come apart and fit together. Additionally, children often collaborate as they build models, for example, a ramp for cars or a counter and stools for a restaurant. In this social process, they learn to assist one another and practice resolving conflicts.

Drawing and painting materials. As with three-dimensional (modeling) materials, young children benefit from unhurried time to discover the properties of two-dimensional art supplies and tools. Working with line, shape, color, and texture develops their overall aesthetic sense.

---

shape). Pliable materials typically found in a High-Scope classroom include clay, dough, beeswax, and damp sand. Fixed or rigid materials include blocks of all sizes and shapes made of different types of materials such as wood, cardboard, foam, and plastic (for example, snap-together blocks). Other materials that can be used to make models include paper, stones, and twigs, wood scraps (a local lumberyard will often donate the latter), cartons and boxes, plastic containers, pipe cleaners, and other household recyclables. HighScope classrooms also provide tools to mold pliable substances and to create impressions on them, such as kitchen items (egg cartons, cookie cutters, garlic presses) and carpentry tools (clamps, awls, chisels, screws, nuts, and bolts). Finally, young children need supplies and tools for resizing and fastening modeling materials — tools such as scissors, staplers, tape, glue, rubber bands, string and yarn, hole punches, hammers and nails, saws, and hand drills.

> *At work time in the toy area, Carey used the Magnatiles. She put four squares on the floor and a triangle at the top. She said, "This is the horses' house."*

▲ **Provide a variety of materials for drawing and painting.** Typical materials include paints, paper, paintbrushes, markers, crayons, colored pencils, and stamps and inkpads. Paper (including scrap and recycled paper) should be of many different textures, sizes, and colors, not just plain white sheets or multicolored construction paper. Materials for making two-dimensional art

---

Open-Ended Questions and Comments Can Encourage Children to Talk About Art

Too many questions can end rather than extend a conversation (see Chapter 5). However, a well-timed inquiry, in which the adult invites a child's ideas, can lead to an instructive exchange. Here are some ways to phrase questions and comments that convey an adult's genuine interest and will encourage children to respond thoughtfully about art.

How does the (material) feel (or smell or other appropriate sense)?

> For example, "How do the beads feel?" or "How does the clay smell?"

What does the (material or tool) remind you of?

> For example, "What else does the straw make you think of?"

What can we do with _____ (material or tool)?

> For example, "What do you think we could do with these shells and pebbles?"

How did [will] you make that? What did [will] you use?

> For example, "How did [will] you build the boat?" or "What did [will] you use to make your boat?"

What did you find out about the _____ (material or tool)?

> For example, "Jason used the tapestry hook today. Jason, what did you learn about using the tapestry hook?"

How did you make this _____ (point to and name a line, shape, or artistic effect)?

> For example, "How did you make this shape that's open at one end and narrow at the other?"

How did you get that color?

> For example, "I wonder what paints you mixed to get this peachy color." or "How did you make all the different shades of green in your picture?"

Tell (another child) about the _____ (materials or tools) you used.

> For example, "Elizabeth, Ali would like to know how you glazed your cup yesterday. She wants to glaze her bowl today."

What made you think of making/doing that?

> For example, "Chris, what made you decide to make a doghouse?"

How else could you use the (material or tool)?

> For example, "What is a different way you can think of to fold the paper?"

What do you think would happen if _____ (suggest a manipulation of a material or tool)?

> For example, "What do you suppose would happen if we dipped the yarn in water first?"

I'd like to hear more about _____ (material, tool, or action).

> For example, "I'd like to hear more about the way you used these brushes on the wood."

I wonder what's the same (or different) about these _____ (materials or tools).

> For example, "I wonder what's the same about the watercolor and acrylic paints" or "I wonder how the clay and dough are different."

180

Children are creative in creative ways! This girl swings on her stomach to investigate the effect of her movements on the marks she is making on the paper she has spread on the ground.

can be stored not only in the art area, but also in the writing or house area.

Over and above these basic materials, it is also important to provide young children with tools to make marks and create textures. These can be conventional writing objects (such as pens and pencils, rulers, shapes for tracing, brushes of different widths), but keep in mind that unconventional tools also encourage creativity. HighScope classrooms provide young children with cooking and eating utensils (such as basters, rolling pins, forks), woodworking tools (such as screwdrivers, pliers, and chisels), and other assorted objects (for example, wheels and other toy parts, hairbrushes and toothbrushes, string and yarn, and screens with different mesh sizes) that create interesting artistic effects when used with paint or ink on paper, for example.

In addition to the materials children manipulate directly, there are also several computer drawing programs that are suitable for preschoolers. Because it is sometimes easier for young children's hands to manage a mouse or keyboard than to manipulate certain art materials, these programs give them the flexibility to move and transform lines and objects as they create two-dimensional representations. Computer programs also allow children to explore color mixing, light and shadow, pattern and texture, and other visual effects.

HighScope teachers also offer different types of surfaces on which children can create two-dimensional artwork. In addition to providing easels and table surfaces, classrooms allow the flexibility to move furniture and create a large space on the floor for children to paint, draw, or create murals and collages. Taping paper to the wall provides a vertical surface to supplement easels. The outdoor environment also offers many opportunities for making art — for example, painting or drawing on the pavement or weaving various materials into a chain-link fence.

▲ **Encourage children to explore art materials.** To facilitate children's explorations of art materials, allow children ample time to work with materials throughout the daily routine.

In addition to making a wide variety of supplies and tools available at work time and small-group time, encourage children to represent their plans and recall their activities by illustrating their ideas and experiences. Introduce new art materials, and let children discover additional properties of familiar materials at small- and large-group time. Accept what children represent and stress the process of exploring art materials rather than expecting them to make a prescribed product. Explore the art materials with them. Art researcher Anna Kindler (1995) observed that when adults simply work alongside them, children are more likely to use the art materials for a longer time and talk spontaneously about what they are doing.

Acknowledge children's descriptive statements about the materials and how they are using them. Do not presume to know what a child has made or even assume a child has made anything. Never force children to talk about the materials or the artwork they are creating with them. Instead, listen

Talking to Parents About Children's Artwork

Sometimes parents pressure children, and their teachers, to produce "refrigerator-ready" artwork. By explaining to parents how and why the process of using and enjoying art materials is educationally more valuable than making a specified product, HighScope teachers help them understand and appreciate the value of artistic exploration rather than production at this age. By using the key developmental indicators to label children's artwork, teachers further help parents appreciate what their children are learning as they freely explore materials.

to children and invite them to share their actions and observations with adults and classmates. Finally, acknowledge children's artwork in meaningful and nonjudgmental ways. (See "praise vs. encouragement" in Chapter 5).

▲ **Display and send home children's artwork.** HighScope teachers create opportunities for children to share their artwork with others. For example, teachers display children's artwork on the wall and on shelves or pedestals throughout the room. Keeping these at children's eye level guarantees children will notice them and increases the likelihood children will talk spontaneously about the intentions and ideas behind their creations. Teachers also send children's artwork home with parents. Displaying and sharing artwork, regardless of its artistic content or skill level, conveys to children that their creations are important.

▲ **Expose children to the materials and techniques used by visual artists.** There are many ways to help young children appreciate the work of visual artists. Illustrated storybooks are a wonderful source of artwork done in different styles (for example, realistic and abstract, simple and complex, color and black and white) and using many types of media (paint, pen and ink, photographs, collage, and so on). With both new and familiar books, call children's attention to the pictures and draw out their thoughts about the artwork. Keep in mind, however, that sometimes children can more easily focus on the pictures as works of art if they are first familiar with the story.

Other ways in which adults can acquaint children with fine art include bringing in reproductions such as postcards and posters, inviting artists to the classroom, taking children to visit artists in their studios, asking parents to share their artistic skills and talents with the children, and encouraging family members to bring in art from home, such as pottery, wall hangings, and framed photos. Young children can also go on field trips to museums and galleries, provided teachers work with docents beforehand to make sure the experience will be appropriate for preschoolers. Many museums, for example, have "hands-on" opportunities for young children to explore sculptures, relate the subject matter in paintings and sculptures to their own lives, and use real art materials in studio workshops.

Art educator Suzanne Kolodziej (1995) describes a project where preschoolers created their own Picture Museum before visiting the International Museum of Photography in Rochester, New York. The children brought in favorite photographs of themselves and gave them titles, which led to discussions about where and when each picture was taken and why it was important to the child who it belonged to. The children also labeled the photographs and made a catalog with their comments. This experience involved children in many participatory ways. In choosing a photograph for the Picture Museum, they expressed an aesthetic preference. By describing the image, they engaged in art criticism. While creating titles, labels, and an exhibit catalog, the children acquired a sense of how museums are organized and operate. As a result, when the children later visited the museum, they had a firsthand basis for understanding such concepts as museum, art collection, and photography as an art form.

> 🔑 **HighScope Key Developmental Indicators in Dramatic Art**
> ❖ Imitating actions and sounds
> ❖ Pretending and role playing

Dramatic Art

Dramatic art in young children involves both **imitation** and imagination. When children imitate, they use gestures, sounds, and props to represent and tell stories about the world they know. In using their imagination, preschoolers express their fantasies. They act out the "what if's" that fill their thoughts and reveal their feelings and intentions. Recreating or modifying the events in their lives also helps young children understand and feel a sense of control over their environment.

At work time in the house area, Ella, Talia, and Sue (a teacher) played together with the dolls. Talia pretended to be a doctor and Ella pretended to be the pharmacist. Sue took prescriptions from Talia and gave them to Ella. Ella filled bottles with sand and gave them back to Sue.

In preschool, the purpose of dramatic art is discovery and exploration, not performance — just as HighScope emphasizes process over product in the early development of visual art. **Pretending** and **role playing** are also inherently social activities. Children interact with one another and partnering adults; they contribute ideas and build on the ideas of others. And although HighScope teachers do not pressure preschoolers to put on dramatic productions, they recognize that children can and do enjoy watching and discussing the performances of others. Live theater, especially productions whose length and content are created with young children's interests and developmental levels in mind, present exciting opportunities for children to experience and reflect on theater as yet another means of creative representation.

HighScope has two key developmental indicators in dramatic art. The first encourages children to be aware of and imitate the movements and sounds in their environment. *Imitation* refers to children's attempts to reproduce the actions and sounds they encounter in their everyday experiences. It need not be an exact duplication, but is rather children's interpretation or identification of what is meaningful in these movements and

sounds. The second focuses on pretending and role playing — a type of play that is a significant part of preschoolers' spontaneous activity. When children pretend and act out various roles, they go beyond reproducing their experiences to inventing or creating new scenarios. By acting out what they see and hear, young children make sense of the people and events in their daily lives, much as adult storytellers try to find meaning or impart lessons with the tales they create. Following are **support strategies** you can use to encourage and extend this natural and rewarding process.

▲ **Imitate and extend children's actions and sounds.** Children use their bodies and voices to imitate or reproduce the actions and sounds around them. You can support this type of representation by in turn imitating what the children do. For example, if a child "meows" and pretends to lap milk from a bowl on the floor, you might meow and do the same.

Imitating a child's action may lead to an **action dialogue.** For example, Corinna, a preschooler, announced she was leading an aerobics class at work time. She stretched her arms high over her head. Her teacher, Gary, imitated her stretching action. When Corinna kicked one foot and then the other forward, Gary did the same. After she performed each part of the exercise routine, Corinna paused and looked at Gary to see if he would imitate her. Only after he reproduced her actions did Corinna go on to the next one.

▲ **Build opportunities for imitation into the daily routine.** You will find there are many natural opportunities for children to imitate or recreate actions and sounds throughout the day. For example, at recall time, they can pantomime what they did at work time. After a teacher reads a book at greeting circle or small-group time, children can imitate the actions of the characters in the story. When children sing a song during large-group time, they can act out familiar verses (for example, "rowing" their boat) or make up new verses and accompany them with appropriate actions ("This is the way we brush our hair").

Imitation, especially of creative and unusual movements or sounds, is also a way to make cleanup time fun for children. For example, when Andee walked backward to put away the blocks, her teacher, Jeannette, copied her movements. Soon, the entire class declared it a "backward cleanup day." On another occasion, Charles "flew"

In pretending and role play, children represent experiences from their everyday lives and use their imaginations to invent new ones. They create props with diverse materials in the classroom.

each item to the shelf and made buzzing airplane sounds as he put away the toys he'd been playing with. His teacher imitated both the gestures and noises while cleaning up alongside him.

Children also see and hear many new things to imitate by going on field trips. A good way to help children recall and reflect on these experiences is by having the children recreate the actions and sounds that were meaningful to them. Once they get started, children will spontaneously imitate what they saw and heard on their own. You can also initiate this activity on the ride back to the classroom, at snacktime, or during a follow-up small-group activity.

> *The class went on a field trip to the zoo where they visited the Penguin House. The next day, at work time at the water table, Dahlia used the small dinosaur figures and said, "I'm pretending they're penguins." She walked them around the edge of the water table and then pretended that they went diving into the water. She said, "They are swimming and diving."*

▲ **Provide materials and space for pretending and role play.** In each area of your classroom, keep a wide variety of materials for children to use in pretending and role playing. For example, equipment and dress-up clothes in the house area might encourage children to role play in family, restaurant, or office scenarios. Children also create their own props, using supplies from around the room. So, for the examples just given, children might sculpt food with clay from the art area, add up the bill with a calculator from the mathematics area, or write letters with a program in the computer area.

> *At work time in the house area, Theo pretended to be a doctor by wearing a stethoscope and taking care of a doll. He said, "When I get sick, I help myself because I'm a doctor."*

Be observant of the people and events children choose to portray in their role playing activities so you can provide additional materials and props to support these interests. For example, in one classroom, when several children who had gone camping with their families during summer vacation began to act out these experiences,

Pretending and Role Play at Large-Group Time

In a classroom in which one group of children had been pretending with "boats" made of large blocks, another group had been pretending with a real camping tent the teachers had set up in the classroom, and a third group had been playing mermaids, the teacher built on elements from all three groups by starting a large-group time with an invitation to the children to pretend to sail to an exotic land with her. The teacher planned a few prompts, such as, "What should we take onboard?" and "What do we see?" to get things started, but then followed the children's leads as the fantasy unfolded; for example, when they discovered "jewels in a treasure chest" (buttons in a box) and swam away from the sea monsters they saw with their "spyglasses" (empty paper towel tubes).

teachers added flashlights and a sleeping bag to the house area. Parents, informed of the children's interest, contributed a tent and a cookstove.

Pretending and role play also occur outdoors. Wheeled toys (such as bicycles or wagons) may serve as buses, trains, airplanes, or boats. Climbing structures become houses, forts, tents, and igloos. And small items from nature, such as pebbles and leaves, are feast for a banquet or birthday party. Additional materials from the classroom (for example, scarves, dolls, dishes) can be brought outside to further help children extend and elaborate their dramatic activity.

Keep in mind that large and fluid spaces inspire and enable pretending and role playing. An open area can become anything the children want it to be — for example, a planet, a campground, or a doctor's office. Also note that dramatic play often overlaps play areas. For example, as children play in the house area they may "build" a backyard barbecue in the block area. By arranging the program space with these two areas next to one another, teachers encourage this type of expansive and creative play.

> *At work time in the block area, Noel worked with Dennis to build a tent. Noel got chairs from his small-group table and*

184

put them together on the carpet, then covered them with a blanket he retrieved from the house area. He made another tent for Rose, and said to her, "It can be anything, like a ship."

▲ **Provide experiences that encourage pretending and role play.** Group times provide many opportunities to introduce the idea of pretending to children. Because they act out their own experiences and fantasies, these activities are most successful when they build on the children's interests and play themes.

At small-group time, for example, you might ask a child to describe a picture he or she has made, or to make up a story. The rest of the group might then act out the ideas in the picture or the story. A familiar storybook, read by a teacher at small-group time, can also inspire the children to portray the characters and events. At large-group time, the children can gather props from around the room and act out a collective fantasy.

In addition to encouraging pretending and role play during regular parts of the daily routine, HighScope teachers plan special experiences that inspire and provide added depth to this kind of play — experiences such as field trips and special visitors to the classroom. Visitors include adult family members, people from the community (artists, storekeepers, construction workers), babies (younger siblings brought in by parents), and even family pets and other animals. Children are naturally interested in all these things, so they are appropriate starting points for acting out roles and elaborating fantasies. Visitors can often leave behind props (for example, cash register receipts or measuring tapes) that add authenticity to the children's play.

▲ **Participate as a partner in children's pretend play.** Child development and theater expert Vivian Paley (1990) concludes that adults who

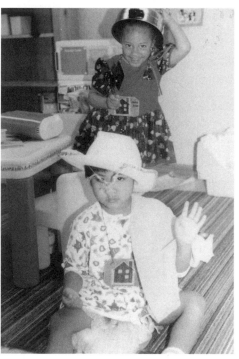

Children enjoy dressing up and using classroom materials in inventive ways. They act out the stories they read and hear, and elaborate on characters and events with their own fantasies.

participate as partners in children's play are better observers, understand children more, and communicate with children more effectively. However, partnering must be done with sensitivity so that children retain control of the play. HighScope teachers therefore observe children's pretend play and take time to understand children's intentions before joining in. The adults either wait until they are invited or pick up on other cues that suggest their involvement would be welcomed.

At work time in the house area, LaMarr, Rona, and Dawn (a teacher) played "restaurant." LaMarr served Dawn chicken soup. He typed letters on the computer, printed out the document, and showed it to Dawn. He said that it was the recipe. Dawn asked LaMarr to tell her what was in the soup.

To make sure they do not "take over," HighScope teachers follow several guidelines. One is to continue with the play theme set by the children — for example, being another dog or baby rather than adding a new type of character. A second rule of thumb is to stay within the play situation when offering suggestions; for example, if the children are pretending to visit the doctor, a teacher would not suggest an emergency ambulance trip from the office to the hospital. A third guideline is to match the complexity of the children's play — that is, to interact and scaffold learning at their developmental level rather than trying to "push" them to a much higher level. Finally, teachers acknowledge and accept children's responses to their suggestions. If children do not pick up on the adult's idea, they let it go. Or they will ask the players, "What do you think we should do?"

▲ **Expose children to the materials and techniques used by dramatic artists.** Young children are generally more interested in child-initiated pretending for themselves than they are in putting on an adult-conceived performance for others. However, they can gain an appreciation of dramatic arts by attending live productions. An increasing number of community theater groups stage performances specifically for young audiences, keeping in mind both the appropriate length and content that will hold their interest. Some performance artists might also be open to allowing children to attend rehearsals or to watch how stage sets are built. Actors and storytellers can also come to the classroom to perform and interact with children. If they contribute props, or use classroom materials in their performances, children are likely to incorporate these in their subsequent play.

In preparing for these experiences (as with visits to museums), learn as much as possible about the performance. That way, you can involve children in related activities ahead of time and make the live performance more meaningful to them. For example, if a play is based on a classic children's story, you might read it several times at small-group time in the weeks before the field trip or visit. Also look for ways to extend the theater experience afterward, planning opportunities for children to represent their experiences. For example, you might add large empty cartons to the block area and socks and yarn to the art area for children who want to recreate a puppet show they saw.

Finally, because movies and television are a pervasive part of young children's lives, there may be appropriate opportunities for selective viewing of recorded performances. For example, the children might view a video or DVD of the school play or of a puppet show they have seen live. Watching a tape never substitutes for the real thing, but — like looking at photographs — it can help children recall the live performance they experienced firsthand.

Further, guided television and movie viewing with adults can be a springboard for more active learning. For example, at small-group time, children might use art and construction materials to represent the characters and events portrayed. Or they may develop a play theme at work time based on a movie or show they've seen with their families. To help children move beyond mere repetition of scripted lines, HighScope teachers encourage more complex play by adding related

materials, entering in as a co-player, offering ideas to extend the play (while not straying far from the children's themes), and providing the children with a broader store of real-life experiences (through field trips and visitors) so the children have more interests on which to base their pretend play.

Music

Young children and music are natural partners. As with other areas of art, the emphasis in music is on exploration and discovery — not production or performance — and also on music appreciation. HighScope has six key developmental indicators in music, encompassing a wide range of developmental experiences with sound, singing and melody, and simple musical instruments. Following are **support strategies** you can use to foster children's musical exploration.

> ### 🔑 HighScope Key Developmental Indicators in Music
>
> ❖ Moving to music
> ❖ Exploring and identifying sounds
> ❖ Exploring the singing voice
> ❖ Developing melody
> ❖ Singing songs
> ❖ Playing simple musical instruments

▲ **Encourage children to explore and identify sounds.** Because of their new ability to represent things, preschoolers enjoy listening to different sounds and identifying the things that make them. Call children's attention to the sounds that naturally occur around them, both inside and outside the classroom. These might include birdsong, wind, traffic, school bells, ticking clocks, a door opening and closing as people enter and leave the classroom, older children playing in the schoolyard, rain on the roof, the telephone, and so on. Also provide a variety of noise-making materials (such as musical instruments, music players, metronomes, timers, wind-up clocks, or computer programs that talk) and things children can use or combine to make their own sounds (for example, beads or pebbles

186

shaken in a pan, wooden sticks banged together, sandpaper rubbed on different types of surfaces, or water squirting from a hose on the pavement).

In addition to providing a wide variety of sounds, intentionally create opportunities for children to listen. For example, just before taking the class outside, you might say, "I wonder what we'd hear if we were quiet for a minute." You might also play sound guessing games at small- and large-group times using musical instruments or a tape recording of familiar sounds from the classroom or playground. Including unusual and less frequent sounds (for example, a basketball being dribbled or a creaky door) can also inspire children to do some creative problem solving.

Encourage children to describe the sounds they hear. Children may do this spontaneously ("I hear a siren!"), in which case you might respond with a comment ("That sounds like the fire engine — let's look out the window"). Occasionally ask sound-related open-ended questions ("Listen to that rain. How does it sound?"). Finally, keep in mind that if a teacher briefly comments on the sound a child is making ("You're banging the blocks together"), the child might continue the exchange ("They're going *click, clack, click, clack*"). Accept the words children use to describe sounds ("It's my whizzle stick because it goes *whizz*"), and help children expand their vocabulary by providing labels for the sounds that interest them.

▲ **Encourage children to explore sounds and singing with their own voices.** Invite children to explore their own voices in two ways — through the sounds they make in general and through their singing voices in particular. When children play, they often use their voices to create characters ("Waaa, I'm a baby"), imitate the sounds of machines ("Crrrch" or "Jing, jing"), and call attention to their own actions and discoveries ("Mmmm, yummy mud cakes!").

In addition to making sounds to enrich their play, children just enjoy creating and listening to the range of sounds

Preschoolers enjoy singing familiar songs and making up words to the melodies they know. Exploring their singing voices helps children develop language and music skills at the same time.

Introducing a New Song

To introduce a new song, HighScope teachers learn to first establish a steady beat (for example, by patting it on their knees with both hands) and encourage children to pat the beat with them. Adults then sing the song through so children can hear the melody and the words. The song's pitch should be on the high side (children's short vocal cords make it easier for them to sing in a higher range). The entire song should be sung through several times. Gradually, more children will be able to join in as the melody and words become familiar. Repeating the song several days in a row will enable more children to learn it.

their voices can produce. Adults can support this exploration by listening to and imitating sounds (for example, when Mara waved a scarf and said "Whoosh," her teacher did the same), offering comments and acknowledgments ("At work time today, I heard Billy say, 'Whee, I fell on my knee'"), and encouraging children to try vocal variations ("I wonder if we can make our voices go up really high"). When children use their voices expressively, as in the last example, they are also exploring one of the attributes that distinguishes music from other types of sounds. Children also enjoy humming and singing, often repeating the same notes and phrases over and over again.

By putting together bits and pieces of familiar songs, or making up their own songs, children develop a sense of melody. You can support this awareness in several ways. If you hear children singing, join in. Often an adult voice helps to stabilize the children's pitch and they can follow along. Or, an adult can sing the first few notes of a familiar song (such as "Old MacDonald") as children gradually chime in. Singing comments to children is also fun and often heightens their attention (for example, singing "Aletha's making big red circles" to the tune of "Mary Had a Little Lamb").

You can also initiate different types of singing games. For instance, you might play "guess this tune," in which you hum or play the first few notes of a familiar song and ask the children to guess what it is. After a few rounds of this, children may take turns humming songs as the others try to identify what it is. It does not matter if the children's humming or guessing is accurate; the significance of the experience is for children to create and listen for melody. Another type of game is **pitch-matching.** For example, a teacher might sing or play two notes and ask children to repeat them. Again, it does not matter if they match the pitch exactly. With time and experience, children will begin to hear and replicate pitches more accurately.

▲ **Play a wide variety of recorded and live music.** Children need many opportunities to hear and move to a wide range of music. In stocking the music area and choosing what to play at group times and transitions, provide an assortment that can include folk music from around the world, classical music, jazz and modern music, march and circus music, and waltzes, tangos, and ballets. Include styles of music representative of local cultures and communities and invite family members to loan the class their favorite music tapes and CDs. Live music is also a special treat for everyone, adults and children alike. Teachers, other staff members, parents, and musicians from the community can all provide music in the classroom.

Depending on the planned activity, music may be played as part of large- and small-group times, outside time, or during transitions. Children may also choose to listen to CDs or tapes in a music area or quiet area at work time. However, HighScope classrooms do not have music playing as "background noise" throughout the day. Constant music can be distracting and may make it harder for children to focus on the thoughts and actions of interest to them, or to converse with others. Treating music as background also does not allow children and adults to actively engage with it and pay attention to music's valuable qualities.

▲ **Sing with children.** Just as children enjoy listening to different types of music, they also enjoy singing in different musical styles. They like nursery rhymes with their sing-song rhythms, such as "Rain, Rain, Go Away" or "Baa, Baa, Black Sheep"; traditional children's songs such as "The Farmer in the Dell" or "If You're Happy and You Know It"; simple folk songs such as "She'll Be Comin' 'Round the Mountain" or "Are You Sleeping?"; and songs for special occasions such as "Happy Birthday," "Jingle Bells," or "The Dreidl Song." Gradually introduce these and other songs, and allow many opportunities for repetition. By the end of the program year, preschool children can have quite a repertoire of songs that they recognize and are able to sing.

Simple instruments, for example, rhythm sticks, help children develop basic musicality and time concepts, such as starting and stopping. Playing together also creates a sense of community.

To help make singing a regular part of children's experience, plan ways to include it throughout the daily routine. Large-group time is a natural occasion for singing familiar songs and introducing new ones. Less experienced singers can easily join in and hone their skills along with those who are more practiced.

Adults and children can also sing together at planning and recall times. For example, to the tune of "Row, Row, Row Your Boat," everyone can sing, "Work, work, work, today, where do I plan to work?" before each child names the area where he or she will play.

There are many opportunities to sing during children's ongoing play at work or outside time, for example, singing lullabies as children rock a doll to sleep or singing "The Wheels on the Bus" while they pretend to be drivers and passengers on the playground. Children often make up their own songs and chants to accompany their actions during play, for example, "Up and down, up and down, I am swinging up and down." You can encourage other adults and children to take up the song, thereby acknowledging the child's singing and giving him or her the satisfaction of being the leader. There are also storybooks that illustrate songs, which adults and children can read and sing during work or small-group time. Playing back tape recordings of children singing is also a favorite small-group activity. Children like to identify their own and others' voices, which helps them develop both their listening and representational skills.

Transitions, such as cleanup time, are always easier when accompanied by singing. For example, the song "This Is the Way We…" can be adapted for singing about cleaning and putting things away (for example, "This is the way we wash the table" or "This is the way we stack the blocks").

Finally, singing is a wonderful way to begin and end parent meetings. It draws the group together and provides an opportunity for family members to share the songs they know and find personally meaningful. Similarly, singing during staff meetings can be a way to bring coworkers together and foster a collaborative spirit, particularly before or after the group solves a problem.

▲ **Encourage simple ways of moving to music.** When young children hear live or recorded music, they naturally want to move to it. Providing

Children in HighScope programs listen to many types of music and move to music in many different ways. This variety reflects the musical diversity of their homes, schools, and communities.

children the opportunity to hear a variety of music styles in the classroom will encourage them to move in different ways, such as fast and slow, bouncy and smooth, intense and relaxed, and to try different specific motions, such as swaying and marching.

To further promote moving to music, imitate children's actions and call attention to the different movements of their classmates ("Li Yuan is swinging his arms back and forth" or "Eleanor is sliding across the floor"). You can also create simple movement sequences to music together with children. For example, you might take a song with two parts (such as "Yankee Doodle") and come up a different motion for each part — for example, marching to the verse and waving arms during the chorus.

At large-group time, Vanna marched to the march music being played. When it changed to a slower tempo, she glided across the floor.

▲ **Provide simple instruments.** HighScope classrooms typically have a wide range of musical instruments that young children can play. The music area might include wood blocks, drums, xylophones, tambourines, triangles, bells, spoons, maracas, washboards, pots and spoons, wooden sticks, and a wide variety of homemade noisemakers (filled, for example, with beads, dried pasta, rice, pebbles, metal washers, or wood chips). Instruments that reflect the children's cultures are also included in the music area mix.

At work time, Eddie set up the hand drums and some other percussion instruments in the style of a drum set. He sat on the floor and played various drum patterns.

You will find that children enjoy playing these instruments on their own, for example, at work or outside time. You can also introduce them during small- and large-group times. Children can play them as they sing a familiar song or parade around the room or playground, taking turns being the leader. Another option is to divide the group in half so that the children in one group play the instruments while those in the other dance; then have children switch roles. Some stories lend themselves to being represented with musical instruments — for example, playing different pitches on the xylophone for the baby, mama, and papa bear of *The Three Bears* or asking the

Strategies for Supporting the Arts: A Summary

Visual Art

__ Provide models, photographs, and pictures.

__ Encourage children to compare models and illustrations with the real things they represent.

__ Provide a variety of model-making materials.

__ Provide a variety of materials for drawing and painting.

__ Encourage children to explore art materials.

__ Display and send home children's artwork.

__ Expose children to the materials and techniques used by visual artists.

Dramatic Art

__ Imitate and extend children's actions and sounds.

__ Build opportunities for imitation into the daily routine.

__ Provide materials and space for pretending and role play.

__ Provide experiences that encourage pretending and role play.

__ Participate as a partner in children's pretend play.

__ Expose children to the materials and techniques used by dramatic artists.

Music

__ Encourage children to explore and identify sounds.

__ Encourage children to explore sounds and singing with their own voices.

__ Play a wide variety of recorded and live music.

__ Sing with children.

__ Encourage simple ways of moving to music.

__ Provide simple instruments.

__ Expose children to the materials and techniques used by musical artists.

---

children to choose an instrument for each creature in *Where the Wild Things Are.*

Musical instruments can also enrich the stop-and-start games that help children develop concepts about time and timing (see Chapter 15). For example, musical chairs can be played to a drum (or other instrument) that is played by a teacher or child. (*Note:* This game is appropriate for preschoolers as long as there are no winners and losers — that is, the focus is simply on everyone finding a chair when the leader stops playing the instrument.)

Finally, transitions can be accompanied by instruments. For example, a teacher or child might play one to signal the beginning of cleanup time, varying the tempo so the other children move fast or slow as they put things away.

▲ **Expose children to the materials and techniques used by musical artists.** As with other art forms, developing an appreciation for music begins with children's interests and experiences. Virtually all children have been exposed to **environmental music** at home, in the car, in the supermarket, and so on. (Similar to the concept of

"environmental print," environmental music is the music children encounter all around them as they go about their daily lives.) Find out what types of music children's families typically listen to, and invite parents to bring examples to share with the classroom. If family members (including older siblings), other staff, or members of the community play instruments or sing, ask them to share their talents with the group. Some communities have programs (for example, those sponsored by Wolf Trap Foundation for the Performing Arts, headquartered in Vienna, Virginia) that pay for local performing artists, such as musicians, to come into the classroom.

Also take children on field trips to hear live musical performances. These may be school choir, band, or orchestra concerts or more "formal" concerts specifically planned for children. But there may also be many informal opportunities; for example, the street performances during a weekly farmer's market or an outdoor art fair.

Keep in mind that the best way to support music awareness and appreciation in young children is by exposing them to many different types

190

of music. Although HighScope teachers begin with what is familiar, they understand that children are interested in and open to hearing all kinds of musical styles and themes. In exploring these with children, teachers may discover new interests and preferences themselves!

Try These Ideas Yourself

1. List the five most important things you think preschoolers need to know or be able to do in each area of the arts when they enter kindergarten. Be sure to include knowledge and skills in visual arts, dramatic arts, and music. Why do you think these are important? How can teachers support young children's development in each of these areas?

2. In the following scenario, identify the key developmental indicators that are taking place in visual art. What types of learning are occurring in other areas of development? How could you as a teacher support and extend the learning? (Refer to the list of KDIs on p. 11.)

> *Susan's plan is to work in the art area and "paint a fence for my doghouse." After putting on a smock. she pumps red, yellow, and white paint into three cups and carries them to the easel. Then she chooses three brushes: thin, medium, and thick. Beginning on the left side of the paper, she makes a thin white stripe, a medium yellow stripe, and a wide red stripe. She paints three more stripes just like them. Then she puts the red brush into the yellow paint and says, "Look, I made orange." She paints the rest of the paper with wide orange stripes.*

3. Visit an art museum or gallery with someone you trust. As you walk around the exhibit, tell one another what you see and think (intellectually and emotionally) about the artwork on display. Pay attention to how the artwork looks (its color, shape, size, and so on), how it was made (the medium and technique used), the subject matter (whether it is realistic or abstract, what the artist is trying to say), and how it makes you feel. Listen carefully and patiently to what your companion has to say. Take time to find the words to express your own thoughts and feelings. What ideas does this give you for fostering art appreciation with young children?

4. List words you can use with children related to the features of a visual work of art, for example, *color, white space, line, shading,* and *shape.* Do the same in relation to drama (a play, movie, or television show); for example, *happy, scary, sad, exciting, characters,* and *dialogue.* Now list words that describe music; for example, *fast, slow, loud, soft, tinkly, booming, jumpy,* and *smooth.* Share your lists with a colleague and ask for additional ideas. Select some of these words to use each time you talk to children about artwork, drama, or music.

5. What type or types (styles, themes) of movies, plays, or television shows do you like? Why? In what ways did your experiences growing up influence your preferences as an adult? How can adults introduce children to a variety of dramatic styles?

6. Choose a character from the last movie, play, or television show you saw. In what ways is your personality or your life the same or different from that of this character? How could you encourage young children to compare themselves to characters they encounter in the media?

7. Do you tend to listen to one type of music? Or do you enjoy a mixture of styles and artists? Why? In what ways did your experiences growing up influence your preferences as an adult? How can adults introduce children to a variety of musical styles?

8. Listen to a piece of music. Move your body to the music and/or paint or draw a picture. Change to a different piece of music, for example, one with another mood or tempo. Move a different way and/or make another picture as you listen. How did each type of music make you feel? How were your feelings reflected in the way you moved your body or the image you created? How can you apply this experience to working with children in the classroom?

HighScope Assessment

This part of the book provides a comprehensive look at how HighScope assesses children and programs that serve them.

Chapter 18 explains the value of authentic assessment tools in evaluating and planning for children and describes HighScope's validated child assessment tools.

Chapter 19 looks at the value to children, teachers, and families of valid and reliable program assessments and describes HighScope's validated assessment tool.

How Does HighScope Assess Children?

Think About It

Lucy and her doctor are going over the blood tests from her annual physical exam. "Your total cholesterol level is 275, which is too high," says the doctor. "Anything over 240 puts you at risk for heart disease. I'm going to suggest some lifestyle changes and prescribe medication to lower your cholesterol level." The doctor explains the difference between "bad" and "good" cholesterol and shows Lucy her numbers on the lab report. She tells Lucy to reduce the amount of fat in her diet and gives her an information sheet on healthier eating. She also recommends that Lucy exercise at least 30 minutes a day, and together Lucy and her doctor discuss different options (walking, swimming, using the treadmill machine) and how Lucy can fit this regular activity into her schedule.

In the above scenario, both Lucy and her doctor are concerned about a potentially serious medical condition. By measuring Lucy's cholesterol before and after the recommended changes, they can assess whether the new diet, regular exercise, and prescribed medication are having the intended

Because HighScope teachers work closely with individual children, they can accurately assess their development. Looking at children as learners helps us look at ourselves as teachers.

effect of lowering her cholesterol level. If the results are good, Lucy can continue the new behavior pattern. If not, she and her doctor can explore additional options, such as trying a new medication.

In addition to simply being concerned about her own patient, Lucy's doctor, like other medical researchers, wants to know how different treatments work for the population as a whole. Does an old drug continue to be effective for many patients or for the same patient over time? Do new drugs work without having dangerous side effects? Are different medications effective for different people? How can doctors help patients understand and follow recommended lifestyle changes? Should other family members be included in the treatment plan?

Even in other types of situations where there is not a "problem," we may want to know if our day-to-day behavior is good for us, our associates, and our possessions, leading us to seek objective answers about our actions and their consequences. Sometimes the answer is obvious (for example, stepping on the scale tells us if we are losing weight), but other times we are not sure what questions to ask or how to measure the response.

194

Chapter Learning Objectives

By the end of this chapter, you will be able to

❖ Define *authentic assessment* and describe its benefits

❖ Describe the Child Observation Record (COR), a comprehensive measure of child development, and how it is used

❖ Describe the Early Literacy Skills Assessment (ELSA), a measure of early literacy development, and how it is used

Also, though we may be able to assess changes in our own behavior, there are times when we want or need to know how we compare to others. In this chapter's opening scenario, for example, it is not enough for Lucy and her doctor to know whether her cholesterol has gone down. They need to know whether it is at or below the safe level recommended by experts in the field.

Similarly, good early childhood assessment tools provide all these types of information about children and their progress in our programs. They help us focus on important child behaviors, especially in areas where we may not have expertise. For example, detailed measures in specific curriculum content areas can help us know what milestones to look for in early language development or emerging relationships between children. Appropriate, comprehensive instruments also allow us to step back and take a broader view of the young children in our programs and whether we are meeting their needs. Looking at the children as learners thus helps us to look at ourselves as teachers.

Systematic assessment can help us organize our impressions and use them to create objective, numerically based reports. Although numbers do not replace the "words" in detailed anecdotes, they are handy for summarizing data gathered over time about one individual or for grouping information about the class as a whole. Numerical summaries also make it easier to communicate

with others, especially those who are not familiar with the individuals being assessed. Systematic assessment is especially useful for communicating with administrators, funders, policymakers, taxpayers, and others who care about the effectiveness of the program as a whole.

Because HighScope is concerned about individual children and teachers in the classroom, as well as system-level public policymakers, the Foundation's tools for assessing children serve multiple purposes. They are designed to look at meaningful educational outcomes, gather information in ways that are natural and comfortable for children and adults, and provide accurate data that can be used for individual child planning and policy-level decision making. Also, because HighScope is an advocate for sound early childhood practices in general, its assessment tools are designed for use by non-HighScope programs as well as by those that do use the HighScope Curriculum.

The Benefits of Authentic Assessment

If I could change one thing about teaching here, it would be to limit the busywork of evaluating children. I feel like I spend the whole first month out in the hall testing one child at a time, when I should be in the classroom with all the children. To top it off, once I've finished the testing, the information that I'm left with is not that useful in my teaching. What I need is something meaningful that doesn't take much time. (Detroit, Mich., Head Start Teacher)

Educators assess young children to see how they are developing and to measure how the programs the children attend contribute to the children's growth. Traditional **testing** — such as a series of multiple-choice questions — is one way to measure children's learning. But, as expressed by the teacher in the quote above, this type of test provides only limited information. It typically

---

Terms Used in This Chapter

• testing • authentic assessments • reliability • validity • standardized • Child Observation Record (COR)
• Early Literacy Skills Assessment (ELSA)

looks at learning for which there is one right answer. It does not indicate how children solve problems or collaborate with others. Moreover, it only shows how children do in the testing situation, not how they perform in real educational settings and everyday life.

Another way to measure children's development is with **authentic assessments.** These include objective observations, portfolios of children's work, and teacher and parent ratings of children's behavior. Authentic assessments are more naturalistic. They take place in the real world or duplicate a familiar situation instead of creating an artificial testing environment. As such, they provide a more accurate picture of what children normally do and reflect their true capabilities.

Authentic assessments add to what we can learn from tests. They provide teachers with valuable and practical information to understand and plan for the developmental needs of their students. Authentic measures can look at a broader range of children's behavior than can tests, which tend to focus on a single area of learning. With authentic assessments, the assessment process itself is more open ended — that is, it can allow for multiple answers and may even look at how children arrive at them. Finally, authentic measures often assess children over a longer period of time than a single test, so results do not depend on how children feel or on children's willingness to perform on a particular day.

HighScope recognizes that tests can be informative and are sometimes necessary — for example, for research or diagnostic purposes. Tests may be the only feasible option in large-scale program evaluations and are often required by a funding source. However, the Foundation is a strong proponent of authentic assessment, especially with young children. It therefore develops authentic tools to measure overall development, as well as learning in specific curriculum content areas.

The assessment instruments HighScope develops are always validated, meaning they meet the same rigorous scientific standards for **reliability** and **validity** as do conventional tests. A reliable assessment produces the same results when completed by different observers or at two closely-spaced points in time. A valid instrument measures what it claims, is consistent with findings from similar measures, and may also predict future behavior. When developed according to these strict requirements, authentic measures can and should be as **standardized** as conventional tests.

This chapter describes two authentic assessment tools developed and validated by HighScope. One is the **Child Observation Record (COR),** which is an objective observational assessment that looks at all areas of early development. The COR comes in preschool and infant-toddler versions. The other is the **Early Literacy Skills Assessment (ELSA),** which recreates the natural situation of an adult reading a book to a child and

Advantages of Authentic Assessment

- ❖ Based on real performance of the child, rather than an artificial testing situation
- ❖ Can focus on a broad range of developmental areas
- ❖ Assesses thinking and problem-solving abilities, not just factual knowledge
- ❖ Produces a profile of change and development over time
- ❖ Helps adults develop objective observational skills
- ❖ Helps adults become more knowledgeable about child development
- ❖ Encourages programs to become more child-oriented (view learning from child's perspective)

- ❖ Provides child-focused information adults can use to plan activities
- ❖ Makes adults pay attention to the "invisible" child
- ❖ If done as part of regular ongoing activities, does not add to program time or cost
- ❖ Can be done by all staff, including aides and assistants, with proper training
- ❖ Provides feedback to program administration and funding agencies
- ❖ Provides valuable and meaningful information for staff and parents to share

196

then examines early literacy development in four key areas.

HighScope has also developed, or is developing, authentic tools to observe children's behavior during other types of experiences, such as those involving visual arts, mathematics and science, movement and music, conflict resolution, and intergenerational programs for seniors and young children. Because all these authentic measures assess universal characteristics of children's development, they can be used by any early childhood program, not just those implementing the HighScope Curriculum.

Child Observation Record (COR)

COR Overview

The Child Observation Record (COR) is an observation-based instrument that provides systematic assessment of young children's knowledge and abilities in all areas of development. The Preschool COR (HighScope Educational Research Foundation, 2003a) is used to assess children from the ages of two-and-a-half to six years. The Infant-Toddler COR (HighScope Educational Research Foundation, 2002) is for programs serving children between the ages of six weeks and three years. Because children develop at different rates, rather than according to an exact timetable, the two measures overlap in the age range covered. They are also useful for programs serving children with special needs, whose chronological and developmental ages may differ widely on one or more dimensions. As noted above, these authentic instruments can be used by any programs serving children in these developmental ranges, not just those using the HighScope Curriculum.

COR Components

The COR kit is made up of several components designed to assist observers in collecting and using the assessment data. It is available in paper-and-pencil format, on CD-ROM, and on the internet at *www.onlinecor.net*. In all versions, the *User Guide* provides the rationale for the COR, reports on its reliability and validity in national and state research studies, and explains how to use each

component of the kit. It includes step-by-step instructions for collecting anecdotal records and scoring the COR. However, the *User Guide* is not intended as a substitute for COR training, which HighScope strongly recommends and makes available through numerous courses and workshops (see Chapter 21).

COR Content

The COR is organized into **categories** of development. Within each category is a list of **observation items.** The items are based on the key developmental indicators (KDIs) in each content area for the age range covered. There are six categories and 32 items on the Preschool COR and six categories and 28 items on the Infant-Toddler COR (see the sidebar on p. 197). Under each of the items are five **developmental levels** that describe behavior ranging from simple (1) to more complex (5).

Completing the COR

Using the COR is a continuous process. Adults record objective anecdotal notes on children throughout the year (see Chapter 9) and use them to score the COR at periodic intervals. Raters may also use information from portfolios, photographs, or other types of documentation to complete COR ratings. Although teachers do not record an anecdote on every child, every day, in every category (which would not be feasible), they do make several observations per week per child. They periodically review their collection of anecdotes to make sure each child's behavior is documented in each of the COR categories. If they notice a gap, they pay special attention to that child and area over the next few days and record what they observe.

Using the notes or other documentary evidence relevant to each item, raters score or "level" the entries on a scale of 1 to 5 to reflect each child's current level of development. Depending on a program's needs and reporting requirements, the anecdotes are used to complete and score the COR two or three times a year, for example, at the beginning, midpoint, and end of the program. Less frequent measurement does not permit one to track development over time. More frequent measurement does not allow sufficient time between assessments for any changes to show up.

Categories and Items on the Child Observation Record (COR)

Preschool COR	Infant-Toddler COR

I. Initiative

A. Making choices and plans
B. Solving problems with materials
C. Initiating play
D. Taking care of personal needs

I. Sense of Self

A. Expressing initiative
B. Distinguishing self from others
C. Solving problems
D. Developing self-help skills

II. Social Relations

E. Relating to adults
F. Relating to other children
G. Resolving interpersonal conflict
H. Understanding and expressing feelings

II. Social Relations

E. Forming an attachment to a primary caregiver
F. Relating to unfamiliar adults
G. Relating to another child
H. Expressing emotion
I. Responding to the feelings of others
J. Playing with others

III. Creative Representation

I. Making and building models
J. Drawing and painting pictures
K. Pretending

III. Creative Representation

K. Pretending
L. Exploring building and art materials
M. Responding to and identifying pictures and photographs

IV. Movement and Music

L. Moving in various ways
M. Moving with objects
N. Feeling and expressing steady beat
O. Moving to music
P. Singing

IV. Movement

N. Moving parts of the body
O. Moving the whole body
P. Moving with objects
Q. Moving to music

V. Language and Literacy

Q. Listening to and understanding speech
R. Using vocabulary
S. Using complex patterns of speech
T. Showing awareness of sounds in words
U. Demonstrating knowledge about books
V. Using letter names and sounds
W. Reading
X. Writing

V. Communication and Language

R. Listening and responding
S. Communicating interest nonverbally
T. Participating in give-and-take communication
U. Speaking
V. Exploring picture books
W. Showing interest in stories, rhymes, and songs

VI. Mathematics and Science

Y. Sorting objects
Z. Identifying patterns
AA. Comparing properties
BB. Counting
CC. Identifying position and direction
DD. Identifying sequence, change, and causality
EE. Identifying materials and properties
FF. Identifying natural and living things

VI. Exploration and Early Logic

X. Exploring objects
Y. Exploring categories
Z. Developing number understanding
AA. Exploring space
BB. Exploring time

Sample Item From the Preschool COR

198

Below, you can look at a sample item from the Preschool COR, adapted from its *Observation Items* booklet. An item includes a short explanation, the five scoring levels, and examples of anecdotes that illustrate each level. All items in the Preschool COR and the Infant-Toddler COR follow this same format. For additional examples of COR items, see the HighScope Web site, *www.highscope.org*.

Item Q. Listening to and understanding speech

Level 1. Child responds with actions or words to a suggestion, request, or question.

The child acts on his or her understanding of a verbal request, suggestion, or question. The child may respond with speech or an action directed to the speaker or to someone else in the vicinity.

▲ *4/4: During cleanup time, when Lee drops the basket of markers on the floor and Eli says, "You need some help!" Eva looks up from her puzzle, walks to the art area, and helps Lee and Eli pick up the markers.*

▲ *9/13: During recall time, the teacher calls James on the phone and asks, "Where did you work today?" With the phone up to his ear, James points to the computer.*

▲ *11/30: At work time in the book area, Marla [a teacher] reads* Big Red Barn *(by Margaret Wise Brown and Felicia Bond) to Lonnette. Marla says, "I wonder where the kitty is?" Lonnette points to the kitty in the picture.*

Level 2. When listening to a story, rhyme, or narrative, child anticipates and fills in a word or phrase.

The child listens to a familiar spoken text and supplies the appropriate next words when the reader or teller pauses, hesitates, or speaks slowly.

▲ *10/20: At greeting time, Hector listens to Paul's dad read* The Very Hungry Caterpillar *(by Eric Carle). When Paul's dad reads, "And on Tuesday he ate through two…," Hector says, "Pears!"*

▲ *1/17: At large-group time, T.J. fills in the phrase "And do not let them in!" when the teacher pauses at the end of the song "Open, Shut Them."*

Level 3. When listening to a story, rhyme, or narrative, child comments on or asks a question about it.

The child listens to a spoken text, forms an idea or question about it, and then expresses it.

▲ *1/16: At greeting time, after hearing Renee [his teacher] tell a story about a dog on a boat, Nathan asks, "Why didn't the dog have a house?"*

▲ *4/19: At snack time, when his teacher reads the book* Pizza, *Sunil says, "My mommy made me a pizza last night."*

Level 4. Child contributes to an ongoing conversation.

The child listens to a conversation between two other people, has an idea of what they are talking about, and makes a bid to join it by making a related comment.

▲ *10/21: In the house area during work time, David and Willis talk about birthday parties. Justin listens and adds, "My mom and dad are going to buy me a big dinosaur for my birthday."*

▲ *7/11: At greeting time, Kendra watches and listens as Dewan and his dad discuss an upcoming zoo field trip. Kendra moves closer and asks, "Are we going to see seals there?"*

Level 5. Child sustains a dialogue, taking three or more conversational turns.

By now, the child attends to conversation and helps to keep it going by making statements the other person can respond to. The child may or may not initiate the conversation.

▲ *6/12: At work time in the block area, after building a block structure, Caitlin and Debi take a look at it.*

> *Caitlin: This is the princess's bedroom over here.*
> *Debi: Okay, then I'm gonna be the princess.*
> *Caitlin: I'll be your sister.*
> *Debi: You can have the bedroom next to mine.*

Caitlin: Let's go put our dresses on.

Debi: You wear the blue one, and I'll get the purple. (They do.)

Using the COR

The COR can be used by different people and for different purposes. Anyone who is familiar with the child(ren) being observed and who has been trained to record and score anecdotal notes can complete the COR. The COR is primarily used by teachers and caregivers responsible for daily planning and regular reporting on their program. It is also used extensively by researchers and evaluators studying child development and how it is affected by program participation. The COR may also be completed by parents, program volunteers and paraprofessionals, curriculum supervisors, and other program or administrative staff directly involved with the children. Training by a designated HighScope trainer is necessary to insure that all these individuals use the COR correctly.

> *In using the* Child Observation Record *to heighten their observational skills, teachers get excited about things they hadn't noticed before. This tool helps them focus and formalize the notes made on each child. Observation is good early childhood practice and should be the primary assessment tool!* (Houston, Texas, Early Childhood Program Supervisor)

Teachers are trained to write objective anecdotal notes about children's behavior and to use this systematic documentation to complete and score the Child Observation Record (COR).

Of particular value to those who use the COR for planning (that is, adults who work directly with children) is the booklet in the COR kit titled *What's Next: Planning Children's Activities Around Preschool [or Infant-Toddler] COR Observations.* This book helps teachers follow up on their observations by providing activities, ideas, and strategies directly tied to the levels of development highlighted in the COR. For each developmental level in each item, this booklet offers corresponding strategies for supporting and extending children's learning at that level. Below is an example for one of the sample items and levels presented above — Item Q, level 4, of the Preschool COR.

Sample From *What's Next*

Item Q: Listening to and understanding speech

Level Q-4: Child contributes to an ongoing conversation.

The following strategies will help you support children at level 4 as they contribute to classroom conversations throughout the day. (*Note:* The *focus child* is the one who the COR observation is written about.)

▲ Be available for conversation with the focus child throughout the day by placing yourself at the child's physical level; listening carefully to what the child is saying; giving the child control of the conversation by making comments and observations; accepting the child's hesitations and nonverbal utterances; learning and remembering the child's particular interests.

▲ Encourage the focus child to talk with other children throughout the day by providing opportunities for cooperative projects and play; putting this child in the same planning and recall group as the child(ren) this child often plays with; referring other children to this child with questions the child can answer.

▲ Include time for children's conversation, ideas, comments, and suggestions at small-group time and large-group time.

Sample Page From a COR Family Report Form

I. Initiative (Iniciativa)

Developmental summary (Resumen del desarrollo):

Lorena expresses a choice with a short sentence. She identifies a problem with materials and asks for help. Lorena engages in pretend play and accomplishes all parts of a self-care activity.

Supporting anecdotes (Anécdotas que lo complementan):

9/27   *At planning time, when asked what she was going to do at work time, Lorena pointed to the puzzles.*

10/24   *Outside, Lorena tried to reach the high swing and said, "I can't get it. Teacher, will you help me up?"*

Parent observations (Observaciones del padre o madre):

Mom said that Lorena wants to get out the dress-up clothes more often than she used to.

II. Social Relations (Relaciones Sociales)

Developmental summary (Resumen del desarrollo):

Lorena initiates an interaction with an adult. She invites another child to play and she identifies the problem in a conflict with another child. Lorena talks about an emotion.

Supporting anecdotes (Anécdotas que lo complementan):

11/2   *At work time, as Andee, the teacher, walked by the house area, Lorena said, "I made a pancake for you, a big pancake!"*

10/21   *At work time in the house area, Lorena told Andrew, "I'm mad — don't take my steering wheel!"*

Parent observations (Observaciones del padre o madre):

Lorena's grandma told us that just the other day when Lorena saw a neighbor walking her dog, Lorena invited the neighbor to bring the dog and come over to play.

Source: *COR User* Guide (HighScope Educational Research Foundation, 2003a, p. 38)

▲ Acknowledge the focus child's contributions to others' planning time and recall time conversations.

In addition to providing teachers with the basis for daily planning, anecdotal records and COR scores can be shared with a variety of audiences. Teachers share anecdotes with parents to involve them in their child's program experience and to educate them about how to extend their child's learning at home (see Chapter 8 on sharing anecdotes with parents; see the sample page from a COR Family Report form, above). Administrators use COR results to monitor their programs and identify areas for staff inservice training. Finally, policymakers and funders, interested in holding programs accountable for their effectiveness, can rely on the COR to provide accurate and objective information about how children are learning and developing.

Early Literacy Skills Assessment (ELSA)

ELSA Overview

The Early Literacy Skills Assessment (ELSA; HighScope Educational Research Foundation, 2004) is an authentic standardized assessment in the form of a children's storybook. It was designed for use with three- to five-year olds in preschool settings, but can also be used in kindergarten. The ELSA is founded on scientifically-based reading research and measures the four essential areas of early literacy: comprehension, phonological awareness, alphabetic principle, and concepts about print (see Chapter 11). These components of early reading were established by the National Reading Panel (2000) and National Early Literacy Panel (Strickland & Shanahan, 2004), and are included in educational legislation, such as the federal No Child Left Behind Act (08 January 2002).

The ELSA has been field tested and meets scientific standards of reliability and validity (DeBruin-Parecki, 2004). Like other authentic assessments, it engages children in a task that is personally meaningful to them and takes place in a naturally occurring activity familiar to most children. Reading a storybook with an adult is pleasurable and captivating for young children, which means they are likely to participate in the activity and answer the adult's questions to the best of their interest and ability.

There are two versions of the ELSA, both available in English and Spanish. One is titled *Violet's Adventure (La Aventura de Violeta)* and the other is *Dante Grows Up (El Cambio en Dante)*. To measure literacy development over the course of one program year, the same version (book) is used twice, as a pre- and post-program assessment. To measure literacy development over a longer period of time — for example, in a two-year early childhood program — one version of the ELSA would be used as a pre-post assessment the first year and the other version would be used pre-post the next year.

The ELSA makes it possible to measure all four areas of early literacy using one instrument. As the adult reads the story, he or she engages the child in conversation and asks questions about the book and its content. Based on the child's answers and comments, the adult can obtain raw scores and also assess the child's developmental level in the four early literacy areas.

For example, the child's ability to retell what happened in the story, to predict what might happen next, and to connect the story to his or her own life are all indicators of reading comprehension. So, during the course of reading the ELSA storybook, the adult asks the child questions designed to reveal these aspects of comprehension (for example, "What has happened in the story so far?" "What do you think will happen next in the story?" "Violet is scared. What do you do when you're scared?"). The ELSA enables the teacher to assess the child's ability to identify letters in a similar, natural way. The story reads, "When the animals came to the edge of the woods, they walked through a patch of small-letter bushes. Please help them again! What letters on the small-letter bushes can you point to and name?" (The illustration shows bushes covered with lowercase letters.) Because the ELSA uses such authentic methods to assess key aspects of literacy, the child enjoys the experience and never feel pushed to respond, as he or she might in a more structured testing situation.

Using the ELSA

The ELSA has multiple applications. Teachers use it to understand both the literacy level of each child in their classroom and also that of the class as a whole. This information allows teachers to plan appropriate instructional experiences and monitor children's developmental progress. In addition to developmental levels in each content and topic area, the ELSA provides raw scores, for example, the exact number of letters a child can name. This more detailed data permits analyses that are useful for reporting to school districts, state and federal departments of education, and other funding sources. Like the COR, the ELSA also provides a simple and concrete way to share information with parents about their child's emerging literacy skills and how to promote further language and literacy development at home.

The Early Literacy Skills Assessment (ELSA) measures early literacy abilities in all four areas identified as essential by the National Reading Panel and National Early Literacy Panel.

Because the ELSA meets rigorous psychometric standards for reliability and validity, it can be used in research studies and program evaluation. Researchers can track the developmental progress of children in all four areas of early literacy. The ELSA is the only assessment that makes this possi-

202

ble within one instrument. Program evaluators can examine whether a literacy program, or early intervention as a whole, contributes significantly to literacy development. As with the COR, use of the ELSA is not limited to HighScope programs. Regardless of their curriculum model, Head Start classrooms, state-funded preschools, or other early childhood programs can use these authentic instruments to assess program effectiveness. The results can be shared with funding agencies and policymakers seeking accountability for public and private investments in early childhood programs.

Try These Ideas Yourself

1. Write three anecdotes about children in your own program or one you arrange to observe. (See Chapter 9 for more information on observing children and writing anecdotes). Review your anecdotes to see whether they are objective. Do they factually describe the behavior ("Rachel frowned and threw the puzzle on the floor") or make subjective judgments ("Rachel tested the teacher's patience by hurling the puzzle to the floor")? When necessary, rewrite the anecdotes to objectively describe the children's behavior. (Variation: Write three anecdotes about a family member or friend. Review them to see if they are objective. Rewrite them as necessary.)

2. Although researchers perform sophisticated statistical analyses, teachers and administrators often have to interpret simple data. The chart below lists the mid-year scores of five preschoolers on the Social Relations items of the Preschool Child Observation Record (Preschool COR). What can you say about the children individually and as a group?

3. Below is a sample from "About Your Child as a Reader" (Family Report) from the Early Literacy Skills Assessment (ELSA). How would you discuss this information at a parent-teacher conference? What questions might the parent have? What would you recommend the family do at home to promote further literacy development in this child?

Comprehension (making sense of what is said) — *Your child can* tell the story by looking at the pictures. Emily makes reasonable guesses about what will happen next.

Phonological awareness (knowing that words are made up of sounds) — *Your child can* tell when words begin with the same sound, such as *bat* and *ball*. She can identify rhyming words, such as *tree* and *bee*.

Alphabetic principle (knowing the letters and the sounds they make) — *Your child can* recognize and say the sounds of the letters in her name. Emily also knows many other letters.

Concepts about print (knowing how a book works) — *Your child can* hold a book right side up. She knows where a book begins and ends. Emily also knows that signs and posters have information in print.

Preschool COR Social Relations Item	Lisa	Don	Ari	Molly	Nema
E. Relating to adults	3	2	4	5	2
F. Relating to other children	3	2	4	4	3
G. Resolving interpersonal conflict	2	2	1	4	2
H. Understanding and expressing feelings	2	2	3	4	3

How Does HighScope Assess Programs?

Think About It

Consider the following two scenarios:

Scenario #1: *Jeanne teaches second grade. Every spring at Jeannie's school, staff are given an annual performance review to see if they qualify for a merit increase in the next year's pay. They are not told ahead of time which day their evaluation will take place.*

One morning in mid-April, Mr. Beaudette, the principal, comes to Jeanne's classroom. It is his first visit since last fall, when he'd stopped by briefly to welcome the students back. This time, Mr. Beaudette goes directly to the back of the room without saying hello. He sits there for 30 minutes, filling out a form, while Jeanne conducts her regular reading lesson. The students keep turning around to watch him. Ten days later, Jeanne finds a copy of the completed form in her mailbox. Mr. Beaudette has marked "Satisfactory" on grooming, clarity of speech, accuracy of information presented, and assigning homework. He's checked "Needs to Improve" on maintaining order in the classroom, following curriculum standards, allowing sufficient time for each subject, and neatness of student desks and papers. Jeanne will get a letter in two months informing her whether she has gotten a merit increase.

Scenario #2: *Pat teaches second grade at a different school. On a mutually decided day in the fall, Mrs. Lowell, the curriculum supervisor, spends a morning in Pat's classroom to observe how things are going. The students know that Mrs. Lowell, who is a familiar figure to them, will be visiting. When she arrives, they greet her and go back to work. As she observes, Mrs. Lowell takes notes on the materials available to students, how Pat interacts with students, how much students contribute to class discussions, the amount of time allotted to required subjects, and what happens during "open" times of the day.*

After dismissal, Pat and Mrs. Lowell go over the notes and ratings. Mrs. Lowell tells Pat her room is well-stocked with interesting materials, and she suggests additional items other second-grade teachers have found helpful. She says Pat is on target to cover reading, mathematics, and social studies but might have trouble meeting the science requirement. Together Pat and Mrs. Lowell brainstorm ideas for adjusting the schedule to allow more time for science, and Mrs. Lowell says she'll drop off some program brochures from the new hands-on children's museum.

Pat says her main goal this year is to get more student participation, especially during book discussions. Pat and Mrs. Lowell review several ways Pat might do this, such as supplementing the required reading with students' book choices and letting them lead the discussions. They agree Mrs. Lowell will observe a book discussion in two months, using the sections of the observation form that address teacher-student interaction and student participation.

204

Chapter Learning Objectives

By the end of this chapter, you will be able to

❖ List the components of program quality

❖ Describe the importance of program assessment

❖ Describe the features and uses of effective program quality measures

❖ Describe and understand the features of the Preschool Program Quality Assessment (PQA) and how this validated instrument is used

A performance review can make anyone nervous, even an experienced and respected employee. Yet an evaluation like that in the second scenario above would be much less anxiety-provoking for most of us than that of the first. For one thing, we'd know *when* we would be observed. Additionally, the supervisor would look at meaningful educational practices that could be objectively measured, such as the number and variety of materials we provided our students. We also wouldn't be judged according to arbitrary and subjective factors, such as grooming (suppose the supervisor just didn't like our taste in clothing and hairstyle!). The observation would be followed by a meeting where the supervisor would acknowledge what was working well. After this encouragement, we'd discuss potential problems and how to address them. There would also be a chance to share our own goals for professional growth and receive support in reaching them. Follow-up observations during the year would show what was effective and what still needed fine tuning.

In sum, this teamwork approach to evaluation would be much more comfortable and certainly more informative. Its purpose would not be to judge us as passing or failing some test but, rather, to *collaborate* on achieving what was best for the children in our program.

The HighScope approach to assessing programs is consistent with the second scenario. HighScope recognizes that valid assessment relies on objective information collected on meaningful variables. Whether we are evaluating teachers or administrators, the underlying concern is always *what will help children and families.*

In this chapter, we discuss why this approach to program assessment is an important component of any comprehensive curriculum model. Additionally, you will read about and see sample items from the **Preschool Program Quality Assessment** (PQA; HighScope Educational Research Foundation, 2003b) — an instrument used to objectively measure how well programs meet the needs of children, families, and staff. Because it is based on documented best practices, the PQA can be used by any developmentally based early childhood program, not just those using the HighScope Curriculum.

Trained observers use objective anecdotal notes to score the validated Preschool Program Quality Assessment (PQA), a comprehensive measure of teaching behavior and program management.

Terms Used in This Chapter

• Preschool Program Quality Assessment (PQA) • program quality • (program) structural components • (program) process • interrater reliability • (program) self-assessment and monitoring

HighScope staff use the results of ongoing program assessment to highlight program strengths, identify areas for improvement, and plan effective staff development strategies.

The Importance of Program Assessment

Decades of research, summarized in the National Research Council report *Eager to Learn* (2000a), make it clear that program performance is positively and significantly related to child performance. In order to evaluate and understand children's performance and progress (see Chapter 18), we need to measure the educational experiences that the programs they attend are providing. Put another way, *programs,* rather than children, should be held accountable for learning. To help programs meet their obligation to educate children, early childhood educators need valid tools to assess how well their programs promote learning in all areas of development. How are such tools developed? To answer this question, we'll first look at what we mean by **program quality.**

Every dedicated early childhood professional cares about program quality. We want to do what is best for children, families, and society as a whole. But program quality, like child development, is complex and has many dimensions. It includes the **"structural" components** of the classroom — that is, how the learning environment is set up and what happens during the program day. Additionally, quality is especially dependent on **"process"** — notably, how adults interact with children and plan and carry out meaningful learning experiences. The ways in which staff relate to parents, one another, and the community can also affect children and are part of quality processes. Finally, agency-wide factors influence what happens in the classroom and directly or indirectly impact children. These include how staff are recruited and trained and how the program is financed and managed overall.

While we know all these quality components are important, we are still faced with the challenge of defining and measuring them. Only valid assessment instruments can guarantee we are looking at the right ingredients of quality in an honest and accurate manner. They give us the information to evaluate whether we are achieving appropriate levels of quality, and if not, where and how we can improve. Good assessment tools also give us a common language with which to share this information with parents, administrators, researchers, and policymakers. An objective program evaluation tool is essential to encouraging self-assessment and promoting communication among everyone concerned about program quality and its implications for early childhood development.

The Characteristics of Effective Program Quality Measures

With these goals in mind, HighScope developed and validated the Preschool PQA. (A version for settings serving younger children, the Infant-Toddler PQA, is in development.) To determine the most effective format and content for the instrument, the Foundation examined other program quality measures in the field. Only one besides the PQA has been widely used and validated: the Early Childhood Environment Rating Scale (Harms, Clifford, & Cryer, 1998). In building on the strengths and filling in the gaps of existing tools, HighScope identified the following characteristics as being essential for an effective and user-friendly program quality measure.

▲ **The most effective program assessment tools define quality along a continuum.** In talking to practitioners and researchers, we found

206

many were frustrated by assessment instruments that permitted only "yes-no" (or "pass-fail") responses to each item. Such measures were often used to measure compliance with regulations but did not allow for the fact that quality is achieved in stages. An assessment tool that rates quality along a continuum helps practitioners see where their programs are now and what steps they need to take to continue making improvements.

▲ **Program assessments are most helpful if they provide users with many examples.** For the assessment tool to be used accurately and objectively, it should clearly describe typical behaviors at each level of quality. Concrete examples allow different raters to interpret and score the same behavior in the same way, which is what researchers call **interrater reliability.** Multiple examples also help staff to see what level they fit into and to know by example what they are striving to achieve.

▲ **Program assessments are most informative if they are comprehensive.** HighScope has identified two aspects of comprehensiveness. First, *assessment tools should look at both the structure and the process of a program.* Most instruments cover structural qualities, such as safety or the diversity of materials. However, many fail to pay equal — if not more — attention to processes such as adult-child and child-child interactions. Yet research, such as that cited in *Eager to Learn* (National Research Council, 2000a) shows these program features are crucial to defining quality and promoting child development.

The second aspect of comprehensiveness refers to *looking at the program from multiple perspectives.* Although our top concern is children, we should also pay attention to how programs serve families and staff. A complete program assessment tool should therefore look at how teachers interact with parents, how staff work together to plan for the children, how supervisors support staff development, and how management secures adequate resources. In other words, a program quality assessment should look at the classroom, the agency, the home, and the community — and the activities and experiences of the participants in each.

▲ **Program assessments make the greatest contribution to the field if they have been tested and validated.** Because we each want to capture our program's uniqueness, it is tempting

Supervisors and teachers use findings from the Preschool Program Quality Assessment (PQA) to improve the learning environment, daily routine, adult-child interaction, and adult team planning.

to create our own assessment tools. The problem with this approach is that we end up talking only to coworkers and a few other people who know our program well. When we do this, we cannot communicate or share successful models outside our own agencies or understand how our program fits within the broader scheme of early childhood initiatives. Moreover, "reinventing the wheel" by making up our own measurement tools fails to make use of decades of valuable research. If we instead build assessment systems on standard best practices, we can advance the early childhood field as a whole and use its knowledge to our own benefit as well. For that reason, HighScope concluded that the most effective assessment tools can and should be applied across program settings, including those using other developmentally based curriculum models.

The Uses of Effective Program Quality Measures

Good program quality measures offer the following options and benefits across a wide array of uses and in different types of settings.

▲ **Effective program quality assessments also serve as training tools.** Evaluation highlights program strengths and identifies areas to be improved through staff training. Concrete examples define good practice for new teachers. They help experienced ones reflect on what they do

Effective Program Quality Measures...

(1) Have the following characteristics:

❖ Define quality along a continuum, not just "yes" or "no"

❖ Provide users with many examples

❖ Are comprehensive

❖ Have been field tested and validated

(2) Can be used in the following ways:

❖ To support the curriculum implementation of teaching teams

❖ To plan and carry out a program of staff development

❖ To carry out research and program evaluation

❖ To communicate to many audiences

ment tools avoid jargon. They speak to professional and lay audiences, including teachers, administrators, parents, researchers, and policymakers. If all these audiences understand the language used in an assessment tool, they are in a better position to collaborate on achieving high program quality.

With these principles in mind, HighScope develops, field-tests, and validates various program quality measures. These include assessments of overall quality, as well as specific content areas (for example, the arts) and specialized settings (for example, those serving children with special needs and those offering intergenerational programs). The most widely used HighScope measure, developed over many years, is the Preschool Program Quality Assessment (PQA). It is a comprehensive assessment that looks at all aspects of program quality. By collecting feedback from many programs, including both HighScope and non-HighScope settings, the Foundation refines and revises this measure periodically. The current version of the PQA for preschool programs is described below.

and encourage them to continue growing as professionals.

▲ **Effective assessment tools allow supervisors to observe individual staff members and provide them with constructive feedback.** Assessment can be anxiety-provoking if the rules are arbitrary and the intention is judgment rather than improving performance. But a well-constructed tool can provide the person being assessed with clear expectations and opportunities for growth. Properly used, a good assessment tool allows a supervisor and a teacher to work as a team, as in the second scenario at the beginning of this chapter. (See Chapter 9 on using the PQA to support staff development.)

▲ **Valid program quality measures are essential for research and program evaluation.** We often evaluate our programs to meet individual funding requirements. Beyond that, practitioners share a responsibility to contribute to the field as a whole. Assessments should serve both local and broad interests. They should meet rigorous scientific standards and produce results that are clear and concise. Instruments that work for researchers and practitioners build bridges between them. Researchers can ask meaningful questions and practitioners can use the results in their programs.

▲ **Effective program assessment tools communicate to many audiences.** Good assess-

The Preschool Program Quality Assessment (PQA)

PQA overview

The PQA is a rating instrument designed to evaluate the quality of early childhood programs and identify staff training needs. It is a comprehensive assessment that examines all the components of program quality. These range from the activities and interactions in the classroom, to relationships with families, to the policies and practices of agency managers. Because the PQA is based on "best practices" in the early childhood field as a whole, it is appropriate for use in all center-based settings, not just those using the HighScope Curriculum. [*Note:* A PQA for use in family day care homes is in development.]

The PQA allows raters to systematically collect information through classroom observations and interviews with teachers and administrative staff. The PQA can be implemented by trained outside

The Preschool Program Quality Assessment (PQA)

Form A — Classroom Items

I. Learning Environment

A. The class provides a safe and healthy environment for children.

B. The space is divided into interest areas that address basic aspects of children's play and development.

C. The location of the interest areas is carefully planned to provide for adequate space in each area, easy access between areas, and compatible activities in adjacent areas.

D. An outdoor play area (at or near the program site) has adequate space, equipment, and materials to support various types of play.

E. Classroom areas and materials are systematically arranged, labeled, and accessible to children.

F. Classroom materials are varied, manipulative, open ended, authentic, and appeal to multiple senses.

G. Materials are plentiful.

H. Materials reflect human diversity and the positive aspects of children's homes and community culture.

I. Child-initiated work (work designed and created by children) is on display.

II. Daily Routine

A. Adults establish a consistent daily routine. Children are aware of the routine.

B. The parts of the daily routine include time for children to do the following: plan, carry out their plans, recall and discuss their activities, engage in small-group activities, engage in large-group activities, have snacks or meals, clean up, transition to other activities, play outside, and nap or rest (if applicable).

C. An appropriate amount of time is allotted for each part of the daily routine.

D. The program has time each day during which children make plans and indicate their plans to adults.

E. The program has time each day during which children initiate activities and carry out their intentions.

F. The program has time each day during which children remember and review their activities and share with adults and peers what they have done.

G. The program has time each day for small-group activities that reflect and extend children's interests and development.

H. The program has time each day for large-group activities that reflect and extend children's interests and development.

I. During transition times, children have reasonable choices about activities and timing as they move from one activity to the next.

J. The program has a set cleanup time with reasonable expectations and choices for children.

K. The program has time each day for snacks or meals that encourage social interaction.

L. The program has an outside time each day during which children engage in a variety of physical activities.

III. Adult-Child Interaction

A. Children's basic physical needs are met.

B. Children's separation from home and daily entry to the program are handled with sensitivity and respect.

C. Adults create a warm and caring atmosphere for children.

D. Adults use a variety of strategies to encourage and support child language and communication.

E. Adults use a variety of strategies to support classroom communication with children whose primary language is not English.

F. Adults participate as partners in children's play.

G. Adults encourage children's learning initiatives throughout the day (both indoors and outdoors).

H. Adults support and extend children's ideas and learning during group times.

I. Adults provide opportunities for children to explore and use materials at their own developmental level and pace.

J. Adults acknowledge individual children's accomplishments.

The Preschool Program Quality Assessment (PQA) (Cont.)

K. Adults encourage children to interact with and turn to one another for assistance throughout the day.

L. Children have opportunities to solve problems with materials and do things for themselves.

M. Adults involve children in resolving conflicts.

IV. Curriculum Planning and Assessment

A. Staff use a comprehensive and documented curriculum model or educational approach to guide teaching practices.

B. Staff use a team teaching model and share responsibilities for planning and implementing program activities.

C. Staff maintain records on children and families.

D. Staff record and discuss anecdotal notes as the basis for planning for individual children.

E. Staff regularly use a child observation measure of proven reliability and validity to assess children's developmental progress.

Form B — Agency Items

V. Parent Involvement and Family Services

A. The program provides a variety of opportunities for parents to become involved in the program.

B. Parents are represented on program advisory and/or policymaking committees.

C. Parents are encouraged to participate in program activities with children.

D. Staff and parents exchange information about the curriculum and its relationship to children's development.

E. Staff and parents interact informally to share information about the day's activities and children's experiences.

F. Staff and parents exchange information about how to promote and extend children's learning and social development at home.

G. Staff members schedule home visits and formal parent conferences to share information with parents and seek input from parents about the program and their children's development.

H. The program or its host agency provides diagnostic and special education services for special needs children.

I. Staff provide parents with referrals and access to supportive services as needed.

J. Program activities are coordinated with community agencies and/or the public schools to facilitate delivery of services to families and/or children's transition to kindergarten.

VI. Staff Qualifications and Staff Development

A. The program director has the appropriate education, training, and experience.

B. Instructional staff have the appropriate education, training, and experience.

C. Support staff and volunteers receive the appropriate orientation and supervision.

D. Staff participate in ongoing professional development activities.

E. Inservice training sessions are specific to early childhood and apply the principles of adult learning.

F. Instructional staff are regularly observed in the program setting and provided with feedback by someone familiar with the curriculum's goals, objectives, and methods for working with children.

G. The director and teachers are affiliated with a local, state, and/or national early childhood professional organization.

VII. Program Management

A. The program is licensed based on regulations passed by the state and/or local licensing agencies.

B. Program policies promote continuity of care by classroom adults (paid staff who work directly with children).

C. Staff regularly conduct a program assessment and use the results to improve the program.

D. The program has a child recruitment and enrollment plan.

E. The program has a fully developed set of operating policies and procedures.

F. The program is accessible to those with disabilities.

G. The program is adequately funded.

evaluators or used as **a self-assessment** — that is, by individuals or teams to evaluate their own program. Based on objective evidence (including anecdotal notes, diagrams, and interviews), PQA raters complete a series of five-point scales describing a broad array of program characteristics. To assure reliable and valid ratings, the endpoints and midpoint of each scale are defined by behavioral indicators and illustrated with examples (see samples on pp. 211–212). Unlike compliance measures that permit only "yes-no" scores, PQA ratings are made along a continuum, which results in more accurate information. It also helps raters pinpoint a program's current level of quality and, if needed, a path for moving up to a higher level.

PQA Components

A PQA kit has several components. The *Administration Manual* describes the instrument, explains how to use it, and reviews the research demonstrating its reliability and validity. A final section aligns the items of the PQA with the Head Start Performance Standards (U.S. Department of Health and Human Services, 2002). The PQA can also be aligned with state and local program performance standards. There are two PQA forms or booklets: *Form A: Classroom Items* is used to observe in the classroom and to interview teachers; *Form B: Agency Items* is used to interview administrative staff. Each form has room to record anecdotal notes and score each item. At the end of each form is a *Summary Score Sheet*. Users can purchase multiple copies of the forms.

Although the PQA *Administration Manual,* as well as each form, contains instructions for conducting and scoring the PQA, HighScope recommends that raters receive training in using the instrument. Training results in the most effective, reliable, and valid use of the measure.

PQA Content

The PQA has a total of 63 items, divided into seven sections. Each item is scored on a five-point scale from a low (1) to a high (5) level of quality. *Form A, Classroom Items,* contains Sections 1 though IV: Learning Environment (9 items), Daily Routine (12 items), Adult-Child Interaction (13 items), and Curriculum Planning and Assessment (5 items). *Form B, Agency Items,* contains Section V through VII: Parent Involve-

ment and Family Services (10 items), Staff Qualifications and Staff Development (7 items), and Program Management (7 items). PQA sections and items are listed on pages 208–209.

Completing the PQA

When the PQA is used as a self-assessment, or by a supervisor to support teachers' curriculum implementation (see Chapter 9), one or more sections can be completed during a single session. If a comprehensive self-assessment is being conducted with the entire PQA, each section may be completed at a different time. However, to get an accurate picture of the program at a single point in time, this period should be limited to several days or a week at most. When trained outside evaluators conduct a PQA, they allow one day for data collection. A minimum of a half-day should be spent collecting classroom items (Form A) and a half-day collecting agency items (Form B). Two raters may visit a program, with one rater collecting classroom data and the other, agency data. If an agency has several classrooms, each one should be observed for at least half of a day. However, the agency-level data only needs to be collected once.

Raters are instructed to complete every row in every item of the PQA in order to obtain a score for that item. Sections I–III are designed to be completed mainly through observation, while Sections IV–VII are interview-based. Forms list the standard questions to be asked during the interviews.

Preschool Program Quality Assessment (PQA) classroom-level items focus on how teachers support early learning on a day-to-day basis. Agency-level items look at overall program operations.

Once each item is scored on the appropriate form (A or B), raters complete a summary score sheet at the end of the form. It is possible to calculate a total and a mean PQA score, as well as a total and a mean score for each of the seven areas. PQA calculations can be done by hand or entered into a computer and analyzed with a spreadsheet or other appropriate statistical program.

Sample PQA Items

Table 19-1 shows two sample items from the Preschool PQA. The first item (III-F) is from Form A (classroom items) and the second (V-I) is from Form B (agency items). Depending on which boxes are checked in the rows of each item, raters assign an item score on a scale of 1 to 5 points following the instructions provided in the *Administration Manual* and repeated at the beginning of each form.

Using the PQA

The PQA can be completed by a trained independent rater such a researcher, program evaluator, outside consultant, or agency administrator. It may also be done as a self-assessment by those directly involved with the program, such as center directors, curriculum specialists, education or parent coordinators, individual teachers or teaching teams, or parents. Students who are preparing to become early childhood teachers and caregivers may also conduct a PQA. They can do it on someone else's classroom or as a self-assessment of their own student teaching. They can then discuss the results with their instructor and classmates as part of their training and professional development.

Uses for the PQA include training, monitoring, staff support and supervision, and research and evaluation. Results can be shared inside the program with instructional and support staff, administrators, parents, and funders and can also be presented to practitioners, researchers, and policy-

Table 19-1. Sample Items From the Preschool PQA

III-F. Adults participate as partners in children's play.			
Level 1 Indicators	**Level 3 Indicators**	**Level 5 Indicators**	**Supporting Evidence/Anecdotes**
❏ Adults do not participate in children's play.	❏ Adults sometimes participate as partners in children's play.	❏ Adults participate as partners in children's play.	
❏ Adults are not partners in children's play.	❏ Adults use some strategies as partners in children's play.	❏ Adults use a variety of strategies as partners in children's play: • Observe and listen before and after entering children's play. • Assume roles as suggested by children. • Follow the children's cues about the content and direction of play. • Imitate children.	
❏ Adults attempt to dominate children's play (e.g., by redirecting play around adult ideas, telling children what to play with, how to play, or whom to play with).	❏ Adults quickly offer suggestions or ideas after entering children's play or offer suggestions outside the children's play theme.	❏ Adults support children at their developmental level and help add complexity to their play. • Match the complexity of their play. • Offer suggestions for extending play. • Stay within the children's play theme.	

Table 19-1 (Cont.) Sample Items From the Preschool PQA

V-I. Staff provide parents with referrals and access to supportive services as needed.			
Level I Indicators	**Level 3 Indicators**	**Level 5 Indicators**	**Supporting Evidence/Anecdotes**
❑ Staff are not aware of family needs.	❑ Staff have some knowledge of family needs.	❑ Staff are familiar with family needs (e.g., staff conduct or have access to needs assessments, intake interviews, or other information-gathering activities with families).	
❑ Staff are not aware of available community resources.	❑ Staff have some knowledge of community resources.	❑ Staff are familiar with resources available in the community (e.g., staff maintain a library of services and referral procedures; staff attend community service workshops).	
❑ Staff do not make referrals to needed family services.	❑ Staff sometimes make referrals to needed family services.	❑ Staff make referrals to needed family services (e.g., brochures and other information are readily available to parents; staff keep lists of local service providers).	
❑ Staff do not facilitate access to family services.	❑ Staff sometimes facilitate access to family services.	❑ Staff facilitate access to family services (e.g., staff provide documentation for parents to share with providers; staff make initial phone call to help arrange appointment; staff help families find child care or transportation so they can use community resources).	

makers in the field as a whole. Findings from the PQA can be used to define and illustrate best practices and to focus attention on program enhancement in training. Statistical analyses can examine the relationship between program practices and child development and can shape policies for improving the quality of early childhood programs. These multiple uses are described below.

▲ **Training.** Both preservice and inservice training activities are enriched by the PQA. It can be used in its entirety to provide trainees with a comprehensive picture of quality. Individual sections can be used to focus on specific program components. The detailed examples in the indicators for each item offer concrete illustrations of "best practices." Users often comment that the

PQA defines the term developmentally appropriate practice by translating an idea or ideal into specific implementation strategies. Even experienced teachers find the PQA's depth and specificity helps them reconsider long-established practices from a new perspective.

▲ **Self-assessment and monitoring.** The PQA is a valuable tool for administrators and teachers to assess their own practices and identify areas for growth. It can also be used by those responsible for quality control to monitor program implementation at a single site or across multiple sites. Because the PQA is objective and quantitative, it can be used to set program goals in one or more areas and to provide a numerical and anecdotal record of progress. HighScope also uses the

PQA to certify teachers and accredit programs according to rigorous performance standards (see Chapter 21).

▲ **Staff support and supervision.** Supervision can be effective and nonthreatening when the PQA is used to conduct observations and the results are discussed as a team. A teaching team and a supervisor familiar with the curriculum and the instrument agree to focus on a particular aspect of implementation (for example, the learning environment). The supervisor then uses the relevant PQA section(s) to observe, record anecdotes, rate the items, and discuss the results with the practitioners. Together, they acknowledge strengths and identify areas for improvement, using the PQA's concrete examples to develop a plan of action. They arrange a time for a follow-up observation to review how the plan is working. (See Chapter 9 for more on this process.)

▲ **Research and evaluation.** The PQA has been used extensively as a research tool administered by trained outside observers (as detailed in the psychometrics section of the *Administration Manual,* pp. 9–15). Studies can be designed to document program practices, compare quality in different program settings, evaluate whether and how staff training improves quality, and examine the relationship between program quality and young children's development.

▲ **Information and dissemination.** With its straightforward language and detailed examples, the PQA can be used to explain research-based practices to a variety of audiences. These include administrators and policymakers, particularly those who may not know the elements of high-quality programs. The PQA can also help support staff understand the actions and requests of the instructional staff. Further, it is an effective tool for explaining the program to parents and for suggesting ways they can carry out similar practices at home. Additionally, PQA results can be easily communicated to researchers. Finally, the many concrete examples help others replicate proven practices in their own settings.

Try These Ideas Yourself

1. Make up a five-point scale for some behavior or skill. For example, a scale for cooking might range from low ("1") for "Knows telephone numbers of at least three takeout restaurants by heart" to high ("5") for "Prepares gourmet dinner for eight guests once a month." List the behavioral indicators that define each level of the scale. Use the scale to take anecdotal notes and rate five people you know. (Variation: Put each level of your scale with its indicators on a different index card. Do not number them. Scramble the order of the cards. Give them to a friend or colleague. See if he or she can identify the behavior you are scaling and put the cards in order.)

2. Table 19-2 on page 214 lists the scores of four teachers on the adult-child interaction items of the Preschool PQA. Identify each person's strengths and areas for improvement. What inservice workshop(s) would you recommend for the staff as a group?

Program assessment can be used to identify training needs, monitor program quality, supervise staff, conduct research and evaluation, and disseminate information about the program.

Table 19-2. Preschool PQA Adult-Child Interaction Items

Adult-Child Interaction Items	Teacher/Classroom Number			
	#1	#2	#3	#4
A. Children's basic physical needs are met.	5	5	4	5
B. Children's separation from home and daily entry to the program are handled with sensitivity and respect.	4	3	2	3
C. Adults create a warm and caring atmosphere for children.	5	5	4	5
D. Adults use a variety of strategies to encourage and support child language and communication.	3	3	3	3
E. Adults use a variety of strategies to support classroom communication with children whose primary language is not English.	2	3	2	3
F. Adults participate as partners in children's play.	4	5	3	4
G. Adults encourage children's learning initiatives throughout the day (both indoors and outdoors).	5	5	3	4
H. Adults support and extend children's ideas and learning during group times.	4	3	2	3
I. Adults provide opportunities for children to explore and use materials at their own developmental level and pace.	5	5	3	4
J. Adults acknowledge individual children's accomplishments.	4	5	4	4
K. Adults encourage children to interact with and turn to one another for assistance throughout the day.	3	3	2	3
L. Children have opportunities to solve problems with materials and do things for themselves.	5	4	3	5
M. Adults involve children in resolving conflicts.	4	3	1	3

HighScope Training Model

This part of the book provides a brief overview of HighScope's approach to staff training. It describes how HighScope works with teachers and child care providers and those who supervise them, to guarantee program quality. While this information presents HighScope's approach to professional development, it is not meant to substitute for actual training by HighScope staff and other designated representatives of the Foundation.

Chapter 20 explains how HighScope applies the principles of active participatory learning to training the adults who work with young children.

Chapter 21 describes HighScope training courses and the Foundation's certification and accreditation procedures.

How Does HighScope Apply Active Participatory Learning to Adults?

Think About It

Rachel had always liked natural sciences. In her sophomore year of high school, she enrolled in a biology class, taught by Ms. Schaeffer. She especially loved the unit on plants. Students gathered samples from the local woods, fields, and riverbank. Ms. Schaeffer also ordered samples from other climates and terrains. Rachel and her classmates examined the plant samples and generated lists of similarities and differences. They grouped them according to their observations and compared their categories with official scientific classifications. Students posed questions and hypotheses, then collected data to test their assumptions. Ms. Schaeffer even taught them simple statistics using a computer program to test whether their findings met scientific standards of significance. The class entered a group project in the school's annual science fair and were invited to present their results at a student auditorium and a special evening session for parents.

In Rachel's junior year, she signed up for a botany course, taught by Ms. Zenda. This class was different. Instead of collecting and comparing their own samples, students were given lists of plant similarities and differences to memorize. There was little laboratory work. Most sessions were lectures, and their content often duplicated the information in the textbook or on the handouts. Students were discouraged from asking questions until the last five minutes of class. The teacher always answered their questions, but Rachel missed gathering data and finding out the answers herself. In the spring, only one student submitted an entry to the school science fair.

When it was time to sign up for senior-year classes, Rachel wasn't sure what to do. Part of her was ready to give up on science, yet she still had fond memories and a lingering interest in the subject. When she saw that Ms. Schaeffer was teaching a course on environmental field work, Rachel took a chance. All year, students collected water samples along the river and tested it for pollutants. They compared wildlife counts to records going back ten years and identified plants and animals whose populations had decreased significantly in the last decade. Ms. Schaeffer arranged for biology students at high schools farther north and south along the river to collect pollution data, too. When they found the worst levels near a manufacturing plant to the north, they wrote their state congressional representative and were invited to make a presentation to the Department of Natural Resources (DNR). Ms. Schaeffer coached them on how to organize and present the information. As a result, the DNR and congressional staffers crafted an antipollution bill. When Rachel graduated, a vote on the bill was pending. Students and teachers at the participating high schools were optimistic about the outcome. When she began college, Rachel immediately signed up for natural sciences courses and eventually majored in environmental studies.

218

Active participatory learning is as important for adults as it is for children. Teachers learn how to implement the HighScope Curriculum in hands-on workshops and classroom exercises.

What made Rachel's experiences so different each year? In her first class, students were engaged in **hands-on learning.** They worked directly with materials, used their powers of observation and analysis, and posed questions and collected data to answer them. Rachel and her classmates were *active learners*. In her second class, the teacher fed them the information, and lectures and book learning replaced lab work. In this case, Rachel and her classmates were *passive learners*. Fortunately, Rachael's experience in her third class not only replicated the hands-on discovery of the first one, it enabled students to apply their scientific knowledge and skills toward making a real difference in the world.

The HighScope model for adult training reflects the principles and strategies that characterized Rachel's experience in her first and third classes. HighScope promotes active learning for adults as well as children. In fact, what distinguishes HighScope training is its combined emphasis on theory, research, and practice. Adults not only gain an understanding of *what* the curriculum is, and *why* it is grounded in theory and research, they also emerge knowing how to implement its practices in the classroom. And, while scripted lessons may also provide teachers with "how to" instructions, HighScope further respects teachers and caregivers as thoughtful individuals who want to know the reasons behind their actions and interactions with children.

In sum, just as HighScope encourages teachers to be thoughtful and active in dealing with young children, so too do its trainers treat teachers as active learners who enjoy and benefit from reflecting on their practices. Or, as a Phoenix, Arizona, teacher said to her HighScope-trained supervisor, "You're helping me learn the way you want me to help children learn." As a result, teachers and caregivers feel more skillful and confident about making a difference in the lives of the children and families they serve. This chapter describes why HighScope's active learning approach to the process of training adults is an important part of serving the best interests of young children.

Why Active Participatory Learning Is Important for Adults

Research shows a strong and positive relationship between teachers' qualifications and young children's development and learning (Barnett, 2003; National Research Council, 2000a). The higher their level of formal education and specialized training, the more likely adults are to use appropriate teaching strategies in their classrooms. In addition, they work more effectively with families

The Value of High-Quality Training

While the amount of education and training is important, its quality may be even more critical in determining the competence of early childhood teachers. The National Association for the Education of Young Children (NAEYC), in its book *Preparing Early Childhood Professionals* (Hyson, 2003), says the value of high-quality education and training is greater than learning specific skills or teaching techniques. As early childhood teachers engage in their own professional development, "they become better able to make connections:

❖ between research and daily practice

❖ between challenging content standards and children's positive outcomes

❖ between a curriculum and an individual child

❖ between homes and schools

❖ between prior knowledge/experience and new information

❖ between national and state policies and their effects on children's lives

❖ between the program and diverse cultural communities

❖ between program staff and other professionals who can serve as sources of expertise and resources" (p. 4).

---

and forge lasting team relationships with their coworkers. Teacher training is also associated with lower turnover rates, which provides essential continuity for children and parents as well as stability for the agencies that employ them and invest in their training (Bloom & Sheerer, 1992).

Early childhood educator Lilian Katz (1995) emphasizes that the best professional preparation encourages teachers to reflect on what they learn and apply it meaningfully in their jobs. For each of us, the goal of reflection is to discover how what we *learn* in the college classroom or teacher workshop translates to what we *do* in the child care setting. A thoughtful teacher does not need to rely on scripted lessons, which may not fit a particular child or group of children. Instead, teachers with appropriate education and training use what they have learned to guide their practice and make decisions about what works best for each child and the class as a whole.

Teacher education and training take place in two ways: through courses at two-year and four-year colleges (Early & Winton, 2001) and through workshops sponsored by an early childhood agency or professional organization (National Institute on Early Childhood Development and Education, 2000). Formal education is sometimes referred to as **preservice training,** while on-the-job training is considered **inservice training.** However, professionals may participate in either or both at any point in their teaching careers. In fact, ongoing education and training is considered

a hallmark of an effective early childhood professional. As the field continues to learn about young children's development and how adults can best support early learning, staying up-to-date with the latest research and practical lessons is a necessity for a committed and competent teacher.

In addition to when and where ongoing preparation takes place, the "how" of such education and training is vital. Research shows that active learning is as important for adults as it is for young children. While grown-ups can deal with ideas and abstractions, they also need to work with materials, connect the information and skills they are learning to their own lives, and observe for themselves the direct effects of their actions upon their students and coworkers. All too often, however, training for early childhood staff covers a series of disconnected topics, is not tied to a theory or the curriculum they are using, lacks practical information, and fails to provide follow-up as teachers attempt to implement new ideas in the classroom (Bloom & Sheerer, 1992).

By contrast, a core proposition of the National Board for Professional Teaching Standards (NBPTS, 2001) is that teachers should think systematically about their practices and learn from their experiences. In its early childhood generalist standards, NBPTS states that "Accomplished teachers examine their practice critically; expand their repertoire; deepen their knowledge; sharpen their judgment; and adapt their teaching to new findings, ideas, and theories" (p. 8). This sentiment is

220

echoed in the standards of other early childhood professional organizations, such as the National Association for the Education of Young Children (NAEYC) and the Council for Exceptional Children/Division of Early Childhood (CEC/DEC).

The HighScope adult training model rests on these principles, too. The HighScope Foundation President, Dr. Larry Schweinhart, advises program administrators to "allocate staff time for monthly inservice training sessions and assure these sessions lead to systematic application of child development principles in the classroom" (Schweinhart, 2004, p. 22). This recommendation is based not only on a philosophical position, but is also grounded in research. The HighScope *Training for Quality* study (Epstein, 1993), summarized in Chapter 4, identified the characteristics of professional development programs that produce real changes in teaching practices and real benefits for young children and their families. The rest of this chapter describes how those critical features of "active participatory learning" for adults are embodied in the HighScope training model.

HighScope Principles of Active Participatory Learning for Adults

HighScope provides professional development programs for teachers and caregivers as well as for the supervisors who train and support these practitioners. HighScope has been training teachers since the 1960s and has worked with supervisors in a "training of trainers" model since the 1980s. Curriculum courses for teachers and caregivers train them to implement the infant-toddler and/or preschool educational approach. Training for supervisors includes not only curriculum courses but also course work on preparing and supporting staff as they implement HighScope programs with young children and families. These training courses and procedures for certifying trainers and teachers and accrediting programs are described in Chapter 21.

All these courses were designed to address the shortfalls commonly found in early childhood teacher preparation initiatives (see the sidebar on p. 221). The *Training for Quality* study, conducted with participants in 80 adult training courses

and 366 HighScope and non-HighScope teachers nationwide, confirmed the value of active participatory learning for adults as well as children. The features listed below, which incorporate active learning and are found in all HighScope training courses and workshops, contribute significantly to improvements in program quality and young children's development.

▲ **Integrated content.** Adults understand and use information when the learning builds on itself. Therefore, professional development works best as a "course" of study in which teachers and caregivers systematically add to their knowledge and skills. Too often, inservice training jumps from one "topic of the month" to another, and the focus and the presenter change

Staff development is most effective when it features a consistent trainer, information that builds on a common core, a proven curriculum, cumulative learning, and follow-up support.

with each session. By contrast, when topics follow a logical sequence, participants can connect what they've already learned with new information. Teachers are able to construct an overall framework of child development and instructional practices to guide their work with children and families.

Each HighScope training course is organized to result in this type of cumulative knowledge and skill. The curriculum is introduced one topic at a time, and participants gain in their depth of understanding as each topic refers to and builds on what has come before. Moreover, because the

Effective Professional Development Programs

Effective professional development programs apply the principles of active participatory learning to training adults. The following chart compares the characteristics of effective and ineffective training programs in helping adults learn and apply the knowledge and skills they need to be good teachers.

In *effective* professional development programs…	In *ineffective* professional development programs…
Inservice training follows a progression of interrelated topics, resulting in knowledge that is cumulative over the course of training.	Topics are not connected in any logical or cumulative fashion.
Training procedures are based on current knowledge about how adults learn. Trainers interact with teachers during group workshop presentations and make individual onsite visits to the classroom for observation and feedback.	Disconnected topics often mean a series of one-time presenters, and their methods of presentation may not be geared toward adult learning styles.
Training uses a curriculum model based on child development principles. The curriculum serves as a framework for applying and implementing new knowledge.	The information presented by trainers is not related to a curriculum or program philosophy, and it is not connected to daily program practices. Consequently, staff may emerge with a few interesting ideas but since they cannot readily fit them into the context of the overall program goals, there is no motivation to implement the ideas in any sustained manner.
Inservice training sessions explore strategies for practical application. Strategies then become practices in the actual work setting.	Theory is not accompanied by practical information. Staff are given no "how-to" guidelines for applying what they have learned.
Training is spread out over many months; staff alternate one week of workshop sessions with several weeks of application at their sponsoring agency. This cycle promotes adaptation and problem solving, and it highlights the progression of skills over time.	Discovery and application are disconnected. There is no natural cycle that alternates learning new ideas and trying them out in an interactive process over time.
The regularity of training and supervision means that follow-up opportunities are built into the model. Trainees can explore issues individually with their trainer as well as in group sessions with their peers.	Follow-up is absent. The real questions surface when staff attempt to implement what they have learned. With no forum for addressing their questions to individuals or groups, staff do not receive the ongoing help they need to apply the lessons of inservice training.

Source: *Training for Quality* (Epstein, 1993, pp. 6–7)

intent is for participants to meet with the same trainer (or team of trainers) over time, there is continuity in how the content is covered and presented. Trainees also have an opportunity to discuss ongoing issues and problem-solve as they study and apply the information to their work in an early childhood program.

▲ **Presentation geared to adult learning.** As noted above, the principles of active participatory learning apply to adults as well as children. Just as HighScope teachers "share control" with children, so, too, HighScope trainers encourage participants to take the initiative in their own learning (see the sidebar on p. 222). Teachers and

222

caregivers in HighScope training courses therefore make plans, carry out course assignments and activities, and reflect on what they have learned.

> *I have decided HighScope training is like being a Grandma for the first time. When you let children satisfy their natural curiosity, give them time to explore their world, and nurture them, you are giving them what they need to learn now and also encouraging lifelong learning. The same is true of my own training. We were encouraged to voice doubts and ask questions, try things for ourselves, and enjoy the support of our trainer and peers. This course turned us all into lifelong High-Scope Curriculum learners. We will continue to use and grow in our knowledge of this successful child- and adult-initiated program.* (Dayton, Ohio, Teacher)

To accommodate individual learning styles, course work includes oral and visual presentations, individual projects, small- and large-group work, practice activities and role playing, and opportunities for discussion and sharing. In addi-

tion, local supervisors who are certified to conduct HighScope training apply the same considerations as they support and mentor staff at their own agencies.

HighScope workshops are a good example of how training helps teachers and caregivers connect the lessons learned to their own work and home lives. Adults, like children of all ages, "learn by doing." HighScope training courses therefore include many opportunities to explore concepts and try out ideas during the workshop sessions. The principles apply equally well to conducting workshops for parents, who also want to understand the curriculum and extend their children's learning at home.

Each HighScope workshop begins with an *opening activity*. Like the "Think About It" section that opens each chapter in this book, the opening activity engages people in remembering an experience or sharing an activity as a way to stimulate or even "shake up" their thinking about the topic.

The second part of the workshop is called *central ideas and practice*. Through a combination of presentations, handouts, group activities, and discussion, participants learn the main concepts about child development and teaching practices that are the focus of that session. This workshop component is analogous to the chapter sections in this book that explain why the topic is important and then detail the relevant HighScope principles and practices.

In planning the session, trained facilitators identify the major learning goals and objectives for participants (just as we identify learning objectives for each chapter of this book). Sometimes the sessions validate for participants what they already believe and do. At other times, the workshop expands their current way of thinking. Often, teachers and caregivers will need to alter their perspective and/or behavior as they take in new information. This process, which is similar to the accommodation and assimilation cycle that Piaget described in children's learning (see Chapter 3), can be both challenging and energizing. Although changing attitudes and practices may be stressful for staff, it can also serve to reinvigorate them.

The third workshop component is the *application activity*. This process allows participants to further internalize the new information by applying it in a related situation, role play, or other

HighScope certified teachers mentor those with less training and experience. Good mentors listen, share ideas, nurture and support others, and are themselves open to learning from peers.

hands-on activity.

Finally, because the ultimate goal of training is to improve teaching practices, participants make *implementation plans* for using what they have learned when they return to their own agencies. For teachers and caregivers, the plan will focus on working with children and/or parents. For supervisors, the implementation plan may be a strategy for introducing curriculum ideas to staff during an onsite workshop or observation/feedback session. The "Try these Ideas Yourself" sections at the end of each chapter in this book likewise help readers solidify what they have learned and explore ways to apply these lessons to their current situation as a student, teacher, or supervisor.

> *As I plan workshops, I balance presenting information with involving participants. Just as we create active learning environments for children, we need to create them for the adults we are training.* (Milwaukee, Wis., Supervisor)

▲ **Articulated curriculum.** A national survey of 671 NAEYC members (Epstein, Schweinhart, & McAdoo, 1996) revealed that most do not use a single, coherent curriculum in their programs. They either use a combination or no curriculum at all. Yet as Chapter 1 of this book emphasizes, early childhood programs can only achieve the highest quality if they implement a unified curriculum model that has been proven to be effective. The curriculum should have written documentation of its philosophy, child development

principles, and teaching strategies to promote and assess children's learning. HighScope's comprehensive curriculum model, as explained and practiced in training, meets all these requirements.

▲ **Distributive learning.** A commonplace observation that HighScope shares with adult learners is that "change is hard." Mastering and applying new knowledge does not happen overnight. People typically resist change because doing what they already know is easier. Even when they are open to altering their behavior, desire often exceeds ability. HighScope therefore spreads out its training courses over several weeks or months. Days that participants spend attending workshops alternate with weeks at their home site. This distribution allows training participants to try out what they have learned, to see what is or is not working, and to bring their successes and questions back to the group. Each session begins with an opportunity to troubleshoot issues and to review previous material, and concludes with a plan for implementing new ideas and solutions. In this way, the HighScope adult learning model employs the plan-do-review sequence that is also a key characteristic of the children's daily classroom routine.

▲ **Follow-up mechanisms.** As noted above, participants in HighScope courses are able to ask follow-up questions at subsequent training ses-

Mentoring

The successful mentor...

❖ Is willing to listen

❖ Is sensitive to the coteacher's needs

❖ Is able to initiate and maintain the relationship

❖ Communicates feelings of acceptance

❖ Demonstrates willingness to share ideas and materials

❖ Is receptive to learning from the coteacher

❖ Is nurturing and supportive

❖ Respects the uniqueness and strengths of the coteacher

❖ Is confident, secure, flexible, altruistic, warm, and caring

"Mentoring in the HighScope Preschool Classroom" (Ranweiler, 2001, p. 383)

224

sions. But what happens when a training course ends? The HighScope Web site, online courses, regular newsletters and publications, and an e-mail "Ask Us" feature provide ongoing information and technical support. In addition, regional, national, and international conferences provide annual opportunities to update information and skills and to network with other practitioners.

However, HighScope recognizes that teachers and caregivers also need and benefit from immediate onsite assistance. Because the Foundation cannot directly reach tens of thousands of HighScope practitioners, HighScope began to offer a training-of-trainers approach in the early 1980s (see Chapter 21). This method of training, in which in-house supervisors learn both the curriculum and how to train adults to implement it, empowers local agencies. HighScope certified trainers are able to conduct observation and feedback with teaching teams in the classroom and plan group workshops that are responsive to the specific professional development needs of their agencies. (See Chapter 9 for a description of HighScope staff support and supervision.)

Another onsite follow-up mechanism is **mentoring** by HighScope certified teachers who work with less experienced or untrained staff, especially in agencies without in-house trainers. Agencies do not always have sufficient resources to enroll all their teachers in training courses. Turnover also means that new staff enter the program after the agency's contracted training with HighScope is completed. In these situations, certified teachers who have demonstrated high levels of curriculum knowledge and implementation skills can mentor their assistants, coteachers, or other instructional peers in the organization. As they observe, provide feedback, and work alongside teachers-in-training, mentors use the same supportive strategies as do HighScope-trained supervisors (see the sidebar on p. 223).

Try These Ideas Yourself

1. Write down all the ways children learn. Write down all the ways adults learn. How are they the same? How are they different? (Variation: How did you learn best as a child? How do you learn best as an adult? What has remained the same? What has changed as you've gotten older?)

2. Think of a time you taught or mentored someone, for example, teaching a younger sibling to ride a bike, coaching another student for a science test, teaching a friend how to knit or change a tire. In what ways were your teaching strategies successful or unsuccessful? Based on what you learned in this chapter, how would you change your approach to better enable the other person's learning?

3. Keep a daily journal describing a recurring situation in the classroom in which you'd like to change your behavior (for example, to help a child who runs away whenever it is cleanup time; to plan large-group times that will result in increased student attention and participation). What training, mentoring, or other support would help you handle this situation better? How could you go about getting the help and support you need? (Variation: Think of a problematic situation at home. What type of outside help or perspective would help you change your behavior?)

4. Share what you've learned from this book with another student or coworker who has never studied HighScope. What can you do to make the curriculum "come alive" for this person?

5. Below is a list of training methods that can add interest and variety to a presentation or workshop. Which have you experienced or used? What was successful or unsuccessful about using them?

Brainstorming	Field trips	Quizzes
Case histories	Games	Reports
Contests	Interviews	Role playing
Debates	Lectures	Skits
Demonstrations	Press conferences	Small-group work
Discussions	Problem-solving	Songs and poems
Exercises	Projects	Storytelling

Can you think of other strategies? Describe them and why/how you think they will work.

Chapter 21

What Training and Certification Does HighScope Offer?

❓ Think About It

A city building inspector has just informed you that the wiring in your house is outdated and is a fire hazard. To retain your homeowner's insurance, the house must be rewired — a substantial investment. You need to hire an electrician. How will you find someone to do the job?

Word-of-mouth is one option. You could ask your sister and brother-in-law to give you the name of the electrician who worked on their kitchen remodeling job. Getting a recommendation from someone you know and trust can be an effective strategy. On the other hand, if things turn out badly, it could rupture family harmony or end a good friendship.

Another tactic is to get name(s) from the Yellow Pages or classified ads in the local newspaper. You could get one or more bids and choose an electrician based on the one who returns your call, is cheapest, can do it fastest, and/or does not treat you rudely.

Alternatively, you could call a trade association and get a list of licensed electricians in your area. You could contact several, ask for references, and call or visit their past clients to inspect the work yourself. A licensed contractor may cost more than an all-purpose unlicensed repairperson from the phone book or newspaper, but sometimes "the best is cheapest." You want the job done right, the first time, especially when it concerns the structural integrity and safety of your home.

When it comes to the safety of young children, qualified professionals are surely worth the price, too! The "work" that early childhood teachers perform has lifelong implications for the health and development of those in their care. Children's well-being in turn affects family functioning. And, as the HighScope Perry Preschool Study and other research shows, the well-being of children and families determines their ability to become satisfied and contributing members of society.

The importance of hiring qualified professionals is recognized by the government agencies that license child care facilities. Although standards are not uniform, and not always rigorous enough, most licensing codes contain requirements about staff degrees and training. Appropriate teacher training and **credentialing** is also the goal of institutions of higher education that design courses of study and seek accreditation through the National Council for Accreditation of Teacher Education (NCATE). Other professional organizations, such as the National Association for the Education of Young Children (NAEYC) and the National Association for Family Child Care (NAFCC), set objective standards for professional development and program accreditation, too. These organizations base their criteria on child development research and knowledge of best practices.

As an advocate for high-quality early childhood programs, HighScope also feels an obligation to provide professional development

226

Chapter Learning Objectives

By the end of this chapter, you will be able to

❖ Describe why training and certification are important

❖ Identify organizations with professional standards in early childhood education

❖ Understand the types and structure of training courses offered by HighScope, what participants can expect to learn from them, and what type of follow-up support participants can expect to receive

❖ Describe what goes into HighScope certification and accreditation

programs that benefit staff, families, and children (see Chapter 20). The Foundation further seeks to ensure that the staff and programs who claim to use HighScope do in fact have the appropriate training and actually deliver the expected level of quality. Naturally, HighScope wants to protect the integrity of its name by monitoring who can legitimately use it. Even more important, however, the Foundation wants to fulfill the trust placed in HighScope by those who count on the validity and effectiveness of HighScope's research and educational programs. Ultimately, training and credentialing protect the children whose families contract for early childhood services.

When a skilled worker holds a license from an official trade organization, this means the individual has received proper training, has undergone an apprenticeship, and has passed objective tests of knowledge and skill. A customer interested in the worker's services therefore has good reason to believe this person will do the job correctly. Likewise, when an early childhood program holds an early childhood credential from a recognized government or professional group, parents and others can feel reassured that staff members and the agency have met at least minimal guidelines for safety and education. If the

credentials further reflect in-depth training, hands-on apprenticeships, and observed best practices, then it is even more likely that the agency and its staff will provide high-quality services.

Why Training and Certification Are Important

In Marilou Hyson's introduction to NAEYC's *Preparing Early Childhood Professionals* (2003), she summarizes decades of research with the following statement:

> *If early childhood practitioners have higher levels of formal education and specialized training, they are much more likely in their work with young children and families to use the evidence-based practices and possess the ongoing professional commitment we know are necessary to make a positive difference in children's lives* (p. 3).

The previous chapter of this book focused on the training *process*. This final chapter emphasizes why training *content* is also critical. Studies conclusively show that the overall level of teachers' formal education is positively and significantly related to program quality and children's learning (National Research Council, 2000a; Barnett, 2003). For example, cross-national analyses of the HighScope IEA Preprimary Project found that teachers' education when the children they served were four years old was significantly related to the children's language performance at age seven (Montie, Xiang, & Schweinhart, 2006).

Beyond this general educational requirement, however, teacher training must also be *specific and specialized* to achieve maximum impact. That is, early childhood teachers are most effective when the courses and inservice workshops they attend specifically address *early childhood devel-*

Terms Used in This Chapter

• credentialing • HighScope Preschool Curriculum Course • HighScope Training of Trainers Course
• curriculum evaluation • training evaluation • HighScope Certified Teacher • HighScope Certified Trainer
• HighScope Field Consultant • HighScope Accredited Program.

HighScope certification guarantees not only that teachers know about early development and best practices, but that they can apply this knowledge to working with children in the classroom.

opment, early childhood curriculum and assessment, and *early childhood teaching practices.*

Further, it is not sufficient to just provide appropriate content in teacher-training endeavors. The field must also assess whether teachers *understand and use* specialized information to implement high-quality programs. A valid system for *credentialing* teachers should be based on their grasp and application of developmental knowledge and best practices. Without proof of high quality, as implemented by practitioners, there is no guarantee that the immediate and life-long benefits of early childhood education will be realized. This is the enduring message of the HighScope Perry Preschool Study and the Foundation's ongoing work (Schweinhart et al., 2005).

Hyson (2003) continues in discussing NAEYC's standards for professional development:

> *The kind of professional development that provides that sound base is not accomplished cheaply or easily. Degrees matter, but a degree alone...is not a guarantee of professional competence. What does matter is what early childhood professionals know, what they are able to do, and the dispositions or "habits of mind" they possess to nurture and promote children's development and learning as a result of their preparation and continuing development* (p. 4).

Toward that end, organizations such as NAEYC, the National Board for Professional Teaching Standards (NBPTS), and NCATE have advocated for establishing professional standards in early childhood education. They emphasize both knowledge and practice, attempt to define standards in measurable terms, and provide guidelines on how to evaluate whether teachers have met them.

Likewise, HighScope's professional development programs include content specific to early childhood development and practice, and they entail systematic procedures for assessing whether participants understand *and* use the information they learn. Because quality is determined by what takes place in the classroom, the training room, and the office, HighScope certifies teachers and trainers and accredits programs. To qualify, participants must meet objective and rigorous criteria encompassing active involvement in the training, in completion of site-based assignments, in reflective writing, and in observed behavior while teaching, training other adults, and/or administering programs.

In this chapter, you will learn about the types of courses HighScope offers and the Foundation's system for credentialing practitioners, supervisors, and agencies.[1] Training is conducted onsite around the country and the world and is also offered at the Foundation's headquarters in Ypsilanti, Michigan. Distance learning options are also increasingly available. In addition to the courses described below, onsite training can be customized to meet specific programmatic needs, while online training provides the flexibility that allows practitioners to fit training into their busy work and family schedules. HighScope's program development divisions and educational services department continually update the scope and content of courses and the delivery systems available to students of the HighScope Curriculum.

---

[1]This chapter describes course offerings at the early childhood level. The Foundation also offers courses in curriculum, adult training, and assessment at the elementary and youth levels, focusing on both in-school and out-of-school settings. HighScope regional, national, and international conferences offer additional seminars and workshops on other specialized topics such as grant and proposal writing, working with children who have special needs, working with children who are English language learners, designing and evaluating state pre-kindergarten programs, aligning HighScope with state and professional standards, adapting HighScope in other countries and cultures, and other topics.

HighScope Training Courses

HighScope's inservice training and professional development programs in early childhood are organized into two basic categories.

The Foundation offers a multisession **Preschool Curriculum Course** for teachers and caregivers. (An Infant-Toddler Curriculum Course is also available.) These sessions provide comprehensive coverage of the HighScope Curriculum, including its underlying developmental philosophy and approach to adult-child interaction, the learning environment, the daily routine, teamwork, parent involvement, curriculum content in all areas of development, and assessment.

In addition, the Foundation offers advanced curriculum courses on specialized topics, such as language and literacy, mathematics and science, conflict resolution, visual arts, movement and music, intergenerational programs, and child and program assessment. New courses are continually being added to HighScope's catalog, including online training options.

The second type of course offering is the Foundation's **Training of Trainers Course.** For participants who have completed the curriculum training, the Training of Trainers Course prepares them to train and support others to implement the HighScope educational approach. The strategies learned in this course apply not only to curriculum training, but also to performing many other adult education and support activities. Further, learning effective presentation techniques also gives participants confidence in public speaking and leading sessions at professional development conferences. Those who typically enroll in the Training of Trainers Course are in supervisory positions, such as center directors, education coordinators, or curriculum specialists. However, HighScope Certified Teachers may also receive this type of specialized training in order to mentor their colleagues in the classroom.

HighScope courses are aligned with the Child Development Associate (CDA) requirements and undergraduate (two- and four-year) and graduate degree programs. Courses can be taken individually or combined. Students who successfully complete one or both courses can earn Continuing Education Units (CEU's) and college credit through reciprocal arrangements between institutions of higher education and the Foundation.

Curriculum Courses

HighScope offers multisession, multiweek courses in the infant-toddler and preschool curriculum. These courses are geared toward practitioners — that is, teachers and caregivers who work with children every day. Supervisors who wish to become HighScope trainers also take the curriculum courses. The workshops and hands-on practice give them a solid grounding in the curriculum's principles and methods so they can effectively transmit it to others.

HighScope curriculum courses provide in-depth coverage of the topics presented in the second and third parts of this book, namely teaching practices and curriculum content. The sessions on teaching practices focus on adult-child interaction strategies appropriate for that age group, indoor and outdoor learning environments, daily routines and schedules, teamwork, and working with families. Workshops and readings on curriculum content focus on early childhood development and key developmental indicators for the age range covered. Students in curriculum courses also become acquainted with the assessment tools and practice writing objective anecdotes.

Course participants engage in hands-on learning in small- and large-group activities during workshops and in the training assignments they complete at their home agencies. Training sessions are distributed over time so course participants can practice what they are learning in the weeks between sessions. Participants receive a library of texts, audiovisual materials, study guides, and assessment tools. They develop a working knowledge of the HighScope approach through the following course activities:

Workshops. Training sessions cover theory, practice, and assessment with ample opportunities for sharing and reflection. Teachers are actively involved in group work during training weeks.

Thank you [HighScope Early Childhood Specialist] for all the support through modeling, challenges, provision of materials, and time to manipulate thoughts. How could any of the trainees not have internalized active learning since you provided that kind of learning environment all the time! (Lincoln, Nebr., Teacher)

▲ **Practice implementation.** In the weeks between sessions, teachers apply what they have learned in their own classrooms. At the beginning of each week, they review implementation and assessment issues with their trainer and coteachers and share problems and solutions.

HighScope curriculum courses feature workshops, practice, reflective assignments, and mentoring. Training of trainers courses prepare supervisors to train and support their teachers.

> *I'm glad we have time each training week to talk with one another about concerns we have regarding our training. I feel sometimes that I'm the only one who has problems with implementation, and after talking with my peers I realize I'm not alone. It helps me to brainstorm with them for ideas, and then I'm all charged up and ready to go again!* (Alpena, Mich., Teacher)

▲ **Training assignments.** Participants complete reading and reflective writing assignments during and between training sessions. Through these assignments, they learn and internalize the central components of the HighScope early childhood curriculum.

▲ **Site visits and ongoing mentoring.** The HighScope trainer visits each classroom to observe and provide feedback on implementation. An agency-based trainer, certified through the Training of Trainers Course (described below), continues to provide this support after the training program ends.

Training of Trainers Course

The HighScope Training of Trainers Course is designed for those who have completed extensive training in the curriculum (infant-toddler and/or preschool) and want to extend their skills to training others in the educational approach. As is true for the curriculum courses, the Training of Trainers Course is a multisession, multiweek endeavor in which active learning workshops and seminars alternate with practical learning assignments at the participants' home agencies.

The Training of Trainers Course covers in depth the principles of adult learning and the strategies of adult supervision and support presented in Chapters 9 and 20 of this book. Participants learn how to design and present workshops and to conduct observation and feedback with staff. They also study the HighScope program and child assessment instruments (Preschool Program Quality Assessment, or PQA, and Child Observation Record, or COR) in greater detail and practice using them to reach standard levels of reliability and validity. Perhaps one of the most important lessons participants learn is that change can be difficult, and that teaching staff require understanding along with instruction. The Training of Trainers Course therefore explores effective strategies to bring about gradual but authentic change in teaching practices.

> *I have altered my attempts to change it all, teach it all. HighScope has provided me with the information to decide which content is most relevant, appropriate, and useful in any given situation rather than trying to force all the change in a short period of time. Select a slice, a modifiable issue, then give support and allow time for change.* (Dayton, Ohio, Supervisor)

In addition to the knowledge and skills they gain, participants network with their colleagues throughout the training course. These associations extend well beyond the training period. Because HighScope's onsite training projects bring together agencies in close geographic proximity, participants may establish arrangements to share and exchange training resources and expertise. When many participants are drawn from the same central source, such as a statewide pre-kindergarten initiative, the training can help them coordinate their implementation and dissemination efforts.

> *Seven weeks with one group with a particular focus was delightful. We formed*

230

professional partnerships that will continue, I am sure. Already, groups are beginning to engage others for site training. (Los Angeles, Calif., Supervisor)

One important aspect of this training is that it brought together the Education Coordinators of South Carolina Head Start and finally got us into the same curriculum, same assessment procedures, and same training content. It also got us all on the same "wavelength." We really became coordinated and united. (Orangeburg, S. C., Head Start Education Coordinator)

Each participant in the Training of Trainers Course identifies a "training classroom," usually at his or her home agency, and works with teachers at that site to train them in the use of the HighScope Curriculum. Throughout the course, participants keep extensive notes (called "trainer reports") to document their work with staff in the training classroom. Near the end of the Training of Trainers Course, participants answer "questions from the field" to show their mastery of the curriculum. They also make daily routine demonstration videotapes in their training classroom, which they review with their trainer to document their implementation skills and ability to reflect on their own strengths and modifiable issues. In addition, each participant presents a workshop to his or her peers and conducts observation and feedback sessions with staff in the training classroom. These activities are observed and evaluated by the HighScope trainer. Finally, course participants keep extensive anecdotal notes on one child in the training classroom, develop plans based on their observations, and complete a COR for a "child study."

At the end of the training course, the participants are evaluated on both their curriculum and training knowledge and skills. For the **curriculum evaluation,** the HighScope trainer grades the child study, accurate administration of the PQA, and demonstration daily routine videotape. The trainer's assessment of the participant's peer workshop, observation/feedback session with staff, and trainer reports are the components of the **training evaluation.** Participants who meet the Foundation's rigorous requirements on both the curriculum and training evaluation become HighScope Certified Trainers. (See the section below on certification and accreditation.)

Follow-Up

When training is completed, participants can update their knowledge and skills by visiting HighScope's Web site (*www.highscope.org*), where they will find articles about new curriculum developments, teaching and training strategies, the latest course offerings, current research reports, and other support materials. They can also join the HighScope Member Association to receive the bimonthly publication *Extensions,* a detailed curriculum and training newsletter. In addition, the Foundation distributes *HighScope ReSource,* a free publication with updates on curriculum, training, research, and publishing activities. Finally, practitioners are updated through the Foundation's annual international conference in Michigan and regional conferences throughout the country. HighScope Institutes in other countries also hold annual conferences for their members.

Belonging to the Member Association is a good way to keep in touch with other trainers and receive newsletters and other publications. It is encouraging to know we are part of a well-established organization with thousands of members, not only in the United States, but also in other countries. (Princeton, N.J., Public School Pre-K Supervisor)

HighScope Certification and Accreditation

Implementing high-quality programs depends on well-trained staff and administrative support. To guarantee quality, HighScope awards *certification to teachers and trainers* and *accreditation to programs* that meet a set of rigorous standards. Certification and accreditation are good for three years, after which they must be renewed through another application and evaluation process.

Individuals and agencies awarded these credentials are listed in the HighScope International Registry and enrolled in the HighScope Member Association, entitling them to various benefits that include scholarships for conference attendance and discounts on HighScope Press products. Following is a summary of the standards and qualifications at each level of recognition.

Levels of HighScope Certification and Accreditation

Level	Requirements and Qualifications
HighScope Certified Teacher	Demonstrates knowledge and skills in one or more curriculum areas[1] Is qualified to teach in a HighScope program in area(s) of curriculum endorsement [1]Curriculum areas are infant-toddler, preschool, youth, and movement and music
HighScope Certified Trainer	Demonstrates knowledge and skills in one or more curriculum areas Demonstrates knowledge and skills in training adults Is qualified to train staff in the HighScope Curriculum at own agency in area(s) of curriculum endorsement
HighScope Field Consultant	Meets all the requirements of a HighScope Certified Trainer Receives additional mentoring and observation/feedback from HighScope staff Is qualified to conduct contracted training in the HighScope Curriculum outside their own agency on behalf of the Foundation
HighScope Accredited Program	Demonstrates knowledge and skills in program operations and management Has lead teachers and/or caregivers who are all HighScope Certified Teachers Has an established relationship with a HighScope Certified Trainer (within agency or in close proximity) Is qualified to operate as a HighScope demonstration program in area(s) for which staff have curriculum endorsement

Teacher Certification

To become a **HighScope Certified Teacher,** a licensed practitioner must attend a curriculum course (or equivalent training) and complete all the assignments. Applicants are then observed in their program setting and must achieve high scores on the first four sections of the PQA (learning environment, schedules and routines, adult-child interaction, and planning and assessment). They also collect anecdotal notes and complete two CORs over several months, complete a series of planning forms, and document and reflect on their implementation practices. Depending on the curriculum course attended,

certified teachers and caregivers also receive an "endorsement" in a specific developmental level or content area (infant-toddler, preschool, youth, movement and music, and so on). A HighScope Certified Teacher is qualified to use that title and teach in a HighScope program in his or her area(s) of curriculum endorsement.

Trainer Certification

To become a **HighScope Certified Trainer,** an individual must complete both a curriculum course (or equivalent training) and a Training of Trainers Course. As noted earlier in this chapter (see "Training of Trainers Course"), applicants are evaluated on their knowledge and skills with regard to both curriculum implementation and adult training practices. Evaluation involves reports and assignments completed during the course, administration and scoring of the PQA and COR, a peer workshop presentation, and successful mentoring and observation/feedback with staff at the training site. HighScope Certified Trainers are qualified to use that title and to train staff in their own or an affiliated agency in the use of the HighScope Curriculum. They can also prepare and recommend teachers for certification and present HighScope workshops at conferences.

I am now the official HighScope trainer for the entire agency. I am responsible for conducting all the training related to the curriculum. I also monitor the classrooms individually and do on-site training in the classroom by way of demonstration teaching and observation/feedback sessions. All of which I've gained superb knowledge about through my training at HighScope. (Detroit, Mich., Supervisor)

Some HighScope Certified Trainers also become **HighScope Field Consultants.** After extensive mentoring and observation/feedback with HighScope staff, these individuals are then qualified to conduct contracted training on behalf of the Foundation (that is, training outside their own agencies, which is contracted through HighScope Educational Services). HighScope depends on its extensive and talented network of field consultants to reach out to communities throughout the United States and abroad to encourage and support high-quality early childhood practices.

Program Accreditation

For a program to become accredited, all of its lead teachers or caregivers must be HighScope Certified Teachers and the agency must have an ongoing relationship with a HighScope Certified Trainer (either within the agency or in close enough proximity to provide regular site visits and support). In addition, programs applying for accreditation must achieve high scores on the last three sections of the PQA (parent involvement and family services, staff qualifications and staff development, and program management). **High-**Scope Accredited Programs** are qualified to use that title and operate as HighScope demonstration programs in the area(s) for which their staff have curriculum endorsements.

Try These Ideas Yourself

1. What do you consider the minimal standards that early childhood programs should meet? What would make a program moderately good? What would characterize a high-quality program? Get a copy of your state's licensing standards for child care programs. Do you consider these standards descriptive of minimal, moderate, or high-quality programs? What (if any) changes to the licensing standards would you recommend?

2. Pick an area or topic from this book that you are particularly interested in applying to your work or personal life (for example, using encouragement rather than praise). Set a goal for achieving "high-quality" knowledge and practice in this area. How will you measure whether you have achieved your goal (that is, what attitudes and behaviors will you look for)? How long will it take you to reach your goal? Using the criteria you set, self-assess your knowledge and skills now. After the amount of time you identified as necessary for reaching your goal has elapsed, do another self-assessment. At that point, ask yourself how much you have changed. Acknowledge your improvement. Decide if you want to continue growing in that area and/or choose another goal and repeat the process.

3. Create your own professional development plan. First, list your professional goals. For example, you might list what degree(s) and certification(s) you want, what kind of agency you want to work in, what kind(s) of children you want to work with, and whether or not you want to teach and/or become an administrator. Then, for each goal, write down the actions (steps) and timeline needed to achieve it. Periodically review your plan to assess your progress and, if necessary, change your goals and the strategies you will use to achieve them. (Variation: Share your plan with a family member, friend, or colleague. Ask that individual for feedback based on what they know of your strengths and interests.)

References

Administration for Children and Families, U.S. Department of Health and Human Services (2003, May). *Head Start FACES 2000: A whole-child perspective on program performance.* Retrieved January 26, 2006, from http://www.acf.hhs.gov/programs/opre/hs/faces/reports/faces00_4thprogress/faces00_title.html

Arnheim, R. (1989). *Thoughts on arts education.* Los Angeles: The Getty Center for Education in the Arts.

Arts Education Partnership. (1998). *Young children and the arts: Making creative connections — A report of the Task Force on Children's Learning and the Arts: Birth to age eight.* Washington, DC: Author.

Barnett, W. S. (2003). *Better teachers, better preschools: Student achievement linked to teacher qualifications.* NIEER Policy Briefs #2, retrieved January 26, 2006, from http://nieer.org/resources/policybriefs.2.pdf

Baroody, A. J. (2000, July). Does mathematics instruction for three- to five-year olds really make sense? *Young Children, 55*(4), 61–67.

Benson, J. B. (1997). The development of planning: It's about time. In S. L. Friedman & E. L. Scholnick (Eds.), *The developmental psychology of planning: Why, how, and when do we plan?* (pp. 43–75). Mahwah NJ: Lawrence Erlbaum.

Bereiter, C., & Engelmann, S. (1966). *Teaching the disadvantaged child in the preschool.* Englewood Cliffs, NJ: Prentice-Hall.

Bergen, B. (1988). Stages of play development and methods of studying play. In D. Bergen (Ed.), *Play as a medium for learning and development* (pp. 27–44 and 49–66). Portsmouth, NH: Heinemann.

Berry, C. F., & Sylva, K. (1987). *The plan-do-review cycle in HighScope: Its effects on children and staff.* Unpublished manuscript. Available from Ypsilanti, MI: HighScope Educational Research Foundation, Research Division.

Black, J. E., Jones, T. E., Nelson, C. A., & Greenough, W. T. (1998). Neuronal plasticity and the developing brain. In N. E. Alessi, J. T. Coyle, S. I. Harrison, & S. Eth (Eds.), *Handbook of child and adolescent psychiatry: Vol. 6. Basic science and psychiatric treatment* (pp. 31–53). New York: Wiley.

Bloom, P. J., & Sheerer. M. (1992). The effect of leadership training on child care program quality. *Early Childhood Research Quarterly, 7,* 579–594.

Boisvert, C., & Gainsley, S. (2006). *Teacher's idea book: 50 large-group activities for active learners.* Ypsilanti, MI: HighScope Press.

Bourtchouladze, R. (2002). *Memories are made of this: How memory works in humans and animals.* New York: Columbia University Press.

Brand, S. (1996, January). Making parent involvement a reality: Helping teachers develop partnerships with parents. *Young Children, 51*(2), 76–81.

Bredekamp, S., & Copple, C. (Eds.). (1997). *Developmentally appropriate practice in early childhood programs.* Washington, DC: National Association for the Education of Young Children.

Case, R. (1985). *Intellectual development: Birth to adulthood.* Orlando, FL: Academic Press.

Clements, D. H. (1999). The effective use of computers with young children. In J. V. Copley (Ed.), *Mathematics in the early years* (pp. 119–128). Reston, VA: National Council of Teachers of Mathematics and National Association for the Education of Young Children.

Clements, D. H. (2004). Major themes and recommendations. In D. H. Clements, J. Sarama, & A-M. DiBiase (Eds.), *Engaging young children in mathematics: Standards for early childhood mathematics education* (pp. 7–72). Mahwah, NJ: Lawrence Erlbaum Associates, Inc.

DeBruin-Parecki, A., (2004). *Early Literacy Skills Assessment user guide.* Ypsilanti, MI: HighScope Press.

DeBruin-Parecki, A., & Hohmann, M. (2003). *Letter links: Alphabet learning with children's names.* Ypsilanti, MI: HighScope Press.

Dewey, J. (1938/1963). *Experience and education.* New York: Macmillan.

DiNatale, L. (2002, September). Developing high quality family involvement programs in early childhood settings. *Young Children, 57*(5), 90–95.

Dobbs, S. M. (1998). *Learning in and through art.* Los Angeles: The Getty Education Institute for the Arts.

Early, D. & Winton, P. (2001). Preparing the workforce: Early childhood teacher preparation at 2- and 4-year institutions of higher learning. *Early Childhood Research Quarterly, 16*(3), 285–306.

234

Elias, M., Zins, J. E., Weissberg, R. P., Frey, K. S., Greenberg, M. T., Haynes, N. M., et al. (1997). *Promoting social and emotional learning: Guidelines for educators*. Alexandria, VA: Association for Supervision and Curriculum Development.

Ellis, M. J. (1988). Play and the origin of species. In D. Bergen (Ed.), *Play as a medium for learning and development* (pp. 23–25). Portsmouth, NH: Heinemann.

Epstein, A. S. (1993). *Training for quality: Improving early childhood programs through systematic inservice training*. Ypsilanti, MI: HighScope Press.

Epstein, A. S. (2002). *Helping your preschool child become a reader*. Ypsilanti, MI: HighScope Press.

Epstein, A. S., & Gainsley, S. (2005). *I'm older than you. I'm five! Math in the preschool classroom*. Ypsilanti, MI: HighScope Press.

Epstein, A. S., Marshall, B., Lucier, R., Delcamp, M., & Gainsley, S. (2001). Walking and talking about art. In N. A. Brickman (Ed.), *Supporting young learners 3: Ideas for child care providers and teachers* (pp. 195–197). Ypsilanti, MI: HighScope Press.

Epstein, A. S., Schweinhart, L. J., & McAdoo, L. (1996). *Models of early childhood education*. Ypsilanti, MI: HighScope Press.

Epstein, A. S., & Trimis, E. (2002). *Supporting young artists: The development of the visual arts in young children*. Ypsilanti, MI: HighScope Press.

Erikson, E. (1950). *Childhood and society*. New York: Norton.

Eshach, H., & Fried, M. N. (2005, September). Should science be taught in early childhood? *Journal of Science Education and Technology, 14*(3), 315–336.

Evans, B. (2002). *You can't come to my birthday party! Conflict resolution with young children*. Ypsilanti, MI: HighScope Press.

Fitch, M., Huston, A. C., & Wright, J. C. (1993). From television forms to genre schemata: Children's perceptions of television reality. In G. L. Berry & J. K. Asamen (Eds.), *Children and television: Images in a changing sociocultural world* (pp. 38–52). Newbury Park, CA: Sage.

Gardner, H. (1991). *The unschooled mind: How children think and how schools should teach*. New York: Basic Books.

Gelman, R., & Baillargeon, R. (1983). A review of some Piagetian concepts. In P. H. Mussen (Ed.), *Handbook of child psychology* (pp. 167–230). New York: John Wiley & Sons.

Gelman, R., & Brenneman, K. (2004). Science learning pathways for young children. *Early Childhood Research Quarterly, 19*(1), 150–158.

Gelman, R., & Gallistel, C. R. (1978/1986). *The child's understanding of number* (2nd ed.). Cambridge, MA: Harvard University Press.

Ginsburg, H., Greenes, C., & Balfanz, R. (2003). *Big math for little kids: Prekindergarten and kindergarten*. Parsippany, NJ: Dale Seymour Publications.

Ginsburg, H. P., Inoue, N., & Seo, K-H. (1999). Young children doing mathematics: Observations of everyday activities. In J. V. Copley (Ed.), *Mathematics in the early years* (pp. 88–99). Reston, VA: National Council of Teachers of Mathematics and National Association for the Education of Young Children.

Goodwyn, S. W., Acredolo, L. P., & Brown, C. A. (2000, Summer). Impact of gesturing on early language development. In *Journal of Nonverbal Behavior, 24*(2), 81–103.

Goswami, U. (Ed.). (2002). *Blackwell handbook of child cognitive development*. Malden, MA: Blackwell Publishers.

Graves, M. (1997). *The teacher's idea book: 100 small-group experiences*. Ypsilanti, MI: HighScope Press.

Graves, M. (2000). *The teacher's idea book: The essential parent workshop resource*. Ypsilanti, MI: HighScope Press.

Greenough, W. T., and Black, J. R. (1992). Induction of brain structure by experience: Substrates for cognitive development. In M. R. Gunnar, & C. A. Nelson (Eds.), *Minnesota symposium of child psychology: Vol. 24. Developmental behavioral neuroscience* (pp. 155–200). Hillsdale, NJ: Erlbaum.

Harms, T., Clifford, R. M., and Cryer, D. (1998). *The early childhood environment rating scale: Revised edition*. New York: Teachers College Press.

Hart, B., & Risley, T. (1995). *Meaningful differences in the everyday experience of young American children*. Baltimore, MD: Brookes Publishing.

Hart, B., & Risley, T. (1999). *The social world of children learning to talk*. Baltimore, MD: Brookes Publishing.

HighScope Educational Research Foundation. (1996). *The HighScope approach to indoor and outdoor learning environments: Two-day workshop participant guide*. Ypsilanti, MI: HighScope Press.

HighScope Educational Research Foundation. (2002). *Adult learning participant guide*. Ypsilanti, MI: HighScope Press.

HighScope Educational Research Foundation. (2002). *Child Observation Record (COR) for Infants and Toddlers*. Ypsilanti, MI: HighScope Press.

HighScope Educational Research Foundation. (2003a). *Preschool Child Observation Record (COR), Second Edition*. Ypsilanti, MI: HighScope Press.

HighScope Educational Research Foundation. (2003b). *Preschool Program Quality Assessment (PQA), Second Edition*. Ypsilanti, MI: HighScope Press.

HighScope Educational Research Foundation. (2004). *Early Literacy Skills Assessment (ELSA)*. Ypsilanti, MI: HighScope Press.

HighScope Educational Research Foundation. (2005). *Growing Readers Early Literacy Curriculum (GRC)*. Ypsilanti, MI: HighScope Press.

Hohmann, M. (2005). *Growing Readers Early Literacy Curriculum teacher guide*. Ypsilanti, MI: HighScope Press.

Hohmann, M., & Weikart, D. P. (2002). *Educating young children: Active learning practices for preschool and child care programs* (Second edition). Ypsilanti, MI: HighScope Press.

Hyson, M. (Ed.) (2003). *Preparing early childhood professionals: NAEYC's standards for programs*. Washington, DC: National Association for the Education of Young Children.

Iverson, J. M., & Goldin-Meadow, S. (2005). Gesture paves the way for language development. *Psychological Science, 16*(5), 367–371.

Janofsky, M. (2005, Oct. 27). New Nevada school will serve super-smart kids. *The New York Times* (reprinted in *The Ann Arbor News*, p. A6).

Jantz, R. K., & Seefeldt, C. (1999). Early childhood social studies. In C. Seefeldt (Ed.), *The early childhood curriculum: Current findings in theory and practice* (3rd ed.), (pp. 159–178). New York: Teachers College Press.

Kagan, M., & Kagan, S. (2003). *The five major memory systems SmartCard*. San Clemente, CA: Kagan Publishing.

Kagan, S. L., Moore, E., & Bredekamp, S. (Eds.). (1995, June). *Reconsidering children's early development and learning: Toward common views and vocabulary*. (Goal 1 Technical Planning Group Report 95–03). Washington, DC: National Education Goals Panel.

Katz, L. (1995). *Talks with teachers of young children: A collection*. Norwood, NJ: Ablex.

Katz, L., & McClellan, D. (1997). *Fostering children's social competence: The teacher's role*. Washington, DC: National Association for the Education of Young Children.

Kindler, A. M. (1995). Significance of adult input in early childhood artistic development. In C. M. Thompson (Ed.), *The visual arts and early childhood learning* (pp. 1–5). Reston, VA: National Art Education Association.

Kohn, A. (1993). *Punished by rewards: The trouble with gold stars, incentive plans, A's, praise, and other bribes*. Boston: Houghton, Mifflin.

Kolodziej, S. (1995). The picture museum: Creating a photography museum with children. In C. M. Thompson (Ed.), *The visual arts and early childhood learning* (pp. 52–55). Reston, VA: National Art Education Association.

Marzano, R. (2001). *Designing a new taxonomy of educational objectives*. Thousand Oaks, CA: Corwin Press.

Montie, J. E., Xiang, Z., & Schweinhart, L. J. (2006). Preschool experience in 10 countries: Cognitive and language performance at age 7. *Early Childhood Research Quarterly, 21*(3), 313–331.

Namy, L. L., Acredolo, L., & Goodwyn, S. (2000, Summer). Verbal labels and gestural routines in parental communication with young children. In *Journal of Nonverbal Behavior, 24*(2), 63–79.

National Association for the Education of Young Children. (2005). *Early childhood program standards and accreditation performance criteria*. Washington, DC: Author. Retrieved August 2005, from http://www.naeyc.org/academy/standards/

National Board for Professional Teaching Standards. (2001). *Early childhood generalist standards* (2nd ed.) Online at http://nbpts.org/standards/complete/ec_gen_2ed.pdf.

National Center for Health Statistics (2004). *2003–2004 national health and nutrition examination survey*. Retrieved August 2005 from the National Center for Health Statistics Web site: http://www.cdc.gov/nchs/products/pubs/pubd/hestats/obese03_04/overwght_child_03.htm

National Council for the Social Studies. (1994). *Expectations of excellence: Curriculum standards for the social studies*. Washington, DC: Author.

National Council of Teachers of Mathematics. (2000). *Principles and standards for school mathematics*. Reston, VA: Author.

National Institute on Early Childhood Development and Education, U.S. Department of Education. (2000). *New teachers for a new century: The future of early childhood professional preparation*. Jessup, MD: U.S. Department of Education, ED Publishing.

236

National Reading Panel. (2000). *Teaching children to read: An evidence-based assessment of the scientific research literature on reading and its implications for reading instruction.* Washington, DC: National Institute of Child Health and Human Development, National Institutes of Health.

National Research Council. (2000a). *Eager to learn: Educating our preschoolers.* Washington, DC: National Academy Press.

National Research Council. (2000b). *Neurons to neighborhoods: The science of early childhood development.* Washington, DC: National Academy Press.

National Research Council. (2005). *Mathematical and scientific development in early childhood.* Washington, DC: National Academy Press.

Necombe, N. (2002). The nativist-empiricist controversy in the context of recent research on spatial and quantitative development. *Psychological Science, 13*(5), 395–401.

No Child Left Behind Act. Public Law (PL) 107–110, 115 stat 1425 (08 January 2002).

Paley, V. G. (1990). *The boy who would be a helicopter.* Cambridge, MA: Harvard University Press.

Piaget, J., & Inhelder, B. (1969). *The psychology of the child.* New York: Basic Books.

Pica, R. (1997, June). Beyond physical development: Why young children need to move. *Young Children, 52*(6), 4–11.

Ranweiler, L. (2001). Mentoring in the HighScope preschool classroom. In N. A. Brickman (Ed.), *Supporting young learners 3: Ideas for child care providers and teachers* (pp. 383–390). Ypsilanti, MI: HighScope Press.

Ranweiler, L. (2004). *Preschool readers and writers: Early literacy strategies for teachers.* Ypsilanti, MI: HighScope Press.

Raver, C. C., Izard, C., & Kopp, C. B. (2002). Emotions matter: Making the case for the role of young children's emotional development for early school readiness. *Society for Research in Child Development Social Policy Report, 16*(3), 1–19.

Rowe, S. M., & Wertsch, J. V. (2002). Vygotsky's model of cognitive development. In U. Goswami (Ed.), *Blackwell handbook of child cognitive development* (pp. 539–554). Malden, MA: Blackwell Publishers.

Sanders, S. W. (2002). *Active for life: Developmentally appropriate movement programs for young children.* Washington, DC: National Association for the Education of Young Children.

Satir, V. (1988). *The new people making.* Mountain View, CA: Science and Behavior Books.

Sawyer, R. K. (2004, June). Improvised lessons: Collaborative discussion in the constructivist classroom. *Teacher Education, 15*(2), 189–201.

Schank, R. C. (1990). *Tell me a story: A new look at real and artificial memory.* New York: Scribners.

Schiller, M. (1995). An emergent art curriculum that fosters understanding. *Young Children, 50*(3), 33–38.

Schweinhart, L. J. (2004). *A school administrator's guide to early childhood programs* (2nd ed.). Ypsilanti, MI: HighScope Press.

Schweinhart, L. J., Montie, J., Xiang, Z., Barnett, W. S., Belfield, C. R., & Nores, M. (2005). *Lifetime effects: The HighScope Perry Preschool study through age 40.* Ypsilanti, MI: HighScope Press.

Schweinhart, L. J., & Weikart, D. P. (1997). *Lasting differences: The HighScope Preschool Curriculum comparison study through age 23.* Ypsilanti, MI: HighScope Press.

Sears, P. S., & Dowley, E. M. (1963). Research on teaching in the nursery school. In N. L. Gage (Ed.), *Handbook of research on teaching.* Chicago: Rand McNally.

Seefeldt, C. (1999). Art for young children. In C. Seefeldt (Ed.), *The early childhood curriculum: Current findings in theory and practice* (3rd ed.), (pp. 201–217). New York: Teachers College Press.

Shore, R. (1997). *Rethinking the brain: New insights into early development.* New York: Families and Work Institute.

Smilansky, S. (1971). Can adults facilitate play in children? Theoretical and practical considerations. In National Association for the Education of Young Children. *Play: The child strives toward self-realization* (pp. 39–50). Washington, DC: Author.

Smith, L. (2002). Piaget's model. In U. Goswami, (Ed.), *Blackwell handbook of child cognitive development* (pp. 515–537). Malden, MA: Blackwell Publishers.

Snow, C. E., Burns, S., and Griffin, P. (Eds.) (1998). *Preventing reading difficulties in young children.* Washington, DC: National Academy Press.

Strickland, D. S., & Shanahan, T. (2004). Laying the groundwork for literacy. *Educational Leadership, 6*(6), 74–77.

Subrahmanyam, K., Gelman, R., & Lafosse, A. (2002). Animates and other separably moveable objects. In E. Forbes & G. Humphreys (Eds.), *Category specificity in mind and brain* (pp. 341–373). London: Psychology Press.

Sylva, K. (1992). Conversations in the nursery: How they contribute to aspirations and plans. *Language and Education, 6*(2), 141–148.

Sylva, K., Smith, T., & Moore, E. (1986). *Monitoring the HighScope training program: 1984–85.* Oxford: Department of Social and Administrative Studies, University of Oxford.

Taunton, M. & Colbert, M. (2000). Art in the early childhood classroom: Authentic experiences and extended dialogues. In N. J. Yelland (Ed.), *Promoting meaningful learning: Innovation in educating early childhood professionals* (pp. 67–76). Washington, DC: National Association for the Education of Young Children.

Theemes, T. (1999). *Let's go outside: Designing the early childhood playground.* Ypsilanti, MI: HighScope Press.

Thomas, A., & Chess, S. (1970). *Temperament and development.* New York: Bruner/Mazel.

Thompson, R. A., & Nelson, C. A. (2001). Developmental science and media: Early brain development. *American Psychologist, 56* (1), 5–15.

Tomasello, M., & Farrar, M. (1986, December). Joint attention and early language. *Child Development, 57*(6), 1454–1463.

U.S. Department of Health and Human Services, Administration for Children and Families, Head Start Bureau. *Program performance standards and other regulations.* (2002, October). Retrieved from http://www2.acf.dhhs.gov/programs/hsb/performance/index.htm.

Veen, A., Roeleveld, J., & Leseman, P. (2000, January). *Evaluatie van kaleidoscoop en piramide eindrapportage.* SCO Kohnstaff Instituut, Universiteit van Amsterdam.

Vygotsky, L. S. (1934/1962). *Thought and language.* Cambridge, MA: MIT Press.

Weikart, P. S. (2000). *Round the circle: Key experiences in movement for young children* (2nd ed.). Ypsilanti, MI: HighScope Press.

Weikart, P. S. (2003). *Movement in Steady Beat* (2nd ed.). Ypsilanti, MI: HighScope Press.

Weist, R. M. (1989). Time concepts in language and thought: Filling the Piagetian void from two to five years. In I. Levin & D. Zakay (Eds.), *Time and human cognition: A life-span perspective* (pp. 63–118). North-Holland: Elsevier.

Wood, D., McMahon, L., & Cranstoun, Y. (1980). *Working with under fives.* Ypsilanti, MI: HighScope Press.

Zelazo, P. D., & Mueller, U. (2002). Executive function in typical and atypical development. In U. Goswami (Ed.), *Blackwell handbook of child cognitive development* (pp. 445–469). Malden, MA: Blackwell Publishers.

Zill, N., Resnick, G., Kim, K., O'Donnell, K., & Sorongon, A. (2003, May). *Head Start FACES (2000): A whole child perspective on program performance: Fourth progress report.* Administration for Children and Families, U.S. Department of Health and Human Services. (Contract HHS-105-96-1912). Washington, DC: Author.

Index

About the Author

Dr. Ann S. Epstein is the Director of Curriculum Development at the HighScope Educational Research Foundation in Ypsilanti, Michigan, where she has worked since 1975. During her career at HighScope, she has developed curriculum and training materials,  directed a team of early childhood specialists who conduct inservice training around the country and abroad, supervised implementation of the NAEYC-accredited HighScope Demonstration Preschool, developed child and program assessment tools, and evaluated federal, state, and local programs. Dr. Epstein publishes books and articles for professional and practitioner audiences. She has a Ph.D. in Developmental Psychology from the University of Michigan and a Master of Fine Arts degree from Eastern Michigan University.